AFRICAN AMERICAN FIRSTS

AFRICAN AMERICAN
·FIRSTS·

Famous, Little-Known and Unsung Triumphs of Blacks in America

JOAN POTTER

FULLY REVISED AND UPDATED

KENSINGTON PUBLISHING CORP.
www.kensingtonbooks.com

DAFINA BOOKS are published by

Kensington Publishing Corp.
119 West 40th Street
New York, NY 10018

All Kensington titles, imprints, and distributed lines are available at special quantity discounts for bulk purchases for sales promotion, premiums, fund-raising, and educational, or institutional use.

Special book excerpts or customized printings can also be created to fit specific needs. For details, write or phone the office of the Kensington Special Sales Manager: Kensington Publishing Corp., 119 West 40th Street, New York, NY 10018. Attn: Special Sales Department. Phone: 1-800-221-2647.

Dafina and the Dafina logo Reg. U.S. Pat. & TM Off.

ISBN-13: 978-0-7582-9241-4
ISBN-10: 0-7582-9241-4

First Trade Paperback Printing: November 2002
Revised Trade Paperback Printing: December 2009
Second Revised Trade Paperback Printing: January 2014

eISBN-13: 978-0-7582-9242-1
eISBN-10: 0-7582-9242-2
First Electronic Edition: January 2014

10   9   8   7   6   5   4   3   2   1

Printed in the United States of America

Text design: Stanley S. Drate/Folio Graphics Co. Inc.

Contents

BUSINESS

WHAT WAS THE FIRST INSURANCE COMPANY OWNED BY AFRICAN AMERICANS?

The Afro American Insurance Company, the first known insurance firm to be owned and managed by African Americans, was established in Philadelphia in 1810 by three businessmen, James Porter, William Coleman, and Joseph Randolph. The original purpose of the company, which stayed in business for thirty years, was to provide African Americans with a proper burial.

◆

WHO WAS THE COUNTRY'S FIRST AFRICAN AMERICAN MILLIONAIRE?

In 1841, William Liedesdorff arrived in San Francisco Bay on his schooner *Julia Ann*. Born in the Virgin Islands around 1810, the son of an African American woman and a Danish sugar planter, Liedesdorff left home to learn the maritime trade, working on ships out of New Orleans. Already a wealthy man when he came to San Francisco, he bought land, built a home, and opened a store. He then proceeded to make a major impact on the city.

As a member of the city council, Liedesdorff was instrumental in setting up the first public school and organizing the first official horse race. He launched the first steamboat on San Francisco Bay and later opened the first hotel. He eventually owned an extensive amount of land in the city as well as a huge estate near Sutter's Mill, in gold-rush country. Liedesdorff died at the age of thirty-eight from what was then called "brain fever." A short street in downtown San Francisco still bears his name.

◆

WHO FOUNDED THE FIRST
AFRICAN AMERICAN LABOR UNION?

Born in Baltimore in 1835, Isaac Myers was apprenticed at the age of sixteen as a ship caulker, an important job in the days of wooden-hulled ships. He was very successful, becoming supervisor of one of the largest shipyards in Baltimore. After the Civil War, white laborers in the city mounted an effort to eliminate all African American skilled workers. In response, Myers organized the ship caulkers and longshoremen who were being forced out of their jobs, raised money from the community, and established a black-owned cooperative shipyard.

The shipyard, the Chesapeake Marine Railway and Dry Dock Company, employed hundreds of African Americans, won a number of government contracts, and provided the impetus for the establishment of the Colored Caulkers' Trade Union Society of Baltimore. Myers then organized the first national African American labor union in United States history—the Colored National Labor Union—and became its first president. Later, Myers held several government positions and was a key member of Baltimore's Republican Party until his death in 1891.

♦

WHO FOUNDED THE FIRST CHARTERED
AFRICAN AMERICAN BANK?

William Washington Browne, born a slave in Georgia in 1849, was still a child when he was sold to an owner in Tennessee. During the Civil War, Browne ran away with the Union Army and became an officer's servant. At fifteen, he joined the army, serving for two years. He then attended school in Wisconsin, returning to the South to become a schoolteacher.

A fervent leader in the temperance movement and an ordained Methodist minister, Browne became the head of an organization for African Americans called the Grand Fountain of the United Order of True Reformers, based in Richmond, Virginia. Browne's organization grew to include an insurance company, a hotel, an office building, a concert hall, and the True Reformers Savings Bank, which, when it opened in 1889, became the first African American bank in the United States to receive a charter. In 2001, the city of Richmond acquired the William Washington Browne House, which had served as the site of the bank, and joined with the National Park Service to restore this National Historic Landmark.

◆

WHO WAS THE FIRST WOMAN IN AMERICA TO BECOME A BANK PRESIDENT?

Maggie Lena Walker was born in 1867 in Richmond, Virginia, where her parents worked in the mansion of a noted abolitionist, Elizabeth Van Lew, who believed in providing her servants with a good education. When Maggie's father found a job as a headwaiter in a hotel, the family moved into its own home. But after he was killed in a robbery, her mother had to support the family as a laundress. A bright student, Walker finished her education and became a teacher. She later took a job with the Independent Order of St. Luke Society, an African American organization that assisted sick and elderly members and provided burial services.

As executive secretary of the Society, Walker expanded it into an insurance company, and in 1903 she founded the St. Luke Penny Savings Bank, becoming its president and the first woman bank president in the United States. Her bank provided small cardboard boxes to children in which they could save their pennies; when they had saved a dollar, they could open a savings account. Walker served as president until the bank merged with two others to form the Consolidated Bank and Trust Company, for which she served as chairman of the board.

Walker started a department store in the African American neighborhood of Richmond and worked for women's suffrage. The house in Richmond where she died in 1934 was named a National Historic Site. During Women's History Month, in March 2001, Virginia Congressman Robert C. "Bobby" Scott honored this remarkable woman in a speech before the House of Representatives, in which he described her accomplishments.

◆

WHAT WAS THE FIRST AFRICAN AMERICAN–OWNED CAR COMPANY?

The Patterson family of Greenfield, Ohio, began manufacturing the Patterson-Greenfield line of cars, trucks, and buses in 1915. The patriarch of the family was Charles Richard Patterson, who had escaped from slavery in West Virginia and settled in Ohio, where he ran a blacksmith business. It was there that he founded the Charles R. Patterson Carriage Company, which started making horse-drawn vehicles in the 1860s. After Patterson died, his son, Frederick, took over and decided to manufacture automobiles. The first car sold for $850. The company went out of business in the 1930s, when it could no longer compete with large car manufacturers.

◆

WHAT WAS THE FIRST RECORD COMPANY OWNED BY AN AFRICAN AMERICAN?

In 1921 Harry Pace formed the Pace Phonographic Corporation, which issued records on the Black Swan label. It was the first record company owned and operated by an African American. The label was named for the renowned singer Elizabeth Taylor Greenfield, who was called "the Black Swan." Earlier, in 1908, Pace had organized a music publishing company in Memphis, Tennessee, with the blues composer W. C. Handy. The Pace and Handy Music Company moved to New York in 1918, but the partnership dissolved three years later when Pace formed his record business.

For his record company, Pace brought in Fletcher Henderson as recording manager and William Grant Still as arranger. His first releases featured performances of light classical music, blues, spirituals, and instrumental solos. Black Swan's first hit was a recording of "Down Home Blues" and "Oh, Daddy," sung by Ethel Waters. Although Pace recorded many outstanding artists, he was unable to withstand the competition from white-owned companies, and was forced to declare bankruptcy in December 1923. A few months later he sold the Black Swan label to Paramount Records.

◆

WHO ORGANIZED AND SERVED AS THE FIRST
PRESIDENT OF THE FIRST MAJOR
AFRICAN AMERICAN TRADE UNION?

One of the country's leading spokesmen for African American workers, A. Philip Randolph was born in Florida in 1889. After moving to New York City at the age of twenty, he worked as a waiter and an elevator operator, and in both jobs he tried to organize his fellow workers to protest deplorable conditions.

In 1925 Randolph decided to organize the poorly paid men and women who worked on railroad sleeping cars. He founded the all-black International Brotherhood of Sleeping Car Porters and served as its first president, a position he held for forty-three years. In addition, he was the first African American to serve as international vice-president of the AFL-CIO, a major labor organization formed in 1955.

Randolph also made history by proposing a major march on Washington to take place on July 1, 1941. It was to be a march of African Americans from all over the country to protest discrimination against black workers in the defense industry. President Franklin Roosevelt tried to dissuade him, but Randolph said the march would take place unless the president issued an order banning discrimination in defense plants. Roosevelt finally gave in and issued the executive order on June 25.

In 1947, Randolph began putting pressure on President Harry Truman, who had created a peacetime draft but had not included a provision to desegregate the armed forces. Finally, the next year, Truman issued an order that did away with discrimination in the military.

Randolph was also the director of the famous 1963 March on Washington, which called for civil rights for African Americans and made Martin Luther King Jr. a national figure. The chief organizer of the march was Bayard Rustin, whose selection caused some opposition because he was known to be a conscientious objector, a socialist, and a homosexual. After Randolph's death in 1979, the crowd of prominent people who attended his funeral was led by President Jimmy Carter.

◆

WHO WAS THE FIRST AFRICAN AMERICAN WOMAN
TO START A MODELING AGENCY?

Ophelia DeVore-Mitchell, one of the first African American models in the United States, was born in Edgefield, South Carolina, in 1922. She moved with her family to New York City in the 1930s, enrolling in the Vogue School of Modeling when she was seventeen. She modeled for several years before deciding to help other African American women overcome stereotypes and succeed in the field.

In 1946 she opened the Grace Del Marco Model Agency, and two years later she started the Ophelia DeVore School of Self-Development and Modeling. But she didn't stop there. She initiated a fashion column for the *Pittsburgh Courier,* created a line of cosmetics, and, in 1959, began publishing a weekly African American newspaper in Georgia, the *Columbus Times.* During her long career, DeVore-Mitchell served on boards and committees under four presidents, including the president's advisory committee on the arts for the Kennedy Center for the Performing Arts.

◆

WHO WAS THE FIRST AFRICAN AMERICAN CAPTAIN
OF A SCHEDULED AIRLINE?

August Harvey Martin was born in Los Angeles, California, in 1919. His mother, a schoolteacher, taught him at home until he was thirteen, when the family moved to New York City. There he graduated from DeWitt Clinton High School before heading back west to attend San Mateo Junior College and the University of California. While in junior college, he washed and fueled airplanes at the Oakland Flying Service to earn money for flying lessons. He soloed in 1940 and continued his flight training at the university.

Martin returned to New York, where he worked as a civilian flight inspector for a year and then joined the Army Air Corps, training in Tuskegee, Alabama. Before he could be sent overseas, World War II ended, and Martin left the air force in 1946. He took an aircraft maintenance job and flew part-time for various airlines. He finally gained the success he had worked for when, in 1955, he was hired by Seaboard World Airlines as the first African American captain of a scheduled airline in the United States.

Martin often used his vacations to fly food and other necessities to struggling African nations. On a mercy flight to Biafra, in 1968, he was killed while trying to land on a highway in a rainstorm. The August Martin High School in Jamaica, New York, named in his honor, is a magnet school for the study of aviation.

◆

WHO WAS THE FIRST AFRICAN AMERICAN PILOT TO FLY FOR A COMMERCIAL AIRLINE?

When Captain Dave Harris was honored by the Organization of Black Airline Pilots in August 2008, he was recognized for his thirty-year career as a pilot for American Airlines—the first African American pilot to fly for a commercial airline. Born in 1934 in Columbus, Ohio, Davis attended a private school and then enrolled in Ohio State University with the goal of becoming a science

CAPTAIN DAVE HARRIS

or physical education teacher. But his experience with the university's Air Force ROTC program led to a change of plans, and after graduation he became an air force pilot, flying planes that were some of the largest in the world at the time.

After more than six years in the air force, Harris decided to seek a position as a commercial pilot. But, unlike his white colleagues, he found that several airlines refused to even hand him an application form. Finally, American Airlines gave him a chance. The chief pilot who interviewed Harris said he wasn't concerned with his color, only his skill at piloting a plane. Harris began training with the airline in December 1964, but his experience was often unpleasant; some of the white pilots refused to speak to him, or would use derogatory language. "It was lonesome for the most part," he told the *South Florida Times*, "because there were no others and it wasn't until six months after I was hired that they got their second black pilot."

Once the training period was over, though, Harris went on to have what he called the "perfect career." When he retired as a captain in November 1994, he was flying the wide-body MD-11, the country's largest airplane at the time. In 2008, when he was honored for his accomplishments, American Airlines vice president of flight, Captain Mark Hetterman, said: "Captain Harris is a role model among African Americans who have since followed in his footsteps to work in the commercial airline industry."

♦

WHAT WAS THE FIRST AFRICAN AMERICAN–OWNED COMPANY TO BE PUBLICLY OWNED AND TRADED ON THE STOCK MARKET?

Those who grew up in the 1950s and '60s can remember the sound of a child's voice on the radio making this plaintive demand: "More Parks Sausages, Mom, please." The Parks Sausage Company, which made this famous product, was founded in 1951 in Baltimore by Henry G. Parks Jr., a marketing graduate of Ohio State University, who had a varied background. Parks's work experience had included stints as a salesman for a beer maker, an owner of a drugstore, and a manufacturer of cinder blocks.

Parks was general manager of his new sausage company, where the sausage was made in the morning and sold in the afternoon. The sausage maker was also the production manager and the entire sales force. One of the two production workers doubled as clerk and demonstrated the sausages in supermarkets on weekends.

The Parks Sausage Company expanded rapidly, and in 1952 Parks hired a new general manager, Raymond V. Haysbert. New products and sales areas were added, and in 1969 Parks Sausage became the first black-owned company to be publicly owned and traded on the stock market. In 1990 the company moved into a new 113,500-square-foot headquarters and meat-processing facility. But the business started going downhill, and by 1996, facing bankruptcy, the company was bought by former football stars Franco Harris, of the Pittsburgh Steelers, and Lydell Mitchell, of the Baltimore Colts. The two were unable to pull the company out of debt, and in 1999 they sold the facility to the Philadelphia-based meat processor Dietz & Watson, which preserved the Parks Sausage name.

◆

WHO WAS THE FIRST AFRICAN AMERICAN TRADER ON THE FLOOR OF THE NEW YORK STOCK EXCHANGE?

On February 12, 1970, for the first time in the one-hundred-and-seventy-eight-year history of the New York Stock Exchange (NYSE), an African American trader was seen on the exchange's floor. The trader, Joseph L. Searles III, a graduate of Kansas State University and George Washington University Law School, had played football for the New York Giants, and was, at the time, a partner at Neuberger, Loeb and Company.

"It's a personal challenge to me as a black man to become part of the economic mainstream of this country," the *New York Times* quoted him as saying when he joined the trading group. "Hopefully, my presence will increase the credibility of the financial community, as far as blacks are concerned."

Searles left the exchange nine months later and joined the public finance department at Manufacturers Hanover Trust Company. He later took leadership roles in minority economic development in New York City. He was a board member of the New York Urban League and president of the New York/New Jersey Chapter of the National Football League Players Association.

◆

WHO WAS THE FIRST AFRICAN AMERICAN DIRECTOR OF GENERAL MOTORS?

Leon Sullivan, born in Charleston, West Virginia, in 1922, was ordained a Baptist minister as a young man. He soon became involved in efforts to improve the economic situation of African Americans, working with A. Philip Randolph in his successful effort in July 1941 to obtain jobs for black workers in the defense industry. Sullivan also served as an aide to New York's Rev. Adam Clayton Powell Jr., in his 1944 Congressional campaign.

In 1951 Sullivan was named pastor of Zion Baptist Church in Philadelphia. It was there that he launched the Opportunities Industrialization Center (OIC), designed to teach people of all races and ages the skills needed for gainful employment and business development. Founded in 1964, by the time of Sullivan's death in 2001 the OIC had provided skills training to more than three million people in the United States and Africa. In 1971, highly respected for his success as an economic development planner, Sullivan was chosen as the first African American to serve on the board of directors of General Motors.

In 1977 Sullivan formulated the Sullivan Principles, which called for fair treatment of South African workers and were instrumental in doing away with apartheid. He expanded his principles to establish fair employment practices throughout the world, and went on to create other programs to improve the lives of African people. His book, *Moving Mountains: the Principles and Purposes of Leon Sullivan,* was published in 1998. Sullivan died of leukemia in 2001 at the age of seventy-eight.

◆

WHAT WAS THE FIRST AFRICAN AMERICAN–OWNED FIRM ON THE NEW YORK STOCK EXCHANGE?

Founded in 1971 by Travers J. Bell Jr. and Willie L. Daniels, two young men with ten years of experience in financial services, Daniels & Bell became the first firm on the NYSE owned by African Americans.

Travers Bell's son, Gregory Bell, was the author of the 2001 book *In the Black: A History of African Americans on Wall Street.* When asked in a *Bloomberg BusinessWeek* interview why it took so long for African Americans to become part of Wall Street, he said, "Back then . . . Wall Street was a rich man's game."

"African Americans in general lacked exposure to business," he continued, "and even if they were fortunate enough to have the knowledge, few had the money to invest."

It took Travers Bell and Willie Daniels a year and a half before they were able to attract financing, Gregory Bell said. "Sadly, there were a number of talented, ambitious people who were not as fortunate."

Daniels left the firm in the mid-1970s, and Bell then became its major figure. Bell died in 1988 at the age of forty-six. After his death, according to his son, "a few bad business decisions led to the firm closing its doors in 1994."

◆

WHO WAS THE FIRST AFRICAN AMERICAN BOARD MEMBER OF THE AMERICAN STOCK EXCHANGE?

Jerome Holland was born in Auburn, New York, in 1916 and earned bachelor's and master's degrees from Cornell University. Holland gained a reputation as a star athlete on Cornell's football team; he was named an All-American for two seasons and eventually was added to the roster of college football's Hall of Fame.

After receiving a Ph.D. from the University of Pennsylvania, Holland was appointed president of Delaware State College. In 1960 he took over the presidency of Hampton Institute. Ten years later,

Holland was named ambassador to Sweden, a position he held until 1972, when he returned to the United States. Starting in 1973, he served on the boards of eleven major corporations and became the first African American named to the board of directors of the New York Stock Exchange.

In 1979 President Jimmy Carter appointed Holland chairman of the American Red Cross, another first. He served as chairman until his death in 1985. Two years later, a research facility, the Jerome H. Holland Laboratory for the Biomedical Sciences, in Rockville, Maryland, was named in his honor.

◆

WHO WAS THE FIRST AFRICAN AMERICAN WOMAN TO FLY FOR A COMMERICAL AIRLINE?

At the age of seventeen, Jill Brown began piloting single-engine planes in her native Maryland when she and her parents took up flying as a hobby. She soloed in a Piper J-3 Cub and later flew the plane that her family bought for itself, a single-engine Piper Cherokee that they named "Little Golden Hawk." Brown became a home economics teacher after graduating from the University of Maryland, but she couldn't turn her back on her love of flying.

In 1976 Brown read an article about Warren Wheeler, the African American owner of a commuter airline in Raleigh, North Carolina. Wheeler hired her as an assistant and she eventually became a copilot. She handled everything: reservations, tickets, baggage, seating, and flying a fifteen-seat plane. By the time she left Wheeler, she had raised her flying time to 1,200 hours, enough to be accepted into the flight training program at Texas International Airlines. In 1978, when she was twenty-eight years old, Texas International hired her as a pilot, a first for an African American woman.

◆

WHO WAS THE FIRST AFRICAN AMERICAN TO HEAD A FORTUNE 100 COMPANY?

In December 1992, Clifton R. Wharton added another item to his extensive list of accomplishments when he was named deputy secretary of state by President Clinton. Wharton, born in Boston in 1926, was the first African American to earn a Ph.D. from the University of Chicago, the first to be president of a major university that was predominantly white, the first to serve as chancellor of the State University of New York, the first to chair the board of a major foundation (the Rockefeller Foundation), and the first to head a Fortune 100 company. In 1987 he became chairman and chief executive officer of the country's largest private pension system, the Teachers Insurance and Annuity Association and College Retirement Equities Fund (TIAA-CREF). He kept that position until President Clinton appointed him deputy secretary of state.

Wharton, whose father, Clifton R. Wharton Sr., was the country's first African American career ambassador, earned his bachelor's degree from Harvard and a master's from Johns Hopkins in Baltimore. He served as president of Michigan State University from 1970 to 1978, and as chancellor of the State University of New York from 1978 to 1987.

◆

WHO WAS THE FIRST AFRICAN AMERICAN BUSINESSMAN TO MAKE THE *FORBES* MAGAZINE LIST OF THE NATION'S 400 WEALTHIEST PEOPLE?

When Reginald Lewis died in January 1993 of brain cancer, at the age of fifty, he was one of the country's richest businessmen and a generous philanthropist. Lewis's business acumen began early in life. Growing up in Baltimore, he started selling newspapers when he was nine years old; he said he earned about twenty dollars a week and saved eighteen.

After graduating from Virginia State University and Harvard Law School, Lewis worked for a prestigious New York City law firm for five years and then opened his own firm. In 1983, fifteen years after he began practicing law, Lewis moved into the world of finance when he established the TLC Group; four years later he bought Beatrice International, a giant food company, for $985 million. In 1992 he was included in *Forbes* magazine's list of the nation's 400 wealthiest people, with personal assets of $400 million. At the time of his death, his company, TLC Beatrice International, was the country's largest black-owned business.

Lewis donated millions of dollars to institutions ranging from homeless shelters and churches to universities such as Virginia State and Howard. His three-million-dollar donation to Harvard Law School in 1992 was the largest from an individual in the school's 175-year history. In return, Harvard named its international law center in his honor, making it the first building at Harvard to be named for an African American. After Lewis's death, his half-brother, Jean S. Fuggett, became CEO of TLC Beatrice. A year later he stepped down and Lewis's widow, Loida Nicolas Lewis, took over. She liquidated the company in 1999.

♦

WHO WAS THE FIRST AFRICAN AMERICAN TO BE NAMED CHIEF PILOT OF A MAJOR AIRLINE?

Louis Freeman is proud of achieving a list of "firsts" that began in his teens, when he and his older brother were two of the first students to integrate Woodrow Wilson High School in Dallas, Texas. Freeman was the first African American cadet corps commander in his high school ROTC unit and filled the same position at East Texas State University, from which he graduated in 1974 with bachelor's degrees in sociology and psychology.

Freeman earned his private pilot's license in college and enjoyed flying his friends around the local skies, but didn't imagine that someday he would fly planes as a career. He decided to take the U.S. Air Force qualifying test, and passed everything except the pilot's section. Studying hard and learning everything he could about airplanes, he took the test again and passed. After finishing pilot

LOUIS FREEMAN

training at Reese Air Force Base in Texas, Freeman was assigned to fly 737s in Sacramento, California.

In 1980 Freeman left the air force to become the first African American pilot to fly for Southwest Airlines, which is based in Dallas. In August 1992 he was chosen to be chief pilot of Southwest's base in Chicago, making him the first black chief pilot for a major U.S. airline. As chief pilot, Freeman is responsible for overseeing all flight operations at the 1,000-pilot base, resolving issues with government agencies, helping determine company policy, and ensuring that pilots meet company objectives.

In November 2007, the Illinois House of Representatives passed a resolution honoring Freeman for "being a man of firsts" and commending him for "his hard work and dedication to his career."

◆

WHAT WAS THE FIRST AFRICAN AMERICAN–OWNED COMPANY TO HAVE ITS OWN LINE OF SUPERHERO COMICS?

Only five months after DC Comics began distributing a line of comic books published by New York's Milestone Media, Inc., buyers snatched up more than three million copies of its first four titles: *Hardware, Blood Syndicate, Icon,* and *Static,* all featuring African American superheroes. Milestone was started by four African American men: Derek Dingle, Denys Cowan, Dwayne McDuffie, and Michael Davis. Their aim was to present colorful heroes battling in a realistic world. "We hope to help readers of all backgrounds to believe in the power they have as individuals that transcends racial and class lines," said the company's president, Derek Dingle.

Milestone's characters represented a variety of aspects of African American life. Its first superhero, Hardware, was by day a brilliant scientist named Curtis Metcalf, whose villainous boss was exploiting his talents. Icon, an alien being with superhuman powers, was actually Augustus Freeman IV, a conservative lawyer who promoted middle-class values. And the daring superhero called Static was really Virgil Hawkins, a studious fifteen-year-old who suddenly acquired electrostatic powers.

Dwayne McDuffie, editor-in-chief of Milestone's comic book line, created a number of series and also wrote for dozens of other comics. And Milestone's president, Derek Dingle, accepted an additional challenge when he became an editor-at-large for *Black Enterprise* magazine. He wrote Milestone's children's book *First in the Field: Baseball Hero Jackie Robinson* and the adult book *Titans of the B.E. 100s: Black CEOs Who Redefined and Conquered American Business.*

◆

WHO WAS THE FIRST AFRICAN AMERICAN PRESIDENT OF NATIONAL PUBLIC RADIO?

National Public Radio is a network that provides news, information, and cultural programs to several hundred radio stations with a total audience of more than fourteen million. Delano E. Lewis, the first African American president of this influential, prize-winning organization, was appointed in August 1993. He left the position in 1998 and a year later was appointed U.S. ambassador to South Africa.

With degrees from the University of Kansas and the Washburn School of Law, Lewis was an attorney for the U.S. Department of Justice, and a Peace Corps director in Nigeria and Uganda. From 1969 to 1973 he worked on Capitol Hill, first as an assistant to Senator Edward Brooke of Massachusetts and then to Congressional Delegate Walter E. Fauntroy of the District of Columbia.

Before joining National Public Radio, Lewis was president and chief executive officer of the Chesapeake & Potomac Telephone Company, an organization that he joined in 1973. Under his leadership, Chesapeake & Potomac, which served the Washington, D.C., area, was one of the first telephone companies in the country to become involved with cable television. After leaving the South African ambassadorship in the summer of 2001, Lewis joined the

DELANO E. LEWIS

boards of directors of the Eastman Kodak Company and Colgate-Palmolive.

In September 2006, Lewis was appointed a senior fellow of New Mexico State University with the responsibility of developing an institute for international relations at the university. He was later elected to the boards of the Meridian International Center and the American Institutes for Research, both in Washington, D.C.

◆

WHO WAS THE FIRST AFRICAN AMERICAN TO LEAD A FORTUNE 500 COMPANY?

When Franklin Raines was a child in Seattle, where he was born in 1949, he saw his father struggle to raise a large family on a janitor's wages. Determined to pursue a path toward an excellent education, Raines achieved high grades in high school and won a scholarship to Harvard, where he earned undergraduate and law degrees, and studied at Oxford University in England as a Rhodes scholar. After serving in the administration of President Carter, he joined the New York investment banking firm of Lazard Freres & Company, resigning after eleven years to become vice chairman of the mortgage lending company Fannie Mae.

He left the company to serve as key negotiator for President Clinton in talks leading to the passage of the Balanced Budget Act of 1997. He also advised the president on other federal issues. In 1998 Raines returned to Fannie Mae, the largest non-bank financial services company in the world, to become chairman and CEO, the first African American to lead a Fortune 500 company. Raines stepped down from the position in 2004, when he and two other executives faced a lawsuit alleging they had committed securities fraud.

In September 2012, a federal judge dismissed the eight-year lawsuit against him, ruling that there was "no direct evidence" that Raines intended to deceive investors. After learning of the judge's ruling, Raines said, "Today's decision puts to rest unwarranted allegations that I have spent eight years refuting. These reckless charges have wreaked untold damage on me, my family, my career, and my reputation."

◆

WHO WAS THE FIRST AFRICAN AMERICAN BILLIONAIRE?

Robert L. Johnson may be best known as the founder of Black Entertainment Television, but when he sold the company to Viacom in 2001 for $3.2 billion, he became the first African American billionaire.

Johnson was born in 1946 in Hickory, Mississippi. He grew up in Freeport, Illinois, and earned a bachelor's degree from the University of Illinois and a master's from Princeton University. In his job with the National Cable Television Association, Johnson became aware of the lack of African American programming. In 1979, with borrowed money, he founded Black Entertainment Television, and in 1991, it became the first African American–owned company to be traded on the New York Stock Exchange.

After selling the company to Viacom, Johnson founded and became president of RLJ Companies, which provides strategic investments in a diverse portfolio of companies, including hotel real estate, automobile dealerships, sports, and entertainment. In January 2013, RLJ acquired R. Thompson Trucking, "the leading transportation company in the Mid-Atlantic," according to Johnson.

◆

WHO WAS THE FIRST AFRICAN AMERICAN WOMAN
TO LEAD A MAJOR U.S. CORPORATION?

As Ursula Burns told a 2012 Class Day audience at Columbia University's School of Engineering and Applied Science, "I grew up in a single-parent household in a public housing project in lower Manhattan." And that housing project, she added, was "just a few miles from here yet light years away in so many respects."

Burns, born in 1958, said that her mother, whose highest income in her life was $4,400 a year, "saw education as a way up and out of the projects." Making whatever sacrifices were necessary, she was able to send Burns and her two siblings to private Catholic schools from kindergarten through high school.

With the help of a scholarship, Burns enrolled at the Polytechnic Institute of New York University, earning a bachelor's degree in science, and went on to Columbia, where she was awarded a master of science degree in mechanical engineering. She joined

URSULA BURNS

the Xerox Corporation in 1980 as a summer intern and later became involved in product development and planning.

At Xerox, Burns ascended from a senior vice president position in 2000 to become chief executive officer in 2009. A year later, she was named chairman, the first African American woman to lead a Fortune 500 company. In *Forbes* magazine's 2012 list of "The World's 100 Most Powerful Women," Burns was seventeenth, and in its list of the "50 Most Powerful Women in Business," she was number seven.

Reflecting on her race and gender in an interview with National Public Radio in May 2012, Burns said, "There's nothing I can do, or wanted to do, about being a black female. I kind of like both of those things. So at the end of the day, the people who were around me had to do a little more adjusting than I did."

◆

EDUCATION

WHEN DID THE FIRST SCHOOL FOR AFRICAN AMERICAN CHILDREN OPEN IN NEW YORK CITY?

In November 1787, the New York Manumission Society, one of the abolition societies that sprang up after the American Revolution, opened a school for African American children. The African Free School, as it was called, began with a class of forty students.

Starting in a one-room schoolhouse with a class of forty boys and girls, most of whom were children of slaves, the school's mission was to educate these young people to prepare them for life as free American citizens. A number of notable people were educated there, including James McCune Smith, the first African American to earn a medical degree, and Henry Highland Garnet, the prominent minister and abolitionist. The first school grew to seven, and by 1847 all had been incorporated into the New York City public school system.

◆

WHO WAS THE FIRST AFRICAN AMERICAN COLLEGE GRADUATE?

Alexander Lucius Twilight was born in 1795, the son of a farmer who had moved to Vermont from Plattsburgh, New York. As a youngster, Twilight was indentured to work on a neighboring farm, where he stayed until the age of twenty. He went on to attend Randolph Academy and in 1823 graduated from Middlebury College, in Middlebury, Vermont. Claiming Twilight as the country's first African American college graduate, Middlebury later named a building in his honor.

Twilight was licensed as a preacher in 1827 and preached on Sundays in towns around Peru, New York, and Vergennes, Vermont,

ALEXANDER TWILIGHT

where he taught school during the week. He and his wife moved to Brownington, Vermont, around 1930. There he became minister of the Congregational Church and principal of the county secondary school, which was called Brownington Academy. It was a two-story frame schoolhouse with no dormitory; students boarded with neighboring families.

Somehow Twilight managed to finance the construction of a huge stone building to serve as a dormitory and provide extra classroom space for the school. Some said he quarried the granite blocks from nearby fields and erected the building himself with only the help of an ox. The stone house, named Athenian Hall, had a kitchen, dining room, parlor, classrooms, and rooms for students to live in, all heated with fireplaces and stoves. In 1836, to prevent the state from reducing the funding for his school, Twilight got himself elected to the Vermont State Legislature for a two-year term, becoming the first African American state legislator.

In 1847 Twilight resigned as headmaster to teach at other schools, but came back to Brownington Academy in 1852. He died five years later, and both he and his wife were buried in the village cemetery overlooking the Academy campus. His students remembered him as a tough disciplinarian but an outstanding teacher with a vivid personality and a lively sense of humor. Twilight's amazing building became the home of the Old Stone House Museum of the Orleans County Historical Society.

◆

WHAT WAS BOSTON'S FIRST SCHOOL FOR AFRICAN AMERICAN CHILDREN?

In 1787, Prince Hall, an activist from Boston known as the founder of the first black Masonic lodge, petitioned the Massachusetts legislature to allow African American children to attend public schools. His request was denied. Eleven years later, after more petitions were also rejected, African American parents set up a community school in Prince Hall's home. The school was later moved to the African Meeting House, a church building.

In 1835 a brand-new school was opened for Boston's African American children. It was named the Abiel Smith School, after a white businessman who had left an endowment of $2,000 for the education of black children. A few years later, a controversy erupted in the city over the issue of segregated schools, and William Cooper Nell, an African American lawyer who led a group called the Equal School Association, organized a boycott of the Abiel Smith School.

In 1848 a Boston resident, Benjamin Roberts, tried to enroll his young daughter Sarah in each of five white schools that stood between their house and the Abiel Smith School, but she was refused. Roberts sued the city, joined by abolitionists, and lost the case when the judge decided the Abiel Smith School was not inferior to the other public schools. But through the efforts of Nell and his organization, a bill outlawing school segregation in Massachusetts was passed in 1855. The Abiel Smith School was closed and the building was used for various purposes over the years, including housing the offices of the Museum of Afro-American History. Renovation of the school building was completed in 2000, and the structure was transformed into an exhibit space with a gallery, classroom, and museum store.

♦

WHO WAS THE FIRST AFRICAN AMERICAN PROFESSOR AT A PREDOMINANTLY WHITE COLLEGE?

Charles L. Reason was born in New York City in 1818, the child of immigrants from Haiti. He attended the African Free School, where he exhibited a special aptitude for mathematics. At the age of fourteen he became an instructor there himself, at a salary of $25 a year. He used part of his earnings to hire tutors to advance his own education, and decided to pursue a teaching career.

Reason became a strong advocate for educational opportunities for African Americans, and in 1847, with Charles B. Ray, he formed the Society for the Promotion of Education among Colored Children, which oversaw New York City schools for African American students. In 1849, New York Central College was founded by anti-slavery Baptists in upstate McGrawville, New York, with the intention of admitting African American students. The college hired Reason as a professor of belles-lettres, Greek, Latin, French, and mathematics, making him the first African American professor to teach at a predominantly white college.

Three years later, Reason left Central College to become principal of the Institute for Colored Youth in Philadelphia, and returned to New York City in 1855 to embark on a thirty-seven year career as a teacher and administrator in the city's schools. He led a successful fight to end racial segregation in the New York City school system and, at the same time, devoted himself to expanding civil rights for all African Americans. He died in New York City in 1893.

♦

WHAT WAS THE FIRST UNIVERSITY FOR
AFRICAN AMERICAN STUDENTS?

The first college expressly intended for the education of African American students was established in Chester County, Pennsylvania, in 1854. It was called Ashmun Institute, after the first president of Liberia, and its student body was limited to young men. In 1866 its name was changed to Lincoln University, in honor of the slain president, and it was expanded into a full university that admitted students of all races. In 1953 it began accepting women. Lincoln University's graduates include former U.S. Supreme Court Justice Thurgood Marshall, the poet Langston Hughes, and Kwame Nkrumah, the first president of Ghana.

Cheyney University, in Pennsylvania, is sometimes considered the first African American college, but for many years it was actually a high school and preparatory school. It was started in 1837 by thirteen members of the Religious Society of Friends, who were carrying out the terms of a will left by a Quaker named Richard Humphrey. Called the Institute for Colored Youth, the school was established on a farm about seven miles outside Philadelphia.

In 1852 the Institute was moved into a three-story building in the city of Philadelphia, where it provided classes for both boys and girls. Fanny Jackson Coppin came to teach at the Institute in 1865 and eventually served as principal. The school was moved away from the city again in 1903, to the town of Cheyney, and in 1914 became the Cheyney Training School for Teachers. Cheyney was made a fully accredited college in 1951, and in 1983 was given university status.

◆

WHO WAS THE FIRST AFRICAN AMERICAN WOMAN
TO JOIN A COLLEGE FACULTY?

Sarah Jane Woodson Early was born in Chillicothe, Ohio, in 1825. Her father, Thomas Woodson, helped found the all African American community of Berlin Crossroads, Ohio, where she grew up. In 1852 she enrolled in Oberlin College, one of only two colleges that were open to both women and African Americans in the

1850s, and earned a bachelor's degree. During her college years she taught at several schools in the area that were sponsored by the African Methodist Episcopal (AME) Church, and in 1859, she was asked to become an English instructor at Wilberforce University, making her the first African American woman to join a college faculty.

Wilberforce closed for about a year during the Civil War, and when it reopened Early rejoined the faculty, teaching English and Latin. In 1868 she left the college to teach at an African American girls' school in North Carolina, and that same year she married Jordan Winston Early, a widowed AME minister. For the next twenty years she taught wherever her husband's career took them, and by the time she retired in 1888, she had taught more than six-thousand children and been the principal of schools in four cities. After her retirement she wrote a book about her husband's work, *The Life and Labors of Rev. Jordan W. Early,* published in 1894. She died in 1907.

♦

WHO WAS THE FIRST AFRICAN AMERICAN WOMAN TO EARN A B.A. DEGREE?

About ten years after her birth in North Carolina in 1840, Mary Jane Patterson's father moved the family to Oberlin, Ohio, so his children could receive an education at Oberlin College, which was the first white college to accept black students. Patterson graduated from Oberlin in 1862, becoming the first African American woman to earn a bachelor of arts degree, and devoted the rest of her life to the education of African American children.

After earning her degree, Patterson went to Philadelphia to teach at the Institute for Colored Youth. In 1869 she joined the faculty of the Preparatory High School for Colored Youth in Washington, D.C., later named Dunbar High School, and became its first African American principal. She held that position until 1884, when an African American man was appointed principal, but she continued there as a teacher until her death ten years later.

♦

WHO WAS THE FIRST AFRICAN AMERICAN COLLEGE PRESIDENT?

Born in Charleston, South Carolina, in 1811, Daniel A. Payne attended school and also learned mathematics and several languages from private tutors. By the time he was eighteen, he was working as a schoolmaster and teaching adult slaves in the evening. In 1834 the state passed a law making it a crime for African Americans, either free or enslaved, to be educated. Payne traveled north, entering a theological seminary in Pennsylvania. After two years he was made pastor of a Presbyterian church in Troy, New York, but soon returned to Philadelphia and joined the Bethel African Methodist Episcopal Church. In 1845 he became pastor and eight years later was elected a bishop.

In 1863 Payne encouraged the African Methodist Episcopal Church to purchase Wilberforce University, in Xenia, Ohio, which had been founded eight years earlier for the education of African American students. Wilberforce thus became the first institution of higher learning owned and operated by African Americans, and Payne was named its first black president. Wilberforce was the first school to offer a work-study program, and under Payne's leadership, it became one of the country's leading African American universities.

♦

WHO WAS THE FIRST AFRICAN AMERICAN TO EARN A PH.D.?

Patrick Francis Healy was born near Macon, Georgia, in 1834; his parents were an Irish planter and an African slave. Healy was one of eight children. His brother James Augustine became the country's first African American Catholic bishop.

Healy studied at a Quaker school on Long Island, attended Holy Cross University, became ordained as a Jesuit priest, and taught at Holy Cross for a time before traveling abroad for further study. In 1865 Healy received a Ph.D. from the University of Luvain in Belgium and joined the faculty of Georgetown University in Washington, D.C. In 1873 he was named its president; he was the first

African American to head a primarily white university. Healy was buried on the school's campus after his death in 1910.

◆

WHO WAS THE FIRST AFRICAN AMERICAN ELECTED TO PHI BETA KAPPA?

Born a slave in Clarke County, Virginia, in 1850, George Washington Henderson was employed as a servant for a Vermont infantry officer during the Civil War, when he was about fourteen years old. At the end of the war, he accompanied the officer to his home in Belvidere, Vermont. After receiving an education at two Vermont academies, he entered the University of Vermont, graduating in 1877 at the top of his class. That year he was elected into Phi Beta Kappa, the oldest collegiate academic honor society in the country. He was the first African American to earn this honor.

GEORGE WASHINGTON HENDERSON

Henderson was principal of both the Jericho and Craftsbury academies in Vermont, earned a bachelor of divinity degree from Yale Divinity School, and continued his religious studies at Yale and the University of Berlin in Germany. He traveled south in 1888 to serve as a congregational pastor in New Orleans, and later taught theology and classical languages at Straight (now Dillard), Fisk, and Wilberforce universities. He returned to Vermont for a short visit in 1896 to receive an honorary degree of Doctor of Divinity from the University of Vermont. He retired from Wilberforce in 1932 and died four years later.

A roadside marker in Belvidere, Vermont, commemorates Henderson's accomplishments, and in 1998 a portrait of Henderson was hung in the Memorial Lounge in a University of Vermont building. He was the first person of color whose portrait was displayed in the lounge.

◆

WHAT WAS THE FIRST AFRICAN AMERICAN UNIVERSITY IN THE DEEP SOUTH?

Two of the country's most outstanding black educational institutions, Morehouse College and Spelman College, are offshoots of Atlanta University, which grew out of classes formed to educate freed slaves. Shortly after the end of the Civil War, the American Missionary Association began holding classes in collaboration with African American residents of Atlanta. The classes developed into Atlanta University, which was established in 1866 with a young Yale graduate named Edmund Asa Ware as principal. James Weldon Johnson, the distinguished writer, diplomat, and teacher, graduated from Atlanta University in 1894, and W. E. B. DuBois taught there from 1897 to 1910.

In 1929 Atlanta University became the graduate school in a group that also included Morehouse, for men, and Spelman, for women. Later, Clark College and Morris Brown College were added. Martin Luther King Jr. graduated from Morehouse in 1948. In 1988, Clark College and Atlanta University merged to become Clark Atlanta University. That same year, just after Johnnetta Cole had become Spelman's first African American woman president, comedian Bill Cosby gave the college a $20-million gift, the largest single donation to a black school at that time.

◆

WHO WAS THE FIRST AFRICAN AMERICAN WOMAN TO HEAD AN INSTITUTE OF HIGHER LEARNING?

A lthough she was born a slave, Fannie Coppin never wavered in her pursuit of education, and by the time she was in her early thirties she had been named principal of the Institute for Colored Youth in Philadelphia. She was the first African American woman educator to hold such a high position. When Fannie was a child in Washington, D.C., her aunt worked for six dollars a month until she had saved the $125 necessary to buy her young niece's freedom. Once free, Fannie went to live with another aunt in Massachusetts and later worked for a family in Newport, Rhode Island, where she went to public school and then attended a state teachers' college.

In 1860 Coppin enrolled in Oberlin College, in Ohio, where she organized classes for freed slaves, gave music lessons, was named senior class poet, and served as the school's first African American student teacher. When she graduated, she became the second black woman to earn a bachelor's degree.

Coppin went to Philadelphia to teach Greek, Latin, and mathematics at the Institute for Colored Youth, where Ebenezer Bassett was principal. When Bassett was appointed United States Minister to Haiti in 1869, Coppin took his place as principal, remaining in that position for thirty-three years. After resigning in 1902, she and her husband, the Rev. Levi J. Coppin, traveled to South Africa, where, for the next ten years, she worked among the native women. She returned to Philadelphia, where she died in 1913. Coppin State College, in Baltimore, Maryland, was named in her honor.

◆

WHAT WAS THE FIRST STATE-SUPPORTED SCHOOL FOR THE TRAINING OF AFRICAN AMERICAN TEACHERS?

T he institution that is now Alabama State University in Montgomery began in 1867 as Lincoln Normal School, a private school for African American students in Marion, Alabama. In 1899 a new building was constructed. Its cost was covered by a group of black citizens, by the Freedmen's Bureau (an agency formed by Congress in 1865 to provide aid to African Americans and impoverished whites), and by the American Missionary Association, whose teachers ran the school. In 1874 Lincoln Normal School was recognized as a state-supported institution for the education of African American teachers.

The school was moved to Montgomery in 1887, its name was changed to Alabama Colored People's University, and the campus was expanded as new buildings were constructed over the years. As the school grew to a four-year college and then added a graduate school, its name was changed several times. In 1969 it received university status, and Alabama State University grew to include colleges of arts and sciences, business administration, education, music, and aerospace studies.

◆

WHO WAS THE FIRST AFRICAN AMERICAN TO EARN A PH.D. IN THE U.S.?

E dward Alexander Bouchet, born in 1852 in New Haven, Connecticut, received a Ph.D. in physics from Yale University in 1876. He was the first African American to earn a doctorate in the United States. He taught chemistry and physics for twenty-six years at the Institute for Colored Youth, in Philadelphia, and was on the faculty of Bishop College in Marshall, Texas, when, because of illness, he retired in 1916. He died two years later.

◆

WHO WAS THE FIRST AFRICAN AMERICAN WOMAN TO SERVE ON A SCHOOL BOARD?

Mary Church Terrell was born in Memphis, Tennessee, in 1863 and studied at Oberlin College, earning a degree in 1884. For two years she taught at Wilberforce University in Ohio. Then, after teaching at a Washington, D.C., high school for a time, she traveled in Europe for two years, earned a master's degree from Oberlin, and married Robert H. Terrell, a lawyer who became the first African American municipal court judge in the District of Columbia.

Terrell was appointed to the Washington, D.C., school board in 1895, the first African American woman to hold that position. She was a founder of the National Association of Colored Women and served as its first president. She also was the first black woman to belong to the American Association of University Women, and was an active worker for women's suffrage.

Terrell published her autobiography, *A Colored Woman in a White World*, in 1940. In her late eighties this energetic woman was still going strong; she was a plaintiff in a lawsuit challenging discrimination in Washington restaurants that resulted in a 1953 Supreme Court decision ending segregation in public accommodations in the nation's capital. Terrell died in 1954 in Annapolis, Maryland.

♦

WHO WAS THE FIRST AFRICAN AMERICAN TO DINE AT THE WHITE HOUSE WITH A PRESIDENT?

Booker T. Washington, the most influential African American of his time, was born a slave on a Virginia plantation in 1856. His white father ignored him, and he was raised by his mother, a cook on the plantation. After the Civil War they moved to West Virginia, where he worked in coal mines and at a salt furnace. He was able to attend school, and in 1872 he returned to Virginia to enroll in Hampton Institute. He stayed on to teach at Hampton, and when he was twenty-six years old he was chosen to head a newly established school for African American students, called Tuskegee Institute.

Washington started at Tuskegee with thirty students, meeting in an abandoned church. He believed in the value of learning a trade; young men at Tuskegee were taught to be farmers, carpenters, painters, plumbers, and blacksmiths, and young women learned cooking, sewing, and nursing. Washington soon became the country's leading advocate of vocational education.

As president of the rapidly expanding Tuskegee Institute, and a popular lecturer, Washington was an authoritative voice throughout the nation. He won the praise of three presidents, McKinley, Taft, and Theodore Roosevelt, even dining with Roosevelt at the White House, and was often called upon to recommend African American candidates for political appointments.

Washington discouraged black Americans from fighting for social and political equality, a view that was rejected by newer leaders such as W. E. B. DuBois, who also differed with Washington by promoting the importance of an academic education. Because of his philosophy of appeasement, Washington was popular with whites, and in 1896 he became the first African American to be awarded an honorary degree from Harvard. He published his autobiography, *Up From Slavery,* in 1900. He died in 1915 at the age of fifty-nine, and in 1940 he became the first African American to have his portrait on a postage stamp, a ten-cent stamp that was first placed on sale at Tuskegee Institute.

◆

WHEN DID PHI BETA KAPPA INDUCT ITS FIRST AFRICAN AMERICAN WOMAN?

Born in Shoreham, Vermont, in 1874, Mary Annette Anderson was educated at Northfield Seminary for Young Ladies in Massachusetts and entered Middlebury College in 1895. Valedictorian of the class of 1899, she was inducted into Phi Beta Kappa, the national honor society. After college she taught for one year at Straight College (now Dillard University) in New Orleans and went on to teach English and history at Howard University in Washington, D.C. After getting married in 1907, she retired from teaching. She and her husband eventually bought a home in Shoreham, Vermont, where she died in 1922.

◆

WHO WAS THE FIRST WOMAN TO ESTABLISH A SCHOOL THAT BECAME A FOUR-YEAR ACCREDITED COLLEGE?

Born in 1875 on a plantation in Mayesville, South Carolina, Mary McLeod Bethune was unable to begin her education until she was eleven years old, when a school opened five miles from her home. Eager to learn, the young Bethune walked back and forth every day. She went on to graduate from Scotia Seminary in Concord, North Carolina, and, aspiring to be a missionary, earned a degree from Moody Bible Institute in Chicago. But when her application to the Presbyterian Mission was rejected because of her race, she became a teacher, first in Georgia and North Carolina and then in Daytona Beach, Florida.

Bethune soon decided to open her own school, the Daytona Normal and Industrial Institute, and got permission to use an old cottage not far from the city dump. With desks made from packing crates salvaged from the dump, she started her first class in October 1904 with an enrollment of five little girls and her own son. When the run-down schoolhouse became crowded, Bethune offered to buy some nearby land. To help raise money for the purchase, she and her students baked sweet-potato pies and sold them to railroad workers. On her new land, Bethune created the school that eventually became one of the most outstanding educational institutions in the South, Bethune-Cookman College, a fully accredited four-year institution.

Bethune went on to found the National Council of Negro Women in 1935, and a year later she became the first African American woman to head a federal office, when President Franklin D. Roosevelt appointed her Director of Negro Affairs for the National Youth Administration. This inspiring educator and advisor to presidents died in Daytona Beach in 1955.

◆

WHAT WAS THE FIRST LIBRARY
FOR AFRICAN AMERICANS?

Before the Louisville Western Branch Library opened its doors in 1905, libraries throughout the country were closed to African Americans. When this Kentucky city passed an ordinance in 1902 that created a public library system, some African American residents challenged the legislation. Spurred on by Albert E. Meyzeek, a black activist and educator, they urged the city's library committee to allow African Americans to have access to the new system. By the time the library system opened in 1905, its plan called for a branch library for black citizens, funded by the wealthy industrialist Andrew Carnegie. Until a new building was opened in 1908, the African American branch was housed in three rooms of a private residence in the heart of Louisville's predominately black neighborhood.

The Rev. Thomas Fountain Blue was chosen as branch librarian, the first African American in the country to head a public library. This innovative librarian and his African American staff created many programs to serve the community, such as a yearly children's storytelling contest and a debating club for high school boys, and built an extensive collection of black history and literature. The Louisville Western Branch Library became a landmark in the city.

◆

WHO WAS THE FIRST AFRICAN AMERICAN TO BE
SELECTED AS A RHODES SCHOLAR?

An educator, writer, historian, and social critic, Alain Locke has been called the dean of the African American literary movement of the 1920s. Born in 1885 in Philadelphia, where his father was a schoolteacher, Locke graduated with honors from Harvard University. His brilliance was recognized in 1907 when he was chosen as the first African American to win a Rhodes scholarship to study at Oxford University in England.

After completing his education abroad, Locke returned to the United States and joined the faculty of Howard University, later becoming chairman of the philosophy department. He taught at Howard for thirty-six years. A scholar who focused on the achievements of African Americans, Locke published a book, *The New Negro,* in 1925, which made him a nationally known figure. He encouraged the work of black writers during the Harlem Renaissance, was an expert on African American theater, and amassed a renowned collection of African art.

In 1945 Locke was elected the first African American president of the American Association for Adult Education, a predominantly white organization. He was a popular lecturer and the recipient of many honors. In 1954 he suffered a fatal heart attack while work-

ALAIN LOCKE

ing on a book, *The Negro in American Culture,* which was later completed by his collaborator, Margaret Just Butcher.

◆

WHEN DID THREE AFRICAN AMERICAN WOMEN BECOME THE FIRST TO EARN DOCTORAL DEGREES IN THE UNITED STATES?

The year 1921 was a momentous one for three women scholars. It was then that the three—Georgiana Simpson, Sadie Tanner Mossell, and Eva Beatrice Dykes—became the first African American women to earn Ph.D.s. Each received the degree at around the same time—first Simpson, then Mossell, then Dykes.

Georgiana Simpson, born in Washington, D.C., in 1866, earned a bachelor's degree in German literature and language from the

SADIE TANNER MOSSELL

University of Chicago in 1911. While teaching at Dunbar High School in Washington, she began pursuing graduate work at the University of Chicago. Her presence in the dormitory there led to protests by white students, and she was asked to live off-campus. Taking most courses during the summer and through correspondence, Simpson earned a Ph.D. in German philology in 1921 at the age of fifty-five. Ten years later, she joined the faculty of Howard University. She died in 1944.

Sadie Tanner Mossell was born in Philadelphia in 1898. Her father, Aaron Albert Mossell, was the first African American awarded a law degree from the University of Pennsylvania. His daughter followed in his footsteps; after earning bachelor's and master's degrees and a Ph.D. in economics from Penn, she went on to become the first African American woman to earn a law degree there and the first to practice law in Pennsylvania. According to the University of Pennsylvania *Almanac,* Mossell was "a lifelong champion of civil rights and equal opportunity for all, regardless of race or gender." She practiced law until 1982 and died seven years later.

Eva Beatrice Dykes was the first to complete her Ph.D. requirement but the third to actually receive her degree. Born in Washington, D.C., in 1893, Dykes earned bachelor's degrees from both Howard University and Radcliff College as well as master's and Ph.D. degrees from Radcliff. She specialized in English, Latin, German, and Greek languages. After teaching at Walden University in Nashville and Dunbar High School and Howard University in Washington, Dykes joined the faculty of the small Seventh-day Adventist college, Oakwood University, in Huntsville, Alabama, where she taught for more than fifty years. She died in 1986 at the age of ninety-three.

◆

WHO CREATED THE FIRST BLACK HISTORY WEEK?

Carter G. Woodson, born in 1875, was known by many as the "father of black history." Forced to work in the coal mines of West Virginia as a teenager, Woodson was unable to attend high school until he was twenty. A brilliant student, he went on to study at the University of Chicago, Harvard, and the Sorbonne in Paris.

Working as a public school teacher and principal in Washington, D.C., Woodson saw that his students had little knowledge of the contributions made by African Americans to the country's history and culture. To help fill this void in American education, he founded the Association for the Study of Negro Life and History in 1915, and a year later he began publishing the *Journal of Negro History,* for which he wrote hundreds of articles and book reviews.

In 1926 Woodson created the first of what was to be an annual celebration of African American achievement. In the beginning, the celebration lasted for one week and was called Negro History Week. In 1976 it was extended to last for the entire month of February, and is now known as African American History Month.

◆

WHO WAS THE FIRST AFRICAN AMERICAN PRESIDENT OF HOWARD UNIVERSITY?

In 1867 a new university for African Americans was opened in Washington, D.C. It was named Howard University, after General O. O. Howard, the head of the Freedmen's Bureau. The university did not appoint its first African American president until June 1926, when Mordecai Wyatt Johnson began his thirty-four-year tenure. Headlines in the *Washington Post* read: "Negro at Last Heads Howard University. Acquisition of Dr. Mordecai W. Johnson as President Places Local University as Capstone of Negro Education in America."

Mordecai Johnson was born in Paris, Tennessee, in 1890, and graduated from Atlanta Baptist College—later to become Morehouse College. He also earned degrees from the University of Chicago, Rochester Theological Seminary, and Harvard University, and served as pastor of a Baptist church in West Virginia before going to Howard.

During his university presidency, Johnson concentrated on attracting African American scholars as administrators, deans, and heads of departments, but was also proud of the school's varied faculty and student body. A skilled orator and debater whose remarks sometime made enemies, Johnson often said, "The Lord told me to speak, but He did not tell me when to stop."

◆

WHO WAS THE FIRST AFRICAN AMERICAN TO EARN A PH.D. FROM HARVARD?

A sociologist, historian, writer, teacher, and civil rights leader, William Edward Burghardt DuBois was born in Great Barrington, Massachusetts, in 1868, of African American, French, Dutch, and Native American ancestry. He studied at Fisk University and the University of Berlin and earned three degrees from Harvard University, culminating in a Ph.D. in 1895. He taught at Wilberforce University, in Ohio, then won a fellowship to the University of Pennsylvania to do research on residents of an African American community. His sociological study, *The Philadelphia Negro,* the first of its kind, was completed in 1899.

W. E. B. DuBois came into conflict with the educator Booker T. Washington, disagreeing with Washington's opposition to academic education for African Americans and his apparent acceptance of an inferior role for blacks. DuBois challenged Washington's beliefs in his collection of essays, *The Souls of Black Folks,* published in 1903.

Two years later, DuBois convened a group of African Americans in Niagara Falls, Canada, to examine ways to improve the social and political lives of black people. The members of the Niagara Movement called for civil rights for all African Americans, and their effort was the forerunner of the National Association for the Advancement of Colored People (NAACP). DuBois became that organization's director of publications and research and started a magazine, *The Crisis,* which he edited until 1934. DuBois left America in 1961 and settled in Ghana, where he died two years later at the age of ninety-five.

◆

WHO WAS THE FIRST AFRICAN AMERICAN STUDENT TO ENROLL IN THE UNIVERSITY OF ALABAMA?

On February 3, 1956, a courageous twenty-six-year-old African American woman named Autherine Lucy braved a tradition of segregation and enrolled as a graduate student in library science at the University of Alabama after a federal court ordered the school to admit her. But three days later, mobs of people rioted on campus, threw rotten eggs at Lucy as she hurried to class, and threatened to kill her. The university quickly suspended her.

The NAACP, which had been handling Lucy's case for three years, went to court to seek reinstatement, charging that the school's administrators were responding to the white mob. But the lawsuit did not succeed, and the university expelled her permanently. Lucy finally abandoned her effort, and the University of Alabama remained segregated for another seven years. Thirty-two years after she was expelled, Lucy received a letter from the university telling her that it had overturned her expulsion and encouraging her to enroll again. A year later, she entered the university to earn a master's degree in education. Her daughter enrolled as an undergraduate at about the same time, and in the spring of 1992, they both received degrees. The university named an endowed scholarship after Lucy and placed her portrait in the Ferguson Center on campus.

◆

WHO WAS THE FIRST AFRICAN AMERICAN TO GRADUATE FROM HIGH SCHOOL IN LITTLE ROCK?

In September 1957, three years after the U.S. Supreme Court's *Brown v. Board of Education* decision ended segregation in the nation's public schools, nine young African Americans attempted to enroll in Central High School in Little Rock, Arkansas. The state's governor, Orville Faubus, summoned the National Guard to surround the school and keep the students out. A federal court ordered Faubus to remove the troops, and when the nine young people arrived to attend classes they entered the school through a side door. But a vicious, shouting mob threatened to take over the school, and the nine students were driven quickly away in two cars. The next day, President Eisenhower sent troops to protect the area, and while soldiers with bayonets held back the crowds, the nine young African American students walked into the school.

Since he was the eldest of the so-called Little Rock Nine and the only senior, Ernest Green was the first to graduate; he received his diploma on May 27, 1958. Green went on to earn undergraduate and graduate degrees from Michigan State University. He served as assistant secretary of labor for employment and training under President Carter and later formed a consulting firm in Washington, D.C., that specialized in employment and training services for minority groups.

ERNEST GREEN

In 1987 Green joined Lehman Brothers, an investment banking firm, as a senior vice president, and by 1991 had become a managing director of the company, based in its Washington, D.C., office. After the 1992 elections, he was appointed to President Bill Clinton's transition team. On September 25, 1997, President Clinton and the Little Rock Nine met on the steps of Central High School to commemorate the fortieth anniversary of the school's desegregation. In 1999, the nine former students were awarded the Congressional Medal of Honor. Nine years later, Green and the others received special invitations to attend the inauguration of President Barack Obama.

◆

WHEN DID THE FIRST AFRICAN AMERICAN CHILD ATTEND AN ALL-WHITE ELEMENTARY SCHOOL IN THE SOUTH?

On the morning of November 14, 1960, six-year-old Ruby Bridges and her mother were driven by federal marshals to an elementary school just five blocks from their home. Ruby, who was about to enter first grade, was one of six African American students chosen to integrate the New Orleans public schools.

As Bridges describes it on her website, they arrived at the school to be met by crowds of angry people, shouting and shaking their fists. With two marshals in front and two behind, the child, holding her mother's hand, walked through the crowd and into the school. White parents rushed in to remove their children, and Ruby and her mother spent the whole day in the principal's office. When she returned the next day, Ruby was greeted by a kind white teacher, a native of Boston, who taught her in an empty classroom for the entire school year.

Bridges' family suffered repercussions: her father lost his job, and her grandparents, who'd been sharecroppers on a Mississippi farm for twenty-five years, were asked to leave. By the next year, more African American students had enrolled in the elementary school, and things gradually calmed down. After high school, Bridges went to business school, studied travel and tourism, worked as a travel agent for fifteen years, married, and raised four sons.

She began lecturing around the country on faith, forgiveness, race, and her experiences with desegregation. In 1999, she created the Ruby Bridges Foundation to promote tolerance, respect, and the appreciation of differences through educational programs. In July 2011, Bridges was in the White House Oval Office with President Obama, viewing a painting by Norman Rockwell that showed her striding to the school accompanied by marshals.

"The girl in that painting at six years old knew absolutely nothing about racism," Bridges said. Her elementary school experience taught her a valuable lesson, she added, "that we should never look at a person and judge them by the color of their skin."

◆

RUBY BRIDGES

WHO WAS THE FIRST
AFRICAN AMERICAN WOMAN TO INTEGRATE
THE UNIVERSITY OF GEORGIA?

In 1961, Charlayne Hunter-Gault and her fellow student, Hamilton Holmes, ended segregation at the University of Georgia when they enrolled as the school's first African American students. Because of her desire to become a journalist, Hunter-Gault agreed to be a test case in the integration of the university, which was the only school in the state with a journalism school.

She and Holmes were met with cross burnings, screaming mobs of white students, and a riot outside the dormitory. Claiming it was

CHARLAYNE HUNTER-GAULT

trying to keep the peace, the school suspended the two students, but the action was overruled by a federal court and they returned to classes. Before graduating, the two succeeded in desegregating the swimming pool, cafeteria, and other university facilities.

Holmes was elected to Phi Beta Kappa and, after graduation, continued his education at Emory Medical School. Hunter-Gault's first job after college was at *The New Yorker* magazine. She then won a scholarship to study at Washington University, where she served on the staff of *Trans-Action* magazine, and later joined the news team at WRC-TV in Washington. In 1968 Hunter-Gault began a ten-year stint as a metropolitan reporter for the *New York Times,* covering the urban African American community. In 1978 she became a national correspondent for the public television program, *The MacNeil/Lehrer Newshour,* where she won many awards for her outstanding reporting. After twenty years with the *Newshour,* she joined National Public Radio and then moved to CNN as the Johannesburg, South Africa, bureau chief and correspondent. She left CNN in 2005 to pursue independent projects. Her memoir, *In My Place,* was published in 1992, and in her 2006 book, *New News Out of Africa: Uncovering Africa's Renaissance,* she examined developments in Africa that are rarely covered by the American media. An historical memoir, *To the Mountaintop: My Journey Through the Civil Rights Movement,* was published in 2012.

♦

WHO WAS THE FIRST AFRICAN AMERICAN STUDENT AT THE UNIVERSITY OF MISSISSIPPI?

Fourteen months after air force veteran James Meredith applied for admission to the segregated University of Mississippi, a federal court ruled on September 10, 1962, that the school had to accept him. But ten days later, the Mississippi governor, Ross Barnett, physically blocked Meredith from entering the school. In response, a federal appeals court threatened the university with contempt and secured a promise that Meredith would be registered.

On September 25, Meredith, accompanied by the chief United States marshal, attempted to register; once again, Barnett rejected him. In a lengthy series of telephone calls, Attorney General

Robert Kennedy warned the recalcitrant governor that he had to comply with the federal court order. The next day a *New York Times* headline read: "U.S. Is Prepared to Send Troops as Mississippi Governor Defies Court and Bars Negro Student."

A day later, Meredith and his escorts traveled to the university campus in Oxford. They were met by the state's lieutenant governor, backed by rows of state troopers and sheriffs, who denied him admission. Meredith tried to reach the university again the next day, but the attempt was called off when thousands of rowdy Mississippians gathered, some carrying rifles and other weapons.

When he came to the campus again on September 30, accompanied by a force of federal marshals, riots broke out among university students and adults from surrounding communities. Rocks, iron spikes, and fire bombs were thrown, and about thirty marshals were hit by gunfire. In the end, two people were killed, including a reporter from London, and hundreds were injured. Finally, on October 1, Meredith was allowed to register and attended his first class. Federal troops remained to guard him until the end of the term, when he graduated with a bachelor's degree in political science. In September 2012, the University of Mississippi commemorated fifty years of integration. Meredith was invited to the celebration but did not attend. In an interview with *Esquire* magazine, he said, "What I did had nothing to do with going to classes. My objective was to destroy the system of white supremacy."

◆

WHO WAS THE FIRST AFRICAN AMERICAN PRESIDENT OF THE NATIONAL EDUCATION ASSOCIATION?

In 1968 Elizabeth Duncan Koontz was elected president of the National Education Association, and served in the position until 1969, when President Nixon appointed her director of the Labor Department's women's bureau. A native of North Carolina, where she was born in 1919, Koontz received degrees from Livingstone College and Atlanta University. A teacher in several North Carolina schools, Koontz was active in local, state, and national teachers' organizations. She died in 1989.

◆

WHO WAS THE FIRST AFRICAN AMERICAN PRESIDENT OF THE AMERICAN PSYCHOLOGICAL ASSOCIATION?

Born in Panama in 1914, Kenneth Bancroft Clark conducted groundbreaking research on the psychological harm to African American children caused by segregation. His findings made a major contribution to the historic 1954 United States Supreme Court decision in *Brown v. Board of Education,* which outlawed segregation in public schools.

Clark, who earned degrees from Howard and Columbia Universities, was a founder of Harlem Youth Opportunities Unlimited, an organization designed to provide job training for young people. In 1970 he was elected the first African American president of the American Psychological Association. He later formed a consulting firm specializing in matters dealing with race relations. He published several important sociological studies, including *Dark Ghetto: Dilemmas of Social Power,* an overview of housing, schools, psychology, and politics in New York City's Harlem. Clark died in 2005 at the age of ninety.

◆

WHO WAS THE FIRST AFRICAN AMERICAN PRESIDENT OF THE AMERICAN LIBRARY ASSOCIATION?

In 1976, the American Library Association named its first African American president, Clara Stanton Jones, the creator of an innovative information and referral system for libraries. Born in St. Louis, Missouri, in 1913, Jones earned a bachelor's degree from Spelman College and a library science degree from the University of Michigan. Her library career began at Dillard University in New

Orleans, and in 1944 she joined the staff of the Detroit Public Library. Starting as a children's librarian, she rose through the system until she was named the library's director in 1970. She remained the director until she retired in 1978. That year, she was appointed by President Carter to the National Commission on Libraries and Information Sciences, where she served until 1982. She died in 2012 at the age of ninety-nine.

◆

WHO WAS THE FIRST WOMAN IN THE COUNTRY TO HEAD A MAJOR RESEARCH UNIVERSITY?

Mary Frances Berry, born in 1938 to a poor family in Nashville, Tennessee, graduated from high school with honors and worked her way through college and graduate school as a lab technician, earning undergraduate and graduate degrees from Howard University and a Ph.D. from the University of Michigan. Berry taught college history while pursuing a law degree and then joined the staff of the University of Maryland, where she was given positions of increasing administrative responsibility. All the while, she was an energetic participant in antiwar and civil rights activities.

In 1976 Berry was named chancellor of the University of Colorado at Boulder, making her the first woman in the country to head a major research university. The next year, President Jimmy Carter asked her to join the Department of Health, Education and Welfare as assistant secretary for education. In 1980 Berry earned another honor when President Carter appointed her to the U.S. Commission on Civil Rights. But after Ronald Reagan became president, Berry found herself in conflict with his conservative policies. When Reagan tried to fire her from the commission, she sued him to retain her job and won.

In 1993 Berry, while serving the first year of her third six-year term on the commission, was appointed chairwoman. She was reappointed to the commission by President Clinton in January 1999. She resigned from the commission in December 2004. During her tenure there, the commission issued a number of important reports on topics such as police practices in New York City, church

MARY FRANCES BERRY

burnings, and conditions on Native American reservations. Berry remained a professor at the University of Pennsylvania, where she began teaching the history of American law in 1987, as well as advising graduate students in legal history and African American history.

◆

WHO WAS THE FIRST AFRICAN AMERICAN PRESIDENT OF AN IVY LEAGUE UNIVERSITY?

At a special meeting in November 2000, the fifty-four officers of the Corporation of Brown University unanimously elected Ruth J. Simmons as the eighteenth president of this Providence, Rhode Island, institution. Responding to her appointment in an interview on the television show *60 Minutes,* Simmons said, "I would not have thought it possible for a person of my background to become president of Brown University."

The background she was referring to includes a childhood in a corrugated-tin shack balanced on blocks on a farm in the East Texas town of Grapeland, where she and her eleven brothers and sisters lived with their mother and father, a tenant farmer. The family moved to Houston, where her father worked in a jelly factory and her mother cleaned houses.

When she was a senior in high school, Simmons won a scholarship to Dillard University, in New Orleans, graduating with hon-

RUTH J. SIMMONS

ors in 1967. After earning her master's and doctoral degrees at Harvard, she began her academic career teaching French at the University of New Orleans, and later served as assistant dean of the college of liberal arts. She moved to California State University in 1977 as visiting associate professor of pan-African studies and acting director of international programs. From 1979 to 1983 she was assistant, and later, associate dean of graduate studies at the University of Southern California. She then went to Princeton University to direct Afro-American studies, rising to become associate dean of the faculty. After two years as provost at Spelman College in Atlanta, she returned to Princeton as vice provost, a position she held until 1995, when she became president of Smith College in Massachusetts. In the fall of 2001, Simmons moved into the Ivy League when she took the helm of Brown University. In June 2009, President Obama appointed Simmons to the President's Commission on White House Fellowships. Simmons stepped down from the presidency of Brown in June 2012, and she continued at the university as professor of comparative literature and Africana studies.

ENTERTAINMENT

WHAT WAS THE FIRST MUSICAL
PRODUCED ON BROADWAY WITH AN
ALL-AFRICAN AMERICAN CAST?

*O*riental America, produced by John W. Isham in 1896, demonstrated for the first time that African Americans could excel at material that previously had been reserved for whites. Rather than featuring the usual minstrelsy and burlesque, the show ended with a medley of operatic arias performed by distinguished African American singers, including J. Rosamond Johnson. The show had a short run on Broadway at Palmer's Theatre.

That same year, *Black Patti's Troubadours,* with music by Bob Cole and featuring the popular concert singer Sissieretta Jones, opened at Proctor's 58th Street Theatre. A great success, the show toured throughout the North and South before traveling abroad.

◆

WHAT WAS BROADWAY'S FIRST SHORT
MUSICAL WRITTEN AND PERFORMED BY
AFRICAN AMERICANS?

*I*n July 1898, an hour-long series of musical skits called *Clorindy; or, the Origin of the Cakewalk* opened at the Casino Theatre Roof Garden on New York City's Broadway. A cast of twenty-six African American performers presented songs, dances, and comedy numbers. The songs were composed by Will Marion Cook with lyrics by the poet Paul Laurence Dunbar. Cook, who was trained as a classical violinist, came to New York to study composition and became fascinated by black vaudeville performers. He decided to write a musical that would explore the cakewalk, an African American dance that had become a national craze.

It was said that when Cook's mother heard his songs, written in dialect, she burst into tears, fearing that he would never become the classical musician she had hoped for. Cook conducted the orchestra for the run of *Clorindy* and continued his career in musical theater, composing music for several shows and writing Broadway's first interracial musical, *The Southerners,* which opened in 1904.

♦

WHO CREATED THE FIRST FULL-LENGTH MUSICAL INVOLVING ONLY AFRICAN AMERICANS?

Bob Cole was a songwriter and performer from Athens, Georgia, who had made a name for himself with the music he wrote for the successful show, *Black Patti's Troubadours.* Expanding on the short pieces he had written earlier, Cole created a full-length musical that ran at New York's Third Avenue Theater during the 1898–99 season. The show, *A Trip to Coontown,* was the first musical entirely written, produced, performed, and owned by African Americans. Called a landmark in the history of black theater, the show toured for several years.

♦

WHAT WAS THE FIRST FULL-LENGTH BROADWAY MUSICAL WRITTEN AND PERFORMED BY AFRICAN AMERICANS?

In 1903, comedian Bert Williams and his partner, George Walker, presented *In Dahomey* at the New York Theatre on Broadway. The show played to packed houses until it left New York for London, where it was presented at the Shaftesbury Theatre. Londoners gave the show only a mild response until it was chosen for a command performance at the birthday celebration of the young Prince of Wales.

After being presented to royalty, *In Dahomey* became the hit of London, where the theater was full night after night for months. Williams himself became immensely popular, and was invited to the homes and clubs of London's leading citizens.

♦

WHO WAS THE FIRST AFRICAN AMERICAN PERFORMER TO STAR ON BROADWAY?

Born Egbert Austin Williams in 1874 in Antigua, British West Indies, Bert Williams was a natural musician from early childhood. His family settled in California, and while he was still in his teens, Williams began performing in saloons and road shows. In San Francisco, he teamed up with George Walker, another traveling entertainer. After a couple of years on the West Coast, the two moved on to Chicago and then New York, becoming famous in 1896 for a musical called *The Gold Bug*, in which they performed the cakewalk. They played in a few other small musicals, but their fame began to spread in 1903 when they starred in the wildly popular musical comedy *In Dahomey*, the first full-length Broadway show to be written and performed by African Americans.

Williams and Walker played in two more musicals, *In Abyssinia* and *Bandana Land*, before Walker became ill and was forced to retire. Williams then struck out on his own, starring in 1909 in another all-black show, *Mr. Lode of Koal*. In 1910 Williams's popularity grew even greater when he was featured in the *Ziegfield Follies*, becoming the first African American performer to star in a white show. He received rave reviews, stopping the show every night with his rendition of the song that became his signature, "Nobody."

Williams performed with the *Follies* until 1919, appearing with such top comedians as W. C. Fields, who called Williams "the funniest man I ever saw." But despite the honors that were heaped upon him for his work in the theater, Williams suffered the pain of racism, unable to ride the elevator or eat in the dining rooms of hotels where he stayed when on the road. He had reached the top of his profession, he once said, "not because of what I am, but in spite of it." Williams died in 1922 after collapsing during the performance of his new show, *Under the Bamboo Tree*.

◆

WHAT WAS THE FIRST AFRICAN AMERICAN MUSICAL TO RUN MORE THAN FIVE HUNDRED PERFORMANCES?

The first all-black musical of the 1920s, *Shuffle Along* was a model for all Broadway shows that followed, and its success was an inspiration for many African American composers and songwriters. The show was written by Eubie Blake, a pianist and composer, and Noble Sissle, a singer and lyricist; the two had teamed up in 1915.

Shuffle Along opened in May 1921 at New York City's Sixty-Third Street Theatre. Blake led the orchestra, which included an oboist named William Grant Still, later to become a famous composer. Many members of the cast also reached stardom, such as Florence Mills, the singer, and Josephine Baker, who danced in the chorus. The show introduced a number of songs that became hits; "I'm Just Wild About Harry" and "Love Will Find a Way" were two of the favorites.

Soon after it opened, *Shuffle Along* became so popular that crowds gathered on the sidewalk waiting to buy tickets, and cars and taxicabs jammed the street. Finally, the city's traffic department had to declare 63rd Street a one-way thoroughfare. After a record 504 performances on Broadway, *Shuffle Along* went on the road to play for two more years.

◆

WHO WAS THE FIRST AFRICAN AMERICAN WOMAN TO RECEIVE THE FRENCH LEGION OF HONOR?

Born in St. Louis, Missouri, in 1906, Josephine Baker spent much of her childhood cleaning houses to help support her struggling family. She joined a vaudeville show, and by the time she was fifteen she was in Manhattan, dancing in the chorus of *Shuffle Along,* a hit show written by the African American musical collaborators Noble Sissle and Eubie Blake. Her vivid features and energetic style won many admirers, and in 1925 she was offered a major role in *La Revue Nègre,* an American production that opened in Paris. Baker became an international sensation, dancing the Charleston and the black bottom and sometimes wearing only

JOSEPHINE BAKER

a string of bananas around her waist. In 1930 Baker added singing to her act, and while she was appearing with the Folies Bergère, she is said to have received 40,000 love letters and 2,000 offers of marriage. Her film appearances attracted even more fans.

After World War II broke out, Baker, who had become a French citizen, served as a Red Cross volunteer and a spy for the French Underground, for which she was awarded the French Legion of Honor. In the 1950s she bought a spacious estate and adopted twelve orphaned children of many nationalities, who became known as her Rainbow Tribe. Baker, who had always refused to perform wherever

African Americans were not allowed, participated in the 1963 March on Washington and gave a civil rights benefit in Carnegie Hall.

Baker died in Paris in April 1975. At her funeral she was honored with a twenty-one-gun salute, the first such tribute given to an American woman.

◆

WHO WAS THE FIRST AFRICAN AMERICAN ENTERTAINER TO BECOME AN INTERNATIONAL STAR?

Florence Mills, born in 1895, was only eight years old when she made her stage debut in the Williams and Walker musical *Sons of Ham*. The audience went wild when she warbled "Miss Hannah from Savannah." Known as Baby Florence Mills, she won medals in cakewalk contests, and as a teenager she joined her sisters in a singing and dancing act called the Mills Trio.

Soon after she went out on her own, Mills became a star of the 1921 Broadway show *Shuffle Along,* in which her rendition of "I'm Craving for That Kind of Love" was a show-stopper. She was featured in *Plantation Revue* in 1922 and toured Europe in *From Dover to Dixie*. Back in New York, Mills starred in *Dixie to Broadway,* in which her performance of "I'm Just a Little Blackbird Looking for a Bluebird" brought tears to the eyes of her audience and became her theme song. By the time she appeared in *Blackbirds of 1926* she had become an international star; when the show played in London, the Prince of Wales is said to have seen it sixteen times.

Mills was set to star in *Blackbirds of 1928,* but a few months before it was to open she was rushed to the hospital for an emergency appendectomy. Complications ensued and she died; she was only thirty-two years old. More than 100,000 people accompanied her funeral procession as it moved through Harlem. When it neared 145th Street, an airplane released a flock of blackbirds. On her grave in Woodlawn Cemetery was placed a tower of red roses eight feet high with a card signed, "From a friend." Some believed it was a tribute from the Prince of Wales.

◆

WHO WAS THE FIRST AFRICAN AMERICAN WOMAN TO BECOME A WELL-KNOWN COMEDIAN?

Jackie "Moms" Mabley started her career as a singer when she was fourteen years old, appearing in clubs and theaters. Born in North Carolina in 1894 and raised in Maryland, she changed her name from Lauretta Aiken because her family was opposed to her show business career. Mabley became a successful stand-up comedian, very unusual for a woman at the time, and by the early 1920s was appearing in clubs in New York City. In 1947 she appeared in her first film, *Killer Diller.* A year later she was featured in the movie *Boarding House Blues,* in which she played the operator of a boarding house for entertainers.

Mabley, who had adopted a costume of print housedresses, floppy hats, and clunky shoes, became a hit on television's *Ed Sullivan Show,* and made her first comedy record album in 1960. In the 1974 movie *Amazing Grace,* Mabley portrayed an elderly woman determined to remove political corruption from the city of Baltimore. She suffered a heart attack while making the movie and was forced to wear a pacemaker to complete the filming. A year later, Mabley died at her home in Westchester County, New York.

◆

WHO WAS THE FIRST AFRICAN AMERICAN ON NETWORK RADIO?

In November 2008, when Hal Jackson celebrated his ninety-third birthday and his sixty-ninth year in radio, a stage full of artists and radio personalities honored his career in a tribute at the historic Apollo Theatre in Harlem, New York, where Jackson himself had hosted hundreds of shows. Among his many accomplishments, Jackson was the first African American on network radio and the first to be inducted into the Radio Hall of Fame.

Born in Charleston, South Carolina, in 1915, Harold Baron Jackson spent his childhood in Washington, D.C., where his father's successful tailor shop allowed the family to live in a comfortable neighborhood. But when he was about nine years old, both parents died within several months of one another. He stayed with relatives for a time, then moved into a boarding house when he was thirteen, supporting himself with various jobs. After graduating from Dunbar High School, he entered Howard University, where he became a radio sports announcer for the college's baseball games and for local American Negro Baseball League games.

In 1939, when he applied for his first job at a radio station in Washington, the owner told him that no black man would ever work there, so Jackson hired a white advertising agency to buy air time for him. As he recalled in an interview with National Public Radio, when he arrived at the station "we walked right in and went right on the air. There was no stopping. They hit a panic button, but it was too late."

He later hosted *The Bronze Review*, a nightly interview program, at a Washington station, and *The House That Jack Built*, featuring jazz and blues. In the 1950s, he hosted a jazz show on WABC, and in 1971, he and Percy Sutton, a former Manhattan borough president, joined other investors to form the African American–owned Inner City Broadcasting Corporation in New York City. Jackson hosted a weekly program, *Sunday Classics*, on New York's WBLS-FM until a few weeks before his death in May 2012 at the age of ninety-six.

◆

WHAT WAS THE FIRST TELEVISION SERIES TO STAR AN AFRICAN AMERICAN ACTRESS?

The weekly television sitcom *Beulah* made its debut on ABC in October 1950. The title character, portrayed at first by the distinguished actress Ethel Waters, was a congenial black maid working for a white family. Hattie McDaniel, who had played the role on radio, took over as Beulah the next season, and after she died in 1952, the role was played by Louise Beavers.

The show's run ended in 1953 and it remained in syndication for a time, but when African American groups protested its stereotyped characters, *Beulah* was cancelled.

◆

WHAT WAS THE FIRST PRIME TIME TV SHOW TO FEATURE AN AFRICAN AMERICAN CAST?

*A**mos 'n' Andy,* a comedy series that debuted on television in 1951, originated as a radio program in Chicago in 1928, becoming the longest-running radio show in broadcast history. On radio, white actors were used to portray the characters, who were supposed to be African American. On television, though, *Amos 'n' Andy* used an all-black cast.

Almost immediately after it began, the NAACP and other organizations denounced the television series as an affront to African Americans, although it was said that some black viewers enjoyed the show. After two years, CBS took it off the air, but the series was kept in syndication until 1966.

♦

WHO WAS THE FIRST AFRICAN AMERICAN TO HOST A NETWORK TELEVISION SHOW?

*N*at King Cole began his career as a jazz pianist but gained fame as a masterful singer of romantic ballads, becoming so popular that he was given his own television series in 1956. Born Nathaniel Adams Coles in Montgomery, Alabama, in 1917, the singer grew up in Chicago. He started forming bands while still in high school, and after graduation he struggled for several years, playing piano in bars and putting together small groups that soon disbanded. His career took off in the 1940s when he formed the King Cole Trio, which slowly but surely became successful as fans discovered Cole's original piano style.

In 1944 the King Cole Trio recorded its first hit song, "Straighten Up and Fly Right," with Cole singing. Four years later, a record of Cole's rendition of the song "Nature Boy" was a huge success, and he became one of the first African American male singers to succeed in the white market.

From that time on, Cole concentrated on singing, becoming one of the most popular recording stars of his day and a frequent guest on television variety shows. In November 1956 he premiered on NBC as the host of his own weekly television program, *The*

NAT KING COLE

Nat King Cole Show. But despite his enormous popularity the show was unable to find a regular sponsor, and it was cancelled after one year. Frustrated and bitter, Cole criticized the advertising industry for not trying hard enough to sell his show to sponsors. In 1965 he died of lung cancer at the age of forty-six.

◆

WHO WAS THE FIRST AFRICAN AMERICAN PERFORMER TO WIN AN EMMY?

Harry Belafonte appeared on the folk music scene in the early 1950s, singing traditional tunes in New York City clubs. After his album of calypso songs was released in 1956, his versions of "Day-O" and "Jamaica Farewell" swept the country. And by 1960 the talented singer had been awarded an Emmy for his television variety special, "Tonight with Belafonte."

Born in New York City in 1927, Belafonte was sent to live in Jamaica, West Indies, at the age of five after his mother, a domestic worker, decided he and his brother would be safer there. He was twelve when he returned to New York, where his West Indian accent added to his alienation from his high school classmates. After a stint in the U.S. Navy, he became a janitor's assistant in a New York apartment building. One day an actress who lived in the building gave him a ticket to the American Negro Theater. Seeing African

HARRY BELAFONTE

American actors on stage opened a new world to him, and he wanted to be part of it.

Belafonte began theater studies at the New School for Social Research, and when his GI Bill tuition money ran out, he began singing jazz and pop tunes at the Royal Roost, a Broadway club. He then discovered the Village Vanguard, where he listened to the music of folk singers such as Leadbelly and Woody Guthrie. One evening in 1951, he convinced the owner to let him sing there, an event that led to a three-week booking, appearances across the country, and an RCA record contract.

Belafonte's theater training paid off in the 1950s when he was given roles in such movies as *Odds Against Tomorrow* and *Carmen Jones,* in which he costarred with Dorothy Dandridge. In the 1955 film *Bright Road,* he portrayed a shy principal in a Southern school, with Dandridge playing a teacher. Two years later, in *Island in the Sun,* he starred as a labor leader attracted to a white socialite. But his success in films was limited by his refusal to play roles that he felt dehumanized African American men.

A longtime civil rights activist and international human rights advocate, Belafonte was a close friend of Dr. Martin Luther King Jr., an organizer of the 1963 March on Washington, a spokesman against apartheid, and a companion to Nelson Mandela during his visit to the United States. In 1996 he starred in the Robert Altman film *Kansas City,* and a year later his concert film, *An Evening With Harry Belafonte and Friends,* was aired on television. In August 2000, he added another award to his collection, the ASCAP Harry Chapin Humanitarian Award, which recognizes "vital humanitarian work by members of the music community." He later became an outspoken critic of some of the policies of President George W. Bush. On January 20, 2009, he hosted one of the balls celebrating the inauguration of President Barack Obama. *Sing Your Song,* a documentary film about his life and legacy, was released in 2011.

◆

WHO WAS THE FIRST AFRICAN AMERICAN ACTOR TO STAR IN A DRAMATIC SERIES ON TELEVISION?

I Spy, a weekly television show that went on the air in 1965, starred Bill Cosby and Robert Culp as partners in espionage and earned Cosby three consecutive Emmy awards as the most outstanding actor in a continuing dramatic series. Born William Henry Cosby in 1937 in Germantown, Pennsylvania, he received a bachelor's degree from Temple University. He later earned a master's and doctorate from the University of Massachusetts.

Cosby began his comedy career performing in clubs throughout the East. He won six Grammy awards for Best Comedy Album, starting in 1964 for *Bill Cosby Is a Very Funny Fellow . . . Right?* After *I Spy* ended in 1968, he starred in *The Bill Cosby Show,* portraying Chet Kincaid, a high school track coach. In 1972 and 1976 he hosted two variety shows, both unsuccessful, but his Saturday morning animated series, *Fat Albert and the Cosby Kids,* attracted an enthusiastic audience.

Cosby finally hit the television jackpot in 1984 as producer and star of *The Cosby Show,* a weekly series about the Huxtable family, in which he played a doctor whose wife is a lawyer. Before the last episode aired in April 1992, *The Cosby Show* was watched by more people than any other situation comedy on television. Also an author, Cosby wrote the 1986 best seller *Fatherhood,* as well as *Love and Marriage, Childhood,* and *Little Bill,* a series for children. In 2007, he published, with Alvin F. Poussaint, *Come on, People: On the Path from Victims to Victors.*

◆

WHO WAS THE FIRST AFRICAN AMERICAN ACTRESS TO HAVE HER OWN TV SERIES?

Diahann Carroll, whose weekly series *Julia* began in the fall of 1968, was the first African American actress to star in her own weekly television show. (Although *Beulah,* which made its debut in 1950, was the first television series starring a black actress, the title character was actually played by three different actresses over the show's three-year run.) In the title role of *Julia,* Carroll portrayed a war widow who worked as a nurse to support herself and her young son. The series ran until mid-1971.

Carroll, who began her career as a singer, was born in 1935 and grew up in New York's Harlem and the Bronx. At age ten, the talented youngster won a Metropolitan Opera scholarship, and at fourteen, while a student at the High School of Music and Art in New York City, she won first prize on *Arthur Godfrey's Talent Scouts.*

Carroll gained fame in 1954 as the costar of the Broadway musical *House of Flowers,* and eight years later she won a Tony award for her role in *No Strings.* In 1974 Carroll received another honor; the Academy Award committee gave her a Best Actress nomination for her touching performance as a single mother in the film *Claudine.* And in 1984, midway through the run of the hit television series *Dynasty,* Carroll joined the show in the role of Dominique Deveraux, a glamorous, sophisticated, and unscrupulous singer. After *Dynasty* ended its run in 1987, she appeared in several television movies, including *Lonesome Dove,* and the 1997 film *Eve's Bayou.* In 2006, Carroll began the first of many appearances on the television series *Grey's Anatomy* in a role that earned her an Emmy in 2008. That year, her memoir, *The Legs Are the Last to Go,* was a best seller. In 2009, Carroll joined the cast of the USA network series *White Collar,* and in January 2011, she was inducted into the Television Academy Hall of Fame.

◆

WHO WAS THE FIRST AFRICAN AMERICAN ACTOR TO COSTAR IN A TV WESTERN SERIES?

Combining his theater training with his spiritual beliefs, Otis Young became an actor, playwright, pastor, and teacher. Born in Providence, Rhode Island, one of fourteen children, Young joined the Marine Corps at seventeen, serving in the Korean War. He then enrolled in acting classes at New York University on the GI Bill and appeared onstage in New York and Los Angeles. In 1968 he was signed to costar with Don Murray in *The Outcasts,* a Western series that ran on ABC for one season. He later attracted attention as a sailor transporting a prisoner to the brig in the 1973 movie *The Last Detail,* starring Jack Nicholson.

Although he acted occasionally in the 1980s, Young turned to religion, earning a degree from the L.I.F.E. Bible College in Los Angeles in 1983. He moved to Rochester, New York, three years later, serving as a pastor and teaching acting and the art of preaching. He earned a master's degree in communications in 1992 and taught speech and communications and theater at a community college in Rochester until his retirement in 1999. He moved back to Los Angeles the next year, where he worked on his autobiography and wrote plays until he died of a stroke in October 2001.

◆

WHICH AFRICAN AMERICAN ENTERTAINER HOSTED THE FIRST SUCCESSFUL TV VARIETY SHOW?

Clerow Wilson, born in 1933 in New Jersey, was one of eighteen children in an impoverished household. After years of bouncing from foster homes to reform school, sixteen-year-old Wilson lied about his age and joined the air force. His outgoing personality and funny stories made him popular; he was even asked to tour military bases to cheer up other servicemen.

He left the service in 1954 and moved to San Francisco, working as a bellhop and perfecting his comedy routine. He managed to get jobs at various comedy clubs using his nickname, Flip. He eventually became a regular at the Apollo Theatre in Harlem and was a favorite guest on *The Tonight Show, Laugh-In,* and *The Ed Sullivan Show.* Finally, Wilson got his own television program, *The Flip Wilson Show,* debuting on NBC in 1970. He played host to many African American entertainers and performed in comedy sketches. His characters included Reverend Leroy, pastor of the Church of What's Happening Now; and Geraldine, whose line "The devil made me do it" became a national expression. The show aired through 1974, gaining high ratings and great popularity. Wilson won a Golden Globe award for best actor in a television series, and the show won eighteen Emmys in the 1972 and 1973 seasons.

After his show closed, Wilson made attempts to make movies and appear in other television programs, but nothing worked out.

His name faded from show business, and he died of cancer in California at the age of sixty-four.

♦

WHO WAS THE FIRST AFRICAN AMERICAN WOMAN TO COMPETE FOR MISS AMERICA?

In 1970 Cheryl Adrienne Browne became the first African American to enter the contest for the title of Miss America. A native of Jamaica, New York, Browne was a sophomore at Luther College in Iowa when she was chosen to represent that state in the pageant in Atlantic City. She later embarked on what became a lengthy career in banking.

♦

WHO WAS THE FIRST AFRICAN AMERICAN MR. AMERICA?

Chris Dickerson won his first bodybuilding contest, Junior Mr. USA, in 1966. Four years later, he earned a top bodybuilding honor when he was crowned Mr. America. Dickerson, one of triplets born in Montgomery, Alabama, in 1939, was an outstanding athlete in high school. Planning to pursue a singing career, he took up bodybuilding to strengthen his voice and develop breath control. He earned first place in many competitions and, in 1982, won the Mr. Olympia contest in London. After a competitive career that lasted more than three decades, Dickerson retired in 1994.

♦

WHO WAS THE FIRST AFRICAN AMERICAN TO HOST A TELEVISION GAME SHOW?

When Adam Wade was made host of the nationally televised game show *Musical Chairs,* in 1975, he was the veteran of a successful singing career that had ended badly. Wade hit the peak of the popular music industry in the early 1960s. His first

ADAM WADE

record, "Ruby," was a hit, and a year later, in 1961, he had three singles in the Top 10. But the singer, only in his mid-twenties, hadn't learned to manage his money and found himself in debt.

Refusing to be defeated, Wade began taking charge of his career and eventually won the spot of the first African American game show host on national television. Unfortunately, *Musical Chairs* was cancelled after just one season on CBS. Wade found work doing television commercials, for which he won two awards, and acted in TV dramas, on stage, and in the movies.

◆

WHO WAS THE FIRST AFRICAN AMERICAN WOMAN CROWNED MISS AMERICA?

Vanessa Williams, born in Westchester County, New York, was a twenty-one-year-old Syracuse University student when she was crowned the first African American Miss America in September 1983. Ten months later, after revealing photographs of her were published in a national magazine, her title was taken away and awarded to another African American woman, runner-up Suzette Charles, from New Jersey.

Williams started a singing and acting career in 1987, making her record debut a year later with the album *The Right Stuff,* which earned her three Grammy nominations. Over the next ten years, she continued to make popular albums while also becoming a sought-after actress. She was a hit on Broadway in *Kiss of the Spider Woman,* and appeared in the films *Eraser, Dance With Me, Soul Food,* and the 2000 remake of *Shaft.*

Williams received a Tony nomination for her portrayal of Witch in the 2002 revival of the Broadway musical *Into the Woods.* In 2006, she took on the role of the magazine editor Wilhelmina Slater in the popular television comedy series, *Ugly Betty.* From 2010 to 2012, Williams starred in the television series *Desperate Housewives,* and in 2012, she took a featured role in the series *666 Park Avenue.* In March 2013, she opened on Broadway in the Horton Foote play *The Trip to Bountiful,* which also starred Cicely Tyson and Cuba Gooding Jr.

A memoir she wrote with her mother, Helen Williams, *You Have No Idea: A Famous Daughter, Her No-nonsense Mother, and How They Survived Pageants, Hollywood, Love, Loss (and Each Other)* was published in 2012.

◆

WHO WAS THE FIRST AFRICAN AMERICAN WOMAN TO HOST A NATIONAL TV TALK SHOW?

One of the most successful women in the entertainment industry, Oprah Winfrey always worked hard to do her best. Born in Kosciusko, Mississippi, in 1954, Winfrey went to Nashville, Tennessee, when she was a teenager, to live with her father. He encouraged her to study hard in school, where she won prizes for debating.

Winfrey began her broadcasting career in Nashville radio while still in high school. At nineteen, she became the first African American woman to anchor the news at a Nashville television station. She moved on to a Baltimore station to coanchor the six o'clock news, and a year later became cohost of the show *People Are Talking,* where she remained until she went to Chicago in 1984 as host of *A.M. Chicago.* Her skills as a talk show host attracted such a wide audience that one year later the program was expanded and renamed *The Oprah Winfrey Show.* In 1986 the program was syndicated nationally, growing in popularity to become the highest-rated talk show in television history.

Winfrey also pursued a parallel career as an actress; in 1985 she was nominated for an Academy Award for her role as Sophia in the film *The Color Purple.* In 1998 she starred in the film based on Toni Morrison's novel *Beloved.* She also appeared in and produced a number of made-for-television movies.

Her skills as a businesswoman were demonstrated when, in 1988, she became the first African American woman to form her own television and film production company, Harpo Productions. The company's productions include the 2005 adaptation of Zora Neale Hurston's *Their Eyes Were Watching God,* starring Halle Berry, and the 2007 film, *The Great Debaters*, directed by and starring Denzel Washington. In 1996 she started Oprah's Book Club, turning many books into best sellers, and soon launched a charity called Oprah's Angel Network. In April 2000 she started a publication, *O, the Oprah Magazine,* and formed another company, Oxygen Media LLC, which included a women's cable network.

Winfrey revealed the secret to her success in a commencement address at the Young Women's Leadership School in New York City in June 2001 when she said, "In my life I have learned, you do the good work, you be as excellent as possible, because excellence is the best deterrent to racism, to sexism . . . When you are excellent, the world notices."

In January 2011, Winfrey launched OWN, The Oprah Winfrey Network, and the final episode of *The Oprah Winfrey Show* aired five months later. According to *Forbes* magazine, her net worth as of September 2012 was $2.7 billion. *Forbes* reported that she was the highest earning celebrity in 2012 and that she had continued to support educational causes, spending, to that date, more than $100 million on the Oprah Winfrey Leadership Academy for Girls in South Africa.

◆

WHO WAS THE FIRST AFRICAN AMERICAN RINGMASTER FOR THE RINGLING BROS. AND BARNUM & BAILEY CIRCUS?

In 1998, the famed Ringling Brothers and Barnum & Bailey circus introduced its new singing ringmaster, Johnathan Lee Iverson, the youngest in the circus's 119-year history and the first African American. Iverson, a New York City native, was only twenty-two when he first donned the traditional top hat of ringmaster. He began his performing career at the age of eleven with the Boys Choir of Harlem, studied at Fiorello LaGuardia High School, and graduated from the University of Hartford's Hartt School of Music in 1998 with a degree in voice performance.

Iverson was discovered by the circus's director when he was auditioning for a dinner theater job. The director was looking for a performer who could revive the concept of the singing ringmaster. Not only was Iverson a trained singer with a fine voice, but he had self-confidence, charisma, and an impressive six-foot, three-inch frame just made for the ringmaster's glittery outfits. Iverson said he thought of the circus as the forerunner of American entertainment. "Anything flashy and big and incredible you see on TV," he said, "that's the circus's influence."

Iverson left the company in 2004 to pursue musical theater, but after several years he was asked to return. In 2013, he continued his reign as ringmaster with the Ringling Brothers and Barnum & Bailey show Dragons.

JOHNATHAN LEE IVERSON

◆

WHO WAS THE FIRST AFRICAN AMERICAN WOMAN TO CREATE AND PRODUCE A TOP TV SERIES?

Shonda Rhimes grew up in a family that loved to read books and tell stories. Rhimes was born in 1970, the youngest of six children; the family lived in University Park, a suburb of Chicago. When she was around four years old, she began telling stories into her parents' tape recorder, which they would then type up for her. Continuing her interest in literature, she majored in English at

Dartmouth College and became involved in a theater group there. She recalled a high point of her college experience in a 2008 magazine interview. In her senior year, she said, she directed George C. Wolfe's play, *The Colored Museum*, and on opening night, "I stood in the back watching my fellow students acting, and I knew that I wanted to be part of the arts for the rest of my life."

After graduating in 1991, she took a job with an advertising agency, but soon left to enroll in the University of Southern California's School of Cinema-Television, earning a Master of Fine Arts degree. The next two years were spent trying to sell her first screenplay, and when she finally found a buyer, her career took off. She went on to write the screenplays for such films as *Introducing Dorothy Dandridge*, *Crossroads*, and *The Princess Diaries 2*.

Rhimes then came up with an idea for a television series set in a hospital that would focus on the relationships among new surgeons. She turned in a pilot script for the show, *Grey's Anatomy*, just before Christmas 2003, and in early 2004, ABC gave it the go-ahead. The series was a huge success; its fifth season started in the fall of 2008. Rhimes also created a spin-off, *Private Practice*, that debuted in 2007. In 2012, Rhimes launched yet another television series, *Scandal*, a political drama.

FILM

WHO WAS THE FIRST AFRICAN AMERICAN FILMMAKER TO PRODUCE MOVIES WITH BLACK CASTS?

William Foster became interested in theater while living in New York City, where he settled in 1884. He first got a job working with horses and became an authority on the performance records of racehorses. Around 1900 Foster worked as a press agent for the entertainers Bert Williams and George Walker. In 1910 he moved to Chicago, started the Foster Photoplay Company, and began making short films with all-black casts. Since he didn't own any camera equipment, he borrowed some from a local camera store owner. And as a stage manager for the Pekin Theatre, he was able to recruit actors from the company.

Foster's first films were *Birth Mark, The Butler,* and *The Railroad Porter.* He wrote, directed, and filmed most of his movies himself, but he had to rely on financing from white backers. He made eighteen films altogether, and although they were never successful, he continued to insist that African American filmmakers should make movies with black actors for black audiences.

◆

WHAT WAS THE FIRST MOVIE TO FEATURE AN AFRICAN AMERICAN ACTOR?

In 1914 an independent black film company released a movie called *Darktown Jubilee,* starring the African American comedian Bert Williams. A screening of the movie in Brooklyn produced shouts, catcalls, and a near race riot. Realizing that white audiences were not ready for African American movie stars, the producers of *Darktown Jubilee* took their film out of circulation.

◆

WHO WAS THE FIRST AFRICAN AMERICAN ACTOR
TO MAKE A CAREER IN FILMS?

Noble Johnson, born in Missouri in 1881 and raised in Colorado, was one of Hollywood's most active and successful African American actors, appearing in movies for about forty years. In his first film, a Western produced in 1909 by the Lubin Film Production Company of Philadelphia, he played an American Indian. In 1915 he moved to Los Angeles, where he helped found the Lincoln Motion Picture Company, an African American production company. He became president of Lincoln and starred in its first three films, *The Realization of a Negro's Ambition*, in which he played a successful engineer, *The Trooper of Company K*, and *The Law of Nature*.

Johnson then moved to the Universal Film Company, where he specialized in portraying characters of various races. He was a cannibal chief in *Little Robinson Crusoe*, and Chief Sitting Bull in *The Flaming Frontier*; he drove a chariot in *King of Kings*, and in 1932 he played a Russian villain in *The Most Dangerous Game*. Johnson's last screen appearance before he retired in 1950 was in the Roy Rogers film, *North of the Great Divide*.

◆

WHAT WAS THE FIRST AFRICAN AMERICAN–OWNED
COMPANY TO PRODUCE SERIOUS FILMS?

The Lincoln Motion Picture Company was the first production company started by African Americans to make serious films with black performers for African American audiences. It was founded in 1916 by the actors Noble Johnson and Clarence Brooks and a prosperous druggist, James T. Smith; Johnson's brother George soon joined the organization. The only white partner was the cameraman, Harry T. Gant, who filmed all of the company's productions.

Lincoln's first venture was *The Realization of a Negro's Ambition*, starring Noble Johnson as a Tuskegee Institute engineering graduate who leaves his sweetheart to travel to California, where he makes a fortune and then returns to marry the girl back home and live happily ever after. Lincoln's second film, *The Trooper of*

Company K, also starring Noble Johnson, was about the African American Tenth Cavalry fighting in Mexico. Despite the high quality of its movies, Lincoln was often unable to persuade white theater owners to show them. And as an African American company, it was unable to obtain financing in advance and had to rely on profits from finished films.

When Noble Johnson left Lincoln in 1918 to make movies for Universal, Clarence Brooks took over as leading man, starring in two well-received films, *A Man's Duty* and *By Right of Birth.* But by 1923, financial and distribution problems forced the company to dissolve.

◆

WHO WAS THE FIRST AFRICAN AMERICAN PERFORMER AWARDED A LONG-TERM MOVIE CONTRACT?

When Frederick Ernest Morrison was just a small child, his father, a New Orleans chef, moved to Beverly Hills to cook for a rich oilman. Little Frederick was barely five years old when he was discovered by a filmmaker looking for a cute African American child. Billed as Sunshine Sammy Morrison, he made his film debut in 1917. Two years later he was signed by the producer Hal Roach, who cast him as an inquisitive little kid in the comedy films of Harold Lloyd and Snub Pollard. Morrison was so appealing that Roach decided to create a series around his talents, giving birth to the *Our Gang* films, which featured young Morrison from 1922 to 1924. When he grew older, he played Scruno in numerous East Side Kids movies, such as *Pride of the Bowery* and *Spooks Run Wild,* both released in 1941.

In 1945 Morrison left the movie business and joined the aerospace industry, retiring in the early 1970s. He occasionally appeared on television in shows like *Good Times* and *The Jeffersons,* and in 1987, two years before he died, he was inducted in the Black Filmmakers Hall of Fame.

◆

WHO WAS THE FIRST SUCCESSFUL
AFRICAN AMERICAN FILMMAKER?

Oscar Micheaux was born on a farm in Illinois in 1884. He left home in his teens and worked as a bootblack and then a Pullman porter. When he was about twenty-five he settled in South Dakota, becoming one of the few African American home-steaders in the state. After about four years of working the land, Micheaux used his own experiences to write a novel entitled *The Homesteader,* publishing it himself and selling it door to door around the region.

Micheaux moved on to Sioux City, Iowa, where he started his own publishing company and continued to write and sell his books. In 1918 the Lincoln Motion Picture Company, a black-owned com-pany from Los Angeles, approached Micheaux with plans to make a movie of *The Homesteader.* But when they refused Micheaux's offer to direct the film, he decided to produce the movie himself. He established the Micheaux Film and Book Company and began to raise money around Sioux City.

Micheaux finished *The Homesteader* in 1919 and traveled from city to city with prints of the film, asking theater owners to show it and at the same time raising money from them for his next production. Between 1919 and 1948, he produced forty-eight films; his last was *The Betrayal.* He died at the age of sixty-seven in Charlotte, North Carolina, after a heart attack. His body was sent to Great Bend, Kansas, where his parents were buried. His tomb-stone reads: "Pioneer Black Film Maker & Author, a Man Ahead of His Time."

◆

WHAT WERE THE FIRST FEATURE-LENGTH
AFRICAN AMERICAN TALKIES?

The year 1929 marked the release of the first two talking pic-tures with African American casts. The first to be released, *Hearts in Dixie,* produced by the William Fox Studio, featured the first all-black cast ever seen in a full-length film (the only white role

HEARTS IN DIXIE

was that of a doctor). A musical about a farmer and his family on a Southern plantation, the film abounded in stereotypes.

The role of the grandfather of the family was played by Clarence Muse, a lawyer, director, and producer with a background in theater. After starring in *Hearts in Dixie,* Muse had a successful career in films, making more than fifty movies in twenty-five years. The movie also starred the actor Stepin Fetchit in one of his most prominent roles.

Several months later the director King Vidor released his first sound film, *Hallelujah!* The movie was a landmark in films about African American families. Although the characters were hackneyed and the plot was melodramatic, the performances of the leads and the spirituals sung by the Dixie Jubilee Choir made it memorable. *Hallelujah!* told the story of a cotton farmer's son, played by Daniel Haynes, led astray by a cabaret singer named Chick, portrayed by the beautiful young Nina Mae McKinney.

Hallelujah! was given a double premiere, one in the Lafayette Theater in Harlem and the other at a theater in midtown Manhattan. Whereas an attempt was made in the North to keep white and black movie audiences separate, in the South most theaters banned *Hallelujah!* altogether.

◆

WHO WAS THE FIRST AFRICAN AMERICAN HOLLYWOOD STAR?

Lincoln Theodore Monroe Andrew Perry, better known as Stepin Fetchit, was born in 1902 in Key West, Florida, the son of a cigar maker. He was in his early teens when he left to seek his fortune

STEPIN FETCHIT

in show business, eventually hooking up with a vaudeville partner, Ed Lee. Although some say he took his name from a racehorse, another story is that the two called their act "Step 'n' Fetchit: Two Dancing Fools From Dixie." The duo eventually broke up and he took the name with him to Hollywood.

Fetchit's first big break in movies was the 1929 all-black talkie, *Hearts in Dixie*. He appeared in many films during the 1920s and '30s, performing with such stars as Shirley Temple and Will Rogers. The first African American movie star to receive feature billing, he always played the same role: a gawky, shuffling character who mumbled and muttered.

Offscreen, Fetchit's wild escapades made headlines, and he could be seen cruising the streets of Los Angeles in his expensive automobile. But by the late 1930s he had been released from his movie contract, and although he was said to have made millions, he ended up nearly penniless. He was last seen on the screen in a cameo role in the 1976 comedy *Won Ton Ton, the Dog Who Saved Hollywood*. Fetchit died in California in 1985.

◆

WHO WAS THE FIRST AFRICAN AMERICAN ACTRESS TO BECOME A WELL-KNOWN MOVIE STAR?

Nina Mae McKinney was born in 1913 in Lancaster, South Carolina, and was raised by her grandmother until the age of twelve, when her parents sent for her from New York City. When McKinney was fifteen, she joined the chorus line of Lew Leslie's show, *Blackbirds of 1928*. A year later the Hollywood director King Vidor chose her to star in *Hallelujah!*, one of the first sound films with an all-black cast. She portrayed a seductive cabaret dancer named Chick.

After her successful appearance in *Hallelujah!*, MGM studios offered McKinney a five-year contract, but she discovered that there were few leading movie roles for African American actresses. When her contract ended, she left Hollywood to travel abroad and performed all over Europe, singing in nightclubs and cafes. In England she starred with Paul Robeson in the 1935 film *Sanders of the River*. Back in the United States, she made a few minor movies. Her

HALLELUJAH!

last screen appearance was a supporting role in the 1949 film *Pinky*. McKinney died in New York City in 1967.

◆

WHO WAS THE FIRST AFRICAN AMERICAN ACTRESS TO ENTERTAIN AT THE WHITE HOUSE?

The lovely actress and singer Etta Moten captured the hearts of many filmgoers with her interpretation of the Depression-era song, "Remember My Forgotten Man," in the movie *Gold Diggers of 1933*, which starred the actor James Cagney. In January 1934, President Franklin Roosevelt and his wife, Eleanor, invited her to perform for their guests at a White House dinner. She sang songs from the movie, as well as the spiritual "Swing Low, Sweet Chariot."

Moten, who was born in 1902 in San Antonio, Texas, was singing in a recital during her senior year at the University of Kansas when she was asked to join the Eva Jessye Choir in New York City. She sang on Broadway in such musicals as *Sugar Hill* and *Lysistrata*, which also featured the young Sidney Poitier, and appeared in

ETTA MOTEN

the 1933 movie *Flying Down to Rio*. In 1934 Moten married Claude Barnett, founder of the Negro Associated Press. She gave concerts for many years and starred in the 1942 Broadway production of *Porgy and Bess*. In the 1950s she and her husband traveled to Ghana as members of a U.S. delegation. She also represented the United States at the independence ceremonies of Nigeria and Zambia. As a resident of Chicago, she was an active supporter of the DuSable Museum and the Lyric Opera.

◆

WHO WAS THE FIRST AFRICAN AMERICAN MOVIE COWBOY?

While singing in a Detroit nightclub in 1933, Herb Jeffries, a native of that city, was approached by Louis Armstrong, who gave him a note of introduction to the bandleader Erskine Tate. Jeffries sang with Tate for a time until Earl Hines hired him away. Jeffries eventually left Hines and went to Los Angeles in 1937, where he continued his singing career, gaining fame for his rendition of "Cocktails for Two."

The popular vocalist was discovered by Hollywood and soon became the star of a series of musical Westerns with all-black casts. Using the name Herbert Jeffrey, he was featured as a singing cowboy in such films as *Harlem on the Prairie,* released in 1937, and *The Bronze Buckaroo,* in 1938, which was advertised as a "roaring round-up of song-studded thrills!"

Jeffries left Hollywood to devote himself to music, joining Duke Ellington's orchestra and, in 1940, recording his signature tune, "Flamingo." Over the years, he continued to sing and record, leaving the United States to spend a decade in France. In 1994 Jeffries settled in Palm Desert, California. Five years later, at the age of eighty-seven, he released a CD, *The Duke and I.* In November 2000, Jeffries was inducted into the Honored Member Society of an organization called Trail Riders of the West. At the celebration dinner, he sang "Satin Doll," "I Got It Bad," and "It Don't Mean a Thing."

◆

WHO WAS THE FIRST AFRICAN AMERICAN ACTRESS TO STAR IN A MAJOR FILM?

One of the most talented performers in Hollywood, Louise Beavers made dozens of movies but suffered the plight of many fine African American actresses—she could not avoid being cast as a servant. Born in Cincinnati in 1902, Beavers grew up in Pasadena, California, and came to Hollywood as a maid for the silent-film star Leatrice Joy. She began accepting small roles in movies, and after appearing in *Uncle Tom's Cabin* in 1927, she worked steadily, usually playing a cheerful maid for the likes of Mae West and Jean Harlow.

Her great triumph was the 1934 film *Imitation of Life.* She and the actress Claudette Colbert played two widows, each with a child to raise. Critics applauded Beavers's performance in the movie, and many thought she should have been nominated for an Oscar. Beavers continued to play her usual movie roles throughout the 1940s and '50s; she was forced to gain weight and wear padding to maintain her plump appearance.

Her other outstanding roles were in the 1939 film *Made for Each Other* and the 1948 Cary Grant movie *Mr. Blandings Builds His Dream House*. In 1950 she played Robinson's mother in *The Jackie Robinson Story,* and two years later she starred in the television series *Beulah*. Her last movie was *Facts of Life* in 1960—playing a maid. She died two years later.

◆

WHO WAS THE FIRST AFRICAN AMERICAN TO WIN AN ACADEMY AWARD?

When Hattie McDaniel was a child in Wichita, Kansas, where she was born in 1895, her father, a former slave and a banjo player, entered her and her siblings in talent contests. They then formed a traveling vaudeville show. In the 1920s the show broke up and McDaniel went to Hollywood, working as a maid until she started getting movie roles. But even on screen, McDaniel was limited to playing a maid, although she gave her portrayals a certain flair that made audiences remember her. In response to those who criticized her choice of roles, she reportedly said, "It's better to play a maid than to be one."

McDaniel appeared in almost fifty films in the 1930s, and her talent was finally rewarded when she was presented with an Academy Award as Best Supporting Actress for her performance as Mammy, in the 1939 hit movie *Gone With the Wind*. She was the first African American to receive an Oscar, but because of her race, she wasn't allowed to attend the movie's premiere in Atlanta. McDaniel continued to make films throughout the 1940s. Her last substantial role was in the 1944 drama *Since You Went Away,* in which she played a maid.

The next year she became a civil rights activist in her community, organizing her Los Angeles neighbors to fight, and eventually win, a battle against housing segregation. In 1947 she began playing the title role in *The Beulah Show* on radio. She later took over the role on television, leaving in 1952, shortly before she died of cancer at the age of fifty-four.

◆

WHO WAS THE FIRST AFRICAN AMERICAN WOMAN
TO JOIN THE SCREEN WRITERS GUILD?

Mary Elizabeth Vroman was born in Buffalo, New York, in 1924 and raised in the British West Indies. She returned to the United States to attend Alabama State Teachers College. When she was in her twenties and employed as a schoolteacher, she wrote a short story called "See How They Run," which was published in a 1952 issue of the *Ladies' Home Journal*.

Vroman's story was about a rural schoolteacher trying to help a troubled student. The story was bought by MGM studios and released in 1953 as the movie *Bright Road*, starring Dorothy Dandridge as the teacher and Harry Belafonte as the sensitive and devoted elementary school principal. Vroman wrote the screenplay for *Bright Road* and became the first African American woman granted membership in the Screen Writers Guild. She went on to write two novels and one nonfiction book before she died in 1967.

◆

WHO WAS THE FIRST AFRICAN AMERICAN
FILM STAR NOMINATED FOR AN OSCAR
AS BEST ACTRESS?

Dorothy Dandridge started her performing career in Cleveland when she was only six years old, singing, dancing, doing acrobatics, and playing the violin with her sister, Vivian, in an act called The Wonder Children. They performed around the South for several years and in 1930 moved to Los Angeles. After the two were joined by a third young woman, Etta Jones, to form The Dandridge Sisters, they toured the country, recording with the Jimmy Lunceford band and performing at the Cotton Club with Cab Calloway. They appeared in *A Day at the Races* and a few other films before the group broke up in 1940.

Dandridge continued to sing in clubs and played a few bit parts in films. Her big break came in 1953 when she costarred with Harry Belafonte in *Bright Road,* and a year later she won an Academy Award nomination for Best Actress, for her role in *Carmen Jones*—a first for an African American actress. Dandridge's career,

DOROTHY DANDRIDGE IN *BRIGHT ROAD*

built on her image as a seductress, began a gradual decline. She failed at a comeback attempt in the 1960s, and met her tragic end at the age of forty-three when she died in her Los Angeles apartment from an overdose of antidepressants.

◆

WHO WAS THE FIRST AFRICAN AMERICAN ACTOR TO WIN AN ACADEMY AWARD?

Sidney Poitier was born in 1927 in Miami, Florida, and raised on Cat Island in the Bahamas, where his parents were tomato farmers. When he was fifteen he traveled to Miami to join his older brother, and a year later he took a bus to New York City. He worked as a dishwasher and spent a year in the army, returning to

New York to wash dishes again. Responding to a newspaper ad announcing "Actors Wanted," he applied for a job at the American Negro Theater, which rejected him. Undeterred, he polished his speaking skills and reapplied. This time the theater company took him in, and he made his stage debut in the African American version of *Lysistrata*.

In 1949 he captured a leading role in the movie *No Way Out*. After finishing a second film, *Cry, the Beloved Country*, he returned to New York to take the lead in a play, *Detective Story*, which was being produced at the Apollo Theatre in Harlem. The play had a short run, and Poitier decided to open a small barbecue restaurant called Ribs in the Ruff to support himself. In 1954 he was called back to Hollywood for a major role in the groundbreaking film *Blackboard Jungle*.

Poitier went on to play other leading parts in such movies as the 1958 drama *The Defiant Ones* and the 1961 film version of Lorraine Hansberry's play *A Raisin in the Sun*, repeating the role he had played on Broadway two years earlier. In 1963 he won an Oscar for his role in *Lilies of the Field*, becoming the first African American actor to receive an Academy Award.

After making *Guess Who's Coming to Dinner* in 1967, Poitier began concentrating more on directing, while also continuing to appear in films. In 1997 he portrayed Nelson Mandela in the television movie *Mandela and de Klerk*. Among his many honors were life achievement awards from the American Film Institute, the Kennedy Center, and the Screen Actors Guild. At the Academy Awards Ceremony in March 2002 Poitier was given an honorary Oscar for his life's work. Poitier has published three memoirs: *This Life*, in 1980; *The Measure of a Man: A Spiritual Autobiography*, in 2000, and *Life Beyond Measure: Letters to My Great-Granddaughter* in 2008. In 2011, he was honored by the Film Society of Lincoln Center for his contribution to cinema as well as his roles as "diplomat, philanthropist, and humanitarian."

◆

WHO WAS THE FIRST AFRICAN AMERICAN TO PRODUCE AND DIRECT A FILM FOR A MAJOR STUDIO?

Gordon Parks Sr. was born in 1912 in the small town of Fort Scott, Kansas, one of fifteen children. His mother died when he was a teenager, and he set out on his own. To support himself he worked as a piano player, a busboy, and a singer with a band. In 1933 he joined the Civilian Conservation Corps, a government program that gave work to impoverished young men. He then became a waiter on a cross-country train.

But Parks's fate was sealed when he bought a camera in a pawnshop for $7.50 and decided to become a photographer. He got his first break when the owner of a women's clothing store in St. Paul, Minnesota, hired him to photograph her fashions. One day, Joe Louis's wife, Marva, saw his photos and encouraged him to move to Chicago, where he took pictures of fashionable society women but also photographed residents of the city's impoverished South Side.

In 1941 Parks earned a fellowship that brought him to Washington, D.C., to take photographs for the Farm Security Administration and then the Office of War Information. Moving to New York City in 1944, he worked as a freelance photographer for magazines and for the Standard Oil Company, and in 1948 he embarked on a career with *Life* magazine.

In 1969 Parks turned to Hollywood, where he produced and directed the film version of his book *The Learning Tree* for Warner Brothers, making him the first African American to produce and direct a major studio film. His other movie credits include *Shaft, Shaft's Big Score,* and a 1968 documentary, *Diary of a Harlem Family,* which won an Emmy award. A true Renaissance man, Parks composed more than a dozen musical works and wrote many books of poetry, fiction, and nonfiction, including his fourth volume of autobiography, *Voices in the Mirror,* as well as *Half Past Autumn,* a collection of memoirs and images published in 1997. Parks died in his Manhattan home in 2006 at the age of ninety-three.

♦

WHO WAS THE FIRST AFRICAN AMERICAN MAN
TO WIN AN OSCAR FOR BEST SUPPORTING ACTOR?

Louis Gossett, Jr., born in Brooklyn in 1936, began his acting career in high school, where he took an acting class and appeared in a school production. He was only sixteen when he auditioned for a Broadway play, *Take a Giant Step,* and was chosen to play the lead. A talented basketball player, he attended New York University on an athletic scholarship and, after graduation, was drafted by the New York Knicks. He played with the team for a short time before returning to his real love, acting.

His appearance in both the stage and film productions of Lorraine Hansberry's play *A Raisin in the Sun* led to many other roles on stage, in film, and on television. In 1977 he was awarded an Emmy for his portrayal of Fiddler in the TV series *Roots.* And it was his role as Gunnery Sergeant Emil Foley in the 1982 film *An Officer and a Gentleman* that won him an Academy Award as best supporting actor, the first for an African American man. In recognition of his more than fifty-year acting career, in 2008 the International Press Academy presented Gossett with the Mary Pickford Award for outstanding contributions to the entertainment industry. His memoir, *An Actor and a Gentleman,* was published in 2010.

◆

WHO WAS THE FIRST AFRICAN AMERICAN WOMAN
FILMMAKER TO PRODUCE A FULL-LENGTH
FEATURE FILM?

In 1992 the movie *Daughters of the Dust,* directed by the African American filmmaker Julie Dash, opened to critical acclaim. The film was an evocation of the West African culture that is preserved on the islands off the coast of Georgia and South Carolina, a background Dash inherited from her father. Dash, who grew up in a New York City housing project and studied filmmaking at the American Film Institute and the University of California at Los Angeles, spent sixteen years making *Daughters of the Dust.* It was her seventh film and first full-length feature, and won first prize for cinematography at the 1991 Sundance Film Festival in Utah. In 1997 Dash directed a short film for the HBO production *Subway Stories,* and in 2000 she was codirector of the MTV film *Love Song.* Her other films include *Brothers of the Borderland* and the television movie *The Rosa Parks Story.* In 2004 the Library of Congress placed *Daughters of the Dust* in the National Film Registry, which preserves films that are considered culturally and historically significant.

◆

WHO WAS THE FIRST AFRICAN AMERICAN DIRECTOR NOMINATED FOR AN OSCAR?

John Singleton was only twenty-two years old when he made his 1991 film *Boyz N the Hood,* which earned him an Academy Award nomination for Best Director. He was the youngest person and the first African American to be nominated for that award.

Singleton was born in 1968 in South Central Los Angeles and grew up in the neighborhood. He wrote the script for *Boyz N the Hood* (which also gained an Oscar nomination for Best Screen Play) while he was a student in the film writing program at the University of Southern California. The story of young people trying to survive in a danger-ridden Los Angeles neighborhood, the film received rave reviews and attracted a wide audience.

Singleton's second movie, *Poetic Justice,* starred singer Janet Jackson. His later films included *Rosewood,* in 1997, and a remake of *Shaft,* starring Samuel L. Jackson, in 2000. In June 2001, a movie critic for *The New York Times* called Singleton's new film, *Baby Boy,* "a powerful, compassionate and tough-minded critique of contemporary black manhood." In 2011, Singleton directed the thriller *Abduction.*

◆

WHO WAS THE FIRST AFRICAN AMERICAN WOMAN TO WIN AN OSCAR FOR BEST ACTRESS?

On March 24, 2002, the Academy Award for Best Actress was presented to Halle Berry for her performance as the widow of a death row inmate in the film *Monster's Ball*. The first African American to win for Best Actress in the seventy-four-year history of the Academy Awards, Berry, in an emotional acceptance speech, said, "This moment is for . . . every nameless, faceless woman of color that now has a chance because the door tonight has been opened."

As a high school student in a suburb of Cleveland, Ohio, where she was born in 1968, Berry was an honor society member, class president, prom queen, and editor of the school paper. She became a frequent beauty pageant winner, and after majoring in broadcast journalism for a time in a community college, she left school to study acting and pursue a modeling career. In 1989 she won a role in the television series *Living Dolls*, but her big opportunity came two years later when Spike Lee cast her as a crack addict in his film *Jungle Fever*. Her success in that role led to starring parts in a number of movies, including *Boomerang, Losing Isaiah, Bulworth,* and the 1999 television movie *Introducing Dorothy Dandridge,* for which she earned Golden Globe and Emmy awards. Berry's next film was the James Bond thriller *Die Another Day*, and in 2005 she was nominated for Emmy and Golden Globe awards for her performance in the television movie *Their Eyes Were Watching God*. In 2012, Berry appeared in the film *Cloud Atlas*. She starred in a thriller, *The Call*, in 2013.

◆

WHO WAS THE FIRST AFRICAN AMERICAN WOMAN TO WIN BEST DIRECTOR AT THE SUNDANCE FILM FESTIVAL?

Ava DuVernay's film *Middle of Nowhere,* about a young nurse whose husband is serving a prison sentence, is a "plaintive, slow-boiling, quietly soul-stirring drama about a woman coming into her own," according to an October 2012 review in the *New York Times*. It was this film that won DuVernay the best director

AVA DUVERNAY

award at the Sundance Film Festival earlier that year, a first for an African American woman.

DuVernay was born in 1972 and grew up in Lynwood, California, near Compton. After earning a bachelor's degree from UCLA in 1995, she worked as a movie publicist for four years before forming her own company, the DuVernay Agency, which developed marketing strategies for such films as *Dreamgirls, Invictus,* and *The Help.*

During the time that she was working on publicity for a client's 2004 movie, DuVernay was inspired to write the script for *Middle of Nowhere.* "Where I'm from, it's impossible not to look at this real epidemic in black and brown communities of incarceration and the women who are left behind," she told an Associated Press reporter.

"There's something very important about films about black women and girls being made by black women," she said. "It's a different perspective. It is a reflection as opposed to an interpretation. . . ."

During the eight years it took for the film to come to fruition, DuVernay wrote and directed *I Will Follow,* released in 2011, and made documentaries, including *My Mic Sounds Nice: A Truth About Women in Hip-Hop,* which was shown on BET in 2010. She also formed AFFRM, the African-American Film Festival Releasing Movement, a distribution company that promotes black-themed art films.

Speaking about her Sundance award, DuVernay told the *Los Angeles Times,* "I accept it with pride. It changed a lot for me, but I know there were black women before me who were certainly deserving."

HISTORY

WHO WAS THE FIRST MARTYR OF
THE AMERICAN REVOLUTION?

In the year 1770, at a time when people in the American colonies were growing increasingly weary of oppression under the British Empire, an African American man named Crispus Attucks was shot and killed by a British soldier in an event that became known as the Boston Massacre. Attucks, who had run away twenty years earlier to escape slavery and had spent much of his time at sea, was working on the docks in Boston.

On the snowy night of March 5, Attucks stood at the front of a crowd of colonists who had joined some boys pelting the British soldiers with snowballs and chunks of ice. The soldiers fired into the crowd, hitting Attucks in the chest. The tall, imposing man dropped to the ground and died. Four other men fell to their deaths at the hands of the British soldiers that night, but Attucks is remembered as the first colonist to die in the struggle for American independence.

◆

WHAT WAS THE FIRST AFRICAN AMERICAN
MUTUAL AID SOCIETY?

The Free African Society, the first mutual aid organization for African Americans, was founded in Philadelphia in 1787 by Richard Allen and Absalom Jones, who later became prominent religious leaders. Members of the Free African Society promised to lead orderly, sober lives, characterized by decorum and marital fidelity, and to contribute to the assistance of those who became widowed, orphaned, or ill.

One of the society's most remarkable public services took place during the great plague of 1793, when a yellow fever epidemic raced through the entire city. The organization offered to help all citizens who were stricken with the disease, and its members stepped forward to nurse the sick and carry away the bodies.

◆

WHO FOUNDED THE FIRST AFRICAN AMERICAN MASONIC LODGE?

Prince Hall, an African American patriot who fought in the Battle of Bunker Hill during the American Revolution, was born in Barbados in 1735 and migrated to Massachusetts in 1765. A few weeks before the outbreak of the Revolution, Hall and several other African Americans were initiated into the Masons, an international mutual aid society, by a British military lodge then stationed in Boston.

In July 1776 Hall and his fellow Masons were granted a license and became established as African Lodge No. 1, the first organized group of African American Masons in the country. The group finally received a charter from the Grand Lodge in England in 1787, and four years later the African Grand Lodge was established with Hall as grand master. He used his position to speak out against slavery and call for equal rights for African Americans. He fought to allow black children to receive a public education, finally opening a school in his own home. A year after Hall's death in 1807, his Masonic colleagues honored him by renaming their lodge Prince Hall Grand Lodge.

◆

WHO WAS THE FIRST SETTLER OF THE CITY OF CHICAGO?

When Jean Baptiste Pointe DuSable arrived at the mouth of the Chicago River some time in the late 1700s and established a trading post, he was known as a tall, handsome, cultured, Paris-educated fur trader who had friendly relationships with both Native Americans and whites. DuSable was born in Haiti around

1745; his mother was an African slave and his father a French seaman. When DuSable's mother died, his father sent him to France for an education and then put him to work as a sailor on one of his ships.

But when DuSable's ship was wrecked near New Orleans, he was afraid that he might become enslaved. He was hidden by Jesuits until he managed to leave the South for the Northwest, where he became a fur trapper. DuSable eventually reached the mouth of the Chicago River and set up his trading post, creating the first permanent settlement in what is now the city of Chicago. It was there that he built a comfortable five-room home, which he shared with his wife, Catherine, who was a Potawatomi Indian, and their son and daughter.

His trading post gradually expanded and became a major supply center for traders, trappers, and Native Americans. Despite his success, in 1800 DuSable sold his property for a small sum and left Chicago forever. No one knows why. Eighteen years later, he died a poor man and was buried in a cemetery in St. Charles, Missouri.

◆

WHO WAS THE FIRST TO EXPLORE THE DEPTHS OF THE LONGEST CAVE IN THE WORLD?

Mammoth Cave in Kentucky is the most extensive cave system in the world, with more than 350 miles of passageways. There is evidence that Native Americans discovered entrances to Mammoth Cave about 4,000 years ago. Guided by the light of torches made from dried weeds and canes, they explored about twenty miles of underground corridors. White men came to the cave in the 1790s to dig for saltpeter, which is used in making gunpowder, and adventurers arrived to investigate its subterranean wonders. But the most famous name connected with Mammoth Cave was that of Stephen Bishop, a slave.

In 1838 a Kentucky attorney, Franklin Gorin, bought Mammoth Cave. He brought his slave, seventeen-year-old Stephen Bishop, to learn the passageways and become a guide. A year later, Gorin sold both Mammoth Cave and Stephen Bishop to a Dr. John Croghan. Bishop was fascinated by the underground twists and turns of the cave and fearlessly explored its deepest sections, discovering rivers, bottomless pits, and dramatic chambers. Visitors were attracted to the handsome, knowledgeable Bishop, and he was in great demand. He guided many famous people, including painters, writers, and even a Norwegian violinist, who played a concerto in an underground hall.

Bishop eventually gained his freedom, as his master had decreed before he died. Although Bishop had talked of taking his wife and son to Liberia when he became free, he remained at Mammoth Cave. He died in the summer of 1857 and was buried in the Old Guide's Cemetery on the top of a ridge south of the entrance to the cave.

◆

WHO WAS THE FIRST AFRICAN AMERICAN WOMAN TO LECTURE AGAINST SLAVERY?

Born a slave named Isabella Baumfree near Kingston, New York, around 1797, Sojourner Truth changed her name some fifteen years after she was freed by the New York State Emancipation Act of 1827. She took the name Sojourner because of her wanderings, and Truth because she was to speak the truth about the evils of slavery. After years of being a slave, a wife and mother, a domestic worker in New York City, and an evangelist, Sojourner Truth spent much of the rest of her life traveling around the country, lecturing against slavery and in support of voting rights for women.

Nearly six feet tall with a deep voice and impressive features, she wore a satin banner across her chest that read: "Proclaim liberty throughout the land unto all the inhabitants thereof." She was a compelling lecturer, drawing crowds wherever she spoke. She visited President Lincoln in the White House several times, urging him to allow African American troops to fight with the Union forces in the Civil War. In Washington, she nursed wounded soldiers and helped resettle newly freed slaves.

After the war she continued to lecture for women's suffrage and on behalf of her people. In a speech she delivered in 1867, she said: "I come from . . . the country of the slave. They have got their liberty, so much good luck to have slavery partly destroyed; not entirely. I want it root and branch destroyed. Then we will all be free indeed." Sojourner Truth died in 1883 at her home in Battle Creek, Michigan.

In April 2009, First Lady Michelle Obama helped unveil a bust of Sojourner Truth in Emancipation Hall, the main room of the Capitol Visitor Center. Truth is the first African American woman to be honored with a statue in the Capitol. "Now many young boys and girls, like my own daughters, will come to Emancipation Hall and see the face of a woman who looks like them," Obama said.

◆

WHO WAS THE FIRST AFRICAN AMERICAN WOMAN TO BE HONORED WITH HER PICTURE ON A POSTAGE STAMP?

Harriet Tubman, referred to as "Moses" because she led hundreds of her people out of slavery, was born around 1820. Growing up as a slave on a Maryland plantation, she was forced to perform hard labor. When she was twelve years old, an overseer struck her on the head, causing a fractured skull that resulted in frequent seizures.

When her master died, she decided to escape, and in 1849 she left her husband and children and made her way north to Canada. Recalling her escape for her biographer, Tubman said, "When I found I had crossed that line, I looked at my hands to see if I was the same person. There was such a glory over everything."

Starting in 1850, Tubman became a "conductor" on the Underground Railroad, leading slaves to freedom. Large rewards were offered for her capture, but she was never caught and she never lost a passenger. In a ten-year period before the Civil War, she made nineteen trips down South, bringing back three hundred slaves, including her children, her brothers and their families, and her elderly parents, whom she settled in Canada. Her husband had married another woman during her absence. On her travels through New York State, she met a number of abolitionists in the community of Auburn, including William H. Seward, a

HARRIET TUBMAN

United States senator. In 1857 he offered Tubman a two-story brick home, where she relocated her parents.

After serving in the Civil War as a scout, spy, and nurse, she returned to Auburn, settling there with her new husband, Nelson Davis, whom she'd met during the war. In 1908 she built a home for the poor and elderly, where she worked and was later cared for until her death in 1913. She was buried with military honors in Auburn's Fort Hill Cemetery.

◆

WHAT WAS THE COUNTRY'S FIRST AFRICAN AMERICAN TOWN?

In the early 1820s, a group of eleven African American families, both fugitive and free, fled St. Louis, crossed the Mississippi River, and established the community of Brooklyn, Illinois. In 1873, the community was incorporated as a town. Brooklyn began to grow as it attracted other African Americans who commuted to jobs in nearby East St. Louis. Although the early citizens of the town were dedicated to self-determination, their economic opportunities diminished over the years. While industries blossomed in surrounding white communities, most of the businesses in Brooklyn, except nightclubs and illicit establishments, gradually disappeared. In 2007, the town's population was 626 and the median yearly income was less than $20,000.

The Historical Society of Brooklyn, Illinois, was formed to reverse this trend. Revitalization plans were initiated to attract new business and encourage former residents to return. "We will fulfill the dreams of those eleven courageous families that laid the blueprint for us to follow," said the society's founders.

In addition, an archaeology and historical research project was begun with the goal of understanding how ethnicity, class, religion, race, and developing markets influenced Brooklyn's residents.

◆

WHO WAS THE FIRST AFRICAN AMERICAN WOMAN TO DRIVE A U.S. MAIL COACH?

Mary Fields was born in about 1832 in a slave cabin in Tennessee. Little is known about her early life, but she eventually headed west, ending up at about the age of fifty in Montana, where she worked for the Ursuline nuns at their mission in Cascade. Standing six feet tall and weighing about 200 pounds, Fields was an impressive sight in the long dress and apron she wore over a pair of men's pants to protect herself from the cold. The nuns helped her set up a restaurant in Cascade, but it is said that the business failed because Fields gave away too many free meals.

In 1895 Fields got a job carrying the U.S. mail. Known as "Stagecoach Mary," she delivered the mail sitting on the coach smoking a big cigar, sometimes having to fight her way through blizzards and fend off attacks by wolves. She was past seventy when she decided to retire from the mail delivery job and open a laundry. Although this career was less arduous, Fields didn't lose her spirit.

Legend has it that she once punched a man and knocked him onto the street because he neglected to pay his laundry bill.

◆

WHO WAS THE FIRST PERSON TO REACH THE NORTH POLE?

Matthew Henson was born on a farm in a rural Maryland county in 1866. He was still a child when his parents died, and at the age of twelve he went to sea as a cabin boy on a merchant ship. He sailed around the world for the next several years, educating himself and becoming a skilled navigator.

Henson met Commander Robert R. Peary in 1888 and joined him on an expedition to Nicaragua. Impressed with Henson's seamanship, Peary recruited him as a colleague. For years they made many trips together, including Arctic voyages in which Henson traded with the Eskimos and mastered their language, built sleds, and trained dog teams—all talents that made him ideally suited for polar exploration.

In 1909, Peary mounted his eighth attempt to reach the North Pole, selecting Henson to be one of the team of six who would make the final run to the Pole. Before the goal was reached, Peary could no longer continue on foot and rode in a dog sled. Various accounts say he was ill, exhausted, or had frozen toes. In any case, he sent Henson on ahead as a scout. In a newspaper interview Henson said: "I was in the lead that had overshot the mark a couple of miles. We went back then and I could see that my footprints were the first at the spot." Henson then proceeded to plant the American flag.

Although Admiral Peary received many honors, Henson was largely ignored and spent most of the next thirty years working as a clerk in a federal customs house in New York. But in 1944 Congress awarded him a duplicate of the silver medal given to Peary. Presidents Truman and Eisenhower both honored him before he died in 1955.

Finally, in 1988, years of effort and petitions by a Harvard history professor were successful in having Matthew Henson's body moved from a shared grave in New York to Arlington National

Cemetery, where, with full military honors, it was placed in the ground next to Admiral Peary. In 1996, on the 130th anniversary of Henson's birth, the United States Navy named its newest ocean-ographic survey ship the USNS Henson. In November 1998 the ship, carrying twelve of Henson's descendents, sailed to Alexan-dria, Virginia. The family members and many others paid tribute to Henson in a ceremony at his grave, where formal military hon-ors were conducted by the Naval Order of the United States.

◆

WHO WAS THE FIRST AFRICAN AMERICAN WOMAN TO EARN A PILOT'S LICENSE?

As a child in Texas, where she was born in 1892, Bessie Coleman was a hard worker, picking cotton and doing laundry to help her mother meet family expenses. After high school the ambitious young woman joined her brother in Chicago, attended beauty

BESSIE COLEMAN

school, and got a job as a manicurist. Intrigued by flying, she read everything she could find on aviation, but when she applied to flying school she was denied admission because of her race and sex. Taking the advice of a friend, she saved her money, studied French, and, in 1920, traveled to France, where she signed up at a flight training school. On June 15, 1921, she earned an international pilot's license, becoming the first African American woman to be a licensed pilot.

Returning to the United States, Coleman embarked on tours of air shows throughout the country, astounding audiences with her daring maneuvers. Her goal was to earn enough money to open a flying school for African Americans. But during a test flight before an air show in Jacksonville, Florida, in a plane she had just purchased, she unfastened her seatbelt so she could lean out of the cockpit to check the field while her assistant flew the plane. At 1,000 feet the craft suddenly went into a tailspin, flipped upside down, and threw her out of the cockpit. Coleman was hurled to the ground, dying before her dream could be realized.

◆

WHO WAS THE FIRST WOMAN TO RECEIVE THE SPINGARN MEDAL?

The Spingarn Medal was instituted by the NAACP in 1914 to be awarded annually for the highest achievement during the year by an African American. In 1922 the medal was awarded to Mary B. Talbert, the first woman to be so honored. Talbert, a founder and president of the National Association of Colored Women, was chosen "for service to the women of her race and the restoration of the Frederick Douglass home."

Talbert was born in 1866 in Oberlin, Ohio, where her family had settled to take advantage of educational opportunities there. She earned a bachelor's degree from Oberlin College in 1894 and taught school in Little Rock, Arkansas, later becoming principal of a high school and a small university. Under her leadership, the National Association of Colored Women led projects to improve educational opportunities for African American children and to protect them from the harsh juvenile justice system in the

South. During World War I, Talbert served for several months as a Red Cross nurse in France, and after the war she joined the effort for passage of an anti-lynching bill. A strong advocate for African American women leaders, and a fighter for civil rights in the United States and human rights throughout the world, Talbert died in 1923 at the age of fifty-seven.

◆

WHOSE ACT SPARKED THE FIRST MAJOR BOYCOTT OF THE CIVIL RIGHTS MOVEMENT?

In 1955, Rosa Parks, a resident of Montgomery, Alabama, was working as a tailor's assistant at a downtown department store. A quiet but determined woman, Parks, forty-three years old, had been secretary of the Montgomery NAACP for several years before becoming the organization's youth adviser. On December 1, exhausted after a long day of work, she boarded a city bus for the ride home. Although more than three-quarters of Montgomery's bus passengers at the time were African Americans, they were forced to sit in the back of the bus and surrender their seats to whites if asked. When some white passengers boarded Rosa Parks's bus that December day, the driver ordered her to give up her seat and she refused. She was arrested, taken to the city jail, and later convicted and fined.

In response to the arrest of Rosa Parks, Montgomery's black ministers and civil rights leaders met to organize a boycott of the city's buses by African Americans. The new minister of the Dexter Avenue Baptist Church, the Rev. Martin Luther King Jr., only twenty-six years old, was chosen president of the Montgomery Improvement Association, which led the boycott. In an emotional speech to a large, enthusiastic gathering, King said, "We will not retreat one inch in our fight to secure and hold on to our American citizenship."

Thirteen months later, the U.S. Supreme Court outlawed segregation on Alabama's buses, the boycott ended, and African American passengers once again rode on city buses in Montgomery. The courageous Rosa Parks, who had been fired from her tailoring job, moved to Detroit, where she was a special assistant to Congressman John Conyers for twenty-five years.

In December 2000, forty-five years after she refused the bus driver's order to give up her seat, Rosa Parks was back in Montgomery, Alabama, this time to attend the dedication of the Rosa Parks Library and Museum at Troy State University. Dr. Martin Luther King's widow, Coretta Scott King, was among the many who came to honor the eighty-seven-year-old heroine of the civil rights movement. After her death in 2005, her casket was placed in the rotunda of the United States Capitol so people could pay their respects.

In February 2013, the month when Parks would have turned one hundred, she became the first African American woman honored with a life-size statue in the Capitol. The statue depicted her seated, dressed in a heavy coat and clutching her purse, as she waits to be arrested. "In a single moment, with the simplest of gestures," said President Obama, "she helped change America and change the world."

◆

WHO WAS THE FIRST TO POPULARIZE THE SLOGAN "BLACK POWER"?

In the 1960s, civil rights activist Stokely Carmichael adopted the term "black power" as a rallying cry for African Americans who were fighting injustice. Carmichael was born in Trinidad in 1941 and moved to New York City's Harlem when he was eleven years old. He graduated from the prestigious Bronx High School of Science and entered Howard University. While majoring in philosophy there, he became involved in the civil rights movement as a Freedom Rider in Mississippi.

In 1960 Carmichael helped organize the Student Nonviolent Coordinating Committee (SNCC), an organization that focused on voter registration and other civil rights issues in the South, and later became chairman. In a speech in 1966 in Greenwood, Mississippi, he spoke angrily about the years of struggle for civil rights for African Americans and concluded: "What we're going to start saying now is 'black power.'" He began a chant with the audience shouting back: "What do we want?" "Black power!"

In 1967 Carmichael left SNCC to join the Black Panther Party. In a book published that year, written by Carmichael and the African American political scientist Charles V. Hamilton, *Black Power: The Politics of Liberation in America,* they said: "Black power is a call for black people of this country to unite, to recognize their heritage, to build a sense of community."

In 1969 Carmichael went to West Africa, changed his name to Kwame Ture, and settled in Guinea. He died of cancer in 1998. Commenting on his death, civil rights leader Jesse Jackson said Ture had "helped defeat legal segregation in the United States and colonialism in Africa."

◆

FRANKLIN A. THOMAS

WHO WAS THE FIRST AFRICAN AMERICAN TO HEAD A MAJOR FOUNDATION?

In 1979 Franklin A. Thomas was named president of the Ford Foundation, the country's largest philanthropic organization. Born in Brooklyn, New York, Thomas graduated in 1956 from Columbia College. After four years as a navigator in the United States Air Force's Strategic Air Command, Thomas entered Columbia University Law School, receiving a degree in 1963.

His career after law school included such positions as assistant United States attorney, deputy police commissioner for the New York City Police Department, and president of the Bedford Stuyvesant Restoration Corporation, a community development organization. Thomas joined the board of trustees of the Ford Foundation in 1977 and two years later was elected president.

He left Ford in 1996, joined the boards of several corporations, including Conoco, Alcoa, and Citigroup, and became head of the TFF Study Group, a nonprofit initiative assisting development in southern Africa. In October 2001 Thomas was named chairman of the board of the September 11 Fund, which was established to set up guidelines for the distribution of grants to individuals, families, and communities affected by the terrorist attacks on the World Trade Center in New York. The fund distributed grants totaling $528 million before it was dissolved in 2004.

♦

WHO WAS THE FIRST AFRICAN AMERICAN IN SPACE?

On August 30, 1983, Guion S. Bluford Jr. became the first African American astronaut in space when he flew aboard the space shuttle *Challenger* on its night launch from the Kennedy Space Center in Florida.

Born in 1942 in Philadelphia, Bluford showed an early interest in engineering—his father's profession—and in airplanes. He graduated from Pennsylvania State University with a degree in aerospace engineering, received his air force wings in 1965, and served as a

GUION S. BLUFORD JR.

pilot in Vietnam, flying 144 combat missions. He then earned master's and doctoral degrees in his field and, in 1978, was selected as an astronaut candidate.

Two years after his first space flight, Bluford again flew aboard *Challenger* on the nation's first spacelab mission. He flew into space two more times, in 1991 and 1992, aboard the space shuttle *Discovery.* He then left NASA and joined an aerospace consulting firm in Maryland. In 2000, Bluford became a vice president of Northrop Grumman Corporation; he left Grumman two years later to become president of the Aerospace Technology Group, an engineering consulting organization in Cleveland, Ohio.

Another black astronaut, Robert H. Lawrence Jr., was the first African American appointed to the manned orbiting laboratory program, in June 1967, but he never made it into space. He was killed six months after his appointment when his fighter jet crashed on the runway at an air force base in California.

♦

WHO WAS THE FIRST AFRICAN AMERICAN TO BE HONORED WITH A NATIONAL HOLIDAY?

On January 20, 1986, eighteen years after this renowned civil rights leader was assassinated, the birthday of Dr. Martin Luther King Jr. was made a national holiday. Born in Atlanta, Georgia, in 1929, King graduated from Morehouse College when he was only nineteen. He went on to earn a bachelor of divinity degree and a doctorate. When he was just twenty-six, he was named pastor of the Dexter Avenue Baptist Church in Montgomery, Alabama.

On December 1, 1955, when Montgomery resident Rosa Parks was arrested for refusing to give up her bus seat to a white man, King responded by leading a year-long bus boycott that put an end to segregated seating on Alabama's buses. Returning to Atlanta, King became associate pastor of his father's church, Ebenezer Baptist.

In 1957 King was named the first president of the Southern Christian Leadership Conference, an organization dedicated to gaining full rights for African Americans through nonviolent action such as boycotts and sit-ins. Although his home was bombed and he was arrested and jailed, King never backed down in his struggle to gain civil rights for black Americans. He was one of the planners of the 1963 March on Washington, where he made his famous "I have a dream . . ." speech, and a year later he was awarded the Nobel Peace Prize.

King was among the leaders of a four-day march from Selma to Montgomery, Alabama, in 1965, and, in 1967, in a speech at New York City's Riverside Church, he condemned the country's involvement in the Vietnam War. His illustrious career reached its untimely end in 1968, when he traveled to Memphis, Tennessee, to support sanitation workers who had gone on strike for higher pay and more benefits. In March, after leading a march on city hall that turned violent, he scheduled another for April 8. He arrived in the city five days early to address a mass meeting.

CAPTAIN WILLIAM PINKNEY

The next day he and his friends were dressing for dinner at the Lorraine Motel. King stepped onto the balcony to greet some visitors, then turned back to his room. A shot rang out and a bullet pierced his face and neck. He died almost instantly.

◆

WHO WAS THE FIRST AFRICAN AMERICAN TO SAIL ALONE AROUND THE WORLD?

Captain William Pinkney once recalled that when he was a boy on the South Side of Chicago, where he was born in 1935, he read a book about a boy sailing around the world. He couldn't have guessed back then that when he was fifty-seven years old he would become the first African American to reach that goal.

Trained as an X-ray technician, Pinkney spent eight years in the navy. He then took an array of jobs until finally following a career as a makeup artist for movies and television. But his love of sailing never left him; he became a U.S. Coast Guard licensed master in 1986 and raced yachts on Lake Michigan. And on June 9, 1992, he sailed his forty-two-foot boat, *Commitment,* into Boston harbor after completing a solo circumnavigation of the globe, covering 27,000 miles in twenty-two months.

In 1999 Pinkney took to the seas again, sailing the 78-foot ketch *Sortilege,* with nine public school teachers aboard, along the route of slave ships that traveled between Africa and the Americas. And in March 2000, when the schooner *Amistad* was launched in Mystic Seaport, Connecticut, Pinkney was at the helm. The boat was a hand-built replica of the original *Amistad,* which entered Connecticut 161 years earlier carrying a cargo of slaves who had been kidnapped in Africa and sold at auction in Havana, Cuba. The slaves took over the schooner, were seized by a navy ship, towed to New London, Connecticut, jailed, and eventually freed.

The re-created *Amistad,* piloted by Captain Pinkney and supported by a Connecticut organization called Amistad America, was designed to visit ports nationally and internationally, serving as a floating classroom to promote harmony among the races and as a monument to the millions of men and women who were victims of the slave trade. Pinkney's book, *As Long As It Takes: Meeting the Challenge,* about finding goals and persevering to reach them, was published in 2006.

◆

WHO WAS THE FIRST AFRICAN AMERICAN WOMAN ASTRONAUT?

When the space shuttle *Endeavor* left its launching pad at Cape Canaveral, Florida, on September 12, 1992, its crew of seven included Dr. Mae Jemison, the first African American woman to travel into space. A physician and a space engineer, the thirty-five-year-old Jemison was responsible during the seven-day flight for conducting experiments involving weightlessness and motion sickness.

As a young girl growing up in Chicago, Jemison had dreams of someday traveling in space. Her parents, a maintenance supervisor and an elementary school teacher, encouraged her interest in astronomy and other sciences. She was only sixteen when she entered

DR. MAE JEMISON

California's Stanford University, where she received degrees in 1977 in chemical engineering and African and Afro-American Studies.

Jemison earned an M.D. from Cornell University Medical College and then served for several years as a doctor in the Peace Corps, working mainly in Liberia and Sierra Leone. In 1985 she opened a private medical practice in Los Angeles, began taking graduate engineering courses, and applied to the astronaut program. In 1987, out of nearly 2,000 applicants, she was one of fifteen chosen for NASA's astronaut training program. On her 1992 space flight, Jemison carried several small art objects from West African countries, which, she said, symbolized her belief that space belongs to all nations.

After resigning from NASA in 1993, Jemison taught at Dartmouth College and then created the Jemison Group, which works to bring advanced technology to people around the world and to further

DR. BERNARD A. HARRIS, JR.

a love of science in students. In 2004 she was inducted into the International Space Hall of Fame.

◆

WHO WAS THE FIRST AFRICAN AMERICAN ASTRONAUT TO WALK IN SPACE?

Bernard A. Harris, Jr., M.D., has described himself as a "dreamer who believes nothing is impossible." His accomplishments prove that he has lived up to that belief. He is a physician, a business-man, and, as a NASA astronaut, the first African American to walk in space.

Harris was born in 1956 in Temple, Texas. He graduated from Sam Houston High School in San Antonio, earned a bachelor of science degree from the University of Houston, a doctorate in medicine from Texas Tech University School of Medicine, and completed his residency in internal medicine at the Mayo Clinic in 1985. A trained aerospace flight surgeon, he was selected as a NASA astronaut in 1990 and flew his first mission three years later. He traveled into space for a second time in 1995 on the first flight of the joint Russian-American space program. During the flight, Harris accomplished what he said was a childhood dream—he completed a walk in space. When he retired from NASA in 1996, he had logged more than 438 hours in space and traveled over 7.2 million miles.

Harris has used his business talents in companies involved in space products, services, and education, and holds several faculty positions. In 1998 he founded the Harris Foundation to develop math and science education and crime-prevention programs for young people.

◆

WHO WAS THE FIRST AFRICAN AMERICAN TO REACH THE TOP OF MOUNT EVEREST?

Sophia Danenberg, who grew up in Chicago and lives in Seat-tle, got her first taste of scaling heights when she took up rock climbing in 1999. Three years later, when she climbed Mount Rainier

SOPHIA DANENBERG

in Washington State, she decided mountainous terrain had more appeal. With her husband, David, whom she met on a rock climb, she ascended numerous peaks, from Kilimanjaro and Mount Kenya to Mount McKinley and Grand Teton.

In 2006, at the age of thirty-four, Danenberg decided to climb Mount Everest in Nepal, the highest mountain on earth and one of the most hazardous. On March 19, several weeks after making her decision, she flew out of the Hartford, Connecticut, airport and was on her way. Danenberg chose an unguided climb, in which she carried her own gear and made her own decisions. She arrived at the mountain's base camp on April 1. Then, assisted by two Sherpas, she ascended to each of the four camps situated on the side of the mountain, and then finally decided to attempt to reach the peak. At seven in the morning of May 19, she was sitting on the top of the world. But she didn't stay there long; she had a stuffy nose, frostbite on her cheeks, and her oxygen mask was clogged with snow and ice. "So I was like, cool, I made it," she told a reporter from the *Chicago Reader*. "I have to get this oxygen mask fixed and get off this mountain."

Danenberg earned a degree in environmental science and public policy from Harvard. An active Obama campaigner in 2008, she was a delegate to the Democratic National Convention. On her website she says: "I love to snowboard, regularly embarrass myself attempting to surf, and am a lifelong theater buff."

◆

WHO WAS THE FIRST AFRICAN AMERICAN TO FLY SOLO AROUND THE WORLD?

On March 23, 2007, twenty-three-year-old Barrington Irving, a senior majoring in aerospace at Miami's Florida Memorial University, embarked on a 30,000-mile flight around the world in a single-engine plane named *Inspiration*. When he returned to Miami on June 27, after fighting fatigue and bad weather, he had

BARRINGTON IRVING

set two world records: he was the youngest person and the first African American to fly solo around the globe.

Born in Kingston, Jamaica, Irving moved with his family to an inner-city Miami neighborhood when he was six. Inspired by his father's hard work and sacrifice, Irving was determined to follow a positive path. When he was fifteen and working in his parents' religious bookstore, he began talking with a customer, a Jamaican-born United Airlines pilot named Gary Robinson, who invited him to the airport to see the cockpit of his Boeing 777. Fascinated by the idea of flying, Irving began spending time at the airport, washing planes for private owners in exchange for money or short flights.

After high school, Irving rejected a football scholarship and enrolled in a community college, at the same time speaking to school and community groups about career opportunities in aviation. When he was awarded a scholarship that paid for tuition and flying lessons, he enrolled in Florida Memorial University and earned a pilot's license. He started an organization, Experience Aviation, Inc., to introduce middle and high school students to the field.

Then, to demonstrate to young people that there were no limits to what they could achieve, Irving launched his plan to fly around the world. With components contributed by various companies, the manufacturer Columbia built the plane he piloted. After his historic flight, Irving received many honors and awards. And in another history-making achievement, on October 15, 2008, he took off on a test flight from Opa-locka Airport in the cockpit of *Inspiration II*, a plane built entirely by Miami high school students in his Experience Aviation Build and Soar summer program. When encouraging young people to pursue their dreams, Irving has said: "Any career is attainable by any child. The sky is the limit!"

Irving was given the 2012 National Geographic Emerging Explorer award for his endeavor to transform a jet plane into a flying classroom.

JOURNALISM

WHAT WAS THE FIRST
AFRICAN AMERICAN NEWSPAPER?

On March 16, 1827, *Freedom's Journal* began publication in New York City. The opening editorial in the first issue of the first African American newspaper in the United States announced: "We wish to plead our own cause. Too long have others spoken for us . . ."

The paper was started by John Russworm and Samuel Cornish. Russworm, who graduated from Bowdoin College in Maine in 1826, was one of the first African Americans to earn a college degree, and Cornish was a Presbyterian minister. The two agreed that slavery should be abolished, but they differed on whether African Americans should emigrate to Africa. Cornish finally resigned from the paper, and Russworm stayed on to espouse his opinions on resettling black Americans in Africa. In 1829 he acted on his beliefs and settled in Liberia. Cornish returned to the newspaper and tried to give it new life, but it folded in less than a year.

◆

WHO PUBLISHED THE FIRST
AFRICAN AMERICAN MAGAZINE?

David Ruggles, a renowned abolitionist, was editor and publisher of the first African American periodical, *The Mirror of Liberty*. The first issue of this quarterly magazine appeared in July 1838. Its articles promoted the rights of African Americans.

Earlier, Ruggles had opened an African American bookstore on Lispenard Street in New York City, as well as a reading room nearby for use by African Americans, who were not allowed to enter the city's libraries.

◆

WHO WAS THE FIRST
AFRICAN AMERICAN NEWSPAPERWOMAN?

Mary Ann Shadd Cary was born in 1823 in Wilmington, Delaware, and grew up in a home where escaped slaves were given refuge. Unable to receive an education in Delaware, she was enrolled in a Quaker school in Pennsylvania. When she returned to Wilmington she opened a school for African American children. After the Fugitive Slave Law was passed in 1850, giving slave owners sanction to retrieve their runaway slaves, Cary and her brother fled to Windsor, Canada, and were soon joined by the rest of the family.

Shortly after her arrival, Cary wrote and distributed a pamphlet listing opportunities for black Americans in Canada. Seeing the need for a newspaper for African Americans, especially fugitive slaves, she began publishing a weekly paper, *The Provincial Freeman.* Its motto was: "Self-reliance is the true road to independence."

Cary was an eloquent speaker against slavery, and when President Lincoln called for men to fight with the Union Army in the Civil War, she returned to the United States and became an army recruiting officer. She eventually moved to Washington, D.C., enrolled in the Howard University Law Department, and, in 1883 at the age of sixty, became the second African American woman in the United States to earn a law degree. She died ten years later.

◆

WHO PUBLISHED THE FIRST NEWSPAPER
BY AND FOR AFRICAN AMERICAN WOMEN?

Josephine St. Pierre Ruffin was born in Boston in 1842 into one of the city's leading African American families. She attended school in Salem, Massachusetts, where the schools were integrated. When she was fifteen years old, she married George Lewis Ruffin, who was the first African American to graduate from Harvard Law School. After her marriage, Ruffin continued her education in Boston. During the Civil War, she became involved in charity work, civil rights issues, and especially the women's suffrage movement. From 1890 to 1897, she served as the editor and publisher of *Women's*

Era, the first newspaper published by and for African American women. The paper featured the achievements of black women and advocated for their civil rights.

In 1894, together with her daughter and a school principal, she organized the Women's Era Club, an advocacy group for African American women, and the next year created a national organization that later became part of the National Association of Colored Women. She also was one of the founding members of the Boston NAACP. Ruffin died in Boston in 1924.

◆

WHO STARTED THE FIRST FAMILY-OWNED AFRICAN AMERICAN NEWSPAPER?

In 1864 a young African American, John H. Murphy, enlisted to fight in the Civil War and was assigned to the Thirtieth Regiment, U.S. Colored Maryland Volunteers, where he was eventually promoted to sergeant. In a letter he wrote in 1920 recalling his Civil War experiences, Murphy said: "That was a real war for liberty. I went in a slave and came out a freedman. I went in a chattel and came out as a man with the blue uniform of my country as a guarantee of freedom . . ."

Murphy went home to Baltimore and began looking for ways to make a living. Over the years he was a whitewasher, porter, janitor, postal employee, and printer. By the time he founded a newspaper, the *Afro-American,* in 1892, he had a wife and ten children to support. The weekly paper's coverage of black social issues attracted a growing number of readers. After Murphy died in 1922, his five sons took over the paper, with his son Carl as editor.

The *Afro-American* focused on stories that were overlooked by the white press. In a December 1912 edition, for example, a front-page headline read: "Discrimination Charged in Uncle Sam's Navy." In October 1940 another headline announced: "Roosevelt, as Commander-in-Chief, permits Jim Crow in U.S. Navy." And a 1945 article about the atomic bomb plant in Oak Ridge, Tennessee, said the African American workers there were "plagued by Jim Crow at work, in housing and other facilities."

When Carl Murphy died in 1967, a grandson of the founder,

John Murphy III, became publisher. By the year 2001, the paper was publishing editions in Baltimore and Washington, D.C., and was being run by two fourth-generation members of the Murphy family, John J. Oliver Jr. and Frances Murphy Draper.

◆

WHO WAS THE FIRST WRITER TO DOCUMENT THE LYNCHING OF AFRICAN AMERICANS?

Ida B. Wells was born in Holly Springs, Mississippi, in 1862 and orphaned at fourteen when both her parents died in a yellow fever epidemic. Although she had to care for her brothers and sisters, she managed to further her education, attending Rust College and Fisk University. She settled in Memphis, Tennessee, to teach school. Her lifelong fight for justice began in 1884, when a railroad conductor told her to give up her seat to a white man and move to the segregated Jim Crow car. She refused and was forced from the train. She sued the railroad, eventually losing her case, but her articles about the incident led her into a career in journalism. She started contributing to African American and religious newspapers, and in 1889 she became the editor of a Baptist weekly in Memphis, *Free Speech and Headlight*.

In March 1892, when three African American grocery store owners were lynched, she wrote a series of editorials urging that the murderers be punished and encouraging black residents to leave the city. After the newspaper printed a particularly vehement editorial attacking the motives of Southern white men, the *Free Speech* office was vandalized, equipment was destroyed, and Wells, who was visiting in New York at the time, was warned not to return to Memphis.

She settled in New York City and became a writer for *New York Age*, where she continued to publish crusading articles exposing the horrifying crimes of lynch mobs. She set out on a lecture tour of England and the United States, helping to set up anti-lynching societies. In 1895 she married Chicago newspaper owner Ferdinand Barnett and used his paper, the *Conservator*, to carry on her campaign to end injustice toward African Americans. She joined with W. E. B. DuBois and others to form the Niagara Movement, founded the Negro Fellowship League, started a kindergarten for African American children, and organized a suffrage club for black women. She died in Chicago in 1931.

◆

WHO WAS THE FIRST AFRICAN AMERICAN WAR CORRESPONDENT?

After the start of World War I, bowing to pressure from black newspapers, the United States government appointed an African American reporter, Ralph W. Tyler, to cover war news of special interest to black readers. Tyler, of Columbus, Ohio, who had written for the *Columbus Evening Dispatch* and the *Ohio State Journal*, was designated a regular war correspondent and was to file daily reports of activities in which African American troops were involved. Although the war ended less than three months after his appointment, he was able to write important firsthand accounts of the experiences of black soldiers.

◆

WHO IS CONSIDERED THE COUNTRY'S FIRST AFRICAN AMERICAN SPORTSCASTER?

When Sherman L. Maxwell died in 2008 at the age of one hundred, many remembered him as the first African American sports broadcaster. Maxwell was born in Newark, New Jersey, graduated from Central High School there, and served in the army during World War II.

His broadcasting career began in 1929, when he talked the owner of the New Jersey radio station WNJR into letting him read short reports. "He was turned down twenty-five times before someone finally got him to be a sports announcer," his sister, Berenice Maxwell Cross, said in a 1998 *Star-Ledger* story. "He never gave up."

By the early 1930s, Maxwell was broadcasting on the New Jersey stations WHOM and WRNY while working full-time as a

SHERMAN L. MAXWELL

postal clerk. His sportscasting expanded to include interviews, and he became an announcer at Ruppert Stadium for the Negro Leagues team, the Newark Eagles. He also kept records and submitted articles about the team. He contributed to *Baseball Digest* magazine and published two books: *Thrills and Spills in Sports* in 1939 and *Great Black Athletes* in 1972.

"I like a thing, I do it," Maxwell told a *Star-Ledger* reporter in 2001. "I never asked for money."

♦

WHO WAS THE FIRST AFRICAN AMERICAN
REPORTER GIVEN ACCESS TO THE WHITE HOUSE?

A native of St. Louis, Missouri, Harry McAlpin studied journalism at the University of Wisconsin and attended Robert E. Terrell Law School in Washington, D.C. In 1942 he was hired as a Washington correspondent for the *Chicago Defender,* and two years later he became the first African American journalist to be accredited as a White House correspondent. His reports appeared in fifty-one newspapers.

In 1945, as the first accredited African American navy correspondent, McAlpin reported on the war from the Pacific. And during the Korean War, he was an information specialist with the Office of War Information. He then entered private practice as an attorney in Louisville, Kentucky, and eventually became a federal judge.

♦

WHO WAS THE FIRST AFRICAN AMERICAN WOMAN
TO GAIN WHITE HOUSE PRESS CREDENTIALS?

B orn in 1906 in Russellville, Kentucky, Alice Dunnigan attended Kentucky State College and embarked on a teaching career. At the same time, she wrote articles for local newspapers, reporting on African American people and their activities. In 1942 she went to Washington, D.C., and took a job with the U.S. Department of Labor.

After the war Dunnigan moved into journalism, becoming a reporter for the Associated Negro Press and a Washington correspondent for the *Chicago Defender.* She made history when she became the first African American woman journalist to win access to the White House as well as the House and Senate. A high point in her career was in 1948, when she accompanied Harry Truman on his campaign train from Washington to California.

Dunnigan left the Associated Negro Press in 1960 to work for the Kennedy-Johnson campaign and later served as an educational consultant for the Equal Employment Opportunity Commission under both presidents. In 1967 she was appointed to the President's Council on Youth Opportunity, where she worked until she retired in 1971. Three years later she published her autobiography, *A Black Woman's Experience: From Schoolhouse to White House.*

◆

WHAT JOURNALIST WAS THE FIRST AFRICAN AMERICAN WOMAN TO BE A VICE PRESIDENTIAL CANDIDATE?

Charlotta Bass, a pioneering California journalist, was named the Progressive Party candidate for vice president of the United States in 1952, when she was seventy-eight years old. Forty-two years earlier, the young Charlotta Spears arrived in Los Angeles, where she had moved for her health, and took a job with a newspaper called the *Eagle*. The paper had been founded in 1879 as the *Owl*, to provide news and information to African American settlers. She was soon promoted to an editorial job.

When the newspaper's owner died in 1912, the paper went on the auction block, but Spears couldn't afford to bid on it. Anxious to help her, a neighboring secondhand dealer bought the paper for fifty dollars and handed Spears the deed. Spears took over and changed the paper's name to the *California Eagle*. The next year she married Joseph P. Bass, a founder of the Topeka *Plaindealer*, who had journeyed west. The energetic couple began a campaign to end segregation and discrimination in Los Angeles. In 1914 Bass tried to halt the making of D. W. Griffith's film *The Birth of a Nation*, which glorified the Ku Klux Klan. Her effort failed, but she forced the director to cut some especially offensive scenes.

Bass tangled with the KKK again in 1925 when she exposed plans for a Klan takeover of the Watts neighborhood of Los Angeles. She was sued and threatened but she did not back down. Later, just before the beginning of World War II, Bass and her newspaper started a campaign for fair housing for African Americans. In 1934 her husband died, and she was left to run the paper alone.

By 1951, when Bass finally sold the *Eagle*, she had already served as the first African American on the Los Angeles County grand jury and had lost her first political campaign, a city council race, in 1945. She left the Republican Party and joined the new Progressive Party, losing a bid for a congressional seat in 1950. Bass made her last stab at politics when she ran as the Progressive Party's candidate for vice president in 1952. She died in 1969 at the age of ninety-five.

◆

WHO WAS THE FIRST AFRICAN AMERICAN TV NEWS COMMENTATOR?

After Mal Goode was hired by ABC in 1962 as the first African American news reporter on a major television network, he was assigned to cover the United Nations. Two months later he found himself reporting on lengthy UN debates over one of the country's most critical events—the Cuban missile crisis.

Born in Virginia in 1908, Goode attended the University of Pittsburgh. During high school and college he worked as a laborer in the steel mills, a job he kept for five years after graduation. He started his journalism career when he joined the *Pittsburgh Courier,* and a year later he started doing a fifteen-minute radio news show twice a week.

In 1950 Goode became a news reporter for radio station WHOD in Pittsburgh, and was named news director two years later. For six years, he and his sister, Mary Dee, were the only brother-and-sister team on radio. Goode was the first African American member of the National Association of Radio and Television News Directors. He worked into his seventies and died of a stroke in 1995, at the age of eighty-seven.

◆

WHICH JOURNALIST WAS THE FIRST AFRICAN AMERICAN TO SIT ON THE NATIONAL SECURITY COUNCIL?

Carl T. Rowan, who was called the dean of the country's African American journalists, was born in 1925 in a small Tennessee town and grew up in a house without electricity or running water.

CARL T. ROWAN

After two years at Tennessee A&I (now Tennessee State University) he left to serve in the navy in World War II and went on to attend Oberlin College. After earning a master's degree in journalism at the University of Minnesota, he began his newspaper career at the Baltimore *Afro-American,* but soon joined the staff of the *Minneapolis Tribune,* becoming one of the first African American reporters in the mainstream press. His reports on conditions for African Americans in the South won him several awards.

In 1961 he left journalism to serve in various positions in the administrations of Presidents John F. Kennedy and Lyndon Johnson. In 1964 President Johnson named him director of the United

States Information Agency, and he became the first African American to sit on the National Security Council.

Rowan returned to journalism in 1965, writing more articles, books, and syndicated columns and appearing on television and radio. His memoir, *Breaking Barriers,* came out in 1991, and two years later he published a biography of an old friend entitled *Dream Makers, Dream Breakers: The World of Thurgood Marshall.* In 1999 the prestigious National Press Club presented Rowan with its Fourth Estate Award for lifetime achievement in journalism. Rowan wrote his final column just a few days before his death in September 2000. His career reflected his deep concern for civil rights. He has been quoted as saying, "I am a crusader for racial justice, and I will be to the day I die."

◆

WHO WAS THE FIRST AFRICAN AMERICAN ANCHOR OF A TV MORNING NEWS SHOW?

Bryant Gumbel made his debut as an anchor of the NBC news program *Today* on January 4, 1982, and was a familiar face on this national early-morning television show for fifteen years. Gumbel was born in New Orleans in 1948 and raised in Chicago. He earned a liberal arts degree from Bates College in Lewiston, Maine, in 1970 and two years later began his television career as a sportscaster for KNBC in Los Angeles. By 1982 he had become the host of almost all of NBC's sports programs.

During his career on *Today,* Gumbel anchored broadcasts from all over the world, including China, Saudi Arabia, Cuba, and sub-Saharan Africa. He won many awards for his reporting, including a number of Emmys for news and sports. After a decade and a half as the coanchor of *Today,* Gumbel announced he would be leaving at the end of 1996. He launched a new show, *Public Eye with Bryant Gumbel,* on CBS, but it was dropped after two years and he returned to an early-morning time slot on *The Early Show.*

Gumbel left *The Early Show* in 2002 to concentrate on HBO's award-winning *Real Sports with Bryant Gumbel.* By 2009 the show had won twenty Emmys, as well as the 2006 Alfred I. duPont-Columbia University Award for broadcast journalism, the first time in the award's history that it was given to a sports program. The show won the duPont award a second time in 2012 for its series of investigative reports on concussions in sports.

◆

WHO WAS THE FIRST AFRICAN AMERICAN EDITOR AND OWNER OF A MAJOR DAILY NEWSPAPER?

A trailblazing newspaperman who won praise for his efforts to help young African Americans to follow him into journalism, Robert C. Maynard was the editor, publisher, and owner of the *Oakland Tribune* for a decade. Maynard was born in Brooklyn, New York, in 1937 to parents who came from Barbados. He was so fascinated by journalism as a youngster that he cut classes to watch courtroom reporters and finally dropped out of high school to become a writer.

Maynard got his first newspaper job when he was still a teenager, working for the *New York Age,* a Brooklyn weekly. He also worked for the *Afro-American* in Baltimore and the *York Gazette and Daily* in Pennsylvania. After studying at Harvard under a Nieman Fellowship in 1966, Maynard joined the staff of the *Washington Post,* where he was a White House correspondent, national correspondent, and editorial writer.

Maynard left the *Post* to form, with his wife, Nancy, the Institute for Journalism Education in Oakland, California, which trained hundreds of minority students. Maynard was an outspoken advocate for the hiring and promotion of minority employees by news organizations.

In 1979 Maynard returned to newspapers when he was named editor of the *Oakland Tribune* in California. Four years later, he bought the paper and became increasingly prominent in the journalism field, writing a syndicated column, appearing as a news commentator on television, and serving on the boards of newspaper organizations and on the Pulitzer Prize board. During the ten years before he sold the paper, the *Tribune* won hundreds of awards for editorial excellence. Maynard died of cancer in August 1993 at the age of fifty-six.

◆

WHO WAS THE FIRST AFRICAN AMERICAN WOMAN EDITOR OF A MAJOR DAILY NEWSPAPER?

In 1992 the *Oakland Tribune* in California named Pearl Stewart the editor, making her the first African American woman to edit a metropolitan daily newspaper. At the time of her appointment, Stewart had been a journalist in the San Francisco Bay area for more than twenty years, starting as a reporter for United Press International.

A native of Camden, Alabama, Stewart moved with her family to Rochester, New York, when she was five years old. She graduated from Howard University in 1971 and a year later earned a

PEARL STEWART

master's degree in communications from American University, in Washington, D.C. A winner of numerous journalism prizes, Stewart first joined the *Oakland Tribune* in 1976, starting as a reporter and later becoming a features editor. She left the *Tribune* in 1982 to become a reporter for the *San Francisco Chronicle,* where she covered Oakland government, education, and community planning. She returned to the *Tribune* as editor ten years later and resigned at the end of 1993. She accepted a research fellowship at Harvard, taught investigative reporting in Zambia, and lectured at several universities. In 2002, while teaching at Florida A&M University's journalism school, she founded Black College Wire, an online student news service. Three years later she joined the University of Southern Mississippi as an adjunct professor.

◆

WHO WAS THE FIRST AFRICAN AMERICAN EDITOR OF A MAINSTREAM NEWS WEEKLY?

Mark Whitaker grew up in Norton, Massachusetts, where he wrote sports reports for a local newspaper while still in junior high school. He started his career with *Newsweek* magazine in 1977, when he was a nineteen-year-old student at Harvard, from which he graduated with honors two years later. His first stint was as a reporting intern in the magazine's San Francisco bureau, and he later reported as a freelancer and an intern from Boston, Washington, London, and Paris. He joined the New York staff full-time in 1981.

Ten years later, *Newsweek* named Whitaker assistant managing editor; in this position he expanded the magazine's technology coverage, wrote occasional essays on racial issues, and cowrote a cover story, "The Hidden Rage of Successful Blacks," which won awards from the Society of Professional Journalists and the National Association of Black Journalists.

Whitaker was promoted to managing editor of *Newsweek* in 1996, supervising coverage of that year's presidential race. The next year he took over after the magazine's editor fell ill, and became the official editor in November 1998. In an interview in *Black Enterprise* magazine about his new position, Whitaker said: "I'm proud

MARK WHITAKER

and I think it's a great thing for black folks. Whenever one of us shows we can do something that hadn't been possible before, it's good and it just opens people's eyes."

Whitaker left *Newsweek* in 2006 to become editor-in-chief of the digital division of the *Washington Post*. A year later he was named a senior vice president at NBC News, and in 2008 he was made chief of NBC's Washington bureau, succeeding the late Tim Russert. In February 2011, Whitaker was named executive vice president and managing editor of CNN Worldwide, but two years later, after the network hired a new president, Whitaker announced he was stepping down. His book, *My Long Trip Home: A Family Memoir*, was published in October 2011.

◆

WHO WAS THE FIRST AFRICAN AMERICAN TO HOLD A TOP EDITING JOB AT THE *NEW YORK TIMES*?

When Gerald M. Boyd learned he was going to become managing editor of the *New York Times* in September 2001—the first African American to hold one of that newspaper's top two editing jobs—he was quoted in the *Times* as saying, "I hope tomorrow, when some kid of color picks up the *New York Times* and reads about the new managing editor, that kid will smile a little and maybe dream just a little bigger dream. And that's all I'll say about firsts."

Boyd earned a bachelor's degree in journalism from the University of Missouri in 1973 and began his career as a copyboy for the *St. Louis Post-Dispatch,* where he worked his way up to a position as White House correspondent. He founded the St. Louis Association of Black Journalists in 1977 and was its first president. Three years later he attended Harvard as a Neiman Fellow. He joined the *New York Times* in 1983, moving from reporter to editor. He directed the paper's coverage of the 1993 World Trade Center bombing, which won a Pulitzer Prize, and he was coeditor of the series "How Race Is Lived in America," published in 2000, which garnered the paper another Pulitzer.

In June 2003, Boyd and the newspaper's managing editor were forced to resign after it was learned that a young reporter in their department had plagiarized several stories. He died of lung cancer in 2006 at the age of fifty-six.

LAW
AND
GOVERNMENT

WHICH AFRICAN AMERICAN LAWYER WAS THE FIRST TO PRACTICE IN THE UNITED STATES?

Macon Bolling Allen, born in 1816, was a native of Indiana, where he taught school. After deciding to pursue the legal profession, he moved to Portland, Maine, and in 1844 he was accepted to the bar, becoming the first licensed African American lawyer in the country. After experiencing difficulty finding clients in Maine, Allen moved to Boston, where he was admitted to the bar in 1845. He soon became a justice of the peace, the first African American in the United States to hold that position. But prejudice in Boston prevented him from becoming a part of the legal community. During the Civil War he moved to Charleston, South Carolina, where he felt he could put his legal skills to better use. There, he was named judge of the inferior court. He died in 1894.

◆

WHO WAS THE FIRST AFRICAN AMERICAN FEDERAL EMPLOYEE?

William Cooper Nell, a lawyer, author, and prominent abolitionist, was born in Boston in 1816. After completing his legal studies, he refused to take an oath that would admit him to the bar, because he would not pledge allegiance to a Constitution that allowed slavery. As founder of the Equal School Association, he led a campaign that in 1855 brought an end to segregated schools for African American children in Massachusetts.

In 1861 this courageous man mounted an attack against discrimination in federal employment and was appointed a clerk in the Boston post office, making him the first African American to hold a federal civilian job. He remained in the position until his death in 1874. Also a historian, Nell wrote a book called *The Colored Patriots of the American Revolution,* published in 1855.

◆

WHEN DID THE FIRST AFRICAN AMERICAN LAWYER PRACTICE BEFORE THE SUPREME COURT?

By 1865, when John S. Rock was admitted to practice before the United States Supreme Court, he had already been a teacher, doctor, and dentist. Rock, born in 1825 in New Jersey, taught for a time in a one-room schoolhouse before he decided to study medicine. Because of his race he was denied admission to medical school, so he became a dentist. Around 1852 he was allowed to earn a medical degree, one of the first African Americans in the country to do so. He practiced both medicine and dentistry in Boston, where he had settled.

A noted abolitionist, Rock participated in an effort to desegregate Boston's schools and challenged discrimination in jobs and public accommodations. His activities prompted him to earn a law degree, and as a lawyer he was the first African American allowed to argue cases before the Supreme Court.

◆

WHO WAS THE FIRST AFRICAN AMERICAN DIPLOMAT?

Born in Connecticut in 1833 and educated at Yale and the University of Pennsylvania, Ebenezer Don Carlos Bassett was principal of the Institute for Colored Youth in Philadelphia when President Ulysses S. Grant named him minister to Haiti in 1869. The appointment marked the first time a diplomatic assignment outside the United States was given to an African American.

After he had served in Haiti for eight years, the Haitians named Bassett their consul general to the United States. When he retired from that post after ten years, he returned to Haiti and wrote a book about the island entitled *Handbook of Haiti.*

◆

WHO WAS THE FIRST
AFRICAN AMERICAN SENATOR?

Hiram Rhoades Revels was born in 1822 in Fayetteville, North Carolina, the son of an African American Baptist minister and a Scottish mother. Revels was ordained a minister in the African Methodist Episcopal Church in Baltimore, Maryland, in 1845. After the Civil War began in 1861, Revels helped organize the first two African American army regiments from Maryland. He served as a chaplain in the Union Army, and when the war was over he held pastorates in Kansas and New Orleans before settling in Natchez, Mississippi.

In January 1870 the Mississippi legislature chose Revels to represent the state in the United States Senate; he was to fill the unexpired term of Confederate President Jefferson Davis. Withstanding the insults of those who were opposed to an African American senator, Revels was finally sworn in. In his first speech on the Senate floor, he argued that Georgia not be readmitted to the Union unless an effort was made to protect the rights of black citizens. Although his speech was praised, it had little effect, but he became a popular lecturer in Northern cities. Revels left the Senate after a year to become president of Alcorn University, an African American school in Mississippi.

◆

WHO WAS THE FIRST AFRICAN AMERICAN IN
THE U.S. HOUSE OF REPRESENTATIVES?

Until the Civil War began, Joseph H. Rainey worked alongside his father as a barber in Charleston, South Carolina. When the war started, Rainey and his wife escaped to Bermuda, where he continued his trade; on their return in 1866, they settled in Georgetown, South Carolina. Attracted to politics, Rainey became involved in the state Republican Party and was eventually elected to the state senate. He served until July 1870, when he was elected to fill a vacancy in the United States House of Representatives.

As a congressman, Rainey fought for legislation to prevent individuals and groups like the Ku Klux Klan from terrorizing African

Americans and whites and pushed for a bill that would grant equal treatment to African Americans in public places. Rainey, an effective, hardworking congressman, was regularly returned to his seat until 1878 when, largely due to the mudslinging campaign of his opponents, he was not reelected. For the next two years he worked as an agent for the Internal Revenue Service, then resigned and ran for the position of House clerk, which he lost. After failing in the banking and brokerage business, Rainey returned to Georgetown. He died in 1887 at the age of fifty-five. A local newspaper claimed that Rainey's stressful years in Washington had ruined his health.

◆

WHO WAS THE FIRST AFRICAN AMERICAN VOTER?

On March 30, 1870, the Fifteenth Amendment to the United States Constitution went into effect. The amendment gave citizens the right to vote regardless of "race, color, or previous condition of servitude."

The next day, March 31, Thomas M. Peterson of Perth Amboy, New Jersey, cast his vote in a special election to revise that city's charter, making him the first African American to exercise his right to vote under the new amendment. Peterson, a school custodian, was later appointed to serve on the commission set up to revise the charter.

◆

WHO WAS THE FIRST AFRICAN AMERICAN TO SERVE AS A GOVERNOR?

Born in Macon County, Georgia, in 1837, Pinckney Benton Stewart Pinchback went to school in Ohio and worked on riverboats on the Missouri and Mississippi Rivers until finally settling in New Orleans. After becoming active in politics, he served in the Louisiana State Senate from 1866 to 1871, when he was chosen the state's lieutenant governor. In 1872 the governor was impeached and forced to resign. Pinchback took his place for about a month, stepping down in January 1873. He was immediately elected to the United States Senate, but the election was disputed and he was not allowed to take his seat. He later served on the state board of education and as an Internal Revenue agent. He died in Washington in 1921.

◆

WHO WAS THE FIRST AFRICAN AMERICAN WOMAN LAWYER?

When Charlotte Ray decided she wanted to go to law school— unheard of for an African American woman in the 1800s— she applied as C. E. Ray. When the Howard University School of Law found out that she was a woman, they admitted her anyway. Ray, who was born in New York City in 1850, was such an outstanding student at Howard that she was inducted into Phi Beta Kappa, the national scholastic organization.

After graduating in 1872 with a specialty in commercial law, Ray looked forward to a bright future. But because of her race, she was unable to attract enough clients and finally had to give up her practice. She closed her Washington, D.C., law office and returned to New York City, where she worked in the Brooklyn school system. She died in 1911, leaving little information about how she spent her life after ending her legal career.

◆

WHO WAS THE FIRST ELECTED AFRICAN AMERICAN JUDGE IN U.S. HISTORY?

Mifflin W. Gibbs made history twice: he started the first black newspaper in California, and he was the first African American elected a judge. Gibbs was born in Philadelphia in 1823 and grew up to be an antislavery activist, working for the Underground Railroad and lecturing on behalf of abolition. In 1850, intrigued by reports of the California gold rush, Gibbs headed west. Once there, he shined shoes, started a successful clothing store, and became involved in politics. In 1855 he began publishing *Mirror of the Times,* the state's first African American newspaper.

Three years later, the restless Gibbs journeyed to British Columbia looking for gold. He opened a store and was elected a local councilman. Back in the United States, Gibbs attended Oberlin College, graduating in 1869. Four years later he was elected a city judge in Little Rock, Arkansas, making him the country's first elected African American judge. He went on to earn several presidential appointments and toward the end of his life was named consul to Madagascar. Gibbs died in Little Rock in 1915.

◆

WHO WAS THE FIRST AFRICAN AMERICAN TO SERVE A FULL TERM IN THE U.S. SENATE?

In 1875, when he was thirty-four years old, Blanche Kelso Bruce was chosen a United States Senator from Mississippi, and served in that post until 1881. Born a slave on a Virginia plantation, Bruce eventually traveled to Missouri, escaping slavery at the start of the Civil War. He taught school for a time, attended Oberlin College, and worked as a porter on a Mississippi steamboat. In about 1869 he settled in Floreyville, Mississippi, and before long he had established himself as a successful planter and become a respected politician. In 1874 the state legislature named him to represent Mississippi in the U.S. Senate for the term starting the following year.

During his years in the Senate, Bruce vigorously defended the rights of minority groups, including African Americans, Native Americans, and Chinese immigrants. Soon after he left his Senate seat in 1881, President Garfield named him register of the treasury, making him the first African American to sign his name on the country's currency.

◆

WHO WAS THE FIRST
AFRICAN AMERICAN U.S. MARSHAL?

In 1877 Frederick Douglass, the noted abolitionist, orator, editor, and activist, was appointed United States Marshal for the District of Columbia by President Rutherford B. Hayes. Douglass was born in February 1818 on a farm in Maryland, where he lived with his enslaved mother and grandparents. At the age of eight, a year after his mother's death, the youngster was sent to Baltimore to work as a houseboy for a family named Auld. There he learned to read and write, but he was eventually returned to a plantation, where he suffered years of brutal treatment.

When he was twenty-one years old, Douglass escaped to Massachusetts and became an ardent abolitionist. He was hired as a traveling orator by the Massachusetts Anti-Slavery Society for $450 a year, and in 1845 he published his autobiography, *Narrative of the Life of Frederick Douglass, An American Slave.* Because he admitted in his book that he was a runaway slave, Douglass was forced to flee to England, where he stayed until British admirers bought his freedom.

Upon his return, Douglass set up a printing plant in Rochester, New York, and in 1847 he began publishing a newspaper, the *North Star.* He continued to crusade against slavery, and when the Civil War began he recruited African American troops for the army. Two of the first volunteers were his sons, Lewis and Charles. When the war ended, Douglass focused his efforts on gaining civil rights for freed slaves, and after he was named U.S. Marshal he fought against segregationist policies in Washington. In 1881 Douglass was appointed Recorder of Deeds, and he later served as minister to Haiti for three years, returning to Washington to write and struggle against racism until he died in 1895.

◆

WHO WAS THE FIRST AFRICAN AMERICAN TO PRESIDE OVER A NATIONAL POLITICAL CONVENTION?

Although born a slave in Louisiana, John Roy Lynch managed to gain an education; it is said that he sat outside the windows of a white schoolhouse and listened to the teachers. He then settled in Natchez, Mississippi, where he opened a photography shop. He was soon named to the state legislature, becoming speaker of its house of representatives.

In 1872, when he was only twenty-five years old, Lynch was elected to the United States Congress, serving for four years. In 1884 he was made temporary chairman of the Republican National Convention, where he gave a keynote address. Said to be the most respected African American congressman of his time, Lynch later became paymaster of the regular army, retiring with the rank of major. He then opened a private law firm in Chicago and practiced for twenty-seven years.

♦

WHO WAS THE FIRST AFRICAN AMERICAN U.S. ASSISTANT ATTORNEY GENERAL?

William H. Lewis originally gained fame as a football star, the first African American player to be chosen for an All-American team. Lewis was born in Virginia in 1868 and attended school there until his father, a Baptist minister, moved the family to New England. Saving the money he earned working in hotels and restaurants, Lewis eventually was able to enroll in Amherst College in Massachusetts. An outstanding scholar and athlete, he played on Amherst's football team for four years and was captain in 1891. He continued playing while at Harvard Law School and was chosen an All-American in 1892 and '93.

After graduating from Harvard, Lewis became a lawyer in Massachusetts, and in 1911 President Taft appointed him to be the first African American assistant attorney general of the United States.

♦

WHEN DID A NORTHERN STATE ELECT ITS FIRST AFRICAN AMERICAN CONGRESSMAN?

After growing up in Kansas, Oscar Stanton DePriest settled in Chicago around 1899, where he established a painting and decorating firm and a real estate business. He grew to be a well-known figure in Republican politics, serving on the Cook County Board of Commissioners and the Chicago City Council. In 1928 he made history when he became the first African American elected to the United States Congress since Reconstruction, and the first ever from a Northern state.

The arrival of an African American congressman caused consternation in the nation's capital, which was strictly segregated. Some Southern congressmen refused to accept an office adjacent to DePriest's, and some Southerners protested vehemently when President Hoover's wife invited Mrs. DePriest to a tea party at the White House.

As a congressman, DePriest called for several measures that would benefit African American citizens and asked Congress to make Abraham Lincoln's birthday a national holiday. But by 1934, Franklin Delano Roosevelt had become president, and many black Americans were joining the Democratic Party. That year, DePriest was defeated by Arthur W. Mitchell, who became the first African American Democrat elected to Congress. DePriest returned to Chicago, serving once again in the city council and remaining active in his real estate business until his death in 1951.

◆

WHO WAS THE FIRST AFRICAN AMERICAN LAWYER TO WIN A SUPREME COURT CASE FOR THE NAACP?

A grandson of slaves, Charles Hamilton Houston was born in Washington, D.C., in 1895. In 1915 he graduated magna cum laude and Phi Beta Kappa from Amherst College in Massachusetts. During World War I he served for two years in a segregated unit of the American Expeditionary Forces. He then enrolled in Harvard Law School, earning an LL.B. in 1922 and a doctorate a year later. While at Harvard, he was the first African American to serve as an editor of the *Harvard Law Review.*

Houston joined the faculty of Howard University Law School in 1924, becoming its dean and reorganizing the school into an institution that would train African American lawyers to use the law to effect social change. In 1935 Houston successfully argued a Supreme Court case for the NAACP. In *Hollins v. State of Oklahoma,* he convinced the Court to overturn the conviction of a black man on the grounds that African Americans had been illegally excluded from the jury panel.

Soon afterward, Houston joined the NAACP as special counsel, directing his energies to exposing the unsoundness of the *Plessy v. Ferguson* Supreme Court ruling of 1896 that sanctioned segregation. To show that separate facilities for blacks and whites were inherently unequal, Houston argued and won the *Gaines v. Missouri* case in 1938, upsetting the University of Missouri's policy of providing a law school for whites but not African Americans. He later won decisions in *Hurd v. Hodge* and *Shelly v. Kraemer,* which prevented the enforcement of racially restrictive covenants in housing.

Houston's ultimate victory was the creation of the legal strategy that finally struck down educational segregation when the Supreme Court declared it unconstitutional in the landmark 1954 *Brown v. Board of Education* decision. Although Thurgood Marshall argued the case, he gave the credit to Houston, who had died four years earlier. "Charlie Houston," said Marshall, was the "engineer of all of it."

◆

WHO WAS THE FIRST AFRICAN AMERICAN FEDERAL JUDGE?

A Phi Beta Kappa at Amherst College, William H. Hastie graduated at the head of his class in 1925. He was a top student at Harvard Law School, earning a degree in 1930. He went to Washington, D.C., to practice law and joined the faculty of the Howard University School of Law, where his cousin, Charles Houston, was dean. In 1933 Hastie became a lawyer in the Department of the

Interior under President Franklin Roosevelt. Four years later, Roosevelt named him a judge of the federal district court of the Virgin Islands, a territory of the United States, making him the first African American federal judge.

After two years Hastie returned to Howard as dean of the law school. In 1940 he was named a civilian aide to the secretary of war but later resigned in protest against segregation in the military. He ended his tenure as dean of Howard Law School in 1946 when President Harry Truman appointed him the first African American governor of the Virgin Islands. Three years later Truman named Hastie to the United States Court of Appeals, Third District, making him the first African American to serve on a federal appeals court. He died in 1976.

◆

WHEN WAS AN AFRICAN AMERICAN WOMAN FIRST ELECTED TO A STATE LEGISLATURE?

Crystal Bird Fauset, a former teacher and advocate of interracial understanding, was elected to the Pennsylvania House of Representatives in 1938, the first time an African American woman had been elected to a state legislature. Fauset was born in Maryland in 1893 and educated in Boston, teaching school for a time. She then took a job as a field secretary for the YWCA, developing programs for young African American women, and later became a speaker in the interracial section of the American Friends Service Committee. In 1933 she helped establish the Institute of Race Relations at Swarthmore College.

Fauset entered the world of politics in 1934 when she was named director of African American women's activities for the Democratic National Committee. In 1936 she was hired as assistant personnel director in the Philadelphia office of the Works Progress Administration (WPA). After finishing her term in the state legislature, Fauset held several other important posts until her death in 1965.

◆

WHO WAS THE FIRST
AFRICAN AMERICAN WOMAN JUDGE?

In 1939, Jane M. Bolin, then a thirty-one-year-old lawyer in the office of New York City's Corporation Counsel, was summoned to meet with Mayor Fiorello LaGuardia. After conferring briefly with Bolin's husband, also a lawyer, LaGuardia asked the startled young woman to raise her right hand. He then proceeded to swear her in as a judge of the Domestic Relations Court of the City of New York, making Bolin the first African American woman judge in the United States.

When she decided to become a lawyer, Bolin was following in the footsteps of her father, Gaius Bolin, the first black graduate of Williams College, who practiced law in Poughkeepsie, New York. She graduated from Wellesley College and entered Yale Law School, where she was one of only two African Americans in her class and one of three women. With law degree in hand, she clerked in her father's law office and later opened a law practice with her new husband. She worked with him for five years, then joined the corporation counsel's office as the first African American on the staff. She was also the first black woman to join the New York City Bar Association.

Bolin remained on the Domestic Relations Court, which was renamed New York Family Court, for nearly forty years, leaving at the mandatory retirement age of seventy. Continuing her interest in children and families, she served on the boards of several agencies that worked on their behalf. Bolin died in 2007 at the age of ninety-eight.

◆

WHO WAS THE FIRST AFRICAN AMERICAN
SUPREME COURT CLERK?

In 1948, William Thaddeus Coleman Jr., who graduated first in his class at Harvard Law School, was appointed a clerk to United States Supreme Court Justice Felix Frankfurter. He was the first African American ever to serve as a law clerk to a Supreme Court justice.

After his clerkship ended, he worked with law firms in New York and Pennsylvania and helped write the legal argument that resulted in the 1954 Supreme Court decision banning segregation in public schools. In the late 1950s and early '60s he defended numerous civil rights activists in courts in the South. He was named president of the NAACP Legal Defense and Educational Fund in 1971, and in 1975 President Gerald Ford appointed him secretary of transportation, the second African American in history to hold a cabinet post. After stepping down in 1977, he joined a Washington law firm. An advisor to six presidents, Coleman received, among other honors, the Presidential Medal of Freedom and the Legal Defense and Educational Fund's Thurgood Marshall Lifetime Achievement Award.

◆

WHO WAS THE FIRST AFRICAN AMERICAN U.S. AMBASSADOR?

Edward R. Dudley was born in 1911 in Virginia, the son of a dentist. After graduating from Johnson C. Smith College in North Carolina, he became a teacher of African American children in a one-room schoolhouse in Virginia, earning sixty dollars a month. He entered Howard University to study dentistry, but after a year he moved to New York, where he worked as a stage manager for Orson Welles's WPA Federal Theatre Project. After the project ended, he enrolled in law school at St. John's University, earning a degree in 1941. Encouraged by an uncle with political connections, Dudley became involved in a Democratic club in Harlem, and served as an assistant state attorney general for a time. He took a job with the Pepsi-Cola company, then joined the NAACP legal team, where he prepared cases for the admission of African American students to Southern colleges, equal pay for African American teachers, and ending discrimination in public transportation.

In 1948, President Harry Truman appointed Dudley ambassador to Liberia, making him the first African American to hold the post of ambassador. After five years he returned to New York, where he practiced law. He later served as Manhattan borough president and state supreme court judge. Dudley died of cancer at the age of ninety-three.

◆

WHO WAS THE FIRST AFRICAN AMERICAN TO WIN THE NOBEL PEACE PRIZE?

Born in Detroit, the grandson of a slave, Ralph Bunche was always a brilliant student. He was the valedictorian of his high school class in Los Angeles, where he was raised by his grandmother after both his parents died. At the University of California at Los Angeles, where he played football, baseball, and basketball, he graduated at the head of his class, and then made his mark as the first African American to earn a doctorate in political science from Harvard University. He became a professor at Howard University, where he organized and chaired that school's first department of political science.

Bunche became the first African American official in the U.S. State Department in 1944, and four years later he went to work at the United Nations. His efforts in negotiating an armistice in the Arab-Israeli conflict earned him the Nobel Peace Prize in 1950. He went on to negotiate peacekeeping efforts in the Congo, Yemen, Cyprus, India, Pakistan, and the Suez, and in 1963 President John Kennedy awarded him the Medal of Freedom. Bunche became undersecretary general of the United Nations in 1967, a post he held until ill health forced him to retire in 1971. He died in September of that year in New York City.

◆

WHO WAS THE FIRST AFRICAN AMERICAN WOMAN DELEGATE TO THE UNITED NATIONS?

While still employed full-time as a social worker, Edith Spurlock Sampson entered law school and, in 1927, became the first woman to earn a degree from Loyola University. After setting up a law practice with her husband, she concentrated on providing legal services to poor clients. She became involved in international affairs in 1949, when the National Council of Negro Women chose her to participate in a worldwide speaking tour, during which she discussed how a democratic nation could work to overcome racism.

In 1950 President Truman selected Sampson as the first African American woman delegate to the United Nations General Assembly, where she served until the early 1960s, when she was appointed to the North Atlantic Treaty Organization. Two years later she won a municipal judgeship in Illinois, making her the first African American woman judge in that state. She retired in 1978 and died a year later.

◆

WHO WAS THE FIRST AFRICAN AMERICAN WOMAN IN THE U.S. ELECTED TO A STATE SENATE?

On her third try, Cora Brown, a social worker and lawyer from Detroit, was elected to serve in the Michigan State Senate, the first African American woman in the country to hold this position. Brown was born in 1914 in Bessemer, Alabama. When she was seven years old, her family moved to Detroit, where her father opened a tailor shop. After finishing high school, she enrolled in Fisk University in Nashville, Tennessee. To help pay her college expenses, she worked at a summer camp for poor children and her mother took a job as a cook.

After earning a sociology degree from Fisk, Brown returned to Detroit, where she was employed as a social worker and then as a police officer. Her involvement in the legal system inspired her to study for a law degree, which she earned in 1948 from Wayne State University. A Democrat, she became involved in political activities in her district of Detroit, and in 1952 was elected to the state senate. Citing the various causes she espoused—civil rights, education, and health—the *Detroit Press* called her a "champion of the underprivileged."

In 1956 Brown ran for the United States Congress, but because of her support for the reelection of Republican President Dwight Eisenhower, she received little Democratic backing and lost the election. She was rewarded by the Republicans in 1957 by being appointed special associate general counsel of the U.S. Post Office, a position she held until John F. Kennedy took office. She went to Los Angeles, opened a law office, and returned to Detroit in 1970, where she was appointed to the Michigan Employment Security Commission. She died two years later.

♦

WHEN DID THE SECRET SERVICE HIRE ITS FIRST AFRICAN AMERICAN AGENT?

Charles L. Gittens became the first African American agent in the Secret Service in 1956 and went on to protect presidents and lead the agency's Washington Bureau. Gittens was born in 1928 in Cambridge, Massachusetts, the son of immigrants from Barbados. He left high school to join the army, where he rose to the rank of lieutenant. After his discharge, he earned a degree from what is now North Carolina Central University and worked as a high school teacher before deciding to seek a job in law enforcement.

After passing a civil service test, Gittens was recruited by the Secret Service. Although he said he never experienced racism within the agency, he sometimes encountered it in his work. Once, while guarding President Lyndon B. Johnson, he and other agents entered a Dallas restaurant where he was told he wouldn't be served. "The other guys were a lot angrier than I was," Gittens told *Ebony* magazine. "But the manager came out and apologized profusely. And we eventually got served."

Gittens protected other presidents, including Dwight Eisenhower, John F. Kennedy, and Gerald Ford. In 1971, he was put in charge of the Washington field office, where he supervised more than one hundred agents. After retiring from the Secret Service in 1979, he became deputy director of the Office of Special Investigations in the U.S. Department of Justice. He died in 2011 at the age of eighty-two.

"He was a great agent," Mark Sullivan, then the director of the Secret Service, told the *Washington Post*. "A lot of agents, black

CHARLES L. GITTENS

and white, have benefited from the things he had done. He led by example, and he set the standards for all of us to follow."

A biography by Maurice A. Butler, *Out from the Shadow: The Story of Charles L. Gittens Who Broke the Color Barrier in the United States Secret Service,* was published in September 2012.

◆

WHO WAS THE COUNTRY'S FIRST AFRICAN AMERICAN WELFARE COMMISSIONER?

When James R. Dumpson died in November 2012 at the age of one hundred and three, he was mourned by members of New York City's human services community for his long career "as a public servant, educator, administrator, social activist, advocate, humanitarian, and scholar," said a statement in the *New York Nonprofit Press*.

"He had a servant's heart," said Mary Redd, president of Steinway Child and Family Services. "He always wanted to make sure we reached back for those who were disadvantaged and without hope."

Dumpson was born in 1909 in a section of Philadelphia known as Hell's Half-Acre. His father was a bank messenger, and his mother, a former teacher, stressed the importance of education. Dumpson graduated in 1932 from Cheyney College in Pennsylvania and went on to earn bachelor's and master's degrees from the New School in New York City. He taught for a time, was a social worker in Philadelphia, and then moved to New York to become a caseworker for the Children's Aid Society.

He joined the New York Department of Welfare in 1956, and in 1959, Mayor Robert F. Wagner appointed him commissioner, making him the first African American welfare commissioner in the United States. He served on many commissions and advisory boards throughout his career. In 1967, he was named dean of the Graduate School of Social Service at Fordham University. He continued to make contributions as a public servant until he retired from public life in 2002.

On the occasion of Dumpson's one hundredth birthday, Congressman Charles Rangel called him "a familiar, popular, and pioneering leader in New York and in the African American community, an icon who worked tirelessly on behalf of others."

◆

WHO WAS THE FIRST AFRICAN AMERICAN FEDERAL DISTRICT COURT JUDGE IN THE CONTINENTAL UNITED STATES?

Early one morning in August 1961, James Benton Parsons was vacationing at his summer home in Lakeside, Michigan, when he got a telephone call from President John F. Kennedy, saying he intended to appoint him federal district judge for the northern district of Illinois. In earlier years several African Americans had served as federal district judges in the Virgin Islands, but Parsons became the first black district judge in the continental United States.

Parsons was born in Kansas City, Missouri, the son of a minister. He worked his way through James Milliken University in Decatur, Illinois, earning a bachelor's degree in 1934. He taught for several years and served in the navy during World War II. Using the GI Bill to help pay his tuition, he enrolled in the University of Chicago, earning a master's degree in political science in 1946 and a law degree three years later. He was a partner in a Chicago law firm, an assistant U.S. attorney, and a superior court judge before his appointment to the federal district bench in 1961. In 1975 he was named chief judge of the northern district of Illinois, the first African American in history to be chief judge of a federal district court. Parsons retired from trial work in 1992 and died a year later at the age of eighty-one.

◆

WHO WAS THE FIRST AFRICAN AMERICAN MEMBER OF THE FEDERAL RESERVE BOARD?

Andrew F. Brimmer, born the son of a Louisiana sharecropper in 1926, was named by President Lyndon B. Johnson forty years later to be the first African American member of the U. S. Federal Reserve Board. Johnson praised Brimmer at his swearing-in ceremony, saying, "Through his own intelligence and by his own efforts he rose to the highest academic honors. In the process, he developed a deep feeling for Americans in every walk of life."

After finishing high school in Louisiana, Brimmer went to Seattle to join one of his sisters. He served in the army toward the end of World War II, then attended the University of Washington, where he earned a bachelor's degree in economics in 1950 and a master's degree a year later. He studied in India as a Fulbright scholar, returning to the United States where he earned a Ph.D. from Harvard Business School in 1957.

He worked at the Federal Reserve Bank in New York and taught at Michigan State University and at the University of Pennsylvania's Wharton School of Business. He held the post of assistant secretary of commerce for economic affairs before Johnson appointed him to the Federal Reserve Board in 1966, where he remained for more than eight years. He then joined the faculty of the Harvard Business School and started a consulting firm.

While on the board, Brimmer drew attention to the economic conditions of African Americans. He had studied the disparities in income between black and white Americans, and he told the *New York Times* in 1973, "I do feel the economic plight of blacks is a serious matter."

After Brimmer's death in 2012, Roger Ferguson, an African American who later served on the Federal Reserve Board, said, "Andy Brimmer was a trailblazer and a role model for a generation of African Americans who aspired to be economic policy makers."

◆

WHEN WAS THE FIRST AFRICAN AMERICAN POPULARLY ELECTED TO THE U.S. SENATE?

In 1966, Edward Brooke became the first African American to be elected to the United States Senate by popular vote. (Hiram Revels, the first black senator, was chosen by the Mississippi legislature in 1870 to fill the unexpired term of Jefferson Davis, who had become the Confederate president. Blanche Kelso Bruce, the second African American senator, also from Mississippi, was chosen by the legislature in 1875 and served a full term.)

Brooke also made history in 1962 when he was elected a state attorney general, the first African American to hold that office. He served in the post for two terms until his election to the Senate. Brooke, born in 1919 in Washington, D.C., was a graduate of Howard University and Boston University Law School. After serving as a senator from Massachusetts until 1979, Brooke practiced law and served as chairman of the National Low Income Housing Coalition, the Boston Bank of Commerce, and the World Policy Council. In 2006, he published his autobiography, *Bridging the Divide: My Life*.

◆

WHO WAS THE FIRST AFRICAN AMERICAN WOMAN TO BE A FEDERAL JUDGE?

Constance Baker Motley made history for the first time in 1962 when, as a lawyer for the NAACP Legal Defense and Educational Fund, she won the right for James Meredith, an African American, to attend the segregated University of Mississippi.

Motley was born and grew up in New Haven, Connecticut, where her parents had immigrated from the Caribbean island of Nevis. After she finished high school, a local businessman, impressed by her spirit, offered to pay her college tuition. She attended Fisk and New York Universities and graduated from Columbia Law School in 1946. In her senior year of law school she worked as a clerk for Thurgood Marshall, then head of the NAACP Legal Defense and Educational Fund. After earning her law degree she joined the staff, remaining with the Fund for twenty years and eventually becoming an associate counsel, winning nine of the ten cases she argued before the Supreme Court.

Motley left the Fund to enter politics, and in 1964, at the age of forty-two, became the first African American woman elected to the New York State Senate. A year later she was the first woman and first African American to be elected Manhattan Borough President. In 1966, President Lyndon Johnson appointed her to the United States District Court, Southern District of New York, making her the first African American woman to serve on the federal bench. In 1982, Motley was named chief judge of the court, and she became a senior judge four years later. She served until her death in 2005 at the age of eighty-four.

◆

WHO WAS THE FIRST AFRICAN AMERICAN TO SERVE IN A PRESIDENT'S CABINET?

When Robert C. Weaver was appointed a cabinet member in 1966, he could claim a lengthy history in government service. In the 1930s he held a responsible position in the Department of Interior under President Franklin Roosevelt, and in 1961 he became the first African American to head a major government agency when President Kennedy appointed him administrator of the Housing and Home Finance Agency.

Born in Washington, D.C., in 1908 and trained as an economist and educator, Weaver served in New York city and state governments and in 1946 directed foreign assistance to the Soviet Union for the United Nations Relief and Rehabilitation Administration. In January 1966 he became the first African American to attain cabinet rank when President Lyndon Johnson named him Secretary of Housing and Urban Development (HUD).

He served as HUD secretary until December 1968, working to increase the availability of affordable housing and to end housing discrimination. He later held several teaching positions, served as president of Baruch College in New York, and in the 1970s was a director of New York City's Municipal Assistance Corporation. Weaver died in July 1997, and three years later the HUD Headquarters Building in Washington was renamed the Robert C. Weaver Federal Building in his honor.

◆

WHO WAS THE FIRST AFRICAN AMERICAN SUPREME COURT JUSTICE?

When Thurgood Marshall died of heart failure in January 1993 at the age of eighty-four, the country lost one of its most illustrious legal scholars. In 1967, when Marshall was named the first African American on the United States Supreme Court, it was the culmination of a career that had resulted in many historic legal victories.

Born in Baltimore, Maryland, in 1908, Marshall described himself as a "hell-raiser" in high school. It was there that he was exposed to the United States Constitution when, as punishment, the teacher made students learn sections of it. "I made my way through every paragraph," he said. He graduated from Lincoln University, a predominantly black college in Pennsylvania, waiting tables to help pay tuition. Excluded from the all-white law school at the University of Maryland, he attended Howard University Law School, where he graduated first in his class in 1933. His mother had pawned her wedding and engagement rings to pay the school's entrance fee. He subsequently brought successful lawsuits that integrated the University of Maryland and other state university systems, and years later the University of Maryland named its law library after him.

At Howard, Marshall met the man who would become his mentor, Charles Houston, a law professor and dean who later became the special counsel to the NAACP. In fact, he credited Houston with helping shape the strategy that resulted in Marshall's greatest legal victory, the Supreme Court's 1954 decision in *Brown v. Board of Education,* which declared an end to racial segregation in public schools. Marshall won that case while he was director-counsel of the NAACP Legal Defense and Educational Fund, a position he held for more than twenty years.

In 1961 Marshall was appointed a federal appeals court judge by President Kennedy, and from 1965 to 1967 he served as Solicitor General of the United States. By the time President Johnson made him a Supreme Court justice in 1967, Marshall had argued thirty-two cases before the Supreme Court, winning twenty-nine. During his twenty-four years on the Supreme Court, he voted against every death sentence presented to him, believing that capital punishment was inherently unfair and permeated with racism. In 1991 Marshall was forced to retire from the Supreme Court because of his failing health.

◆

WHEN DID A MAJOR U.S. CITY ELECT ITS FIRST AFRICAN AMERICAN MAYOR?

In November 1967, the city of Cleveland, Ohio, elected Carl Stokes to the mayor's office. A Democrat, lawyer, and former state legislator, Stokes won ninety-six percent of the city's African American vote and nineteen percent of the white vote.

Richard Hatcher, also an African American, was elected mayor of Gary, Indiana, that same month, but Stokes was inaugurated first, making him the first African American to become mayor of a large American city.

Stokes served until 1971, deciding not to run for a third term. He later found positions as a television news anchor and a municipal court judge. In June 1991, President Clinton appointed him ambassador to the Republic of Seychelles. He died of cancer two years later. Richard Hatcher, after serving as mayor of Gary for twenty years, joined the faculty of Valparaiso University School of Law in Indiana.

♦

WHO WAS THE COUNTRY'S FIRST AFRICAN AMERICAN ASSISTANT SECRETARY OF STATE?

Born in New York City in 1918, Barbara Watson was a member of an illustrious family. Her father, James S. Watson, was the first African American judge in New York State, and her brother, Douglas, was to become the country's first black aeronautical engineer.

After earning a bachelor's degree from Barnard College in 1943, Watson embarked upon a series of diverse occupations. She was an interviewer for the United Seamen's Service, she managed her own modeling agency, and she was coordinator of student activities at Hampton Institute in Virginia. She then decided to enter New York Law School, graduating third in her class in 1962. A group of prominent jurists selected her as the most outstanding law student in New York City.

With her law degree, Watson held a number of government positions, including Assistant Corporation Counsel for the City of New York, and executive director of the New York City Commission to the United Nations, serving as a liaison between the city and various UN missions. In 1966 her background and talent attracted President Lyndon Johnson, who appointed her to the Bureau of Security and Consular Affairs, U.S. State Department. In 1968 she was appointed Assistant Secretary of State for Consular Affairs. The first woman and the first African American to achieve the rank of assistant secretary of state, she served in that position under Presidents Johnson, Nixon, Ford, and Carter.

In 1980 President Carter named her United States Ambassador to Malaysia, where she negotiated several important trade agreements on behalf of the United States. Her lifelong commitment to African and Caribbean countries brought her many honors, including a designation as Commander of the National Order of the Republic of the Ivory Coast. At her funeral in Washington in 1983, the ninety-three honorary pallbearers included ambassadors, senators, congressmen, mayors, and heads of educational and political organizations.

♦

WHO WAS THE FIRST AFRICAN AMERICAN WOMAN TO SERVE IN THE U.S. CONGRESS?

Born in Brooklyn in 1924, Shirley Chisholm spent her early childhood in Barbados. After returning to New York she attended Brooklyn College and Columbia University to prepare for a teaching career. In her autobiography, *Unbought and Unbossed,* she wrote that there was no other road open to a young African American woman, since law, medicine, and nursing were too expensive, "and few schools would admit black men, much less a woman."

After college Chisholm entered politics, and was elected to the New York State Assembly in 1964. Four years later, running as a Democrat from the Bedford-Stuyvesant section of Brooklyn, she became the first African American woman elected to the United States Congress.

In 1972 Chisholm broke another barrier, becoming the first black woman to actively run for the presidential nomination of a major party, the Democrats. Although she did not win the nomination, her compelling voice was heard on the issues of better education for minority groups, programs for the poor, and equality for minorities and women. In her book *The Good Fight* she explained why she ran for the presidency, saying: "The next time a woman of whatever color, or a dark-skinned person of whatever sex aspires to be President, the way should be a little smoother because I helped pave it."

After a fourteen-year career in Congress, Chisholm returned to education as a professor at Mt. Holyoke College in Massachusetts. She later retired to Florida, where she wrote and lectured. She died on January 1, 2005, at the age of eighty.

♦

WHO WAS THE FIRST AFRICAN AMERICAN MEMBER OF THE FCC?

Best known as the longtime executive director of the NAACP, Benjamin Hooks first made national headlines in June 1972 when he was appointed the first African American member of the seven-person Federal Communications Commission, a government body that oversees the operation of the broadcasting industry.

Born in Memphis, Tennessee, in 1925, Hooks graduated from Howard University and earned a law degree from DePaul University. He practiced law in Memphis, was the first African American public defender in that city, and served for several years as a county court judge. As an FCC commissioner, Hooks worked to improve the portrayal of black people on television and to increase employment and ownership opportunities for African Americans in the electronic media. He served as the executive director of the NAACP from 1977 to 1993. During his tenure, the organization's membership grew to the highest in its history.

After leaving the NAACP, Hooks became a professor in the political science department of the University of Memphis, which established the Benjamin L. Hooks Institute for Social Change in 1996. He also served as pastor of the Middle Baptist Church and president of the National Civil Rights Museum, both in Memphis. In 2007, Hooks was awarded the Presidential Medal of Freedom. He died of heart failure at his home in Memphis in April 2010 at the age of eighty-five.

◆

WHO WAS THE FIRST TO DISCOVER THE WATERGATE BREAK-IN?

On June 17, 1972, an African American security guard at the Watergate Hotel in Washington, D.C., made a discovery that changed history. The guard, twenty-four-year-old Frank Wills, was patrolling the building in the early morning hours when he noticed a piece of tape over a door lock at the garage level. Wills removed the tape, but when he returned about an hour later a new piece of tape had been placed over the lock.

Wills called the police and they in turn were able to capture five men who had broken into the headquarters of the Democratic National Committee. The burglars turned out to be connected with the reelection campaign of President Richard Nixon, a Republican. The ramifications of Wills's discovery led to an effort to impeach Nixon and to the president's eventual resignation in 1974. Wills later played himself in a movie about the event, *All the President's Men.* He died in September 2000 from the effects of a brain tumor.

◆

WHEN DID AFRICAN AMERICANS BECOME MAYORS OF TWO LARGE CITIES?

On November 6, 1973, Thomas Bradley was elected mayor of Los Angeles, and Coleman Young was elected mayor of Detroit. They became the first African American mayors of cities with populations greater than one million. Born in 1917 in Calvert, Texas, Bradley attended the University of California at Los Angeles and earned a law degree from Southwestern University. The son of sharecroppers, Bradley devoted fifty years of his life to public service: two decades as a police officer, a decade as the first African American city councilman, and five terms as mayor. Tom Bradley International Terminal at the Los Angeles airport was one of the institutions named to honor the former mayor, who died in 1998.

Coleman Young was born in Tuscaloosa, Alabama, in 1918. His family moved to Detroit when he was five. After high school, Young worked for the Ford Motor Company and the U.S. Postal Service, and during World War II he served with the Tuskegee Airmen. After the war, he returned to Detroit and got involved in politics. He was serving in the Michigan State Senate when he was elected Detroit's mayor. Young died in 1997.

◆

WHO WAS THE FIRST AFRICAN AMERICAN TO HOLD A DEMOCRATIC LEADERSHIP POSITION IN THE HOUSE OF REPRESENTATIVES?

In 1972 Cardiss Collins's husband, George, a Democratic congressman from Illinois, was killed in a plane crash while returning to Chicago from Washington. Elected to fill her husband's unexpired term, Collins took office in 1973.

Collins's tenure in Congress was filled with firsts. She was the first African American woman to chair the Congressional Black Caucus and the first African American and the first woman to chair the Manpower and Housing subcommittee of the House Government Operations Committee. A fighter for women's health rights, Medicare reform, environmental issues, and airline safety, Collins became the first African American and first woman to hold a Democratic leadership position in the House of Representatives when she was named whip-at-large. She served in Congress until she retired in 1996. She died in February 2013.

◆

WHO WAS THE FIRST AFRICAN AMERICAN TO GIVE A KEYNOTE SPEECH BEFORE A DEMOCRATIC NATIONAL CONVENTION?

Barbara Jordan, born in Houston, Texas, in 1936, the daughter of a Baptist minister, was a graduate of Texas Southern University. Her speaking skills were recognized while she was still in college, where she won first place in junior oratory as a member of the first debating team from an African American university to compete in an annual debate competition at Baylor University. In 1959, after earning a law degree from Boston University, Jordan returned to Houston, and seven years later was elected to the Texas Senate. She was the first African American to serve in that body in eighty-three years.

In November 1972 Jordan was elected to the United States House of Representatives, the first African American woman from the South to win a seat in Congress. During her three terms as a congresswoman, she sponsored bills advocating the causes of the poor and disadvantaged. During the impeachment hearings of President Nixon, her eloquence drew national attention. In July 1976 she became the first African American and the first woman to give a keynote address at a Democratic National Convention. Two years later she retired from public office and became a distinguished professor at the Lyndon B. Johnson School of Public Affairs at the University of Texas, serving until her death in 1996.

◆

WHO WAS THE FIRST AFRICAN AMERICAN WOMAN TO SERVE IN A PRESIDENT'S CABINET?

Patricia Roberts Harris, born in Illinois in 1924, earned a bachelor's degree from Howard University and a law degree from George Washington University School of Law, where she graduated first in a class of ninety-four. While still an undergraduate, Harris took part in a student sit-in aimed at integrating a local cafeteria.

After law school Harris worked for the United States Justice Department for a time and then joined the faculty of Howard University Law School, where she later was named dean. In 1965 she became the first African American woman ambassador when President Lyndon Johnson appointed her ambassador to Luxembourg, a post she held for two years. In 1977 President Jimmy Carter gave Harris a position in his cabinet, naming her Secretary of Housing and Urban Development. Just two years later, he appointed her Secretary of Health, Education and Welfare, an office she held until Ronald Reagan became president.

Harris left government service and in 1982 began teaching at George Washington Law School, where she remained until her death from cancer three years later.

◆

WHEN WAS THE FIRST AFRICAN AMERICAN
APPOINTED SECRETARY OF THE ARMY?

Clifford Alexander, Jr., a distinguished lawyer and public servant, held positions in four presidential administrations during the 1960s and '70s. Born in New York City in 1933, Alexander attended the Ethical Culture and Fieldston schools and graduated from Harvard, where he was elected student body president. After earning a degree from Yale Law School, he returned to New York, where he worked first as an assistant district attorney and then as the executive director of two city agencies.

Officials in the administration of President John F. Kennedy, impressed by Alexander's accomplishments, offered him a position on the National Security Council. After Kennedy's assassination, Alexander was appointed deputy special assistant and, eventually, deputy special counsel, to President Lyndon B. Johnson. He served as special consultant to Johnson on civil rights and voting rights issues. In 1967, Johnson appointed him chairman of the U.S. Equal Employment Opportunity Commission (EEOC), which greatly expanded its activities under his direction, investigating the hiring practices of major industries. He resigned from the post shortly after Richard Nixon took office, saying the new administration did not support the EEOC's goals.

Alexander then practiced law until 1977, when President Jimmy Carter appointed him secretary of the Army. He was the first African American to hold that position. He served until Ronald Reagan took office, and later formed a consulting company, Alexander & Associates, Inc., that advised businesses on increasing minority hiring.

His daughter, Elizabeth Alexander, a poet and the head of the African American studies department at Yale, was chosen by Barack Obama to create and read a poem at his first presidential inauguration.

◆

WHO WAS THE FIRST AFRICAN AMERICAN AMBASSADOR TO THE UNITED NATIONS?

After graduating from Howard University in 1951 at the age of nineteen, Andrew Young decided to study for the ministry. He earned a divinity degree in 1955, was ordained a Congregational minister, and served as a pastor in rural churches in Georgia and Alabama.

In the early 1960s Young became active in the civil rights movement in the South, joining the Southern Christian Leadership Conference and eventually becoming its director. A close associate of the Rev. Martin Luther King Jr., he organized citizen education programs and voter registration drives and helped draft the Civil Rights Act of 1964 and the Voting Rights Act of 1965. In 1972 Young was elected to the United States House of Representatives, becoming the first African American congressman from Georgia in 101 years.

Young served in Congress until 1977, when President Carter named him the first African American ambassador to the United Nations, where he stayed until 1979. In 1981 he was elected mayor of Atlanta, Georgia, serving for eight years. Other achievements followed: in 1994 President Clinton appointed him to head the South African Enterprise Development Fund; he was cochair of the Centennial Olympic Games in 1996; in 1999 Georgia State University named its School of Policy Studies after him; and he served as president of the National Council of Churches for the 2000–2001 term.

◆

WHO WAS THE FIRST WOMAN TO CHAIR THE EQUAL EMPLOYMENT OPPORTUNITY COMMISSION?

Eleanor Holmes Norton, an African American woman of many accomplishments, was born in Washington, D.C., in 1937. The eldest of three girls, Norton earned a bachelor's degree from Antioch College and then entered Yale, where she received a master's in American history and a law degree. She worked with the American Civil Liberties Union for five years and in 1970 was appointed to chair the New York City Commission on Human Rights, where she fought against discrimination in housing and the workplace.

Aware of her outstanding work in New York, in 1977 President Jimmy Carter appointed Norton as chair of the Equal Employment Opportunity Commission, a federal agency created to end discrimination in hiring practices. The first woman to chair that agency, she stayed until President Ronald Reagan took office in 1981. She then became a professor at Georgetown University Law Center and in November 1990 was the first woman elected to represent the District of Columbia in the House of Representatives, where in 2013 she was serving her twelfth term.

♦

WHO WAS THE FIRST AFRICAN AMERICAN AND THE FIRST WOMAN TO HEAD THE PEACE CORPS?

When President Jimmy Carter nominated Carolyn Payton in 1977 to head the Peace Corps, she became the first woman and the first African American to head this volunteer overseas assistance organization. Payton, a native of Norfolk, Virginia, with degrees from Bennett College, the University of Wisconsin, and Columbia University Teachers College, had a history with the Peace Corps at the time of her appointment as director. She started with the agency as a field assessor in 1964 and later became an overseas country director, supervising 130 volunteers in education projects in the Caribbean.

As director, Payton called for increased funding for various Peace Corps programs, as well as efforts to recruit more African Americans and other minorities. But because of budget constraints and lack of political power, she had trouble fulfilling her mandate. She finally resigned after thirteen months in the post after disputes with the director of the agency who oversaw the Peace Corps and other volunteer programs. She said she felt the director was trying to turn the Corps into an arrogant, elitist organization. She rejoined Howard University, where she had taught from 1959 to 1964.

She was serving as dean of counseling services there when she re-tired in 1995. She died in April 2001 at her Washington home at the age of seventy-five.

◆

WHO WAS THE FIRST AFRICAN AMERICAN TO SERVE A FULL TERM ON NEW YORK'S HIGHEST COURT?

Born in Florida in 1926, Fritz Alexander was raised by his uncle, a lawyer in Gary, Indiana. He served in the navy during World War II, graduated from Dartmouth College, and was president of his class at New York University Law School. After graduation, he and two other lawyers, one of whom was David Dinkins, formed a law practice that became the leading African American firm of the time. Alexander was appointed a civil court judge in 1970, served on the state supreme court, and was a member of the State Com-mission on Judicial Conduct. In 1985, Governor Mario Cuomo named him to the Court of Appeals, the state's highest court.

After only seven years, Alexander surprised his colleagues by re-signing from the Court of Appeals to join the administration of his old friend David Dinkins, who had just been elected mayor of New York City. Alexander served as a deputy mayor under Dinkins until his two-year term ended, and then served as special counsel to a Manhattan law firm. Alexander died in April 2000.

◆

WHO WAS THE FIRST AFRICAN AMERICAN WOMAN MAYOR OF A LARGE U.S. CITY?

A lifelong resident of Hartford, the capital of Connecticut, Carrie Saxon Perry was elected mayor in 1987. Perry was educated in Hartford's public schools and attended Howard Uni-versity. Before entering politics she was a social worker, an anti-poverty program administrator, and the director of a group home for adolescent girls.

In 1980 Perry was elected to the Connecticut General Assembly, where she served four terms. As mayor, Perry led efforts for adequate and affordable housing, job training, education, and health care for underprivileged and needy Hartford residents. After completing three terms in office, she became president of the Hartford branch of the NAACP.

♦

WHO WAS THE FIRST AFRICAN AMERICAN WOMAN TO SERVE ON A STATE'S HIGHEST COURT?

On March 3, 1988, Juanita Kidd Stout was inducted into office as a justice of the Pennsylvania Supreme Court, making her the first African American woman in the country to serve on a state's highest court. Earlier, in 1959, when she was elected to the Philadelphia Municipal Court, she became the first black woman in the United States to be elected to a court of record. She was later elected twice to the Common Pleas Court of Pennsylvania.

Stout, a native of Oklahoma, earned a bachelor's degree in music from the University of Iowa and two law degrees from the Indiana University School of Law. She was awarded numerous honorary degrees, and in 1988 was named Justice of the Year by the National Association of Women Judges, and a Distinguished Daughter of Pennsylvania by the governor. Stout left the Pennsylvania Supreme Court in 1989, when she reached the mandatory retirement age of seventy, and returned to the court of common pleas as a senior judge, a position she held until her death in 1998.

♦

WHO WAS THE FIRST AFRICAN AMERICAN TO SERVE AS MAJORITY WHIP OF THE HOUSE OF REPRESENTATIVES?

William H. Gray III, who rose to leadership positions in the House during his twelve-year tenure there while also serving as a Baptist minister, was selected as majority whip by his fellow Democrats in 1989, the first African American to hold that post.

Gray was born in Baton Rouge, Louisiana, in 1941. He earned

a bachelor's degree from Franklin & Marshall College and divinity degrees from Drew Theological Seminary and Princeton Theological Seminary. During much of the 1960s, he was a minister at a Baptist church in New Jersey and taught at several colleges.

In 1972, Gray succeeded his father and his grandfather as pastor of Bright Hope Baptist Church in Philadelphia. He remained pastor there while serving in Congress from 1979 to 1991, commuting from Washington to deliver the Sunday sermon. While chairing the House Budget Committee—a first for an African American legislator—he pushed to provide funding for education and other social services for the poor. A critic of apartheid, he was instrumental in creating legislation that implemented economic sanctions against South Africa.

Gray resigned from Congress in 1991 to become head of the United Negro College Fund; he raised more than $2 billion for the fund before he left in 2004. President Clinton appointed him a special advisor to Haiti in 1994.

Gray died July 1, 2013, after collapsing while attending the Wimbledon tennis tournament in London with his son Andrew. Responding to news of Gray's death, President Obama said, "Bill's extraordinary leadership, on issues from housing to transportation to supporting efforts that ended apartheid in South Africa, made our communities, our country, and our world a more just place."

Philadelphia Mayor Michael Nutter called Gray "a transformative leader among leaders. . . . He knew guys on the corner, and he knew Nelson Mandela and everyone in between."

◆

WHO WAS THE FIRST AFRICAN AMERICAN TO BE ELECTED GOVERNOR?

On January 13, 1990, Lawrence Douglas Wilder was sworn in as governor of Virginia, the first African American to be elected governor in United States history. Wilder, born in 1931 in Richmond, Virginia, was the grandson of slaves. His parents named him after Frederick Douglass, the abolitionist, and the poet Paul Laurence Dunbar. In 1951, just after Wilder earned a bachelor's degree from

Virginia Union University in Richmond, he was drafted into the army and sent to Korea. While serving his country he distinguished himself by earning a Bronze Star for rescuing fellow soldiers and capturing enemy troops.

Back home, Wilder decided to take advantage of the GI Bill to study law, but he had to leave the state because Virginia barred African Americans from attending its law schools. He enrolled in Howard University School of Law, earning a degree in 1959, and returned to Richmond to establish a law firm.

In 1969 Wilder was elected the first African American state senator in Virginia since Reconstruction. He served five terms in the state senate and made history again in 1985, when he was elected Virginia's first African American lieutenant governor. Four years later he was elected governor. He served until his term expired in 1994, and began teaching at Virginia Commonwealth University, which named its School of Government and Public Affairs in his honor. In November 2004, Wilder was elected mayor of Richmond, Virginia, receiving seventy-nine percent of the vote. In the spring of 2008, he announced he would not seek reelection when his term ended in 2009.

◆

WHO WAS THE FIRST AFRICAN AMERICAN WOMAN SHERIFF IN THE U.S.?

Jacquelyn Barrett was elected sheriff of Fulton County, Georgia, in November 1992, making her the first African American woman sheriff in the country. Barrett, forty-two years old when she took office, had been director of the Fulton County Public Safety Training Center. A graduate of Beaver College in Pennsylvania, with a master's degree from Atlanta University, Barrett had sixteen years of law enforcement experience when she became head of the Fulton County Sheriff's Department, where she was responsible for the largest county jail operation in the state of Georgia, with a staff that by the year 2001 had reached 1,000 employees.

After her election, in response to letters she received from other women, Sheriff Barrett said, "If I'm brave enough to run for office, maybe they can too." In August 2004, Barrett left office five months

JACQUELYN BARRETT

before her term ended, after the county jail that she supervised was reported to be in a state of crisis, and she was charged with accepting $40,000 in illegal campaign contributions from businessmen who stood to benefit from her $7 million real estate investment. Eight years later, the Georgia Campaign Finance Commission dismissed the charge relating to the campaign contributions.

◆

WHO WAS THE FIRST AFRICAN AMERICAN WOMAN ELECTED TO THE U.S. SENATE?

Carol Moseley-Braun made headlines as well as history in November 1992 when she became the first African American woman elected to the United States Senate. The daughter of a police officer and a medical worker, Moseley-Braun grew up in Hyde Park, an integrated area of Chicago. A University of Chicago Law School graduate, Moseley-Braun worked for three years in the United States Attorney's office and spent ten years in the Illinois State Legislature, where she was a chief sponsor of bills to improve education and increase school funding in the city of Chicago. She

CAROL MOSELEY-BRAUN

was Cook County Recorder of Deeds at the time of her election to the Senate.

Forty-five years old when elected, Moseley-Braun became the only black member of the Senate and the first African American to serve in that body in its history. She was named to the important Senate Judiciary Committee, which up to that time had been all male and all white, and served on banking, small business, finance, and housing and urban affairs committees. As senator, Moseley-Braun sponsored several education bills and supported gun control laws. She lost her 1998 reelection bid, and the next year was confirmed as ambassador to New Zealand, where she served until the newly elected president, George W. Bush, replaced her in 2001.

In November 2010, Moseley-Braun kicked off a campaign for mayor of Chicago, but she lost the February 2011 election to Rahm Emanuel, President Obama's former chief of staff.

◆

WHICH AFRICAN AMERICAN WOMAN WAS THE FIRST TO BE ELECTED A STATE ATTORNEY GENERAL?

In November 1992, Pamela Fanning Carter was elected attorney general of the state of Indiana. She was the first woman and the first African American to be attorney general of that state, and the first African American woman in the United States to be elected to that position. (In 1962, Edward Brooke of Massachusetts became the first African American state attorney general.)

After her victory, Carter gave credit to her parents, a former teacher and a businessman, and to her paternal grandfather, who lived to be 101 and enjoyed reading law books and quoting legal principles to her when she was a youngster. She also credited a short conversation she had with Dr. Martin Luther King Jr. at a fair housing march in Chicago, when the civil rights leader told the fifteen-year-old Carter to be "courageous in any pursuit."

A native of Indianapolis, Carter earned a bachelor's degree from the University of Detroit, a master's from the University of Michigan, and a law degree from Indiana University School of Law. She

PAMELA FANNING CARTER

worked as a Vista volunteer, a social worker, and a litigation lawyer for the United Auto Workers. In 1987 she became an enforcement attorney for the secretary of state, fighting white-collar crime, and in 1988 she joined Governor Evan Bayh's office, where she rose to deputy chief of staff.

Carter served as Indiana attorney general until 1997. Affected by an earlier bout with breast cancer, from which she fully recovered, she decided to move on. After leaving office, she became the first African American to be parliamentarian of the Indiana House of Representatives. She then joined the private sector as vice president–general counsel and corporate secretary for Cummins Engine

Company, the first African American woman in the country to be general counsel of a Fortune 500 company. After three years she moved to Brussels, Belgium, where she ran one of the Cummins businesses that covered Europe, the Middle East, and Africa. In the summer of 2001 she was promoted to vice president of worldwide sales, marketing, logistics, and distribution for Cummins's Filtration Business Unit, headquartered in Nashville, Tennessee.

◆

WHO WAS THE FIRST AFRICAN AMERICAN TO BE NAMED SECRETARY OF COMMERCE?

On December 12, 1992, the newly elected president, Bill Clinton, named Ronald H. Brown to his cabinet as Secretary of the Department of Commerce. Brown was the first African American chairman of the Democratic National Committee and the first black partner in the Washington law firm of Patton, Boggs & Blow.

Born in Washington, D.C., in 1941, Brown spent most of his childhood in New York City's Harlem, where his father was manager of the Hotel Theresa on 125th Street. He attended private schools in Manhattan and entered Middlebury College in Vermont, where he became the first African American to join a fraternity. The fraternity, Sigma Phi Epsilon, had a whites-only charter and was expelled by its national office when Brown was admitted.

After a stint in the army, Brown attended St. John's Law School in New York and then joined the staff of the National Urban League, where he remained for twelve years. He later served as chief counsel of the Senate Judiciary Committee. In 1988, Brown was chief campaign aide to Jesse Jackson in his attempt to win the presidential nomination.

Brown had served as Secretary of Commerce for four years and three months when he was killed in April 1996 at the age of fifty-four, when his plane crashed in stormy weather near Dubrovnik, Croatia, while he was on an economic tour of the Balkans for the Department of Commerce.

◆

RONALD V. DELLUMS

WHO WAS THE FIRST AFRICAN AMERICAN CHAIRMAN OF THE HOUSE ARMED SERVICES COMMITTEE?

In January 1993, Representative Ronald V. Dellums, a Democratic congressman from Berkeley, California, and a longtime peace advocate, was named chairman of the House Armed Services Committee. When Dellums was first suggested for a seat on the committee twenty years earlier, many resisted his membership because of his opposition to armed conflict.

A congressman since 1970, Dellums, a former marine, opposed the war in Vietnam as well as other foreign military interventions by the United States and espoused diplomacy as the best way to settle international disputes. He also voted against expensive defense systems and advocated cuts in the defense budget as a way to fund social programs.

At a news conference after his colleagues in the House voted to make him chairman of the Armed Services Committee, Dellums said, "I came here as an advocate of peace and I am going to continue to do so."

Dellums retired from the House in 1998, and a year later he inaugurated the Ronald V. Dellums Chair in Peace and Conflict Studies at the University of California at Berkeley. He returned to politics in October 2005, when he announced that he would run for mayor of Oakland, California. After a close vote, he was declared the winner in June 2006, and took office the next January. He served as mayor until 2011.

◆

WHO WAS THE FIRST WOMAN TO HEAD THE NAACP LEGAL DEFENSE AND EDUCATIONAL FUND?

The NAACP Legal Defense and Educational Fund, Inc., with headquarters in New York City, was founded in 1940 to fight for racial and social justice. Its lawyers provide legal assistance in cases involving discrimination in housing, employment, voting, education, health care, the environment, and the administration of criminal justice. The organization became nationally known in 1954 when Thurgood Marshall, then its director-counsel, argued and won the *Brown v. Board of Education* case that outlawed segregation in public schools.

In February 1993 Elaine R. Jones became the first woman to be named director-counsel of the Legal Defense Fund. The appointment was a culmination of her twenty-six-year career as a litigator and civil rights activist. Born in Norfolk, Virginia, in 1944, Jones, the daughter of a teacher and a Pullman porter, was the first African American woman to graduate from the University of Virginia Law School.

After earning her law degree, she became an attorney with the

ELAINE R. JONES

Legal Defense Fund, where she served as counsel of record in *Furman v. Georgia,* a landmark U.S. Supreme Court case that abolished the death penalty in thirty-seven states. In 1975 she left the Fund to become a special assistant to Secretary of Transportation William Coleman. Two years later, she returned to the Fund to head its Washington, D.C., office, where her efforts helped pass scores of civil rights laws. In 1989 Jones was the first African American elected to the board of the American Bar Association.

In August 2011, Jones received the bar association's Thurgood Marshall Award, which honors the recipient's "substantial, long-term contributions to the advancement of civil rights, civil liberties, and human rights in the United States." And in September

2012, the Legal Defense Fund announced that its former president had received the Trailblazer Award from the Just the Beginning Foundation, which has a goal to increase racial diversity in the legal profession and the judiciary.

◆

WHO WAS THE FIRST AFRICAN AMERICAN WOMAN TO HEAD A MAJOR POLICE DEPARTMENT?

When the first African American police officer was hired in Beverly J. Harvard's hometown of Macon, Georgia, he turned out to be her best friend's brother, and she never forgot the celebration surrounding the event. But she didn't think of entering the profession herself until the early 1970s when friends at a party, discussing the idea of hiring women for the Atlanta Police Department, remarked that the recruits should be very tall and weigh at least 200 pounds. Harvard's husband agreed, and she bet him $100 that she, a short and slender woman, could succeed as a police officer. She joined the department in 1973, starting as a patrol officer and moving steadily through the ranks until, in 1994, the mayor of Atlanta appointed her chief of police.

A graduate of Morris Brown College in Atlanta, Harvard earned her master's in urban government and administration from Georgia State University. She was the first woman in the Atlanta Police Department to graduate from the Federal Bureau of Investigation National Academy in Quantico, Virginia. Her first major challenge as police chief was coordinating security for the 1996 Centennial Olympic Games. She made community policing a priority in Atlanta, putting more officers on the street, and established and expanded units within the police department to curb crime and violence. She served until 2002. She then became a director of the United States Transportation Security Administration. In August 2010, President Obama nominated her to the position of United States Marshal for the Northern District of Georgia. She was sworn in two months later.

◆

BEVERLY J. HARVARD

WHEN DID A U.S. PRESIDENT NAME THE FIRST AFRICAN AMERICAN SECRETARY OF STATE?

When General Colin L. Powell retired from the military in 1993, he ended a thirty-five-year career that culminated in serving as the nation's top uniformed military officer—chairman of the Joint Chiefs of Staff. Powell was born in New York City's Harlem in 1937 and grew up in the South Bronx. He graduated from City College of New York with a degree in geology and a commission as a second lieutenant in the army ROTC.

Progressing in the army to command positions in the United States, Korea, Vietnam, and Germany, he was named national security advisor by President Ronald Reagan in 1987. Two years later, President George Bush made Powell the Chairman of the Joint Chiefs; he was the first African American and the youngest man ever to hold that office.

After he retired from the military, Powell published his 1995 bestselling autobiography, *My American Journey*, pursued a career as a public speaker, and chaired America's Promise, a national organization working on behalf of young people. On December 16, 2000, George W. Bush, about to take office as president, nominated Powell to serve as secretary of state. He was sworn in on January 20, 2001. Speaking to African American high school students two weeks later, Powell said, "What you have to do to defeat the people who think you're second class is to make sure that you are first class in your own mind. . . ."

Powell was criticized for presenting evidence before the United Nations Security Council that supported military action against Iraq but was later discredited. Shortly after Bush was reelected in 2004, Powell stepped down as secretary of state. In October 2008, he endorsed Barack Obama for president. He endorsed Obama for a second term two weeks before the November 6, 2012 election, saying, "I think we ought to keep on the track we are on."

◆

WHO WAS THE FIRST AFRICAN AMERICAN WOMAN TO BE APPOINTED SECRETARY OF STATE?

On January 28, 2005, Condoleezza Rice was sworn in as the sixty-sixth secretary of state of the United States. At her confirmation hearing, she said "we must use American diplomacy to help create a balance of power in the world that favors freedom. And the time for diplomacy is now." Yet by the time Rice stepped down in January 2009, she had been criticized for supporting some of President Bush's decisions, particularly the 2003 invasion of Iraq.

Rice was born in 1954 in Birmingham, Alabama. Her parents placed a strong emphasis on education for their only child; she studied music, French, figure skating, and ballet. In 1967 her family moved to Denver, and she attended a private all-girls Catholic high school. She hoped to become a concert pianist, but finally gave up that goal and enrolled in the University of Denver, where she majored in political science. She eventually earned bachelor's and master's degrees and a doctorate in that subject. In 1981 she joined the faculty of Stanford University, where she served as a provost from 1993 to 1999.

Rice served as President Bush's national security advisor during his first term, and after Colin Powell resigned as secretary of state in November 2004, Bush nominated her as his successor. She earned a reputation as a disciplined, dedicated public servant. In an interview with Andrea Mitchell of MSNBC eight days before the first inauguration of Barack Obama, Rice was asked if she had ever envisioned a day when an African American could become president. Obama's election, she said, meant "that we've overcome that impulse to define people by race, to define what they can do by race, and to limit them by race."

In September 2010, Rice joined the faculty of the Stanford University Graduate School of Business. Her book for young people, *Condoleezza Rice: A Memoir of My Extraordinary, Ordinary Family and Me*, was published in 2011. *No Higher Honor: A Memoir of My Years in Washington* came out in September 2012.

♦

WHO WAS THE FIRST AFRICAN AMERICAN WOMAN IN THE COUNTRY ELECTED SPEAKER OF A STATE ASSEMBLY?

Karen Bass, a California State Assembly member since 2005, made history in May 2008 when she was elected speaker of this legislative body; not only was she the first Democratic woman to hold the post in the state's history, but she was the first African American woman in the country to serve in this important position. Reporting on her victory, the *Sacramento Bee* newspaper noted that Bass would "assume a political job considered by many to be second only to the governor in power and prestige in California government."

KAREN BASS

Bass, born in 1953, grew up in the Venice/Fairfax area of Los Angeles. Her father worked as a mail carrier and her mother stayed at home to raise their four children. Bass graduated from Hamilton High School, and earned a bachelor's degree in health sciences from Cal State Dominguez Hills and a physician's assistant certificate from the University of Southern California's School of Medicine.

She worked as a nurse and a physician's assistant, and she also founded and led the Community Coalition, a group that sought to improve conditions in south Los Angeles. In 2006 she was struck by tragedy when her only child, Emilia Wright, was killed along with Emilia's husband, Michael Wright, in a car crash.

Bass entered politics in 2004, when she was elected to the state assembly. She has supported such issues as health insurance coverage, foster care reform, and other Democratic causes. As speaker, she names the chairs of every legislative committee, sets staff budgets, and picks which legislation reaches the assembly floor. The first African American speaker of the California State Assembly, Willie Brown, was elected speaker in 1980 and held the post for fourteen years. He went on to become mayor of San Francisco.

In November 2010, Bass was elected to the United States Congress with eighty-six percent of the vote, and in 2012, she was reelected to a second term. She was chosen to serve on several important committees, including the House Committee on Foreign Affairs. She continued to provide leadership on reforming the country's foster care system and strengthening the relationship between the United States and Russia.

◆

WHO WAS THE FIRST AFRICAN AMERICAN TO BE ELECTED PRESIDENT OF THE UNITED STATES?

When Barack Hussein Obama was sworn in as the forty-fourth President of the United States on January 20, 2009, the nearly two million people who had gathered in Washington to witness this historic event cheered, waved American flags, and shed tears of happiness. While his wife, Michelle, and their young daughters, Malia and Sasha, looked on with pride, Obama recited the oath on the same Bible that Abraham Lincoln had used at his own inauguration 148 years earlier.

Obama's journey to the presidency was extraordinary and inspiring. His mother, Stanley Ann Dunham, grew up in a small town in Kansas. Her parents later settled in Hawaii and it was there, as a student at the University of Hawaii, that she met the man who

BARACK OBAMA

was to become Obama's father, Barack Hussein Obama, Sr., a scholarship student from a small village in Kenya.

Obama was born in Hawaii in 1961; two years later his parents separated and his father returned to Kenya. Obama was to see him only once more before his death in a car accident in 1982. Except for a few years in Indonesia, Obama grew up in Hawaii, raised by his single mother and her parents. His mother died of cancer in 1995, and his beloved grandmother passed away the day before her grandson was elected president.

Obama left Hawaii to attend Occidental College in Los Angeles, transferring after two years to New York City's Columbia University, where he graduated in 1983 with a degree in political science and international relations. After working in New York for IBM and then as an organizer of student volunteers at City College of New York, he moved to Chicago in 1985 and took a job as a community organizer, seeking to improve conditions in poor neighborhoods. Three years later he entered Harvard Law School, where he was elected the first African American editor-in-chief of the *Harvard Law Review*. With his law degree, he returned to Chicago to practice as a civil rights lawyer and teach constitutional law. Entering politics in 1996, he served for eight years as an Illinois state senator, and in 2004, he became the third African American since Reconstruction to be elected to the United States Senate.

Obama made headlines in February 2007 when he announced his candidacy for the 2008 Democratic presidential nomination. After a lengthy campaign, he became the party's nominee in June 2008 after he won the majority of Democratic convention delegates and his opponent, Hillary Clinton, withdrew. And on November 4, crowds danced in the streets all over America and throughout the world when they learned he had been elected the first African American President of the United States.

In his inauguration speech, Obama said that the time had come "to carry forward that precious gift, that noble idea passed on from generation to generation: the God-given promise that all are equal, all are free, and all deserve a chance to pursue their full measure of happiness."

A major accomplishment of Obama's first term in office was passage of the Affordable Care Act, designed to reform the country's health care system. In November 2012, Obama was reelected, defeating the Republican candidate Mitt Romney. On January 21, 2013, his stirring inauguration speech ended with these words: "With common effort and common purpose, with passion and dedication, let us answer the call of history, and carry into an uncertain future the precious light of freedom."

After concluding his address and heading toward the Capitol building, Obama turned for a moment and gazed out at the hundreds of thousands gathered before him. "I want to take a look one more time," he said to people nearby. "I'm not going to see this again."

◆

MICHELLE OBAMA

WHO WAS THE FIRST AFRICAN AMERICAN WOMAN TO BECOME FIRST LADY OF THE UNITED STATES?

Michelle Obama, the wife of President Barack Obama, is proud of her roots in the South Side of Chicago. She was born there in 1964, the daughter of Fraser and Marian Robinson, who lived on the top floor of a small brick house. Her father was a pump operator for the water department, and her mother stayed at home to raise Michelle and her older brother, Craig.

She attended Chicago public schools and graduated from Princeton University, where she studied sociology and African American studies. After earning a law degree from Harvard Law School in 1988, she returned to Chicago and joined the law firm of Sidley & Austin, where she met her husband-to-be. Realizing after a time that corporate law was not her calling, she went to work at city hall, becoming assistant commissioner of planning and development. She then became founding director of the Chicago chapter of Public Allies, an AmeriCorps program. In 1992 she and Barack Obama were married. Their two daughters, Malia and Sasha, were both born on Chicago's South Side.

Obama began working for the University of Chicago in 1996, first as associate dean of student services and then as vice president of community and external affairs for the University of Chicago Medical Center. She has said that as First Lady she would continue her work on issues important to her: supporting military families, helping working women balance work and family, and encouraging national service.

"My first priority," she said, "will always be to make sure our girls are healthy and grounded. Then I want to help other families get the support they need, not just to survive, but to thrive."

During her husband's first term in office, Obama focused on encouraging healthy eating and reducing childhood obesity, while continuing to advocate for military families. In February 2013, she announced a $70 million program, largely funded by Nike, to expand health and physical education programs in schools throughout the country.

◆

WHO WAS THE FIRST AFRICAN AMERICAN NAMED WHITE HOUSE SOCIAL SECRETARY?

The job of White House social secretary entails much more than planning parties. As the social secretary for the Obama White House—the first African American to hold this position—Desirée Rogers was given the responsibility of organizing and overseeing every event that takes place in the White House and on its grounds, including everything from state dinners to Easter egg hunts.

Rogers, forty-nine years old when she was appointed social secretary, had been a Chicago corporate executive and civic leader well-known in that city for her accomplishments, personal style, and ease with people from all walks of life. A native of New Orleans, where her mother ran a preschool and her father was an athletic director in the public schools, Rogers graduated from Wellesley College and earned an MBA from Harvard. In the 1990s, she was director of the Illinois state lottery, and went on to become president of Peoples Gas and North Shore Gas, a two-billion-dollar utility. When she was tapped to join the Obama administration, she was an executive at Allstate Financial.

Barack and Michelle Obama have said they want to open up the White House to a wide range of people, and Rogers supported this goal from the start. In an interview with the *New York Times*, Rogers said: "One of the things that is particularly important for this administration is that we continue along this vein of making it everyone's America. We are inviting all of America and all of the world to share in that splendor."

During her first year on the job, Rogers organized hundreds of White House events, but she was criticized when she attended elaborate fashion shows and posed for magazine photos wearing expensive clothing while the country's economy was in decline. She finally left her position in March 2010, and five months later, she was appointed CEO of the Johnson Publishing Company, owner of the magazines *Ebony* and *Jet*.

◆

WHO WAS THE FIRST AFRICAN AMERICAN TO SERVE AS U.S. ATTORNEY GENERAL?

When Eric Holder was growing up in Queens, New York, he filled two roles: he was a popular basketball player in his neighborhood and an overachieving student in his public school. Holder was born in the Bronx in 1951; his father was a real estate broker who had immigrated from Barbados, and his mother was an Episcopal church secretary from New Jersey. In middle school, aware of the tensions surrounding school integration in the South and affected by the assassination of President Kennedy, he began to delve into American history, reading books on World War II and biographies of public figures. He was admitted to the prestigious Stuyvesant High School, where he joined the Afro-American Society and was co-captain of the basketball team.

Holder entered Columbia University in 1969, majoring in American history. On Saturdays, he volunteered his time to take the poor and mostly African American children who lived near the campus on trips to cultural sites in the city. While in Columbia Law School, he clerked at the NAACP Legal Defense Fund and the Department of Justice's criminal division. After earning his law degree, he joined the staff of the Department of Justice, where he was assigned to the public integrity section, investigating and prose-

ERIC HOLDER

cuting official corruption. In 1988 he was nominated by President Reagan to become an associate judge of the superior court of the District of Columbia, and in 1993, President Clinton nominated him as United States attorney for the District of Columbia, the largest such office in the country; he was the first African American to hold that position. In 1997 Clinton appointed him deputy attorney general, the number two position in the Department of Justice, also a "first" for Holder as an African American. After the Bush administration took over the White House, Holder joined the staff of Covington & Burling, a Washington law firm.

When President Obama nominated him to become the nation's first African American attorney general, he said Holder "has the combination of toughness and independence that we need at the Justice Department . . . I have every expectation that Eric will protect our people, uphold the public trust, and adhere to our Constitution."

◆

WHICH AFRICAN AMERICAN WOMAN IS THE FIRST TO BE AMBASSADOR TO THE UNITED NATIONS?

When President Barack Obama chose Susan E. Rice, an advocate of strong action against genocide, to be ambassador to the United Nations, he was sending the world organization someone who had spoken out forcefully against mass killings, such as those in the Darfur region of Sudan. Throughout her political career, Rice had been recognized for her outspokenness on issues she believed in.

Rice was not only the first African American woman chosen to be ambassador to the U.N., but one of the youngest. Growing up in Washington, D.C., where she was born in 1964, she attended the elite National Cathedral School; she was president of the student council, valedictorian of her class, and a star basketball player. She earned a bachelor's degree from Stanford University, and a master's and doctorate in international relations from Oxford University, where she was a Rhodes scholar. Rice joined President Bill Clinton's

SUSAN E. RICE

National Security Council staff in 1993, rising to the position of assistant secretary of state for African affairs. When Obama announced his candidacy for president, she entered the campaign as a senior foreign policy advisor.

When Rice was on the staff of the National Security Council, she visited Rwanda after the 1994 genocide there. Haunted by the sight of thousands of dead and mutilated bodies, she promised herself to do all in her power to prevent the repeat of such a massacre. "I swore to myself that if I ever faced such a crisis again," she told the *Atlantic Monthly* in 2001, "I would come down on the side of dramatic action, going down in flames if that was required."

Rice appeared to be President Obama's choice to succeed Hillary

Clinton as secretary of state for his second term. But after undergoing intense criticism by some Republican senators, Rice asked the president to take her out of the running. Obama said he accepted her request with regret, describing her as "an extraordinarily capable, patriotic, and passionate public servant."

In June 2013 Obama appointed Rice as his national security advisor. "I think everybody understands Susan is a fierce champion for justice and human dignity," he said when announcing the appointment, "but she's also mindful that we have to exercise our power wisely and deliberately."

◆

WHO WAS CHOSEN TO BE THE FIRST AFRICAN AMERICAN CHIEF OF THE ENVIRONMENTAL PROTECTION AGENCY?

When President Obama announced his choice of Lisa P. Jackson to head the Environmental Protection Agency (EPA), he said that she shared his "commitment to restoring the EPA's robust role in protecting our air, water, and abundant natural resources so that our environment is cleaner and our communities are safer."

Jackson, a chemical engineer with a background of more than twenty years as an environmental regulator, took on the important job of addressing issues such as global warming and the strengthening of clean-air regulations that had been weakened under the Bush Administration.

Born in 1962 in Philadelphia, Jackson was adopted a few weeks after her birth and raised in the Ninth Ward of New Orleans. First in her class at St. Mary's Dominican High School, she graduated from Tulane University's School of Chemical Engineering and earned a master's in chemical engineering from Princeton University. She spent sixteen years at the federal EPA as an enforcement officer before joining the staff of the New Jersey Department of Environmental Protection, becoming commissioner of that agency in 2006. She was named chief of staff by New Jersey Governor Jon Corzine shortly before Obama appointed her to head the federal EPA.

In December 2012, Jackson announced she would soon be leaving the administration. Although she was able to find ways to address climate change during her tenure, she was often challenged by industry and congressional Republicans, and sometimes by the Obama administration itself. She told the *New York Times* that she was proud of expanding the environmental agenda to include little-heard voices, such as low-income communities, Native Alaskans, and American Indians. "Before me," she said, "some people said that African Americans don't care about the environment. I don't think that will ever be the case again."

LITERATURE

WHO WAS THE FIRST AFRICAN AMERICAN TO WRITE A POEM THAT WAS LATER PUBLISHED?

Lucy Terry, born in Africa about 1730, came to America on a slave ship and was brought to Deerfield, Massachusetts, when she was about five years old. She was in her teens when she wrote a twenty-eight-line poem about a Native American raid on white families in a part of Deerfield called The Bars. She named her poem "Bars Fight." People in the area recited the poem through the years until it was finally published in 1855.

Although "Bars Fight" was her only published work, Terry was known as a captivating storyteller and speaker. When she was in her mid-twenties she married a well-to-do African American man named Abijah Prince, who bought her freedom. The couple eventually settled in Vermont, where they raised six children. When one of their sons applied to Williams College, Terry gave an eloquent three-hour speech entreating the trustees to admit him, but she was unsuccessful. Some years later, when a man tried to steal land that she and her husband owned, Terry argued her case before the Supreme Court, and this time she won. When she died in 1821, the illustrious minister Lemuel Haynes preached at her funeral.

◆

WHAT WAS THE FIRST PUBLISHED PROSE WRITTEN BY AN AFRICAN AMERICAN?

According to a narrative written by an African American man named Briton Hammon, his master, a General Winslow of Marshfield, Massachusetts, gave him permission in 1747 to take a sea voyage on a sloop bound for the West Indies. In 1760, after he finally returned to his Massachusetts home, Hammon wrote and published an account of his experiences. Its title was *A Narrative of the Uncommon Sufferings and Surprising Deliverance of Briton Hammon, a Negro Man Servant to General Winslow, of Marshfield, in New-England, Who Returned to Boston, after Having Been Absent Almost Thirteen Years.*

Hammon's narrative told of the many hardships he endured: his ship was captured by Native Americans and the crew murdered; he was imprisoned in a Cuban dungeon for more than four years; he escaped from prison and worked in Cuba until he signed on to a ship headed for London; he lay ill for several weeks in London and then was hired as a cook on a ship bound for Boston. To his amazement, his old master, General Winslow, was on the same ship. Winslow, wrote Hammon, "was exceedingly glad to see me, telling me that I was like one arose from the Dead."

◆

WHAT WAS THE FIRST PUBLISHED POEM BY AN AFRICAN AMERICAN MAN?

Jupiter Hammon was born a slave on Long Island in 1711. It is known that his owners were named Lloyd, that he learned to read in the Queen's Village school (now Lloyd's Neck in the town of Huntington), and that he had the use of his master's library. He was not related to Briton Hammon, who was the first African American to publish a work of prose.

On Christmas Day 1760, his eighty-eight-line religious poem "An Evening Thought, Salvation by Christ, with Penitential Cries" was printed; it was the first poem published by an African American man. The poem was printed on a broadside—one large sheet of paper. His second broadside, published in 1778, was a poem about Phillis Wheatley, the first African American to publish a volume of verse. It was entitled "An Address to Miss Phillis Wheatley, Ethiopian Poetess, in Boston."

In addition to poetry, Hammon wrote some notable prose, including, at the age of seventy-six, *An Address to the Negroes of the*

State of New York. In it he described a heaven where blacks and whites are judged as equals, and he called attention to the irony of the American Revolution, where whites were passionately concerned with defending their own liberty, yet ignored the subjugation of black Americans. But by then, Hammon felt he was too old to enjoy freedom, since, he wrote, "many of us who had grown up slaves, and have always had masters to take care of us, should hardly know how to take care of ourselves. . . ."

◆

WHO WAS THE FIRST AFRICAN AMERICAN TO PUBLISH A BOOK?

Born in Africa around 1753, Phillis Wheatley arrived in Boston on a slave ship when she was about eight years old. She was bought by an affluent tailor and merchant named John Wheatley as a personal maid for his wife. A bright child, Phillis was provided a broad education by the Wheatley family, who encouraged her talent for poetry.

She was just a teenager when she wrote an elegy on the death of the Reverend George Whitefield, a noted evangelist; it was published in 1770. Two years later, when the Wheatleys tried to publish a volume of her poems, the publishers refused to believe that Phillis was the poet. A group of eighteen prominent Bostonians questioned her and then wrote a two-paragraph introduction attesting to her ability.

Accompanied by her master's son Nathaniel, Wheatley sailed to England. She met a number of prominent citizens, and it was there in 1773 that thirty-one of her poems were published in a book entitled *Poems on Various Subjects, Religious and Moral*. It was the first book of writings of any kind to be published by an African American.

After her return to America, Wheatley continued to write poetry. In 1776, after George Washington was named commander-in-chief of the military forces, she wrote him a poem of congratulations and he invited her to visit him at his headquarters. Phillis's life began a downward spiral as one by one the members of the Wheatley family died, and she was left alone. She finally married, but her husband mistreated her. She had two children who died, and her third baby perished in December 1784, on the same day that Wheatley herself passed away.

♦

WHO WAS THE FIRST AFRICAN AMERICAN WOMAN TO PUBLISH A BOOK OF ESSAYS?

Little is known about the life of Ann Plato except that she was born in Hartford, Connecticut, around 1820, and was a teacher of young children when she was about fifteen. Plato has gone down in history as the author of the first book of essays published by an African American woman. The volume, published in 1841, was entitled *Essays; Including Biographies and Miscellaneous Pieces, in Prose and Poetry.*

Plato's book, only the second published by an African American woman, contained sixteen essays on such subjects as religion, education, death, and the seasons. It also included twenty poems, eleven of which had death as their subject.

♦

WHO WAS THE FIRST AFRICAN AMERICAN TO PUBLISH A NOVEL?

Clotel, or The President's Daughter: a Narrative of Slave Life in the United States was written by William Wells Brown and published in London in 1853. It was the story of a girl fathered by President Thomas Jefferson and born to his African American housekeeper. Five years later, Brown published the first drama by an African American, *The Escape; or, A Leap for Freedom.* Among his other works were two volumes of history and the first travel book by a black American, *Three Years in Europe,* published in 1852.

Brown was born about 1814 on a plantation near Lexington, Kentucky, to a mother who was a slave. He grew up around St. Louis, Missouri, where he worked at various jobs, including printer's helper, medical office assistant, and handyman. He finally escaped from slavery in 1834. On his way to Cleveland, Ohio, he was befriended by a Quaker couple, Mr. and Mrs. Wells Brown, whose names he added to his own.

After moving to Buffalo, New York, he worked for nine years on Lake Erie steamboats, while at the same time helping fugitive slaves escape to Canada. A lecturer for an antislavery society, he eventually wrote about his own experiences in his autobiography, *Narrative of William W. Brown, a Fugitive Slave.* In 1849 he traveled to England, where he continued to speak against slavery, and remained abroad until 1854, when some friends bought his freedom. Brown continued fighting for abolition until after the Civil War, when he settled in Boston and practiced medicine until his death in 1884.

◆

WHAT WAS THE FIRST NOVEL PUBLISHED BY AN AFRICAN AMERICAN WOMAN?

Harriet Wilson's 1859 novel, *Our Nig: Sketches from the Life of a Free Black,* was the first published novel by an African American woman and the first novel by a black writer to be published in the United States. The recollection of a free African American woman's experiences as a servant for a white family in Massachusetts, *Our Nig* provided a picture of racism in the antebellum North.

Virtually unnoticed when it was published, the book was rediscovered in 1981 by the African American scholar Henry Louis Gates Jr., who conducted research into Wilson's life. Born in Milford, New Hampshire, about 1828, Wilson married a fugitive slave, gave birth to a son, and was soon abandoned by her husband. Because she was ill, she was forced to place her son in foster care. She wrote the novel, based on her own experiences as an indentured servant, when she was working as a dressmaker in Boston. The book was a desperate attempt to have her child returned to her. In the preface to *Our Nig,* she wrote: "Deserted by kindred, disabled by failing health, I am forced to some experiment which shall aid me in maintaining myself and child without extinguishing this feeble life." But her effort failed; her son died six months after the book was published, at the age of seven. After that tragic event, Wilson disappeared from public record.

In 2001, Henry Louis Gates acquired an unpublished manuscript that he said was the first known novel by an African American slave. The handwritten manuscript, titled *The Bondswoman's Narrative,* was written about 1857 by a slave who had run away from a North Carolina plantation. The novel, signed by Hannah Crafts, tells of a woman's life as a house slave and later as a teacher in the North.

◆

WHO WAS THE FIRST AFRICAN AMERICAN POET TO RECEIVE NATIONAL RECOGNITION?

Paul Laurence Dunbar was born in 1872 in Dayton, Ohio, the child of former slaves. In high school, where he was the only African American student in his class, Dunbar was editor of the school paper, president of the literary society, and class poet. Before he graduated he had already published a poem in a local newspaper. Dunbar's widowed mother could not afford to send him to college, so he found a job as an elevator operator for four dollars a week.

Devoting as much time as possible to his writing, in 1893 Dunbar published his first collection of poems, *Oak and Ivy.* Many of the fifty-six poems were written in an African American dialect. His second collection of dialect poems, *Majors and Minors,* was published in 1895 and received an excellent review from the prominent critic William Dean Howells in *Harper's* magazine. Howells wrote the introduction to Dunbar's next book, *Lyrics of Lowly Life,* which became one of the most popular poetry collections of the time. Dunbar went on to produce novels, short stories, and articles, and wrote the libretto and lyrics for Will Marion Cook's 1898 musical *Clorindy, the Origin of the Cakewalk.*

But the public showed little interest in Dunbar's work unless it was written in dialect, and he was forced to produce writing that he felt was not his best. Near the end of his life, he told his friend James Weldon Johnson that he had not achieved his dream. He contracted tuberculosis, and after his doctor prescribed whiskey for his cough, he developed a drinking problem. When he was only thirty-four years old, Dunbar died of pneumonia in his hometown of Dayton. His childhood home there became a state historic site, containing his bicycle, which was built by his high school friends Wilbur and Orville Wright, his desk and chair, and a ceremonial sword presented to him by President Theodore Roosevelt.

◆

WHICH POET WAS THE FIRST AFRICAN AMERICAN TO PASS THE FLORIDA BAR EXAM?

Poet, teacher, civil rights leader, diplomat: James Weldon Johnson, born in 1871 in Jacksonville, Florida, made his mark in an amazing number of undertakings. After graduating from Atlanta University in 1894, he returned to Jacksonville and was appointed principal of the public school where his mother had been a teacher. At the same time he studied law, becoming the first African American to pass the Florida bar exam.

In 1900, he and his younger brother, Rosamond, an accomplished musician, wrote the song "Lift Every Voice and Sing" for a program given by Jacksonville schoolchildren to celebrate Lincoln's birthday. The song became known as the African American national anthem. The brothers began working on a musical comedy that they hoped to present in New York City, where they went to seek their fortunes in musical theater. There they teamed up with actor and songwriter Bob Cole; over the next several years the partners wrote more than two hundred songs.

But Johnson wanted to broaden his horizons. He took courses at Columbia University and went to Washington, D.C., to take an exam for the consular service. In 1906 he was appointed U.S. Consul to Venezuela and then to Nicaragua, leaving the service in 1912, the same year his first novel, *The Autobiography of an Ex-Colored Man,* was published—first anonymously and later under his own name.

Johnson joined the staff of the NAACP in 1916 and served as executive secretary from 1920 to 1930. Always an activist, he investigated charges of brutality to Haitians and pushed for passage of an antilynching bill in Congress. After retiring from the NAACP he joined the faculty of Fisk University as a creative writing teacher. Best known today for his poetry, his books of verse include *God's Trombones, Fifty Years and Other Poems,* and *Selected Poems.* He published his autobiography, *Along This Way,* in 1933 and died five years later when his car was hit by a train in Wiscasset, Maine, while he was driving to his summer home.

◆

WHO WAS THE FIRST AFRICAN AMERICAN WOMAN TO WIN A GUGGENHEIM FELLOWSHIP?

Nella Larsen was the leading woman writer of the Harlem Renaissance, a period of creative expression by African Americans during the late 1920s. After publishing short stories and two novels, Larsen became the first African American woman to win a Guggenheim Fellowship—a prestigious award made to scholars, writers, and artists. But Larsen never published again, and soon disappeared from the literary scene.

Born in Chicago in 1891, Larsen claimed her parents were an African American woman and a Danish man, although her background remains somewhat mysterious. After attending Fisk University for a year, she graduated from Lincoln Hospital's nursing school in New York City and pursued a nursing career until 1921, when she became a children's librarian at the Harlem branch of the New York Public Library.

Larsen's first writing appeared in *The Brownies' Book,* a magazine for African American children. She published two short stories for adults and then, in 1928, a novel, *Quicksand,* the despairing story of an educated black woman unable to find her place in the world. Her next novel, *Passing,* published the following year, was equally tragic in its portrait of an African American woman searching for her identity.

With the Guggenheim Fellowship that she won in 1930, Larsen traveled to Europe to write another novel, but publishers rejected her work. Back in New York, she returned to nursing, remaining in the profession for thirty years. She retired in 1963 and died a year later.

◆

WHAT WAS THE FIRST MYSTERY NOVEL
BY AN AFRICAN AMERICAN?

The Conjure Man Dies: A Mystery Tale of Dark Harlem, published in 1932, was the first mystery novel published by an African American. Its author was Rudolph Fisher, a physician who was born in Washington, D.C., in 1897 and grew up in Providence, Rhode Island, earning bachelor's and master's degrees from Brown University. He pursued medical studies at Washington's Howard University and at Columbia University in New York City, where he remained to practice medicine.

The Conjure Man Dies told the story of the murder of an African seer in Harlem, a case that was solved with the help of a young African American doctor. The *New York Times* book reviewer at the time called it "a puzzling mystery yarn" and "a lively tale of Harlem." Fisher's first published work, a short story entitled "The City of Refuge," appeared in the *Atlantic Monthly* in 1925. His first novel, *The Walls of Jericho,* was published three years later. *The Conjure Man Dies* was adapted as a play by Arna Bontemps and Countee Cullen for New York's Federal Theatre Project. It opened there in 1936, two years after Fisher's death at the age of thirty-seven. The play was not produced again until 2001, when it was revived in a New Federal Theatre production at New York City's Henry Street Settlement.

◆

WHICH POET WROTE THE FIRST LONG-RUNNING
BROADWAY PLAY BY AN AFRICAN AMERICAN?

Langston Hughes, poet, novelist, and playwright, was the author of the drama *Mulatto,* which opened in 1935 and was performed on Broadway 373 times. Hughes, born in 1902 in Joplin, Missouri, lived in Kansas and Ohio until, in September 1921, he arrived in New York to fulfill his father's wish that he attend Columbia University. Three months earlier his poem, "A Negro Speaks of Rivers," had been published in *The Crisis* magazine. Leaving Columbia after a year, Hughes spent the next three years in an array of menial jobs, also managing to spend a few months in Paris, while continuing to write poetry. With the help of his longtime friend, Carl Van Vechten, he published his first collection of poems, *The Weary Blues,* in 1926.

Already established as a major figure in the Harlem Renaissance, Hughes enrolled in Lincoln University in Pennsylvania, graduating in 1929, and a year later published his first novel, *Not Without Laughter.* After *Mulatto,* which was about interracial relationships in the South, Hughes went on to write other plays, published the first volume of his autobiography, *The Big Sea,* in 1940, and continued to publish verse. In 1942 he began writing a weekly column in the *Chicago Defender* featuring a character called Jesse B. Semple, nicknamed Simple; the lively and perceptive columns continued for twenty years and were collected in five volumes, starting in 1950 with *Simple Speaks His Mind.* Hughes continued to write in various styles for the rest of his life. His final collection of verse, *The Panther and the Lash,* was published a few months after his death in 1967.

♦

WHO WROTE THE FIRST NOVEL BY AN AFRICAN AMERICAN TO BECOME A BOOK-OF-THE-MONTH CLUB SELECTION?

Richard Wright was born on a plantation near Natchez, Mississippi, moving with his mother to Memphis when he was six. They later settled in Jackson, Mississippi, where he attended school and avidly read books he checked out of the public library. In 1924, the *Southern Register,* a local African American newspaper, published his first short story, "The Voodoo of Hell's Half Acre." Wright moved to Chicago in 1927, working as a post office clerk and taking other temporary jobs. He turned to the Communist Party, which he quit twelve years later after publishing articles in the Communist Press. In 1937 he traveled to New York City, where he became Harlem editor of the *Daily Worker.*

Wright's first book, *Uncle Tom's Children,* published in 1938, was a collection of four novellas about the South. Two years later he published his novel *Native Son,* the story of a young black man who commits a murder in a moment of panic. Published in 1940,

RICHARD WRIGHT

it created a sensation, becoming a best seller, the first novel by an African American writer selected by the Book-of-the-Month Club, and the first to enter the mainstream of American literature.

In 1945, Wright's memoir of his southern childhood, *Black Boy,* became an even bigger success. The next year he moved to Paris, where he lived until his death in 1960. He continued to write books, but none were successful, and he died alone and almost penniless of a heart attack when he was only fifty-two. The second part of his autobiography, *American Hunger,* wasn't published until 1977. During the last eighteen months of his life, Wright wrote some four thousand haiku—the three-line, seventeen-syllable Japanese poetic form—and selected 817 to be published as a collection. The book finally appeared in 1998.

◆

WHICH AFRICAN AMERICAN WROTE THE
FIRST NOVEL TO BECOME A BEST SELLER?

In September 2012, a previously unknown manuscript of a 1941 novel by Claude McKay was found to be authentic. The manuscript, *Amiable With Big Teeth: A Novel of the Love Affair Between the Communists and the Poor Black Sheep of Harlem*, had been discovered by a student three years earlier in the archives at Columbia University. A much earlier novel of McKay's, *Home to Harlem*, published in 1928, was the first best-selling novel by an African American writer.

McKay, a poet and novelist who was a key figure in the Harlem Renaissance, was born in Jamaica in 1889. He was just ten years old when he began to write poetry. An avid reader, he was tutored by his older brother, a schoolteacher, and an Englishman who became his mentor. In 1912, he published two collections of poetry, and with an award and stipend he received, he traveled to America, enrolling in Tuskegee Institute in Alabama. After two months he transferred to Kansas State College, and in 1914, he settled in New York City.

The racism McKay encountered in America influenced much of his work. In his writing, he often confronted issues of race and the plight of the working class. One of his best-known poems, "If We Must Die," written in 1919, is a call for resistance by oppressed people. Around 1920, he began lengthy trips abroad, finally returning to New York in 1934 after experiencing ill health and financial problems. In 1944, he moved to Chicago, where he died four years later.

During McKay's career he published poetry, two more novels, a collection of short stories, and numerous essays. The Columbia professor whose student unearthed McKay's long-lost manuscript, Brent Hayes Edwards, said he believed the work would eventually be recognized as "the key political novel of the black intellectual life in New York in the 1930s."

◆

WHAT NOVEL WAS THE FIRST BY AN AFRICAN AMERICAN WOMAN TO SELL OVER ONE MILLION COPIES?

The Street, by Ann Petry, published in 1946, is the story of a young woman struggling to raise her son in New York City's Harlem. Petry's first novel, it was also the first by an African American woman to sell more than one million copies.

Petry was born in 1911 in Old Saybrook, Connecticut, where her father and grandfather ran a drugstore. As a child she loved to read, and at the age of fourteen she knew she wanted to be a writer. She wrote poetry and short plays in high school, but after graduation she followed the family tradition and studied to be a pharmacist. She earned a degree from the Connecticut College of Pharmacy in 1931, worked in the family drugstore for a time, then married and moved to New York City in 1938.

Her first job in New York was in the advertising department of the *Amsterdam News,* an African American newspaper. She then became a reporter and editor for *The People's Voice,* a weekly founded by Adam Clayton Powell Jr. Petry took writing courses at Columbia University and published stories in the NAACP magazine *The Crisis* and in the Urban League's *Opportunity.* Her story, "On Saturday, the Siren Sounds at Noon," appeared in *The Crisis* in December 1943. An editor at a major publishing company who read the story offered her a contract for a novel, which she completed in 1946 and titled *The Street.*

After the success of *The Street,* which sold 1.5 million copies, Petry continued to write, publishing short stories, children's books, and two other novels. Her 1953 book *The Narrows* examined the lives of African Americans in a New England town, and a biography for young readers, *Harriet Tubman: Conductor on the Underground Railroad,* was published in 1955. *The Street,* with its realistic portrayal of life in Harlem in the 1940s, was reissued in 1992, when Petry was eighty-one years old. She died five years later in a convalescent center near her Old Saybrook home.

◆

WHO WROTE THE FIRST NOVEL BY AN AFRICAN AMERICAN TO BE BOUGHT BY HOLLYWOOD?

Frank Yerby became a best-selling author with his very first book, *The Foxes of Harrow,* which was published in 1946. A historical melodrama, it was set in the South before the Civil War. Selling over one million copies, the novel was the first by an African American writer to be purchased by a Hollywood studio; it was made into a 1947 film starring Rex Harrison and Maureen O'Hara.

Yerby was born in 1916 in Augusta, Georgia, and was educated at Paine College, Fisk University, and the University of Chicago. During World War II he worked in defense plants in Dearborn, Michigan, and Jamaica, New York. After the success of his first book, Yerby settled in Madrid, Spain, and went on to write more than thirty historical novels, most of which became best sellers. His books include *An Odor of Sanctity,* set in medieval Spain; *Goat Song,* set in ancient Greece; and *Judas, My Brother,* set in the time of Jesus. His 1971 novel, *The Dahomean,* was an exploration of his African ancestry, and he published a novel about slavery, *A Darkness at Ingraham's Court,* in 1979. Yerby died in 1991.

◆

WHO WAS THE FIRST AFRICAN AMERICAN WOMAN TO PUBLISH SCIENCE FICTION?

Born in 1947 in Pasadena, California, Octavia Butler was a shy, awkward child who spent her happiest hours in the public library. She said that she began writing when she was about ten years old to escape loneliness and boredom. Outstanding in a genre dominated by white male writers, Butler was awarded top honors in science fiction, and a science fiction newsletter, *Locus,* called her books "some of the most powerfully disquieting science fiction of recent years."

Butler starting writing science fiction, she said in an interview, when she was twelve, inspired by a movie called *Devil Girls from Mars.* After attending college in California, she supported herself with a succession of jobs while trying to become established as a writer.

Her first story was published in *Clarion,* an anthology of work from the Clarion Science Fiction Writers' Workshop that she attended in 1970. Five years later, laid off from a job that she hated, she managed to write three books in one year; all were published. They were the first in a string of successful novels.

Butler's leading characters are usually independent African American women, and her themes deal with genetic engineering, alien beings, and the use of power. Her first five novels were set in a universe she called Patternist. The series told of a society run by a specially bred group of telepaths. In 1979 she broke away from that theme with her novel *Kindred,* which used a time-travel device to explore slavery in America. Among her other books were the Xenogenesis trilogy: *Dawn, Adulthood Rites,* and *Imago.* Much of her short fiction was collected in a 1995 volume, *Bloodchild and Other Stories.* And in 1995 she became the first science fiction writer to win the MacArthur Foundation "genius grant." She began her Parable series in 1993; the second volume, *Parable of the Talents,* won the 1999 Nebula award for best novel. Her last book, *Fledgling,* was published in 2005, and one year later, at the age of fifty-eight, she died after falling and striking her head outside her home near Seattle. "I didn't realize that writing was supposed to be work," Butler was quoted as saying. "It was too much fun. It still is."

◆

WHO WAS THE FIRST AFRICAN AMERICAN TO WIN A PULITZER PRIZE?

Gwendolyn Brooks was born in Topeka, Kansas, in 1917, but grew up on the South Side of Chicago, where she lived for the rest of her life. Brooks, who wrote poems and novels about the African American experience from the 1940s to the 1990s, once said: "I wrote about what I saw and heard on the street. I lived in a small second-floor apartment at the corner, and I could look first on one side and then the other. There was my material."

Her parents introduced her to classic literature at an early age, and when she began writing poetry as a young girl, her mother was enthusiastic. Her first poem, "Eventide," was published in a magazine when she was thirteen. She sent some poems to Langston

Hughes and James Weldon Johnson, who both encouraged her. By the age of sixteen, she was a regular contributor to the *Chicago Defender* newspaper. Her first volume of poetry, *A Street in Bronzeville*, based on her South Side neighborhood, was published in 1945. Four years later, her second volume of verse, *Annie Allen*, was awarded the Pulitzer Prize. Her 1953 novel, *Maud Martha*, was followed by more collections of poetry, with Brooks's focus expanding from her neighborhood to the wider world.

In 1967 she started a workshop in her home, for young poets as well as members of a Chicago street gang called the Blackstone Rangers. She continued to give much of her time to nurturing budding poets, including schoolchildren, prisoners, and homeless people. From the 1970s to the '90s she published many volumes of poetry and nonfiction, including two autobiographies. She received awards from several prestigious literary and arts organizations, and when the National Endowment for the Humanities selected her as its Jefferson Lecturer in 1994, she called it "the absolute crown of my career." Brooks died at her Chicago home in December 2000, at the age of eighty-three.

♦

WHO WAS THE FIRST AFRICAN AMERICAN WRITER TO WIN THE NATIONAL BOOK AWARD?

In 1953 Ralph Ellison's novel *Invisible Man* won the National Book Award for fiction, a yearly award for outstanding writing. This one novel, an account of a young African American's confrontation with discrimination and his inability to be seen apart from his race, established Ellison as a major writer of his time. He was born in Oklahoma City in 1914. His father, an ice and coal dealer, died when he was three, and his mother worked as a domestic to support the family. In 1933 Ellison entered Tuskegee Institute, where he majored in music. Three years later he moved to New York City, becoming involved in the Federal Writers Project and developing friendships with the African American writers Langston Hughes and Richard Wright. Encouraged to become a writer himself, Ellison began publishing essays, reviews, and short stories in various publications.

After serving in the merchant marine as a cook during World War II, Ellison took a trip to Vermont to visit a friend. One day, sitting before a typewriter, he wrote, "I am an invisible man." These words became the opening line of his novel, *Invisible Man,* which was published seven years later, in 1952. He spent the rest of his career teaching and lecturing at colleges and universities and published two collections of essays. In 1966, a fire at his home destroyed part of the manuscript of his second novel. For almost thirty years he continued to labor on the work, and when he died in 1994 he left some 2,000 typed pages. Five years later, a 354-page extract from the manuscript was published with the title *Juneteenth.*

◆

WHO WAS THE FIRST AFRICAN AMERICAN POET LAUREATE OF THE UNITED STATES?

Robert Hayden was born Asa Bundy Sheffey in 1913 in a Detroit neighborhood that people called Paradise Valley. His parents, Asa and Ruth Sheffey, separated before he was two years old, and his mother, so she could search for work, placed him in the care of a neighborhood couple, William and Sue Ellen Hayden. His foster parents changed his name, but he didn't completely lose touch with his own mother and father.

Because of Hayden's poor eyesight and the thick glasses he wore, other children often treated him cruelly. His childhood with the Haydens, who were often angry and sometimes violent, left him with periods of depression, which he later called "my dark nights of the soul." His unhappiness led him to escape into books, where he discovered poetry.

He attended Detroit City College (later Wayne State University), and in 1936 went to work for the Federal Writers' Project, researching African American history and culture. In 1940 Hayden published his first volume of poetry, *Heart-Shape in the Dust.* After marrying that year, he adopted his wife's faith, Baha'i, which stresses the unity of all religions.

In 1941 Hayden enrolled in the University of Michigan, where he studied with the poet W. H. Auden. He earned a master's degree and taught at Michigan for several years before beginning a twenty-three-year career as a professor at Fisk University; he returned to Michigan to teach in 1969.

Hayden published numerous collections of poetry, much of which reflected his Baha'i faith as well as his concerns about race; he wrote about such African American figures as Frederick Douglass, Harriet Tubman, and Malcolm X. In 1976 Hayden became the first African American to be appointed consultant in poetry to the Library of Congress, a position that was later renamed poet laureate. He died in Michigan in 1980.

◆

WHO WAS THE FIRST AFRICAN AMERICAN WOMAN TO WIN A PULITZER PRIZE IN FICTION?

A novelist, essayist, short story writer, and poet, Alice Walker had published several books before winning the Pulitzer Prize in 1983 for her novel *The Color Purple*. Walker was born in 1944 in Eatontown, Georgia, where her parents were sharecroppers and dairy farmers. An accident when she was eight years old—she was blinded in one eye after being shot by her brother's BB gun—led her to develop a shy and solitary nature. Much of her time in school was spent reading and writing poetry, and she was the valedictorian of her high school graduating class.

Walker won a scholarship to Spelman College in Atlanta, but in her sophomore year transferred to Sarah Lawrence College in Bronxville, New York. While still a student, she wrote a series of poems about suicide, love, and civil rights. The collection, entitled *Once,* was published in 1968.

After college Walker continued to write and became active in the civil rights movement. She lived for seven years in Mississippi, and while in the South she was writer-in-residence at Jackson State and Tougaloo Colleges. Her first novel, *The Third Life of Grange Copeland,* was published in 1970, and six years later she published her second novel, *Meridian,* about her experiences in the civil rights movement.

Her 1982 novel, *The Color Purple,* the story of an African American woman's life, won not only the Pulitzer but also the American Book Award, and was made into a film in 1985 and a Broadway musical in 2005. Her other books include *The Temple of My Familiar, Possessing the Secret of Joy,* the 1998 novel *By the Light of My Father's Smile,* and *We Are the Ones We Have Been Waiting For,* a collection of essays and lectures published in 2006.

In 2010, a book of Walker's poems, *Hard Times Require Furious Dancing,* was published, and 2011 saw the release of *The Chicken Chronicles,* a collection of short essays.

◆

WHO WAS THE FIRST AFRICAN AMERICAN POET LAUREATE OF NEW YORK STATE?

Audre Lorde was born in 1934 in New York City, where she attended Catholic schools. An avid reader of poetry, she eventually started writing her own; her first published poem appeared

AUDRE LORDE

in *Seventeen* magazine when she was still in high school. She graduated from Hunter College, earned a master's degree in library science from Columbia University, and worked as a librarian and teacher during the 1960s.

The year 1968 was an outstanding one for Lorde: she was appointed poet-in-residence at Tougaloo College in Mississippi, she was a visiting professor at Atlanta University, and she published her first volume of poetry, *The First Cities*. An outspoken feminist and lesbian, during her life Lorde published seventeen volumes of poetry, essays, and autobiography, all reflecting her aversion to racial and sexual prejudice. She became an English professor at Hunter College and lectured throughout the United States, Africa, and Europe. In 1989 a collection of her essays, *A Burst of Light*, won an American Book Award.

In 1980 Lorde wrote *The Cancer Journals*, which described the beginning stages of the disease that finally took her life in 1992 when she was fifty-eight. Before her death she was awarded honorary degrees from Hunter, Haverford, and Oberlin Colleges, and received the Walt Whitman Citation of Merit in 1991, making her the poet laureate of New York State. When he announced her appointment, Governor Mario Cuomo said, "Audre Lorde is the voice of the eloquent outsider who speaks in a language that can reach and touch people everywhere."

♦

WHO WAS THE FIRST AFRICAN AMERICAN POET TO READ AT A PRESIDENTIAL INAUGURATION?

Chosen by President Bill Clinton to create a poem for his January 1993 inauguration, Maya Angelou read her composition "On the Pulse of Morning," to a spellbound nation. Later that year, she published *Wouldn't Take Nothing for My Journey Now*, a collection of essays about such subjects as religion, death, racism, and motherhood.

Born Marguerite Johnson in 1928 in St. Louis, Missouri, and raised in Clinton's home state of Arkansas, Angelou moved to California when she was in ninth grade. At the age of fifteen, after hounding the Market Street Railway Company for weeks, her tenacity was rewarded and she was hired as the first African American street-car conductor in San Francisco.

Angelou's varied and colorful career included a role in the opera *Porgy and Bess* during its twenty-two-nation tour in 1954, and a four-year stint on the staff of the University of Ghana beginning in 1963. Angelou's screenplay *Georgia, Georgia* was the first by an African American woman to be made into a film, and she received an Emmy nomination for her performance in the television mini-series *Roots*.

This actress, singer, dancer, playwright, author, lecturer, and civil rights activist published more than a dozen books of poetry and autobiography, including *I Know Why the Caged Bird Sings*, which was nominated for a National Book Award. In 1981 she was appointed to a lifetime position as the first Reynolds Professor of American Studies at Wake Forest University in North Carolina. She returned to films in 1998, directing *Down in the Delta*, starring Alfre Woodard. The sixth volume of Angelou's autobiography, *A Song Flung Up to Heaven*, was published in 2002.

In 2010, she published a cookbook, *Great Food, All Day Long: Cook Splendidly, Eat Smart*, and the story of her relationship with her mother, *Mom & Me & Mom*, was published in 2013.

◆

WHO WAS THE FIRST AFRICAN AMERICAN WOMAN NAMED U.S. POET LAUREATE?

In May 1993, Rita Dove, a Pulitzer Prize–winning poet, was chosen to be the country's new poet laureate, the first African American and the youngest person to hold that position. Dove was born in 1952 in Akron, Ohio. Her father was the first African American research chemist to be employed by a leading tire manufacturer, and her mother was a homemaker; they both encouraged her love of reading. Already an achiever, in 1970 she was invited to the White House as a Presidential Scholar, one of a hundred in the United States that year. She graduated with a degree in English from Miami University in Oxford, Ohio, spent two semesters as a Fulbright Scholar in Germany, and earned a master's degree from the University of Iowa Writers' Workshop.

RITA DOVE

Her poems had already appeared in magazines and anthologies before she published her first collection of verse, *The Yellow House on the Corner,* in 1980. Her third volume, *Thomas and Beulah,* a collection of poems inspired by the lives of her grandparents, won the 1987 Pulitzer Prize in poetry; she was the second African American poet to receive this prestigious award. Her other works include a novel, *Through the Ivory Gate,* and the poetry collections *On the Bus with Rosa Parks, American Smooth,* and *Sonata Mulattica.*

Dove, who received numerous literary and academic honors, joined the faculty of the University of Virginia in Charlottesville in 1993 as commonwealth professor of English. She was once again named poet laureate when Governor Mark Warner appointed her to this position for Virginia in 2004.

President Obama presented Dove with the National Medal of Arts in 2011, and that same year *The Penguin Anthology of Twentieth-Century American Poetry,* a six-hundred-and-fifty-six-page volume that she edited, was published.

◆

WHO WAS THE FIRST AFRICAN AMERICAN TO WIN THE NOBEL PRIZE IN LITERATURE?

On October 7, 1993, writer Toni Morrison joined her friends in a jubilant celebration—she had just been awarded the Nobel Prize in Literature. In making the announcement, the Nobel Committee said that the novelist "gives life to an essential aspect of American reality."

Morrison was born Chloe Anthony Woford on February 18, 1931, in Lorain, Ohio, a steel town near Cleveland. Her parents taught her to read before she started first grade. She earned degrees in English from Howard and Cornell Universities and then embarked on a teaching career, first at Texas Southern University and then at Howard. There she married a Jamaican architect named Harold Morrison; they were later divorced.

Morrison left Howard in 1965 to work as an editor for Random House. In 1970 she published her first novel, *The Bluest Eye,* about a young African American girl who longs to have blue eyes. Her second novel, *Sula,* published in 1973, was nominated for a National Book Award. Her 1977 book, *Song of Solomon,* became a best seller, winning several prizes including the National Book Critics Circle Award. *Tar Baby,* published in 1981, was also a success.

In 1987 Morrison was named the Robert F. Goheen Professor in the Council of the Humanities at Princeton University. That same year she published *Beloved,* the story of a runaway slave who is captured and cuts her daughter's throat rather than have the child grow up in slavery. It won great critical acclaim and was awarded a Pulitzer Prize. Morrison published two books in 1992: a novel, *Jazz,* and a collection of essays, *Playing in the Dark: Whiteness and the Literary Imagination.* Her novel, *Paradise,* was published in 1998,

Love, in 2003, and *A Mercy,* in 2008, which the *New York Times* called "a small, plangent gem of a story" that "stands with *Beloved,* as one of Ms. Morrison's most haunting works yet." She published her tenth novel, *Home,* in 2013.

Discussing the liberating aspects of being an African American woman writer, Morrison once said, "My world did not shrink because I was a black female writer. It just got bigger."

◆

WHO WAS THE FIRST CHILDREN'S AUTHOR TO RECEIVE A MacARTHUR FOUNDATION "GENIUS GRANT"?

Virginia Hamilton, who grew up to be a prize-winning author of books for children, was born in 1936 on a farm in Yellow Springs, Ohio, where her mother's family had lived since the 1850s. It was there that her grandfather, Levi Perry, had settled after escaping from slavery on the Underground Railroad. He often told his children stories about slavery, and young Virginia's own parents were wonderful storytellers.

After high school, Hamilton attended Antioch College and Ohio State University before traveling to New York City, where she studied writing at the New School for Social Research. Her first book for children, *Zeely,* published in 1967, was about a girl spending a summer on her uncle's farm. In 1975 she won a National Book Award for *M. C. Higgins the Great,* as well as the prestigious Newbery Medal, the first to be given to an African American writer.

After fifteen years in New York, Hamilton and her husband, the poet Arnold Adoff, moved back to Yellow Springs and built their own house near the family farm. Her books continued to win awards, including the 1992 Hans Christian Anderson Medal and two Coretta Scott King awards, one in 1986 for *The People Could Fly: American Black Folktales,* and another in 1989 for *Anthony Burns: The Defeat and Triumph of a Fugitive Slave.*

Hamilton taught and lectured throughout the world, and was the inspiration for an annual event at Kent State University in Ohio: the Virginia Hamilton Conference on Multicultural Literature for Youth. In 1995 she became the first children's book author to be

VIRGINIA HAMILTON

awarded one of the "genius" grants from the MacArthur Foundation, which are given to individuals of exceptional creativity and promise.

In February 2002, this esteemed author of more than thirty-five books for children died of cancer in Ohio at the age of sixty-five.

◆

WHO WAS THE FIRST AFRICAN AMERICAN TO WIN THE NATIONAL BOOK AWARD FOR POETRY?

Lucille Clifton was born in 1936 in the village of Depew, New York, near the city of Buffalo. Although her parents didn't have a formal education—her father was a steel mill worker and her mother was a laundress and homemaker—they taught their children to appreciate reading, especially books by African Americans. Clifton was sixteen when she entered Howard University as a drama major, later transferring to Fredonia State Teachers College in New York.

After college, while working in the Division of Employment in Buffalo and the Office of Education in Washington, D.C., and taking care of her own growing family, Clifton continued to write poetry. In 1969, the African American poet Robert Hayden entered her poems into a contest for the YW-YMHA Poetry Center Discovery Award. She won the award and publication of a collection of her poems, *Good Times*, which was cited by the *New York Times* as one of the best books of the year. She went on to write several collections of poetry, a memoir, and numerous books for young people. Her collection, *Blessing the Boats: New and Selected Poems 1988–2000*, won the National Book Award.

In 1971 Clifton left her position in Washington to become poet-in-residence at Coppin State College in Maryland. She also taught at the University of California, Santa Cruz, and in 1991 she became distinguished professor of humanities at St. Mary's College of Maryland. She was poet laureate of Maryland from 1979 to 1985, and in 2007, she won the Ruth Lilly Poetry Prize of $100,000, which honors a living United States poet whose "lifetime accomplishments warrant extraordinary recognition."

Clifton died in 2010 at the age of seventy-three. *The Collected Poems of Lucille Clifton 1965–2010* was published two years later.

◆

WHO WAS THE FIRST AFRICAN AMERICAN WOMAN TO WIN THE NATIONAL BOOK AWARD FOR NONFICTION?

Almost every day for eight years, Annette Gordon-Reed researched and wrote about the family history of Sally Hemings, the enslaved woman who had a thirty-eight-year relationship with her owner, Thomas Jefferson. All her hard work came to fruition in 2008 with the publication of her acclaimed book, *The Hemingses of Monticello: An American Family*. And in November of that year, on Gordon-Reed's birthday, her book was chosen over 540 entries to win the National Book Award for nonfiction. Five months

ANNETTE GORDON-REED

later, in April 2009, Gordon-Reed was awarded the Pulitzer Prize for History.

Gorden-Reed was born in Conroe, a small town in east Texas. Her father owned a funeral home and a store, and her mother taught tenth-grade English. She said that she first became interested in Thomas Jefferson, the third president of the United States, in third grade, when she read a book about him. She admired him for being, like her, an avid reader, and she puzzled over the fact that, despite his belief in equality of all people and his writing of the Declaration of Independence, he was a slave owner.

Gordon-Reed never lost her interest in Jefferson. She majored in history at Dartmouth, graduating in 1981, and attended Harvard Law School. In 1992 she joined the faculty of New York Law School and also taught history at Rutgers. Her first book about the relationship between Jefferson and Hemings, *Thomas Jefferson and Sally Hemings: An American Controversy,* was published in 1997, and led to much debate about whether or not Hemings had a lengthy relationship with Jefferson and bore him several children. The next year, DNA tests showed that Jefferson had, indeed, fathered children with Hemings.

To counteract the focus on Jefferson by historians, Gordon-Reed decided to tell the story of the Hemings family in a way that hadn't been done before, she told the *New York Times,* so that readers could "see slave people as individuals." Her prize-winning book, *The Hemingses of Monticello,* followed four generations of the Hemings family, from Virginia in the 1700s through the death of Jefferson in 1826. As she worked on the book, Gordon-Reed said in an interview for the National Book Foundation, she "wanted to get a sense of, and convey to readers, the way slavery worked in the day-to-day lives of people."

Her experience as a mother of two children, said Gordon-Reed, made her view the system of slavery in a personal light. When she wrote about separations among family members, she said, "I thought of my children, and that had we lived a century and a half ago . . . we would all be slaves and subject to the same thing."

MILITARY

WHO WAS THE FIRST CASUALTY
OF THE CIVIL WAR?

In April 1861, an African American named Nicholas Biddle, then sixty-five years old, became an orderly for a captain in a militia group from Pottsville, Pennsylvania. When President Abraham Lincoln called for troops to defend the Union, Biddle marched out of Pottsville along with his captain on their way to Washington. While marching through Baltimore, the group was surrounded and attacked by a hostile mob. A brick struck Biddle on his head, injuring him seriously, and making him the first person to shed blood in the Civil War.

Biddle served until the end of the war, then returned to Pottsville and his job as a porter at the Penn Hotel. After he died a pauper in 1876, a local Civil War veterans group paid his funeral expenses. In Pottsville, an elementary school was named after him and a street bears his name. And on April 18, 2001, 140 years after he was injured in Baltimore, he was remembered by the town's citizens. A twenty-one-gun salute was fired above his grave at Bethel African Methodist Episcopal Church, and the post office issued a commemorative postal cancellation in his honor.

◆

WHO WAS THE FIRST
AFRICAN AMERICAN NAVAL HERO?

Robert Smalls was born a slave in Beaufort County, South Carolina, in 1839. Just after the outbreak of the Civil War in 1861, Smalls, who had been hired out by his owner, was made the wheelman of a Confederate steamboat, the *Planter,* which was being used to transport guns and ammunition for the rebel army. On the

ROBERT SMALLS

night of May 12, 1862, when the ship was docked in the harbor at Charleston, South Carolina, the white officers went ashore. After alerting the other black crewmen—all slaves—who remained aboard, Smalls put on the captain's dress uniform, took control of the ship, and steered it out of Charleston harbor.

Heading for Beaufort harbor, which had been seized by Union forces, Smalls and his crew steered the *Planter* past the guns of Fort Sumter and surrendered the ship to the officers of the Union fleet. This amazing exploit earned great praise for Smalls, and he served for the rest of the war as a pilot in the Union Navy.

After the war, Smalls entered politics and in 1868 was elected to the South Carolina State Legislature. In 1876 he became a United States Congressman, serving four terms. President Benjamin Harrison later appointed him customs collector of the port of Beaufort, where he died in 1915 at the age of seventy-six.

◆

WHO WAS THE FIRST AFRICAN AMERICAN TO WIN THE CONGRESSIONAL MEDAL OF HONOR?

Sergeant William H. Carney was a member of the Massachusetts Fifty-fourth Infantry, the first black regiment recruited in the North to fight in the Civil War. On July 18, 1863, the men of the Fifty-fourth led an assault on the Confederate fort, Fort Wagner, which protected the approach to Charleston Harbor in South Carolina. The commander of the regiment, Robert Gould Shaw, and many other soldiers were killed in the battle.

As the fighting raged on, Sergeant Carney was running beside the color-bearer just as the man was hit by a shell. Carney picked up the flag and led the final charge on the fort. The valiant soldier managed to reach the parapet, but was shot twice and severely wounded by Confederate soldiers. As he fell he held the flag high and passed it to his comrades, saying, "Boys, the old flag never touched the ground."

For his heroism, Carney was presented with the Congressional Medal of Honor, becoming the first African American soldier to win it. The highest military award for bravery, the Medal of Honor was established by Congress in 1862 to be awarded for gallantry at the risk of life above and beyond the call of duty. In all, more than 180,000 African Americans fought in the Union Army during the Civil War, and sixteen were awarded the Medal of Honor.

◆

WHO WAS THE FIRST AFRICAN AMERICAN ARMY MAJOR?

Late in the Civil War, Martin Delany, an editor, doctor, lecturer, writer, and antislavery activist, was appointed a major in the Union Army, for which he recruited two regiments of former slaves. Born in Charles Town, West Virginia, in 1812, he later moved with his family to Pennsylvania after it was discovered that the Delany children were being taught to read. Before his military career began, Delany studied medicine, published a newspaper, and in 1852 wrote a book that urged African Americans to emigrate to Latin America or Africa. It was titled *The Condition, Elevation, Em-*

MARTIN DELANY

igration and Destiny of the Colored People of the United States, Politically Considered.

After the Civil War, Delany was an important figure in South Carolina, where he assisted former slaves in making the transition to free citizens. He served on the Freedmen's Bureau for three years, was a customs house inspector, and then became a trial judge in Charleston, South Carolina. In 1861 he wrote the official *Report of the Niger Valley Exploring Party,* which he had led in 1859. His 1879 book, *Principia of Ethnology: The Origin of Races and Color,* pointed out the major contributions African Americans had made to world civilization, a view that had never before been expressed.

Delany, who died in 1885, always emphasized his pride in being an African American. In fact, the distinguished statesman Fred-

erick Douglass wrote: "I thank God for making me a man sim-
ply, but Delany always thanks Him for making him a black man."

◆

WHAT WERE THE FIRST AFRICAN AMERICAN UNITS COMMISSIONED IN THE REGULAR ARMY?

In 1866 Congress passed a law creating six regiments of African
American regular army soldiers. Four of these regiments were infantry (they were later combined into two), and two, the Ninth
and Tenth, were cavalry. The Native Americans of the western United
States, against whom the cavalries often fought, called these men
the Buffalo Soldiers, possibly due to their tightly curled hair or
because of their courage.

For twenty-five years the Buffalo Soldiers patrolled the West,
guarding wagon trains, constructing roads, stringing telegraph lines,
building towns, protecting payrolls, chasing off cattle rustlers, and
serving in the thick of the Indian wars. They fought in New Mexico, Arizona, Texas, Oklahoma, Colorado, and the Dakotas, fend-
ing off bands of Apache, Sioux, Cheyenne, and others. Eighteen
Buffalo Soldiers were awarded the Congressional Medal of Honor
during the western campaigns.

The Buffalo Soldiers were called back east to fight in the Spanish-
American War, participating with Teddy Roosevelt's Rough Riders in the attack on San Juan Hill in Cuba. They went on to serve
with distinction in the Philippines and Mexico and in the First
and Second World Wars, until their units were disbanded in 1944.
Four years later, President Harry Truman issued an order that led
to the end of racial segregation in the armed forces.

◆

WHO WAS THE FIRST AFRICAN AMERICAN WOMAN TO ENLIST IN THE UNITED STATES ARMY?

Cathay Williams was born on property owned by a wealthy farmer
near Independence, Missouri; her father was free and her mother
was a slave. When the Civil War broke out, she was freed by Union

soldiers, and traveled with them for some time, employed as a cook and washerwoman. After the war, as a way to make a living, Williams, disguised as a man, enlisted in the newly formed African American regiment, the Thirty-eighth United States Infantry, one of the regiments later known as the Buffalo Soldiers.

At the time Williams enlisted, in November 1866, medical examinations were not required. Her army papers listed her as William Cathey. In a January 2, 1876, article in the *St. Louis Daily Times*, Williams was quoted as saying "I carried my musket and did guard and other duties while in the army, but finally I got tired and wanted to get off." She complained of being sick and, she says, a doctor discovered her secret. "The men all wanted to get rid of me after they found out I was a woman," she said in the article. She was discharged in October 1868 and settled in Colorado.

◆

WHO WAS THE FIRST BUFFALO SOLDIER TO RECEIVE THE CONGRESSIONAL MEDAL OF HONOR?

Sergeant Emanuel Stance, a former sharecropper, was a member of one of the all-black regiments—known as the Buffalo Soldiers—that patrolled the West for twenty-five years after the end of the Civil War. In May 1870, Stance and his company rode out from their fort in Texas to search for Kickapoo Indians who had raided local settlements. On the trail, he led an attack on a band of Indians herding stolen horses and drove them away. He and his men camped for the night at Kickapoo Springs, and the next day drove off another band that was about to attack a wagon train.

When Stance returned to the fort, his captain commended him for his courage and devotion to duty and recommended him for a Congressional Medal of Honor, which he received on July 24, 1870. He was the first of eighteen African American soldiers to win the Medal of Honor during the Indian wars.

◆

WHEN DID THE U.S. NAVAL ACADEMY ACCEPT ITS FIRST AFRICAN AMERICAN?

James Henry Conyers, a native of South Carolina, was appointed by his congressman to attend the United States Naval Academy in Annapolis, Maryland, and entered in September 1872, twenty-two years after the academy was established. His appointment created a storm of controversy. Since hazing was a popular practice at the academy, some faculty members feared he would be tormented by his fellow midshipmen.

Although Conyers was the object of several hazing incidents, he was said to have borne them stoically. But his teachers eventually decided that he was deficient in mathematics and French, and he left Annapolis after his first year.

◆

WHO WAS THE FIRST AFRICAN AMERICAN GRADUATE OF WEST POINT?

Although he was not the first African American to enter the United States Military Academy at West Point, Henry Ossian Flipper was the first to graduate. In 1870, seven years before Flipper's graduation, a young man named James Webster Smith was admitted to the academy, but in his fourth year he was judged deficient in the study of philosophy and dismissed. While at West Point, Smith was forced to live and eat his meals alone, and constantly suffered racist taunts.

Henry Ossian Flipper, who was born into slavery in Thomasville, Georgia, in 1856, was also mistreated. Although ostracized by his fellow cadets, he was determined to get through the four years and he succeeded. After graduation Flipper was assigned to the all-black Tenth Cavalry, a unit of the Buffalo Soldiers, where he served with distinction. While stationed at Fort Sill, Oklahoma, he perfected a drainage system that eliminated the stagnant water that had plagued the fort. Known as "Flipper's Ditch," it became a national landmark in 1977. But while working as a commissary officer, he was accused of mishandling funds. Although he proclaimed his innocence, he was court-martialed and dismissed from the army in 1882.

Flipper embarked on a long career as a mining engineer, becoming the first African American to gain recognition in that profession. He worked as a special agent for the Department of Justice, an expert on Mexico for the Senate Foreign Relations Committee, and a special assistant to the secretary of the interior. He retired to Atlanta, where he died in 1940 at the age of eighty-four, still trying to clear his name. It was not until 1976 that the army finally reexamined his records, exonerated him, and reburied him with military honors.

In February 1999, President Bill Clinton granted Flipper a full pardon, saying: "Today's ceremony is about a moment in 1882, when our government did not do all it could do to protect an individual American's freedom. It is about a moment in 1999 when we correct the error . . ."

◆

WHO WERE THE FIRST FOUR AFRICAN AMERICAN SOLDIERS TO WIN THE MEDAL OF HONOR IN THE SPANISH-AMERICAN WAR?

On June 30, 1898, members of the all-black Tenth Cavalry along with other troops aboard the USS *Florida* were approaching the harbor in Tayabacoe, Cuba, to deliver food and ammunition to Cuban insurgents. After landing, the forces were fired upon by Spanish troops; most escaped, but sixteen wounded men were taken prisoner by the Spaniards. After several attempts to rescue the men had failed, four members of the Tenth Cavalry, Privates Dennis Bell, Fitz Lee, William Thompkins, and George Wanton, volunteered to try. They rowed to shore, rescued their comrades, and carried them safely back to the ship. For their courage, each of the four cavalrymen was awarded the Congressional Medal of Honor.

◆

WHO WAS THE FIRST
AFRICAN AMERICAN FIGHTER PILOT?

Almost twenty-five years before the famed Tuskegee Airmen took to the skies, the first African American military pilot, Eugene Jacques Bullard, flew with the French Flying Corps during World War I. Born in 1894 in Columbus, Georgia, the adventurous young man left home when he was eighteen, hitchhiked to Virginia, stowed away on a ship to Scotland, and worked his way through England to France.

In 1914, soon after the beginning of World War I, Bullard joined the French Foreign Legion. He was wounded in battle twice and declared disabled. Still wanting to serve, he trained as a pilot and was accepted by the French Flying Corps. When the United States entered the war in 1917, he volunteered to transfer into the U.S. Army Air Corps but was rejected because of his race.

During the war, Bullard flew more than twenty missions with the French against the Germans and shot down at least five enemy aircraft. He was decorated more than ten times, earning the Croix de Guerre and the Legion of Honor, France's highest award. He stayed in France, and when World War II broke out he fought with the French Underground until the Germans occupied Paris in 1940. He then returned to the United States and lived in New York until his death in 1961.

◆

WHO WAS THE FIRST AFRICAN AMERICAN IN THE
U.S. ARMY TO WIN A CROIX DE GUERRE?

During World War I, Henry Johnson, a former porter in the Albany, New York, train station, joined the army and was assigned to the all-black 369th Infantry Regiment. In May 1918, Johnson's unit, serving alongside French troops, was guarding a line of trenches. One night while he was on sentry duty, a German patrol suddenly attacked. Johnson shot one soldier, wounded two others, and continued to fight until the Germans retreated. Then, ignoring his own injuries, he went to the aid of a wounded comrade. In recognition of his courage, the French government awarded Johnson its highest military decoration for bravery in action—the Croix de Guerre with Gold Palm.

In 1996, New York Governor George Pataki initiated an effort to award the Medal of Honor to Johnson. "Sergeant Johnson was a true American hero," said Pataki, "and I am committed to seeing to it that this courageous New Yorker receives the nation's highest military honor."

♦

WHO WAS THE FIRST AFRICAN AMERICAN GENERAL?

Benjamin O. Davis Sr., born in Washington, D.C., in 1877, enlisted in the infantry when he was twenty-one years old, starting a military career that would last for fifty years. Davis saw action in the Spanish-American War, World War I, and World War II, amassing many honors, including the Bronze Star and the Distinguished Service Medal.

From the time that he enlisted, Davis rose through the ranks, becoming a lieutenant colonel in 1920 and being named the first African American brigadier general in the army in 1940. Before his retirement in 1948, Davis played a major role in the movement toward desegregation of the armed forces. In 1954, his son, Benjamin O. Davis Jr., became the first African American brigadier general in the air force.

♦

WHO WAS THE FIRST HERO OF WORLD WAR II?

When Japanese planes attacked Pearl Harbor on December 7, 1941, Doris Miller, known as Dorie, a United States Navy mess attendant aboard the battleship *West Virginia*, was in the process of collecting laundry when an alarm sounded. As planes roared overhead, Miller rushed on deck. First he carried wounded sailors to safety. Then an officer ordered him to the bridge, where the captain lay gravely wounded. Miller manned a machine gun and fired at the attacking planes until he ran out of ammunition and was ordered to abandon ship. It is uncertain how many planes Miller actually downed during his attack.

Miller's exploit made him the first hero of the war, and within six months he was personally awarded the Navy Cross for extraordinary courage by Admiral Chester W. Nimitz. But what made his feat really remarkable was the fact that he, like most African American sailors, was serving as a noncombatant in a segregated navy that had given him no training in the operation of guns.

After he was given the Navy Cross, Miller was sent to African American communities around the country to promote the sale of war bonds. When this tour of duty ended, he was returned to the war in the Pacific—as a mess attendant. In 1943 his ship, the aircraft carrier *Liscombe Bay*, was torpedoed by a Japanese submarine and sank within minutes. Six hundred and forty-six sailors died, including Dorie Miller, who was only twenty-four years old. Over the years since the end of World War II, many efforts have been launched to posthumously award Miller the Congressional Medal of Honor.

◆

WHO WERE THE FIRST AFRICAN AMERICAN FIGHTER PILOTS IN THE U.S. AIR FORCE?

On March 7, 1942, the first group of African Americans ever to undergo training as combat fighter pilots graduated from flying school at Tuskegee Institute in Alabama. Known as the Tuskegee Airmen, the first classes to finish training were organized into the Ninety-ninth Pursuit Squadron. Led by Captain Benjamin O. Davis Jr., who was to become the first African American brigadier general in the air force, the pilots were ordered to combat duty in North Africa. As more pilots graduated from the Tuskegee training school, more squadrons were formed, and in July 1944, the Ninety-ninth joined three other squadrons of Tuskegee Airmen to form the 332nd Fighter Group, led by Davis.

The Tuskegee Airmen continued flying and fighting until the war in Europe ended in May 1945. By then, 992 men had graduated from pilot training at Tuskegee, 450 of whom were sent overseas for combat assignments. About 150 lost their lives while in training or on combat flights. The Airmen were involved in more than 15,000 combat sorties, winning 150 Distinguished Flying Crosses, 744 Air Medals, eight Purple Hearts, and fourteen Bronze Stars.

◆

WHO WAS THE FIRST AFRICAN AMERICAN TO COMMAND A U.S. MERCHANT SHIP?

Although the United States Army and Navy were segregated during World War II, the merchant marine had been integrated from the start; it was not part of the armed forces, and its members belonged to a labor union that prohibited discrimination. Before the end of the war, fourteen Liberty ships (cargo ships built during World War II) had been named after well-known African Americans, four after black colleges, and four after African American seamen who had lost their lives in the service.

In September 1942, when the Liberty ship *Booker T. Washington* was launched, an African American captain, Hugh Mulzac, was in command. Mulzac was the first of four African Americans assigned to command Liberty ships. By May 1944, he had guided the *Booker T. Washington* through the dangerous, submarine-infested waters of the Atlantic Ocean seven times.

◆

WHO WAS THE FIRST AFRICAN AMERICAN NURSE TO SERVE IN THE NAVY NURSE CORPS IN WORLD WAR II?

Phyllis Daley, a graduate of the Lincoln School for Nurses in New York City, was commissioned an ensign in the United States Navy Nurse Corps in March 1945, two months after the navy dropped its color ban. Daley was the first of four African American nurses to serve in World War II, and her appointment was a milestone in the effort to integrate the U.S. Navy.

◆

WHO WAS THE FIRST AFRICAN AMERICAN COMMISSIONED OFFICER IN THE U.S. MARINE CORPS?

In June 1941, President Franklin D. Roosevelt signed the Fair Employment Act, barring discrimination in all federal agencies, including the marine corps. But when Frederick C. Branch entered the marines two years later, the training facility at Montford Point, North Carolina, where he was sent, was still segregated and would remain so until 1949.

Branch was born in Hamlet, North Carolina, the fourth of seven sons of an African Methodist Episcopal Zion minister. He graduated from high school in Mamaroneck, New York, attended Johnson C. Smith University, and was a student at Temple University when he was drafted in 1943. He applied to officer candidates school and was turned down. But later, while serving in the South Pacific, he made a good impression on his commanding officer, who recommended him for officer's training; he was the only African American in a class of two hundred and fifty.

Branch was commissioned a second lieutenant in November 1945. Since the war was over by then, he joined the reserves and returned to Temple, graduating two years later with a degree in physics. He created a science program at a Philadelphia high school, where he taught until he retired in 1988. He was recalled to active duty during the Korean War and was promoted to captain before leaving the military in 1955.

When Branch was honored at the annual NAACP convention in 2004, Marine General Cornell Wilson said, "For a person of color to aspire to be an officer in the marine corps was a danger. We still had Jim Crow laws. . . . He could very well have been lynched or injured in some way."

In 1997, the marine corps named a training building for Branch at Marine Officer Candidates School in Quantico, Virginia. And a year after Branch's death in 2005, the Naval ROTC created the Frederick C. Branch Marine Corps Leadership Scholarship in his honor. The scholarship is available for students at seventeen historically black colleges and universities affiliated with NROTC.

◆

WHEN DID THE FIRST AFRICAN AMERICAN GRADUATE FROM THE U.S. NAVAL ACADEMY?

From the time the United States Naval Academy opened in Annapolis, Maryland, in 1845 until Wesley Brown was appointed in 1945, only five African Americans had been admitted, the first in 1872. All resigned or were dismissed, allegedly because of poor grades or disciplinary problems. When two black midshipmen left in the 1930s, one within his first month at the academy, African American organizations protested, charging discrimination.

In June 1945, Wesley A. Brown of Washington, D.C., was ap-

WESLEY A. BROWN

pointed to the naval academy by New York Congressman Adam Clayton Powell Jr. As a student at Dunbar High School in Washington, Brown had excelled academically; was active in German, chess, and photography clubs; and participated in tennis and track. His teachers encouraged him to pursue a military career.

Brown's first year at the naval academy was an ordeal; he was harassed by classmates and reprimanded by teachers at any provocation. But he persevered, and in June 1949 became the first African American to graduate from the academy. After a twenty-year career in the navy, serving in the civil engineering corps, Brown retired as a lieutenant commander and continued working in engineering and construction until he retired again in 1988. In 1989, when he celebrated the fortieth anniversary of his graduation from the naval academy, Brown received tributes from many other graduates, including former President Jimmy Carter, who had run with Brown on the academy track team. Brown died in May 2012 at the age of eighty-five.

◆

WHO WAS THE FIRST AFRICAN AMERICAN NAVY PILOT?

Ensign Jesse L. Brown, born in Hattiesburg, Mississippi, in 1926, was the first African American to be commissioned as a pilot in the United States Navy. In December 1950, Brown was shot down near the Chosin Reservoir in North Korea. He had just taken off from the aircraft carrier *Leyte* when his plane crashed into a snow-covered mountain. Seeing that Brown was trapped in the wreckage, a white pilot from Massachusetts, Lieutenant Thomas J. Hudner, Jr., landed his plane on the icy slope and rushed to Brown's side, where he tried unsuccessfully to free the injured flyer. Hudner radioed for help, but the rescue pilot arrived too late to save Brown's life.

After his death, Brown was awarded the Distinguished Flying Cross and Air Medal for bravery. In March 1972 he was further honored when the navy christened a new member of its fleet, the USS *Jesse L. Brown*. It was the first time a naval vessel had been named for an African American.

◆

WHO WAS THE FIRST AFRICAN AMERICAN TO EARN A MEDAL OF HONOR IN THE KOREAN WAR?

When William Thompson was just a youngster, a minister noticed him sleeping in a park and took him to the New York Home for Homeless Boys. Thompson remained a resident there until just after his eighteenth birthday in 1945, when he was drafted into the army. Thompson was honorably discharged a year and a half later and returned to New York, but he had trouble adjusting to civilian life and eventually reenlisted in the regular army.

Thompson was with the first American troops to arrive in South Korea in June 1950. Six weeks later, in the dark of night, his platoon came under a surprise attack by enemy forces. Private First Class Thompson set up his machine gun in the enemy's path and swept them with his fire, allowing the rest of the platoon to withdraw to a better position. Although the foe continued to charge toward him, tossing grenades and firing, Thompson, badly wounded, refused orders to retreat. Finally an enemy grenade exploded nearby, killing him. In June 1951, Thompson was posthumously awarded the Congressional Medal of Honor.

◆

WHEN DID THE AIR FORCE APPOINT ITS FIRST AFRICAN AMERICAN BRIGADIER GENERAL?

In October 1954, Benjamin O. Davis Jr. made air force history by becoming the first African American brigadier general in that branch of the service. The son of Benjamin O. Davis Sr., the first black general in the army, the younger Davis graduated in 1936 from the U.S. Military Academy, the first African American West Point graduate in the twentieth century.

BENJAMIN O. DAVIS JR.

Davis's treatment at the academy was almost intolerable, he once told a group of students. "The greatest indignity was neglect," he said. "No cadet speaking to me the entire time I was at West Point except in the line of duty . . . I made up my mind that I wasn't going to let these people make me leave. I said to myself, 'I'm a better man than they are because I'm more human.'"

Soon after the start of World War II, when the military was still racially segregated, Davis was chosen to head the Ninety-ninth Pursuit Squadron, consisting of African American pilots trained at Tuskegee Institute, and later the 332nd Flying Group, a larger black unit. His outstanding performance earned him several military decorations, including the Distinguished Flying Cross and the Silver Star. He spoke out against segregation in the armed forces, and after President Truman's 1948 order putting an end to this practice, Davis assisted the air force in making plans to desegregate its bases.

After the war, Davis held a number of command posts, rising to the rank of three-star general before his retirement in 1970. After leaving the air force, he served as an assistant secretary of the Department of Transportation. In 1998, President Clinton, in a White House ceremony, presented the eighty-six-year-old Davis with a fourth star, making him one of the few military officers to become a four-star general during retirement. Davis died on July 4, 2002, at the Walter Reed Army Medical Center in Washington, D.C.

◆

WHO WAS THE FIRST AFRICAN AMERICAN SOLDIER AWARDED THE CONGRESSIONAL MEDAL OF HONOR IN THE VIETNAM WAR?

Milton Lee Olive III, a young resident of Chicago, joined the army in 1964. A year later he was sent to Vietnam. On October 22, 1965, sixteen days before his nineteenth birthday, Olive and his platoon were creeping through the jungle when they stumbled into a Viet Cong ambush. A grenade landed near Olive and four other soldiers. He immediately grabbed the grenade and threw his body on it as it exploded, sacrificing his own life to save the lives of his comrades. He was buried in the West Grove Missionary Baptist Cemetery, not far from his birthplace in Lexington, Mississippi.

Six months later, President Lyndon Johnson posthumously awarded the Congressional Medal of Honor to the courageous African American soldier, presenting the award to Olive's father in a White House ceremony. In Chicago, on a site on Lake Michigan called Olive Park, a monument stands in honor of Milton Olive.

◆

WHO WAS THE FIRST AFRICAN AMERICAN ADMIRAL IN THE U.S. NAVY?

Samuel Gravely, born in Richmond, Virginia, in 1922, began his navy career at the age of twenty when he enlisted in the United States Naval Reserve. He was later commissioned as an ensign and served in various assignments during World War II until he was released from active duty in 1946. Three years later he returned to the navy, where he was given increasingly responsible duties.

In January 1962 Gravely was made commander of the destroyer

SAMUEL GRAVELY

escort USS *Falgout,* becoming the first African American to command a warship since the Civil War. He was later made captain of another warship, the USS *Taussig.* Gravely made military history once again in 1971 when he became the first African American to reach the rank of admiral in United States naval history. He retired in 1980.

◆

WHO WAS THE FIRST AFRICAN AMERICAN TO COMMAND A U.S. ARMY DIVISION?

Before beginning his illustrious army career, Major General Frederic Davison graduated from Howard University in 1938 and, after completing his ROTC training, was commissioned a second lieutenant in the infantry reserve. In March 1941, soon after the United States entered World War II, Davison was called to active duty and served as an infantry officer in Italy. After the war he filled various posts in the United States and South Korea.

In 1968, during the Vietnam War, Davison led the 199th Infantry Brigade in the Tet offensive, the first African American to command an army brigade in combat. Four years later he took command of the Eighth Infantry Division in Germany, making him the first African American to lead a United States Army division. Davison retired from the military in 1974 and served as executive assistant to the president of Howard University for the next decade. This decorated veteran of two wars died in January 1999 at the age of eighty-two.

♦

WHO WAS THE FIRST AFRICAN AMERICAN FOUR-STAR GENERAL?

Daniel James Jr., who was nicknamed "Chappie," was born in Pensacola, Florida, in 1920. His mother, Lillie James, ran a school for African American children in their home. James studied at Tuskegee Institute in Alabama and became a pilot with the Tuskegee Airmen. He flew 101 combat missions as a fighter pilot during the Korean War and seventy-eight more in Vietnam. In 1976 he became the first African American four-star general in United States military history. After he received his fourth star, James said: "I've fought in three wars, and three more wouldn't be too many to defend my country." Widely known for his speeches on patriotism, James died of a heart attack in 1978, only a few weeks after his retirement.

♦

WHEN WAS THE FIRST AFRICAN AMERICAN WOMAN ADMITTED TO THE U.S. NAVAL ACADEMY?

Women were admitted to the United States Naval Academy in Annapolis, Maryland, for the first time in 1976. Of the eighty-one women who entered the academy that year, one was an African American—Janie Mines, an eighteen-year-old from Aiken, South Carolina. A member of the Navy Junior ROTC at her high school, Mines majored in political science at the naval academy, where she was a squad leader, a midshipman drill instructor, and a regimental adjutant.

Mines graduated from the U.S. Naval Academy in 1980 with a bachelor's degree in engineering. She later earned a master's degree in business administration from the Massachusetts Institute of Technology. During her military career, she filled various posts as a supply corps officer. After leaving the military, she held management positions at several corporations, including Procter & Gamble and Hershey Foods. She founded the Boyz to Men Club in Fort Mill, South Carolina, an organization that teaches life skills and entrepreneurship to young men who would otherwise not have these opportunities. She also became a strategic partner in Queen Associates, a technology and engineering consulting firm.

◆

WHO WAS THE FIRST AFRICAN AMERICAN WOMAN GENERAL?

Five years after completing her nurse's training in 1950 at Harlem Hospital in New York City, Hazel Johnson joined the United States Army Nurse Corps, and in May 1960 she was commissioned a second lieutenant. While in the service she earned a bachelor's degree from Columbia and a Ph.D. from Catholic University. In 1979, at the age of fifty-two, she was promoted to brigadier general, the first African American woman general in United States military history.

Johnson was chief of the army nurse corps from 1979 to 1983, when she retired. She then embarked on a second career in academia; she was a professor of nursing at Georgetown University and later at George Mason University in Virginia. She retired from teaching in 1997.

Responding to her death in August 2011 at eighty-three, the American Nurses Association called Johnson "a leader and educator whose determination and dedication to the profession provided inspiration to generations of nurses."

◆

WHO WAS THE FIRST AFRICAN AMERICAN
FOUR-STAR GENERAL IN THE ARMY?

After General Roscoe Robinson, Jr., died of leukemia in 1993, his West Point classmates wrote a tribute to him, saying he would be remembered for many reasons, but especially as the first African American four-star army general. "As a class," the tribute said, "we are proud of Robby's accomplishments . . . [He is] the role model for thousands of young black soldiers during his thirty-five years of service and to this day."

ROSCOE ROBINSON, JR.

Robinson, born in St. Louis, Missouri, in 1928, graduated from the United States Military Academy at West Point in 1951, and after being commissioned in the army he served first in segregated units. He then served in the Seventh Infantry Division in the Korean War and with the First Cavalry Division during the Vietnam War, and later was brigade commander of the Eighty-second Airborne Division. He was awarded his fourth star in 1982, when he was assigned to be the United States representative to NATO's military committee. After his retirement, the army often called on him to contribute his experience and expertise to various committees.

In May 1993, Robinson was presented with West Point's Distinguished Graduate Award; two months later, many classmates, friends, and Washington officials attended his funeral. He was buried in Arlington National Cemetery. In April 2000, Robinson was again honored by West Point at a ceremony in which the Thayer Hall auditorium was renamed the General Roscoe Robinson, Jr. Auditorium. In his keynote address, West Point's superintendent said Robinson was "first and foremost a combat infantry soldier" and that his "every fiber reflected the academy's motto of duty, honor, country."

In 2010, Harris was appointed by President Obama to serve as a member of the Board of Visitors for the United States Air Force Academy.

◆

WHO WAS THE FIRST AFRICAN AMERICAN WOMAN GENERAL IN THE AIR FORCE?

Early in life, Marcelite J. Harris, a native of Houston, Texas, wanted to be an actress. Harris, born in 1943, enrolled in Atlanta's Spelman College to study speech and drama. During her senior year, she joined a USO tour of military bases in France and Germany, and a year later, in need of a job and remembering the excitement of her travels abroad, she decided to join the U.S. Air Force.

Her first assignments were in California and Germany, and during the Vietnam War she was an aircraft maintenance supervisor at an air base in Thailand. She went on to fill military assignments

MARCELITE J. HARRIS

in different parts of the country and in Japan—including a stint as a White House social aide to President Jimmy Carter—and to win a number of decorations and awards.

Harris, the first woman aircraft maintenance officer in the air force, was promoted to brigadier general in September 1990 and became vice commander of the Oklahoma City Air Logistics Center at Tinker Air Force Base. In July 1993 Harris was assigned to Randolph Air Force Base in Texas as director of technical training, air education, and training command. A year later, she was named director of maintenance at the United States Air Force Headquarters in Washington, and in 1995 was promoted to major general. Two years after her retirement in 1997, Harris joined United Space Alliance, a company that contracted with NASA on the manned space program. In 2002, the chancellor of the New York City Department of Education hired her as his chief of staff. She resigned less than six months later.

In 2010, Harris was appointed by President Obama to serve as a member of the Board of Visitors for the United States Air Force Academy.

◆

WHO IS THE NAVY'S FIRST AFRICAN AMERICAN FOUR-STAR ADMIRAL?

In 1861, when the Union Navy began enlisting African Americans, most served as stewards and cooks. Although the navy later desegregated its ranks, it took 135 years before an African American was promoted to four-star admiral. Several months after J. Paul Reason was awarded the four stars in 1996, he said in a speech, "I totally attribute my success to those who have gone before me—all minorities. People who have broken down barriers by showing others they're capable of doing the expected task, that they can perform, and it has nothing to do with the color of skin or ethnicity . . ."

Reason was born in 1943 in Washington, D.C. His parents were both educators, and Reason himself attended Howard University before entering the U.S. Naval Academy, graduating in 1965. Reason has said that his interest in the navy came from the loves of his childhood: swimming, fishing, canoeing—anything to do with water. After graduation, he entered the navy's nuclear propulsion program and served on three ships, a destroyer escort, a nuclear-powered guided missile cruiser, and a nuclear-powered aircraft carrier.

In 1976 Reason joined President Gerald Ford's administration as naval aide to the White House and kept the position for two years under President Carter. When he was named a four-star admiral, he became commander-in-chief of the Atlantic Fleet, which comprises about half of the entire U.S. Navy. After his retirement in 1999, he held several top corporate positions, and was a member of the National Research Council, the National Science Foundation, and the Naval Studies Board.

◆

WHO WAS THE FIRST AFRICAN AMERICAN WOMAN ADMIRAL IN THE U.S. NAVY?

When Lillian E. Fishburne was promoted to rear admiral on February 1, 1998, she became the first African American woman admiral in the United States Navy. Born in 1949 to a naval family in Patuxent River, Maryland, and raised in Rockville, she graduated from Lincoln University in Oxford, Pennsylvania. Less than two years later, she completed women's officer school training at Newport, Rhode Island, and was commissioned an ensign in 1973.

Fishburne served in many positions during her career in the navy, starting as a personnel and legal officer at the naval air test facility in Lakehurst, New Jersey. After earning a degree from the naval postgraduate school, she held such positions as executive officer at the naval communications command in Yokosuka, Japan, and chief of the command and control systems support division in Washington. After commanding the naval computer and telecommunications area master station in Hawaii, she was promoted to rear admiral in 1998. When Secretary of Defense William Cohen made a speech honoring Fishburne and others, he said that her story "helps us to understand the truth that women are an indispensable part of today's military."

In May 2001, three months after her retirement, Fishburne gave the commencement address at her alma mater, Lincoln University, and was awarded an honorary degree.

◆

WHO WAS THE FIRST AFRICAN AMERICAN WOMAN TO COMMAND AN AIR FORCE FLYING SQUADRON?

"Why ride when I can fly?" has been the philosophy of Stayce Harris, whose love of aviation set her on a path that led to her position as the commander of an Airlift Squadron located at the March Air Reserve Base in California. Born in Los Angeles in 1959, Harris earned a bachelor's degree in engineering

BRIG. GEN. STAYCE HARRIS

from the University of Southern California, receiving a commission in the air force through that school's ROTC program. She was assigned to a civil engineering squadron at an air force base in Utah, but her sights were set on becoming a pilot. She received pilot training in Arizona and later earned a master's degree from Embry-Riddle Aeronautical University.

Harris separated from active duty in the air force in 1990 and began flying for United Airlines as a first officer on a Boeing 747. She joined the air force reserve, spending four years as a pilot, then filled assignments at the Pentagon until she returned to March Air Reserve Base in 2000. One year later, in February 2001, Harris took command of the 729th Airlift Squadron, directing more than one hundred personnel who fly C-141 Starlifter cargo planes to deliver combat forces or humanitarian aid.

Some of Harris's mentors, former Tuskegee Airmen, honored her by attending the ceremony at the March base when she was named the first African American woman to command an air force or air force reserve flying squadron. Harris was promoted to brigadier general in April 2009, and in 2012, she became mobilization assistant to the commander, 18th Air Force, Scott Air Force Base, in Illinois.

MUSIC

WHO WAS THE FIRST AFRICAN AMERICAN CONCERT ARTIST TO WIN RECOGNITION OUTSIDE THE UNITED STATES?

Elizabeth Taylor Greenfield was born in 1809 in Natchez, Mississippi, the daughter of an African father and a Seminole Indian mother. She was brought to Philadelphia when she was one year old and raised by a Quaker woman, Mrs. Greenfield. Her musical talent soon became evident, and she was encouraged to pursue it. Said to be awkward and unattractive, she was mostly self-taught, since white teachers refused her as a student. However, the quality and range of her voice—three and one-half octaves—made her increasingly popular.

When her patron died in 1844, Greenfield moved to Buffalo, New York, and made her professional debut there in 1851, singing to great acclaim before the Buffalo Musical Association. A year later, she performed in Albany for an audience that included the New York governor and his family, members of both houses of the legislature, and other officials. After touring throughout the country, where she became known as "The Black Swan," she sailed for England in 1853 to give a command performance for Queen Victoria at Buckingham Palace.

Despite Greenfield's success, her African American fans were either denied admission to her concerts or forced to sit in the balcony. When she made her New York debut in 1953 at Metropolitan Hall, African Americans were not allowed to attend, and she gave a second performance for them at another theater.

After the Civil War, Greenfield settled in Philadelphia, where she gave concerts, opened a studio, and taught voice. She died in 1876.

◆

WHO WAS THE FIRST AFRICAN AMERICAN TO GAIN FAME AS A CONCERT PIANIST?

Born into slavery in 1849 near Columbus, Georgia, Thomas Greene Bethune was blind from birth and suffered from a condition that today might be considered a form of autism. His father was named Domingo Wiggins and his mother, Charity Greene. As a slave, Tom was given the name of his owner, James Bethune. One day, when he was about four years old, young Tom wandered into the living room, sat at the piano, and began to play tunes that he had heard his master's children play. Amazed by his ability to imitate any piece by ear, the Bethune family encouraged him to use the piano whenever he wished, got him music teachers, and played music for him so he could develop a repertoire.

By the time he was about five, Bethune was performing for private groups. He made his formal debut in 1857 at Temperance Hall in Columbus. Known as "Blind Tom," he started giving concerts throughout the country, with his master keeping most of the profits. He continued performing throughout the Civil War, but only in the South. Even after the emancipation of slaves, the Bethune family maintained control over him. For almost thirty years he performed throughout the United States, Europe, and South America. It was said that he could play 7,000 pieces and that he composed more than one hundred. He died after suffering a stroke at the age of fifty-nine.

◆

WHAT WAS THE FIRST SINGING GROUP TO PERFORM SPIRITUALS THROUGHOUT THE WORLD?

Trying to save their struggling college, nine student singers at Fisk University—five young women and four young men, all but two of whom had emerged from slavery—left their Nashville, Tennessee, campus in October 1871, accompanied by their music teacher. Stopping in Ohio, the group, which called itself the Fisk Jubilee Singers, gave its first concert of spirituals, on a cold night in Cincinnati. They went on to Wilberforce University, an African American school, where a bishop gave them his blessing.

As the singers traveled northward through the cold countryside, their skimpy clothing offered little protection from the icy weather. In many towns they were turned away from hotels and driven out of railroad station waiting rooms because of their race.

A concert they gave in Oberlin, Ohio, was praised in the press, and word of the talented singers began to spread across the country. They made their way east to New York State and stopped for a time in Brooklyn, where the theologian Henry Ward Beecher had arranged a concert. As their fame grew, they performed before eminent citizens of New York City and were asked to sing for President Ulysses S. Grant.

After returning to the Fisk campus three months after their departure to present the money they had earned, the Fisk Jubilee Singers, with two additional members, responded to invitations to perform across the country and overseas. They traveled and sang abroad for seven years and managed to raise $150,000 to give to Fisk University. Part of the money was used to build the first brick building on the campus; it was named Jubilee Hall.

◆

WHO WAS THE FIRST AFRICAN AMERICAN VIOLINIST TO TOUR THE UNITED STATES?

Joseph Douglass, born in 1871, was the grandson of the great abolitionist Frederick Douglass. Both Joseph's grandfather and father were violinists, so as a youngster he, too, was given lessons on the instrument. When he was not yet twenty, his grandfather sent him to Boston to study at the New England Conservatory of Music.

Douglass returned to his native Washington, D.C., and began giving concerts. On August 25, 1892, at the World's Columbian Exposition in Chicago, a group of African Americans proclaimed Colored People's Day. The main speaker, Frederick Douglass, then seventy-four years old, and his favorite grandson, Joseph, began the program by playing a violin piece along with their friend Will Marion Cook.

Douglass soon embarked on what was to be thirty years of touring throughout the United States. It was said that he played at every African American educational institution in the country and in most of the churches. At the same time, he taught at Howard University and occasionally conducted orchestras.

♦

WHO IS SAID TO BE THE FIRST JAZZ MUSICIAN?

Charles "Buddy" Bolden, a cornet player who is thought to be the first musician to lead a jazz band, became known throughout the Storyville section of New Orleans for the brass bands he led along the streets, wailing out blues and ragtime on his horn. Bolden and his bands played for dances, funerals, and Mardi Gras celebrations. At funerals, they would parade through the streets to the cemetery and back, marching to the tunes of old hymns they had set to jaunty rhythms.

It was said that Buddy Bolden was one of the loudest cornet players in the world. In fact, a story was told about the two amusement parks that existed in New Orleans at the time, one of which was preferred by Bolden. When he and his band arrived there, he would blow a call on his cornet and all the people in the other park would rush over to hear him play.

Buddy Bolden first improvised in the style later called jazz around 1895, before the first recordings were made. His band, consisting of cornet, clarinet, trombone, guitar, bass, and drums, became one of the most popular groups in the city. But Bolden's behavior became increasingly erratic, and in 1907 he was committed to a mental hospital, where he remained for twenty-four years until his death.

♦

WHAT WAS THE FIRST RAG PUBLISHED BY AN AFRICAN AMERICAN COMPOSER?

In 1897, Thomas Million Turpin, a pianist from St. Louis, Missouri, published "Harlem Rag," the first ragtime piece to be published by an African American composer. Ragtime music, usually played on the piano, is thought to have got its name from its ragged, syncopated rhythm. Turpin, who was born about 1873, was a self-taught musician. When he was young he worked in his father's saloon, and in 1900 he and his brother opened their own place, the Rosebud Café. It became a gathering place for ragtime pianists.

Turpin was an impressive figure; he was over six feet tall, and when he grew older he weighed about 300 pounds. This ragtime pioneer wrote several appealing, tuneful pieces, including "Rag-Time Nightmare" and "St. Louis Rag," in honor of the St. Louis World's Fair. His last published rag, a more complex work, was the 1904 "Buffalo Rag."

◆

WHO WAS THE FIRST COMPOSER OF GOSPEL HYMNS?

Charles A. Tindley was born in Maryland in 1851. The son of slaves, he taught himself to read and write. After moving to Philadelphia, he worked as a church sexton while earning his divinity degree through a correspondence course. After leading congregations in New Jersey and Delaware, he returned to Philadelphia as pastor of Calvary Methodist Episcopal Church, the same church where he had earlier been sexton.

He attracted a large congregation, cared for the city's poor, and wrote many gospel hymns. Two of his most famous are "We'll Understand It Better By and By" and "Stand By Me." It is said that when the famous composer Thomas A. Dorsey heard Tindley's spiritual "I Do, Don't You" at the 1921 National Baptist Convention, he was inspired to leave popular music and start writing gospel songs. Although Dorsey is sometimes referred to as the first gospel composer, he always gave Tindley credit for originating this form of music.

◆

WHO WAS THE FIRST AFRICAN AMERICAN
TO GAIN FAME AS A COMPOSER
OF CONCERT MUSIC?

When Harry Burleigh was just a child, he was inspired to become a singer after hearing performers in his hometown of Erie, Pennsylvania, where he was born in 1866. He was unable to afford lessons but often sang in local churches. When he was twenty-six he went to New York, where he was awarded a scholarship to attend the National Conservatory of Music. He studied with the Czech composer Antonin Dvořák, director of the conservatory, and introduced him to spirituals, which Dvořák incorporated into his *New World* symphony. Two years later he became a baritone soloist at the eminent St. George's Protestant Episcopal Church, a position he held for more than fifty years. In 1900 he was hired as a soloist in another house of worship, Temple Emanu-El; he sang at services there for twenty-five years.

By the late 1800s, Burleigh had become a composer, eventually producing about 300 art songs and arrangements of spirituals. His works, which were favorites of concert artists, include the popular "Deep River" and "Nobody Knows the Trouble I've Seen." He made several trips to Europe and sang for members of the British royal family and President Theodore Roosevelt. Illness forced him to retire as a soloist in 1946, and he died of heart failure four years later.

◆

WHO WAS THE FIRST GREAT JAZZ COMPOSER?

Jelly Roll Morton was born in 1890 in New Orleans. It is believed that his baptismal name was Ferdinand Joseph Lemott, or possibly Lamothe. He acquired Morton from his stepfather, a porter, and he chose to call himself Jelly Roll. As a child, before settling on the piano as his instrument, Morton played harmonica, drums, trombone, violin, and guitar. By the time he was in his teens, he was playing piano in the bordellos of Storyville, the red-light district of New Orleans.

Morton was about seventeen when he began a lifelong career

as a traveling musician. He worked in St. Louis, Chicago, Mobile, Jacksonville, Memphis, New York, and many other cities. He was a pool shark, gambler, bandleader, and nightclub operator. To top it all off, he claimed he invented jazz.

He was still in his teens when he wrote "New Orleans Blues" and "King Porter Stomp," soon followed by "Jelly Roll Blues" and "Wolverine Blues." All big hits at the time, these tunes merged ragtime, blues, and brass band music into a new jazz style. These works alone could have earned him the title of the first great jazz composer, but he went on to write "Black Bottom Stomp," "Kansas City Stomp," "Winin' Boy Blues," and many more. In 1926 he began recording with his group the Red Hot Peppers, seven New Orleans jazz musicians. But in the 1930s, music fans started to turn away from New Orleans jazz, and in 1940 Morton traveled to California, where he died a year later. In all, Morton claimed to have written 1,400 compositions.

◆

WHO FIRST SANG THE BLUES
IN TRAVELING SHOWS?

The influential blues singer known as Ma Rainey was born Gertrude Pridgett in 1886 in Columbus, Georgia. She made her stage debut at the age of fourteen in a talent show at a local opera house. Four years later she fell in love with Will Rainey, a singer and comedian known as Pa Rainey, who had stopped in Columbus with a traveling minstrel show. The two soon married and toured with the Rabbit Foot Minstrels and other traveling shows for many years. Billed as Ma and Pa Rainey, they performed a song-and-dance act, but it was Ma Rainey's blues singing that pulled in the audiences. She is believed to be the first vocalist to sing the blues in minstrel shows, and she became known as the "Mother of the Blues."

Resplendent in glamorous ensembles, Rainey performed for devoted fans throughout the South. In 1923 she started making records; two of her earliest recorded songs were "Bo Weevil Blues" and "Southern Blues." She was accompanied by Lovie Austin's Blue

Serenaders, a group comprised of a clarinet, cornet, violin, and piano. When her recording career ended in 1928, she had cut almost one hundred songs, performing with such outstanding musicians as Louis Armstrong, Kid Ory, and Fletcher Henderson.

Rainey's popularity had begun to diminish by 1930, and she retired three years later. She returned to live in her hometown of Columbus and died of heart disease in 1939, at the age of fifty-three.

◆

WHO WROTE THE FIRST
AFRICAN AMERICAN OPERETTAS?

The multitalented Robert "Bob" Cole entered show business in the 1890s. A singer, dancer, actor, and writer, he created the first full-length musical entirely written, owned, produced, and performed by African Americans. The musical, *A Trip to Coontown,* opened at New York's Third Avenue Theater in 1898. Cole then embarked on a relationship with two talented brothers, J. Rosamond and James Weldon Johnson, who wrote the song "Lift Every Voice and Sing," which became known as the African American national anthem. Rosamond was a classically trained musician and James was a poet. The collaborators wrote more than 200 songs, while Cole and Rosamond put together a vaudeville show and took it on the road.

Bob Cole and J. Rosamond Johnson became the first African American songwriters to sign a contract with a Broadway music publisher, and in 1906 they produced the first true African American operetta, *The Shoo-Fly Regiment,* with lyrics by James Weldon. They both appeared in their second operetta, *The Red Moon,* which opened in 1908. By then, James Weldon had gone on to pursue his interest in literature.

In 1910, Cole and Johnson returned to vaudeville, setting off on a lengthy tour. On the final night of the tour, at New York's Fifth Avenue Theater, Cole collapsed. He was hospitalized for several months, and in August 1911, while in a private sanitarium in the Catskill Mountains, he drowned in a nearby lake. After his

ROBERT COLE AND J. ROSAMOND JOHNSON

partner's death, Johnson turned to more serious music. He published collections of spirituals and folk songs, taught for several years at the Music Settlement School in New York, and composed a number of choral works. He died in 1954.

◆

WHO WROTE THE FIRST RAGTIME OPERA?

Scott Joplin was born into a musical family in Texarkana, Texas, in 1868. His father, a former slave, was a violinist, and his mother played banjo and sang. He learned the basics of classical music from local teachers, and left home to seek his fortune when he was not yet twenty years old.

After touring parts of the country as a traveling pianist, Joplin moved to Sedalia, Missouri, where he enrolled in college to study composition and began composing piano rags. In 1899 his ragtime piece "Maple Leaf Rag" was published, and it soon became a big hit. He moved to St. Louis and continued to write popular rags, but his goal was to compose ragtime pieces that would receive as much respect as classical music. In 1902 he wrote a ballet, *The Ragtime Dance*, which was ignored by the public. A year later he composed a ragtime opera, *A Guest of Honor*, but couldn't get it published.

He wrote another opera, *Treemonisha*, settled in New York City, and spent most of his money in a futile attempt to get it produced. Increasingly depressed, he eventually became gravely ill with dementia and died in 1917 at the age of forty-nine.

Ragtime music experienced a revival in the early 1970s, when Joplin's collected works were published and a recording of his piano rags became a best seller. In 1974 his music reached a mainstream audience when his composition "The Entertainer" was used on the soundtrack of the Paul Newman movie *The Sting*. And his dream finally came true when *Treemonisha* was given a premiere performance in 1972 in Atlanta, and was presented later that year at Wolf Trap Park in Virginia. The opera was produced several times in subsequent years. In June 2000 it opened the summer season of the Opera Theater of St. Louis, in the city where Joplin lived when he began composing it. His home in St. Louis was made a state historic site and ragtime museum.

◆

JAMES REESE EUROPE AND HIS CLEF CLUB ORCHESTRA

WHO WAS THE FIRST TO ORGANIZE
AFRICAN AMERICAN MUSICIANS?

James Reese Europe, considered the most influential African American musician in New York City in the early 1900s, was born in Mobile, Alabama, in 1881 and grew up in Washington, D.C. His mother played piano, and Europe and his brother and sister all became professional musicians. When he was twenty-two, he went to New York and found work playing the piano in small clubs. He was the musical director of two shows: Cole and Johnson's *The Shoo-Fly Regiment* in 1906, and Bert Williams's *Mr. Lode of Koal* three years later.

In 1910 Europe established the Clef Club, the first attempt to organize African American musicians. Members of the Clef Club paid dues and were hired out in various combinations as dance bands. Europe's bands emphasized African American rhythms and leaned heavily on banjos, mandolins, and pianos. In 1912, in a benefit concert at Carnegie Hall, he conducted a 125-piece orchestra that amazed the audience. In 1914 he resigned from the Clef Club and led several other musical groups. Around the same time, he became the bandleader for the popular white ballroom dance team of Vernon and Irene Castle, for whom he composed music and invented some dances, including the fox-trot and the turkey trot. Vernon Castle was killed in a plane crash in 1917, the same year the United States entered World War I, and Europe became the bandmaster of an all-black army unit, the 369th Infantry. Throughout the war, his band, called the Hellfighters, entertained troops and citizens, creating a sensation wherever it played. The band returned to New York in triumph in February 1919 and embarked on a nationwide tour.

Europe's life came to a shocking finale when he was only thirty-eight years old. While his band was performing at Mechanics Hall in Boston, a maddened band member attacked the talented musician with a knife, severing his jugular vein. Europe's death was mourned by so many fans that New York City gave him a public funeral, the first ever for an African American. He was buried with military honors at Arlington National Cemetery.

♦

WHO WAS THE FIRST PERSON TO WRITE A BLUES COMPOSITION?

Born in a log cabin in Florence, Alabama, in 1873, William Christopher Handy was the son and grandson of ministers. When he announced that he wanted to be a musician, a teacher told him that music would bring him to the gutter, and his father said he'd rather follow him to his grave than see him become a musician. But Handy managed to learn to play the cornet without their knowing it. He organized a quartet that sang and played its way to the World's Fair in Chicago, only to find that the fair had been postponed. The group wandered to St. Louis and then disbanded. There, with no money and nothing to eat, Handy found himself sleeping on cobblestones. He learned, he said, "that my teacher's prophecy was true; I had ended up in the gutter."

But Handy pulled himself together. He started touring with Mahara's Minstrels and then formed his own band, ending up in Memphis, where he founded a music publishing company with a businessman named Harry Pace. He began composing songs, using the blues form and the rhythms and tunes he'd picked up listening to laborers and sharecroppers in the streets and saloons of the South. In 1909 he wrote a campaign song for a Memphis mayoral candidate named Edward H. Crump. The tune, with new words, was published in 1912 as "Memphis Blues," which is thought to be the first blues song ever written. Two years later he wrote the classic "St. Louis Blues," inspired, he said, by the hardships he suffered while living on the street twenty-one years earlier.

Handy and Pace moved their publishing company to New York in 1917, and he continued to write blues songs throughout the 1920s. In 1926 he wrote a blues anthology, and in 1938 he published *W. C. Handy's Collection of Negro Spirituals*. His autobiography, *Father of the Blues*, was published in 1941. He died in New York City in 1958.

◆

WHO WAS THE FIRST AFRICAN AMERICAN WOMAN TO BECOME A CONCERT PIANIST?

Hazel Harrison, born in Indiana in 1883, was musically gifted from early childhood. Her mother started providing her with piano lessons before she was five, and encouraged her to pursue a career in music. When she was twenty-one, her teacher arranged a concert tour in Germany, where Harrison played with the Berlin Philharmonic. She went back to Europe several years later to study and perform, returning to the United States after the outbreak of World War I. She made her debut in New York's Town Hall in 1930, to enthusiastic reviews. But because of her race, many of her performances were limited to African American churches and schools.

Harrison decided to concentrate on teaching, and in 1931 joined the faculty of Tuskegee Institute, where she was appointed head of the piano department. She also taught at Howard University and Alabama State College in Montgomery, where she gave her final concert in 1959.

◆

WHO WAS THE FIRST AFRICAN AMERICAN TO EARN A MASTER'S DEGREE IN MUSIC?

Nora Holt was born in Kansas in 1885 and started taking piano lessons when she was still a child. She graduated from Western University in Kansas and in 1918 earned a master's degree in music from Chicago Musical College. For her thesis she composed a symphonic rhapsody for string orchestra, basing it on the spiritual "You May Bury Me in the East."

After college, Holt became an active participant in the world of music. She was a music critic for the *Chicago Defender* newspaper and published a magazine called *Music and Poetry*. She was president of the Chicago Music Association and helped organize the National Association of Negro Musicians. During the 1920s and '30s Holt traveled in the United States and abroad, working for a time as a nightclub entertainer.

After returning to the United States, she taught in Los Angeles schools for a few years, then moved to New York City. In 1944 she was named music critic of the *Amsterdam News* and began producing a classical music program for radio. In 1945 she joined the Music Critics Circle of New York, becoming the first African American member of this professional organization.

◆

WHO WAS THE FIRST SINGER TO RECORD THE BLUES?

When Mamie Smith cut the record of "Crazy Blues" in August 1920, it was because of the persistence of an ambitious songwriter named Perry Bradford. Bradford had been trying to convince record companies to let Smith record his songs, but

MAMIE SMITH

the owners feared there would be no market for records by an African American singer.

Finally, in February 1920, Okeh Studios recorded Smith singing "You Can't Keep a Good Man Down" and "That Thing Called Love." The disc was such a hit that Smith was called back in August to cut "Crazy Blues," the first blues record ever made. "Crazy Blues" was a phenomenal success, selling more than one million copies the first year.

Smith, born in 1883 in Cincinnati, had been a dancer and singer in Harlem clubs. Her recording career lasted until 1931. She toured the country with her own revue and band, the Jazz Hounds, and she starred in musicals and film shorts. It was said that in her heyday she owned two apartment houses and performed in a $3,000 cape trimmed with ostrich feathers. But she reportedly died in the early 1940s in poverty and obscurity.

◆

WHO WAS THE FIRST PIANIST TO RECORD A JAZZ SOLO?

Known as the "father of the stride piano," James Price Johnson was born in New Brunswick, New Jersey, in 1891. As a boy he studied classical music and ragtime. He moved to New York while still in his teens and developed his stride piano style—in

JAMES PRICE JOHNSON

which the left hand plays a steady, driving beat—while playing at rent parties, in small clubs, and in vaudeville shows. He accompanied singers such as Ethel Waters and Bessie Smith and produced hundreds of piano rolls and records. His 1921 recording of "Carolina Shout" is considered the first jazz piano solo on record.

A leading figure in the transition from ragtime to jazz, Johnson began writing scores for shows in the early 1920s. In all, he composed eleven musicals, including *Keep Shufflin'* and *Runnin' Wild*, in which a new dance was introduced with Johnson's tune "The Charleston." He also wrote such favorites as "If I Could Be With You" and "Old Fashioned Love."

Johnson wanted to prove himself a composer of concert music using jazz and African American themes, but his works, including *Yamekraw: A Negro Rhapsody* and *Harlem Symphony* received little attention. He performed in clubs into the 1940s and died in 1955.

◆

WHAT WAS THE FIRST JAZZ BAND TO CUT A RECORD?

The great jazz trombonist Edward "Kid" Ory was born in Laplace, Louisiana, around 1890. For four years starting in 1912, he led one of the most popular bands in New Orleans, hiring such illustrious musicians as Louis Armstrong, Joe "King" Oliver, Johnny Dodds, and Sidney Bechet. In 1919 Ory moved to Los Angeles, assembling a group of New Orleans musicians into a band he called Kid Ory's Creole Orchestra. In 1922, under the name Spike's Seven Pods of Pepper Orchestra, the group became the first jazz band to cut a record.

In 1925 Ory moved to Chicago and played with such groups as Louis Armstrong's Hot Five and Hot Seven and Jelly Roll Morton's Red Hot Peppers. After a lull during the Depression years of the 1930s, when he ran a chicken farm with his brother, he was rediscovered in the 1940s. He revived his Creole Orchestra and performed and recorded until he retired in 1966 and settled in Hawaii, where he died in his mid-eighties.

◆

WHO WAS THE FIRST AFRICAN AMERICAN TO SING WITH A MAJOR SYMPHONY ORCHESTRA?

Roland Hayes was born in rural Georgia in 1887; his parents were struggling tenant farmers and former slaves. When he was thirteen his father died and the family moved to Chattanooga, Tennessee, where the young Hayes found work wherever he could as a laborer, farmhand, waiter, and messenger. He managed to earn enough money to enter Fisk University, and in 1911 toured with the Fisk Jubilee Singers. When the group reached Boston, Hayes decided to settle there. He studied voice and began performing as a concert singer.

In 1920 he traveled abroad, and for the next three years he sang in the major cities of Europe, becoming a celebrity in the music world and bringing spirituals to the international concert stage. Accounts of his concert at Buckingham Palace before King George V attracted the attention of American impresarios, who were interested in representing him when he returned to the United States. His groundbreaking performance with the Boston Symphony Orchestra in November 1923 evoked acclaim from critics, as did his recitals in New York City, where admirers packed the concert halls.

Through the 1940s Hayes was considered the world's preeminent concert tenor. In 1950 he was appointed to the music faculty of Boston University, and in 1962, at his seventy-fifth birthday concert in New York's Carnegie Hall, every seat was filled. Hayes died in 1976 at the age of eighty-nine.

♦

WHO WAS THE FIRST AFRICAN AMERICAN WOMAN TO BE INTERNATIONALLY RECOGNIZED AS A CHORAL DIRECTOR?

Eva Jessye was born in Coffeyville, Kansas, in 1895. From early childhood she had an innate understanding of music, and by the time she was twelve she had organized a girls' singing group. She met the composer Will Marion Cook when he brought a musical production to her town; Cook was to become her mentor.

After studying in Kansas and Oklahoma, Jessye went to New York in 1922 to work with Cook. She organized the Eva Jessye Choir, a leading choral group that performed widely. In 1929 Jessye went to Hollywood to serve as choral director of the all-black film *Hallelujah!,* and in 1934 she filled the same role for the Virgil Thomson opera *Four Saints in Three Acts.* A year later she directed the chorus for the first production of George Gershwin's opera *Porgy and Bess,* traveling with the company from Broadway to England, Germany, Russia, and Australia.

The first African American woman to succeed as a professional choir director, Jessye, who died in 1992, directed the chorus for a number of operas and composed several choral works, including *Paradise Lost and Regained* and *The Chronicle of Job.*

◆

WHAT AFRICAN AMERICAN SINGER WAS THE FIRST TO PERFORM WITH A EUROPEAN OPERA COMPANY?

The famed singer Lillian Evanti was born Annie Lillian Evans in 1890 in Washington, D.C. Her mother, a music teacher, discovered that the child had a lovely voice. When she was only four, she gave her first solo performance. But Lillian chose to study education in college, and after graduation became a kindergarten teacher. Soon, however, she enrolled in Howard University to pursue a music degree. In 1918 she married one of her professors, Roy W. Tibbs, and created a new professional name by combining her name with his.

Evanti gave concerts in Washington for several years and in 1925 traveled to France, where she was awarded a contract with the Paris Opera. She made her debut singing the title role in Delibes's *Lakmé.* When she came home for a visit, her successes abroad were praised by local newspapers but her race was not mentioned.

Evanti continued to perform in operas throughout Europe, not returning to the United States until the early 1930s. She sang at the White House in 1934 for President and Mrs. Roosevelt, and later gave concerts for Presidents Eisenhower and Truman. During

the 1940s and '50s Evanti toured Latin American countries as a
goodwill ambassador for the United States. She died in 1967.

◆

WHO WAS THE FIRST MUSICIAN TO INTRODUCE SCAT SINGING?

The renowned jazz trumpeter Louis Armstrong introduced scat
singing—using the voice as an instrument by substituting non-
sense sounds for words—on an Okeh recording of "Heebie Jeebies"
with the Hot Five band in 1926. Armstrong was born in New Orleans; he claimed the date was July 4, 1900, although his baptismal
certificate lists his birth date as August 4, 1901. Growing up in
poverty, he spent most of his childhood on the streets. A family named Karnofsky, who had hired him to work on their junk
wagon, loaned him money to buy a cornet. When he was about

**LOUIS ARMSTRONG
(THIRD FROM RIGHT) WITH KING OLIVER'S CREOLE JAZZ BAND**

twelve he was arrested for firing a pistol in the air to celebrate New Year's Eve and sent to the Colored Waifs Home. There he was taught to read music and played the cornet in a band.

After young Armstrong's release from the home, he supported himself at various jobs until 1918, when he was befriended by Joe "King" Oliver, a cornetist who led a popular jazz band. Armstrong played cornet on Mississippi riverboats and with the Kid Ory band for a time, and then traveled to Chicago in 1922 to join King Oliver's Creole Jazz Band. He ended up marrying Lil Hardin, a piano player and arranger for the band, who urged him to leave King Oliver. He took her advice and went to New York City to play with Fletcher Henderson. That was when he switched to trumpet and began vocalizing in his distinctive husky voice and demonstrating his scat singing style.

The outstanding recordings of Armstrong's Hot Five and Hot Seven groups in the mid-1920s were to make him a historic figure in jazz history. Known by his nickname "Satchmo," he grew to be an international star, attracting wide audiences around the world; he was referred to as America's Ambassador of Jazz. In 1942 he and his new wife, Lucille, bought a house in the New York town of Corona, Queens, where they lived for the rest of their lives. There, when he wasn't performing, Armstrong wrote memoirs, essays, articles, and letters. He died in his sleep on July 6, 1971. Although he and Lil Hardin were divorced in 1938, she played at a memorial service held in his honor in Chicago. On stage, during her performance, Hardin collapsed and died.

◆

WHO WAS THE FIRST WOMAN TO LEAD AN ALL-MALE JAZZ BAND?

Blanche Calloway was the older sister of the famous bandleader and scat singer, Cab Calloway. Born in 1902 in Baltimore, Blanche sang in the choir of the church where her mother was an organist, and studied music at Morgan State College. But her yearning to be an entertainer soon took over; she dropped out and began performing in clubs and stage shows. In 1923 she joined the touring company of the groundbreaking musical *Shuffle Along* and appeared in the James P. Johnson show *Plantation Days*. She left that show in Chicago to become a nightclub entertainer there and was joined by her younger brother Cab. Together, they sang and led a band.

Calloway started making records in 1925, and over the next ten years she recorded for several labels. She worked at the Ciro Club in New York City and joined the Andy Kirk band. After parting ways with Kirk in 1931, Calloway became the leader of her own all-male band, Blanche Calloway and her Joy Boys, delighting audiences with her combination of conducting, singing, and dancing. The group lasted seven years, and in 1940 she organized an all-female big band. She later moved to Washington, D.C., where she managed nightclubs and directed the career of singer Ruth Brown. In Miami, Florida, where she eventually settled, Calloway embarked on a lengthy career as a radio disc jockey. She died in 1978 in Baltimore, where she had spent the last years of her life.

♦

WHO FOUNDED THE FIRST GOSPEL PUBLISHING COMPANY?

Thomas A. Dorsey, the foremost composer of gospel music, wrote his first successful gospel song, "If You See My Saviour," in 1929 and founded his publishing company, Dorsey House, three years later. Dorsey, born in 1899 in Villa Rica, Georgia, was the son of a country preacher. By the age of twelve, he had become a skilled piano player, and five years later he went to Chicago, where he studied composing and arranging.

As a young musician known as "Georgia Tom," Dorsey played blues piano in saloons and bordellos in and around Chicago. It is said that at the 1921 National Baptist Convention, he heard Charles A. Tindley's gospel song "I Do, Don't You" and decided to turn to composing sacred music. If so, it wasn't long before he returned to the blues. His first hit, "Riverside Blues," was recorded by King Oliver's Creole Jazz Band in 1923. He played for blues singer Ma Rainey's band for a time but returned to religion after the death of a close friend, an event that inspired his first gospel song, "If You See My Saviour." He founded his gospel publishing company, Dorsey House, three years later in 1932.

Dorsey's best-known gospel song, "Precious Lord, Take My Hand," was made famous by Mahalia Jackson, who toured with Dorsey for several years. The song was inspired by a tragic loss that Dorsey suffered when his wife died in childbirth and their baby passed away a day later. In the 1930s Dorsey's music began spreading across the land, and by the time he died in 1993 at the age of ninety-four, he had written more than 1,000 gospel songs.

◆

WHO WAS THE FIRST AFRICAN AMERICAN WOMAN TO BE RECOGNIZED AS A COMPOSER?

Florence Price was born in Little Rock, Arkansas, in 1888. When she was still a baby, she moved to Chicago with her father, a dentist, and her mother, a singer and pianist. She took her first piano lessons from her mother and also learned to play organ and violin. After high school, Price enrolled in the New England Conservatory of Music, where she studied composition and organ and wrote a string trio and a symphony.

Back in Little Rock, she taught music at a local college and gave private lessons, but racial unrest caused her to move with her family to Chicago in 1927. A symphony she composed won an award in a music competition in 1932, and a year later it was performed by the Chicago Symphony Orchestra at the Chicago World's Fair.

Price wrote symphonies, concertos, art songs, chamber pieces, and arrangements of black spirituals; she was especially known for her adaptation of "My Soul's Been Anchored in the Lord." As the first African American woman to gain recognition as a composer, her works were performed by instrumentalists, orchestras, and singers throughout the country. But after her death in 1953, her compositions were largely forgotten.

◆

WHO WAS THE FIRST AFRICAN AMERICAN SINGER
TO APPEAR WITH A MAJOR OPERA COMPANY?

In July 1933, Catarina Jarboro, a soprano, sang the title role in Verdi's opera *Aida* with the Chicago Civic Opera at the Hippodrome Theater in New York City. Long before she became the first African American prima donna of an opera company, Jarboro had sung in the chorus of two popular musicals of the early 1920s: *Shuffle Along* and *Runnin' Wild*. She later traveled abroad to study voice and stayed for seven years, performing to acclaim throughout Europe and making her operatic debut at the Puccini Theater in Milan.

Reports of Jarboro's great success reached the United States, and she finally returned to make her American operatic debut. When she appeared in *Aida,* the theater was filled with opera fans, both black and white, who showered her with applause and flowers as she knelt on stage after the final curtain. But Jarboro was unsuccessful in establishing a career in the United States; she returned to Europe where she continued to perform in leading opera houses. She died in 1986, and in December 1999 she was honored with a star on the Walk of Fame in Wilmington, North Carolina, where she was born in 1898.

◆

WHAT WAS THE FIRST BROADWAY OPERA
WITH AN AFRICAN AMERICAN CAST?

An unusual opera entitled *Four Saints in Three Acts* opened in Hartford, Connecticut, in February 1934 with a cast that was made up completely of African American singers. Composed by Virgil Thomson and written by Gertrude Stein, the opera was about Spanish saints of the sixteenth century. It featured beautiful settings and costumes, colorful lyrics that made little sense, and performers who moved in a dramatic, stylized manner. The opera starred Edward Matthews as St. Ignatius, and the chorus was trained by the African-American choir director Eva Jessye.

Four Saints in Three Acts moved to Broadway, where it ran for sixty performances, making it the longest-running modern American opera to that date. Over the years it was revived several times.

◆

WHO WAS THE FIRST AFRICAN AMERICAN TO CONDUCT A MAJOR SYMPHONY ORCHESTRA?

Born in Woodville, Mississippi, in 1895 and raised in Little Rock, Arkansas, William Grant Still studied violin as a child, but he enrolled in Ohio's Wilberforce University planning to major in science and become a doctor. Soon, however, he formed a string quartet, began writing his own compositions, and became director of the college band. He left Wilberforce to play in dance bands, and in 1916 was hired by the publishing company owned by W. C. Handy and Charles Pace while also playing in Handy's band. He enrolled in the Oberlin College Conservatory of Music in 1917, taking a year off to serve in the navy, and then went to New York,

WILLIAM GRANT STILL

where he worked as musical director of Pace's record company and played the oboe in the 1921 show *Shuffle Along*.

While studying at the New England Conservatory of Music and with the French composer Edgar Varese, Still begin composing large-scale works in the mid-1920s. In 1931 his *Afro-American Symphony* was performed by the Rochester Philharmonic; it was the first time a major symphony orchestra had performed a work by an African American composer. Four years later the symphony received its New York premiere when it was played by the New York Philharmonic in Carnegie Hall.

As his career developed, Still continued to make history in the world of concert music. In 1936 he became the first African American to conduct a major symphony orchestra when he led the Los Angeles Philharmonic in a concert of his own works. At radio station WNBC he was the first African American to direct a white radio orchestra. And his opera *Troubled Island* was the first by a black composer to be performed by a major opera company, the New York City Opera, in 1949. In all, Still composed five symphonies, six operas, four ballets, and many other works.

◆

WHO WAS THE FIRST AFRICAN AMERICAN VOCALIST TO SING WITH A WHITE ORCHESTRA?

Lena Horne was only sixteen when she was hired for the chorus line at Harlem's Cotton Club. Dancing with twelve other young women, she made twenty-five dollars a week, which went to support her family. Born in Brooklyn in 1917, she left high school to work at the famous nightclub, where she stayed until 1935, when she became a vocalist with Noble Sissle's orchestra. After a road tour with Sissle, she joined Charlie Barnet's popular band, becoming the first African American to sing with a white orchestra.

In 1941 Horne went to Hollywood. Singing at the opening of a new nightclub, she was noticed by a scout from the MGM movie studio, which offered her a contract. She appeared in the all-black movies *Cabin in the Sky* and *Stormy Weather* and later was given singing parts in white movies. By design, her scenes had nothing to do with the story and could be cut from the film when it was shown in the South.

Horne's Hollywood career gradually faded, and in 1957 she was beckoned to Broadway, where she was featured in the musical *Jamaica*. She continued to perform, make records, and appear on television. In 1981 she won a Tony award for her Broadway show *Lena Horne—The Lady and Her Music*. She was eighty-one when she released the album *Being Myself,* a collection of ten songs. In January 2006, Blue Note released *Seasons of a Life*, an album containing ten previously unreleased performances recorded during the 1990s, including such Horne classics as "Stormy Weather" and "Willow Weep for Me."

In a message of condolence after her death in 2010, President Obama said Horne had "worked tirelessly to further the cause of justice and equality."

◆

WHO WAS THE FIRST FULL-TIME AFRICAN AMERICAN CONDUCTOR OF SYMPHONIC MUSIC?

Born in New York's Harlem in 1915 to West Indian parents, Dean Dixon was introduced to classical music as a child when his mother took him to concerts at Carnegie Hall. He began violin lessons at an early age and organized his own amateur musical groups, the Dean Dixon Symphony Orchestra and the Dean Dixon Choral Society, while he was still a student at DeWitt Clinton High School.

Dixon earned a bachelor's degree from the Juilliard School of Music and a master's from Columbia Teacher's College. In 1941 he made his first appearance as a conductor of a major orchestra when he led the NBC Summer Symphony in two concerts. He later conducted the New York Philharmonic, the Philadelphia Orchestra, and the Boston Symphony. But by the late 1940s, conducting opportunities in the United States had all but disappeared, and Dixon traveled abroad to do concerts in Paris. He settled in Europe, where he developed a distinguished career, serving as musical director of orchestras in Sweden, Germany, and Australia. In 1970 Dixon returned to his native country to conduct the New York Philharmonic in Central Park, attracting an audience of 75,000 music lovers. He died six years later in Switzerland.

♦

WHO WAS THE FIRST AFRICAN AMERICAN SINGER TO WIN THE NAUMBERG AWARD?

In 1944 the contralto Carol Brice became the first African American musician to win the prestigious Walter Naumberg award, which is presented to young performers with outstanding talent. A year later she made her Town Hall debut in New York City, garnering praise from critics.

Brice was born in 1918 in Sedalia, North Carolina, to a musical family; her parents were singers and her two brothers became professional musicians. She studied at Talledega College in Alabama and the Juilliard School of Music in New York. After winning the Naumberg award, she toured extensively as a soloist. She also appeared in musicals, including *Finian's Rainbow* in 1960 and *Show Boat* a year later.

Brice reached a turning point in her lengthy performing career in 1974, when she and her husband, baritone Thomas Carey, became professors at the University of Oklahoma, where they founded a regional opera company. In 1977 a recording of *Porgy and Bess* on which she sang was awarded a Grammy. Brice died in 1985 in Norman, Oklahoma.

♦

WHO WAS THE FIRST AFRICAN AMERICAN MAN TO SING A LEADING ROLE WITH A MAJOR OPERA COMPANY?

In 1945 the baritone Todd Duncan made his debut with the New York City Opera, singing the role of Tonio in *Il Pagliacci*, thus becoming the first African American man to sing with a major opera company. Duncan, born in Danville, Kentucky, in 1903, sang in an all-black production of *Cavalleria Rusticana* at New York's Mecca Temple in 1934. A year later he was cast in the role of Porgy in George Gershwin's opera *Porgy and Bess,* and recreated the role in the opera's 1942 revival.

Duncan made his concert debut in 1944 at New York's Town Hall, and after his 1945 performance in *Il Pagliacci* he sang a leading role at the New York City Opera in Bizet's *Carmen.* In addition to his operatic performances, he gave concerts throughout the world and served on the music faculty of Howard University. In 1950 Duncan won a Tony and a New York Drama Critics award for his role of the minister in *Lost in the Stars.* After a twenty-five-year singing career, he continued to teach. A student was waiting downstairs for a lesson when Duncan died at his Washington home at the age of ninety-five.

◆

WHEN DID AN AFRICAN AMERICAN WOMAN SING A LEADING ROLE WITH A MAJOR OPERA COMPANY?

When the accomplishments of African American opera singers are recounted, Marian Anderson is often considered the first to sing with a major opera company. It is true that Anderson was the first African American woman to sing at the Metropolitan Opera, but, almost a decade earlier, in 1946, Camilla Williams, a lyric soprano, made her debut with the New York City Opera as the heroine of Puccini's *Madame Butterfly.*

Williams was born in 1919 in Danville, Virginia, the daughter of a chauffeur and a domestic worker. She was raised in a musical family, and by the age of eight, she was singing in her church choir. She earned a bachelor's degree in music education from the Virginia State College for Negroes, now Virginia State University, and taught for a year in a Danville elementary school until she went to Philadelphia to study with a well-known voice teacher.

Williams embarked on a career as a concert singer, and in 1944, she was discovered by the renowned soprano Geraldine Farrar, who helped her secure a recording contract and a manager and audition for the New York City Opera. After singing the lead in

CAMILLA WILLIAMS

Madame Butterfly to enthusiastic reviews, Williams performed with the company regularly until 1954. She also appeared with other opera companies and soloed with orchestras. But although she was the first African American woman to sing with a major opera company, she never sang at the Met, and she never gained the fame of Marian Anderson, who was her friend.

"The lack of recognition for my accomplishments used to bother me," Williams said in a 1995 interview, "but you cannot cry over these things. There is no place for bitterness in singing. It works on the cords and ruins the voice."

She died in February 2012 in Bloomington, Indiana, where she was an emeritus professor of voice at Indiana University.

◆

MAHALIA JACKSON

WHO WAS THE FIRST GOSPEL SINGER TO GAIN INTERNATIONAL FAME?

Before she was five years old, Mahalia Jackson was singing in the choir of her Baptist church in New Orleans, where she was born in 1911. Her father, a devout preacher who worked on the New Orleans docks during the week, allowed only religious music to be played in his home. After her mother died, young Mahalia went to live with an equally religious aunt, and she was strongly affected by the powerful, rhythmic singing of the sanctified church congregation next door.

When she was sixteen, Jackson moved to Chicago to live with another aunt. Working as a maid and laundress to support herself, she became an active member of the Greater Salem Baptist Church and joined a gospel group. She soon began performing alone, singing in African American churches around the country. She met the great gospel composer Thomas Dorsey, and the two sometimes performed together.

In 1934 Jackson made her first record, "God Gonna Separate the Wheat from the Tares," but it received little attention. She opened a beauty salon and a flower business and didn't record again until 1946, when she cut "Move On Up a Little Higher." The record was a hit, selling nearly two million copies, and it made her famous. She sang in concerts, appeared on the Ed Sullivan television show, and in 1950 made her debut in New York's Carnegie Hall. She toured Europe and had her own radio and television programs in Chicago.

After singing at a rally in Montgomery, Alabama, Jackson allied herself with Dr. Martin Luther King Jr. and became a fervent participant in the civil rights movement. During the 1963 March on Washington, her voice rang out in song from the steps of the Lincoln Memorial. After King was assassinated in 1968, she sang one of his favorite songs, "Precious Lord, Take My Hand," at his funeral. Jackson then retreated from public life, and died of a heart attack in 1972.

◆

WHAT AFRICAN AMERICAN SINGER WAS THE FIRST TO PERFORM WITH THE METROPOLITAN OPERA?

As a child, Marian Anderson sang in the choir of the Union Baptist Church in Philadelphia, where she was born in 1897. In her teens she became the student of a distinguished voice teacher; members of her church collected money to pay for her lessons. After giving recitals in Philadelphia and New York, Anderson traveled to Europe, where she studied and gave concerts in several countries. A spellbinding performance in Salzburg in 1935 moved the conductor Toscanini to remark, "A voice like yours comes once in a century."

Six months later, Anderson returned to the United States for

MARIAN ANDERSON

a highly acclaimed concert at New York's Town Hall. Critics hailed her as one of the "greatest singers of our time," and she was invited to sing at the White House for President and Mrs. Roosevelt. Despite Anderson's many triumphs, in 1939, because of her race, she was barred by the Daughters of the American Revolution from singing in Washington, D.C.'s Constitution Hall. Outraged by this insult to the great singer, Eleanor Roosevelt resigned from the DAR in protest and sponsored an Easter Sunday concert on the grounds of the Lincoln Memorial, where Anderson received a tremendous outpouring of support from an audience of 75,000 people.

Although she performed hundreds of recitals around the country, opera houses were closed to her until January 7, 1955, when she sang the part of Ulrica in Verdi's *Un Ballo in Maschera* at the Metropolitan Opera House in New York City. She was the first African American to sing on the stage of the Met. Three years later, President Eisenhower appointed her delegate to the Thirteenth General Assembly of the United Nations. Further recognition came in 1963 when Anderson became the first African American woman to receive the Presidential Medal of Freedom, presented to her by President Lyndon Johnson. Anderson gave her farewell Carnegie Hall concert on Easter Sunday in 1965. Her autobiography, *My Lord, What a Morning,* was published in 1956. Anderson died in April 1993 at the age of ninety-six at the home of her nephew, the conductor James DePriest, in Portland, Oregon.

◆

WHO WAS THE FIRST AFRICAN AMERICAN MAN TO BE A FEATURED SINGER AT THE MET?

On January 27, 1955, three weeks after Marian Anderson made her Metropolitan Opera debut, Robert McFerrin appeared on the stage of the Met, singing the role of Amonasro in Verdi's *Aida.* McFerrin, born in 1921 in Marianna, Arkansas, grew up in St. Louis and studied music in Chicago and New York. A baritone, he began singing professionally in the 1940s.

McFerrin sang in Broadway musicals and with opera companies. In 1949 he appeared in the New York City Opera Company's production of *Troubled Island,* by the African American composer William Grant Still. After his Met debut in January 1955, he became the first African American to accept a permanent position with the Metropolitan Opera. McFerrin resigned from the Met in 1958 after being given only three roles in three years. He went to Hollywood, where he provided the singing voice for Sidney Poitier

ROBERT McFERRIN AS AMONASRO IN *AIDA*

in the movie *Porgy and Bess*, and became a voice teacher. In 1973 he returned to St. Louis, where he taught voice and spent the rest of his life. He died in November 2006. His son, Bobby McFerrin, gained renown as a vocalist and composer.

◆

JOHN BIRKS "DIZZY" GILLESPIE

WHO LED THE FIRST JAZZ BAND SENT ABROAD
BY THE STATE DEPARTMENT?

John Birks "Dizzy" Gillespie was born in Cheraw, South Carolina, in 1917. His father, who was a bricklayer, led a local band. Gillespie was just a youngster when he began learning to play the trumpet, and he was playing professionally while still in his teens. It is said that bandleader Teddy Hill gave Gillespie his nickname because of his eccentric clothing style and his love of practical jokes.

After joining Cab Calloway's band in 1939, he met saxophonist Charlie Parker in Kansas City and they began to work on the style that would soon be called bebop. Referring to Parker as "the other side of my heartbeat," Gillespie joined him in a quartet in 1945 that produced bop's most famous records. It is generally acknowledged that Gillespie, Parker, and Thelonius Monk founded the bebop movement.

Also in 1945, Gillespie formed the first of his big bands. He gradually became interested in Cuban rhythms and is considered the creator of Afro-Cuban jazz. In 1953 someone fell on his trumpet, bending it upward. Gillespie discovered he could hear its sound better that way. His tilted horn and ballooning cheeks became his trademarks.

In 1956 he put together a new big band and, at the request of the U.S. State Department, made a tour of the Middle East and South America. His was the first jazz band to be sent abroad by the United States government. His autobiography, *To Bop or Not to Bop*, came out in 1979, and he won Grammy awards in 1975 and 1980. He died of cancer in 1993. His wife, Lorraine, said one of his songs, "Dizzy's Dime," was playing on his tape player when he passed away in his sleep.

◆

WHO WAS THE FIRST JAZZ PIANIST TO GIVE A CONCERT IN CARNEGIE HALL?

Although Erroll Garner had no formal training and never learned to read music, he became one of the world's most popular jazz pianists. Born in Pittsburgh, Pennsylvania, in 1921, he was the youngest of five children. When he was not yet three years old, he started playing the piano; he could repeat the tunes he heard on his mother's records and those that the music teacher played for his older brother and sisters. As a youngster he performed on a local radio station and played in clubs and on riverboats, learning new tunes and styles by listening to professional pianists.

In 1944 Garner went to New York, where his lilting piano style won him a legion of fans. The first jazz musician to be represented by the leading impresario Sol Hurok, Garner toured widely in the United States and Europe. In 1950 he made his concert debut in the Cleveland Music Hall, and in 1958 he became the first jazz pianist to appear in concert at New York's Carnegie Hall. He continued to travel and record until 1975, when ill health forced him to retire. Garner died of lung cancer in Los Angeles in 1977 at the age of fifty-six. He is especially remembered for his composition "Misty." He said he was inspired to write the song when he saw a rainbow through an airplane window.

♦

WHICH AFRICAN AMERICAN MAN WAS THE FIRST TO WIN A GRAMMY?

The Grammy awards were created to recognize outstanding achievements in the music recording industry. Winners were awarded a trophy in the form of a small, gilded statuette of a gramophone. At the first Grammy ceremony in 1958, Count Basie won two awards—best performance by a dance band and best jazz performance—both for his album *Basie*.

William Basie was born in Red Bank, New Jersey, in 1904. Both of his parents were musicians, and his mother, a pianist, gave Basie his earliest lessons. He worked professionally for the first time as an accompanist for vaudeville acts, and by 1927, he was touring with a group that eventually broke up in Kansas City. He stayed in the city, playing first in a silent movie house and then with various bands. It was during this period that he became known as "Count" Basie. A band that he formed began broadcasting from a Kansas City radio station, and one of the broadcasts was heard by the jazz promoter John Hammond, who encouraged the group to move to New York. In 1937 the Basie band made its recording debut with Decca Records. Its recording of "One O'clock Jump" made the charts and became the band's theme song.

Anchored by Basie's piano, the band grew in popularity, becoming known throughout the world. During the 1940s and '50s, many famous musicians passed through its ranks. Basie won a total of eight Grammy awards throughout his career, as well as numerous

ERROLL GARNER

jazz polls, and was elected to the Down Beat Hall of Fame. He suffered a heart attack in 1976, and his health began to deteriorate. He died of cancer in 1984.

◆

WHO WAS THE FIRST AFRICAN AMERICAN WOMAN TO WIN A GRAMMY?

In 1958, in the first Grammy awards ceremony ever, the singer Ella Fitzgerald won two Grammys. She was given an award for best individual jazz performance for her album *Ella Fitzgerald Sings*

ELLA FITZGERALD

the Duke Ellington Song Book, and best female vocal performance for *Ella Fitzgerald Sings the Irving Berlin Song Book*. Called "the first lady of song," over the next thirty-two years Fitzgerald was to win eleven more Grammys as well as countless other awards.

Fitzgerald was born in Newport News, Virginia, in 1917. After her parents separated, she and her mother moved to Yonkers, New York. When she was a teenager, her mother died in a car accident, and she moved in with an aunt. It was a difficult time for the young girl; she began skipping school, her grades dropped, and, after getting into trouble, she was sent to reform school. She managed to escape, and made her way on her own.

When she was seventeen, Fitzgerald had a chance to compete in amateur night at the famed Apollo Theatre in Harlem. She sang Hoagy Carmichael's song "Judy" and, for an encore, "The Object of My Affection." The saxophonist Benny Carter was playing in the band that night, and, impressed with her talent, began introducing her to other musicians. The drummer and bandleader Chick Webb hired her to sing with his band, and in 1936 Decca released her first record *Love and Kisses*. In 1938 she recorded a version of the nursery rhyme "A-Tisket, A-Tasket"; it sold a million copies and made her famous. She worked with Louis Armstrong on several albums, and recorded a series of albums featuring the songs of composers such as Cole Porter and Rogers and Hart. She appeared in television variety shows and toured around the world.

In 1986 Fitzgerald had coronary bypass surgery, but kept performing. By the 1990s she had made more than 200 albums. She gave her final performance in 1991 in Carnegie Hall, and died in her California home five years later.

◆

WHO WAS THE FIRST AFRICAN AMERICAN SINGER TO PERFORM A LEADING ROLE AT THE MET ON OPENING NIGHT?

Known as the first African American diva, Leontyne Price sang major roles at opera houses throughout the world. Born in 1927 in Laurel, Mississippi, Price's career path was decided when, at the age of nine, her mother took her to a performance of the great singer Marian Anderson. Endowed with a glorious voice, Price earned a degree in music education from Central State College in Wilberforce, Ohio, and won a scholarship to study at the Juilliard School of Music in New York City. When he heard her sing in a student production, the composer Virgil Thomson chose her for a role in his all-black opera, *Four Saints in Three Acts.* She next appeared in a revival of *Porgy and Bess,* touring with the production throughout the world.

Price made her Paris debut in 1952, her New York debut at Town Hall in 1954, and performed at leading opera houses in San Francisco, Vienna, and Milan. In January 1961, Price finally reached the stage of New York's famed Metropolitan Opera as Leonora in Verdi's *Il Trovatore,* receiving a forty-two minute ovation from an ecstatic audience. And on the Met's opening night that fall, she sang the leading role in the Puccini opera *The Girl of the Golden*

West. She was the first African American singer to perform a leading role on an opening night at the Met.

Price retired from the opera stage in 1985 after a performance of *Aida* at the Metropolitan Opera. She continued to give recitals, making what she said would be her final public performance in 1998 in Chapel Hill, North Carolina. But on September 30, 2001, when she was seventy-four years old, Price came out of retirement to sing at a Carnegie Hall concert to honor the victims of the September 11 terror attack on the World Trade Center. The audience responded to her solo of "America the Beautiful" with a lengthy ovation.

♦

WHO WAS THE FIRST AFRICAN AMERICAN TO SING AT THE BAYREUTH FESTIVAL?

Prompting a storm of protest, the grandson of composer Richard Wagner chose the African American mezzo-soprano Grace Bumbry to sing the role of the traditionally blond Venus in the opera *Tannhauser* at the famed Wagner Festival in Bayreuth, Germany, in 1961. Bumbry's performance was a huge success, and she made headlines throughout the world.

Born in St. Louis, Missouri, in 1937, Bumbry sang in school and church choirs. After graduating from high school, she won first prize on the television talent program *The Arthur Godfrey Show* in 1954, singing a Verdi aria. She studied voice at Boston and Northwestern Universities, and made her operatic debut in 1969 with the Paris Opera Company in Verdi's *Aida.* She first performed at the Metropolitan Opera in 1965 in the opera *Don Carlos,* and in the 1970s and '80s she sang with several leading opera companies. In 1997 she gave a farewell operatic performance in *Elektra* in Lyons, France, but continued to sing in concerts and recitals, as well as teaching and judging competitions.

♦

WHO WAS THE FIRST AFRICAN AMERICAN COUNTRY MUSIC STAR?

When he was a child in the cotton-growing region of Sledge, Mississippi, where he was born in 1938, Charley Pride listened to country music every Saturday night on the radio show *Grand Ole Opry*. But Pride's first interest was baseball, and he played for several seasons with the Memphis Red Sox of the Negro Leagues.

Pride began making the switch to a country music career around 1960, when he sang between innings at baseball games. He signed a recording contract with RCA and cut his first record, "The Snakes Crawl at Night," in 1965. Two years later he became the first African

CHARLEY PRIDE

American singer to appear on the favorite show of his childhood, Nashville's *Grand Ole Opry*. In 1969 he first hit the number one spot on the singles charts with "All I Have to Offer You (Is Me)."

Pride went on to produce many more hit tunes, including "Kiss an Angel Good Morning" and "Mountain of Love," and became one of the top-selling country singers of all time. As that rarity— an African American country music singer—Pride said he developed his style from listening to such country stars as George Jones and Hank Williams, as well as African American blues singers B. B. King and Sam Cooke.

On May 1, 1993, Pride finally became a regular member of *Grand Ole Opry*, twenty-six years after first appearing there as a guest. He sang at a special performance hosted by President and Mrs. Clinton at the White House, and in 2000 he was inducted into the Country Music Hall of Fame. He continued to tour, and, along with several compilation albums of his greatest hits, released a studio recording, *Comfort of Her Wings*, in 2003.

Pride sang the national anthem before game five of the 2010 World Series, released an album of new recordings, *Choices*, in 2011, and in 2013, he was still touring.

◆

WHO WAS THE FIRST AFRICAN AMERICAN DIRECTOR OF A MAJOR ORCHESTRA?

Henry Lewis was born in Los Angeles in 1932 and, like many professional musicians, started piano lessons at an early age. He expanded his musical education, and by the time he reached sixteen he had become such an accomplished double bass player that he was hired to play with the Los Angeles Philharmonic Orchestra. Lewis served in the army in 1955 and '56, playing the bass in an army orchestra and conducting.

In 1961 Lewis made his professional debut as a conductor when he led the Los Angeles Philharmonic in two concerts. He was named musical director of the Los Angeles Opera Company in 1965, and three years later he left to become musical director of the New Jersey Symphony Orchestra, making him the first African American director of a major orchestra in the United States. In 1972 Lewis made his debut with the Metropolitan Opera, conducting Puccini's *La Boheme*. He was the first African American to lead an orchestra at the Met. He continued as director of the New Jersey Symphony until 1976 and toured as a guest conductor until his death at the age of sixty-three.

◆

WHO WAS THE FIRST AFRICAN AMERICAN WOMAN TO CONDUCT MAJOR SYMPHONY ORCHESTRAS?

Margaret Rosezarian Harris, a musician and educator, was the first African American woman to conduct the Los Angeles Symphony, the Chicago Philharmonic, and the orchestras of fourteen other cities. Born in Chicago in 1943, she gave her first recital

MARGARET ROSEZARIAN HARRIS

when she was three years old, playing eighteen short classical pieces and three encores from memory. Soon she began performing outside of Chicago, traveling as far as San Francisco. The touring stopped when she was six, and she entered school. At the age of ten, she played with the Chicago Symphony, and later won a scholarship to the Curtis Institute in Philadelphia, moving there with her mother. She went on to earn bachelor's and master's degrees from the Juilliard School of Music.

Harris continued to play piano recitals in the United States and abroad, but she gained more fame as a conductor. As well as leading symphony orchestras, she worked on Broadway as the music director of the musical *Hair,* in 1970. She also composed music, including an opera and two piano concertos. In February 2000, Harris was appointed associate dean of the Pennsylvania Academy of Music. But only one month later she suffered a heart attack and died.

♦

WHAT WAS THE FIRST RAP MUSIC HIT?

Hip-hop music leaped onto the national scene when "Rapper's Delight," a fifteen-minute rap song by the Sugarhill Gang, was released on October 13, 1979. The trio that made up the Sugarhill Gang were Henry "Big Bank Hank" Jackson, Guy "Master Gee" O'Brien, and Michael "Wonder Mike" Wright. They were put together by Sylvia Robinson, owner of Sugarhill Records in Englewood, New Jersey. When she spotted Henry Jackson, a native of the Bronx, he was working in a pizza shop in Englewood and managing another rap singer. She asked Jackson if he wanted to make a record, and he quickly rounded up his two companions.

Although completely improvised and recorded in one take, "Rapper's Delight" changed the world of hip-hop, paving the way for future rap musicians. It became a huge success, selling many millions of copies. The Sugarhill Gang recorded a few more songs, but they were never to equal "Rapper's Delight." The group finally disbanded in 1985.

♦

WHO WAS THE FIRST WOMAN INDUCTED INTO
THE ROCK AND ROLL HALL OF FAME?

The Rock and Roll Hall of Fame, with headquarters in Cleveland, Ohio, began inducting members in 1986, and a year later installed its first woman—the famed singer Aretha Franklin. Notoriously shy and afraid of flying, Franklin did not attend the January 1987 induction ceremony; her award was accepted by her brother, the Rev. Cecil Franklin. When musician Keith Richards announced that "Lady Soul" would be the first woman in the Hall of Fame, the crowd that had gathered to attend the ceremony roared its approval.

Aretha Louise Franklin was born in 1942 in Memphis, Tennessee, and grew up in Detroit, where her father, the Rev. C. L. Franklin, was pastor of the New Bethel Baptist Church. Young Aretha, who played piano for the church choir and sang in a gospel quartet, performed her first church solo at the age of twelve and recorded her first single at about the same time for Chess Records.

In 1960 Franklin decided to move to New York City and try to make it as a singer. She was soon signed by Columbia Records, which issued her 1961 album, *Aretha*. She recorded a total of nine albums in a range of styles for Columbia before her contract ran out in 1966 and she was signed by Atlantic Records, where she began to focus on rhythm and blues. At Atlantic, where she was encouraged to freely express her gospel piano style, Franklin came into her own as a great soul singer. Her recordings of "I Never Loved a Man" and "Respect" hit the top of the charts. Her albums for Atlantic, *I Never Loved a Man* and *Lady Soul,* are considered soul masterpieces. Her career had its ups and downs during the 1970s and '80s, but she produced two major albums, *Amazing Grace* and *Who's Zoomin' Who?,* and many of her best numbers for Atlantic were collected in a four-CD set. Franklin won her eighteenth Grammy award in 2008 for her duet with Mary J. Blige, "Never Gonna Break My Faith." That same year *Rolling Stone* magazine ranked her number one on its list of the 100 greatest singers of all time. On January 20, 2009, she gave a riveting performance of "My Country, 'Tis of Thee" as she sang before millions of people at the inauguration of President Barack Obama.

◆

WHO WAS THE FIRST AFRICAN AMERICAN MUSICIAN TO WIN THE NAUMBERG PIANO COMPETITION?

In May 1992, twenty-six-year-old Awadagin Pratt won first prize in the Naumberg International Piano Competition, held at New York City's Lincoln Center. The award created a wave of interest sparked not only by Pratt's outstanding talent, but also by his long dreadlocks, the jeans and casual shirts he wore when performing, and the small lamp table he sat on instead of a piano bench. Pratt had already distinguished himself as the first student in the history of Baltimore's Peabody Conservatory to earn diplomas in three areas: piano, violin, and conducting.

Pratt was born in Henderson, Texas, in 1966, and moved with his family to Normal, Illinois, when his parents became professors at Illinois State University. He was still a child when they intro-

AWADAGIN PRATT

duced him to classical music and gave him lessons in piano and violin. His father, a native of Sierra Leone, had been an organist in his youth. At sixteen, Pratt entered the University of Illinois on a violin scholarship, later transferring to the Peabody Conservatory, where he studied for six years.

As the winner of the Naumberg competition, Pratt was granted a two-year tour of the United States as guest soloist with several top orchestras, and a debut recording. When asked in a radio interview if he regarded himself as a role model, Pratt said that as an African American in a white male profession, he would "try to do what I believe in and not be swayed."

Pratt went on to make several records and to perform with orchestras in the United States and abroad. He occasionally returned to his early love of conducting, and in June 2001 he led the National Symphony Orchestra in Beethoven's Eighth Symphony at the Kennedy Center in Washington. In 2004 Pratt joined the faculty of the College-Conservatory of Music at the University of Cincinnati as assistant professor of piano.

His Pratt Music Foundation was formed in 1997 to support talented young music students in the Bloomington/Normal area of Illinois. By the end of 2012, the foundation had provided two hundred and two scholarships.

RELIGION

WHO WAS THE FOUNDER AND FIRST BISHOP OF THE AFRICAN METHODIST EPISCOPAL CHURCH?

Born in 1760 to parents who were slaves, Richard Allen grew up in Delaware, where he developed a Christian faith so strong that he was able to convert his owner, who had allowed him to study religion. Allen purchased his freedom and eventually settled in Philadelphia, where he preached at St. George's Methodist

BISHOP RICHARD ALLEN

Episcopal Church. The church had a white congregation, but Allen encouraged African Americans to join.

Most white churches of the time forced black communicants to sit in certain pews at the back of the church or in the gallery. One Sunday morning in 1787, when Allen and his colleague, Absalom Jones, were kneeling in prayer, a trustee insisted that they move to the rear of the church. The two African American leaders walked out of St. George's and never returned. That same year they formed the Free African Society, a mutual aid organization that later built the St. Thomas African Episcopal Church, naming Jones as its pastor.

Allen gathered his own congregation and formed the Bethel African Methodist Episcopal Church, which was dedicated in 1794 in a blacksmith shop hauled to the site by horses. The ground on which the church was created, and where the current Bethel Church now stands, is the oldest piece of property in the United States continually owned by African Americans.

African Methodist Episcopal Churches sprang up around Pennsylvania, Maryland, Delaware, and New Jersey, eventually uniting in 1816 to form a separate branch of Methodism with Richard Allen as its first bishop.

◆

WHO WAS THE FIRST AFRICAN AMERICAN EPISCOPAL PRIEST IN THE UNITED STATES?

Absalom Jones, a deeply religious former slave from Delaware, bought his freedom and settled in Philadelphia, where he and his colleague Richard Allen formed the Free African Society, a mutual aid society for African Americans. Both men worshipped at St. George's Methodist Episcopal Church, but after being told they could not sit in the front pews they left the congregation and decided to start an African American church. Jones, however, preferred the Anglican religious tradition, whereas Allen was a Methodist.

Although they remained friends, the two took separate paths. Jones organized the St. Thomas Protestant Episcopal Church in 1794 and became its first pastor. He was the first African American in the nation to be ordained as an Episcopal priest.

◆

WHAT WAS THE FIRST AFRICAN AMERICAN
ORDER OF CATHOLIC NUNS?

In July 1829 in Baltimore, four black women—two from Haiti, one from Baltimore, and one from Cuba—took their vows as nuns. Sister Mary Elizabeth Lange, whose parents were born in Haiti and who immigrated to Baltimore from Cuba, became the order's mother superior.

Soon after arriving in Baltimore, Lange started a school in her home, for children of Haitian refugees. A priest, Father Joubert, hearing of the school, approached Lange with the idea of founding a religious community that would concentrate on education. The four women made their vows and formed the Oblate Sisters of Providence. The sisters established a school and orphanage and were praised for their service to the poor during a cholera epidemic in 1832. The order expanded to several states and Latin American countries.

◆

WHO WAS THE FIRST AFRICAN AMERICAN
CATHOLIC PRIEST AND BISHOP?

James Augustine Healy was born on a Georgia cotton plantation in 1830. His father, an Irish immigrant, had challenged the state's laws by marrying Healy's mother, a slave. Since James and his siblings were considered slaves, they were forbidden to attend school. Their parents sent the youngsters north to attend Quaker schools in New York and New Jersey. They went on to Holy Cross College in Massachusetts, where James was valedictorian of his graduating class. Deciding to become a Catholic priest, he attended seminaries in Montreal and Paris, and was ordained in 1854 at the Cathedral of Notre Dame in Paris.

When Healy returned to the United States, it was as the first African American Catholic priest in the country. He was assigned to parishes in Boston, where he became known for his work with needy youngsters. His generous efforts on behalf of destitute and troubled people brought him to the attention of Pope Pius IX, who in 1875 named him Bishop of Portland, Maine—the first African

American Catholic bishop in the United States. In his twenty-five years as bishop, Healy established sixty new churches, sixty-eight missions, and eighteen convents, and worked to give autonomy to Native American tribes and to end child labor.

Healy's brother, Patrick Francis, also had a distinguished career. He was the first African American to earn a Ph.D. and was president of Georgetown University from 1873 to 1881.

◆

WHO WAS THE FIRST AFRICAN AMERICAN CHAPLAIN COMMISSIONED IN THE ARMY?

Bishop Henry McNeal Turner was born free in South Carolina in 1834. He studied for the ministry and joined the Methodist Church, later transferring to the African Methodist Episcopal Church.

BISHOP HENRY McNEAL TURNER

Starting as an itinerant preacher, Turner soon became a prominent minister. In 1863 President Lincoln appointed him the first African American chaplain in the United States Army.

Turner was not only an outstanding clergyman, he also rose to prominence in politics. In 1867 the National Republican Committee assigned him to supervise the political organization of African Americans in Georgia, and that same year he was elected to the State Constitutional Convention. The following year he won a seat in the state legislature, but in 1869 all African American legislators were illegally removed. He served briefly as postmaster of Macon, and in 1870 was again elected to the legislature.

During the 1870s Turner became increasingly disillusioned about the future for African Americans in the United States, and began arguing for black migration to Haiti or Africa. In 1880 he was named the twelfth African Methodist Episcopal bishop of Georgia, and he served for twelve years as chancellor of Morris Brown College in Atlanta. He died in 1915 in Windsor, Canada.

◆

WHO WAS THE FIRST AFRICAN AMERICAN MINISTER TO PREACH BEFORE THE HOUSE OF REPRESENTATIVES?

Although Henry Highland Garnet was only twenty-four years old when he went to Troy, New York, to serve as a minister, his life had been marked by many dramatic events. Garnet was born in 1815 in Maryland, where his family were slaves. When he was a child his father, pretending to be traveling to a funeral, got passes for his family to leave the plantation. The Garnets escaped into Delaware, and with help from an antislavery advocate they were able to reach New York City.

There, young Henry studied at the African Free School and then accepted an invitation to attend Noyes Academy in Canaan, New Hampshire. Soon after Garnet and two friends arrived at the school, local farmers destroyed the building. Garnet ended up at the Oneida Institute in Whitesboro, New York, where he gained a reputation as a brilliant student.

When Garnet went to Troy in 1839, it was to serve as pastor of the Liberty Street Presbyterian Church and to start a school for African American children. Active in the Underground Railroad in Rensselaer County and a passionate spokesman for African American freedom, Garnet was invited to speak at a national convention in 1843 in Buffalo, New York, at which black Americans gathered from throughout the country to find ways to end slavery. Garnet made an eloquent plea for African Americans to resist slavery, by armed rebellion if necessary. By 1849 he was supporting emigration to Africa. In 1881, Garnet traveled to Africa as minister to Liberia; he died in Monrovia two months after his arrival.

◆

WHAT WAS THE FIRST SEMINARY FOR TRAINING AFRICAN AMERICAN PRIESTS?

At the turn of the century, a Catholic priest, Father Aloysius Heick, left Illinois and traveled to Mississippi, intending to open a mission chapel and an industrial arts school for African Americans in the town of Merigold. But opposition to his plan was so intense that he was forced to leave, and the project was abandoned.

Heick moved to Vicksburg, Mississippi, and in 1905 his order, the Society of the Divine Word, asked the Vatican for permission to start a seminary to train African American priests and brothers. Permission finally was granted in 1920. The first seminary, called Sacred Heart College, was opened in Greenville, Mississippi, with fourteen students.

In 1923 the seminary moved to Bay St. Louis, Mississippi, and was renamed St. Augustine's Mission House. The first African American priests were ordained in 1934, and that same year the first black candidates for brothers enrolled in the seminary. Although some black priests had been trained in integrated seminaries before St. Augustine's was established, it was the first set up exclusively to train African American Catholic clergy.

◆

WHEN DID THE EPISCOPAL CHURCH ORDAIN ITS FIRST AFRICAN AMERICAN WOMAN PRIEST?

Pauli Murray was born Anna Pauline Murray in Baltimore in 1910. When she was only three her mother died, and she went to live in Durham, North Carolina, where she was raised by her grandparents and an aunt, a first-grade teacher who taught the little girl to read. She graduated at the top of her high school class, and from Hunter College with honors. But the University of North Carolina law school refused to admit her because she was African American, and Harvard University turned her down because she was a woman.

She earned a law degree from Howard University, a master's in law from the University of California at Berkeley, and a doctorate from Yale. Active in the civil rights movement and a founder of the National Organization for Women, Murray was a civil rights lawyer, professor, poet, college vice president, and a deputy attorney general of California. In 1956 she published a memoir, *Proud Shoes: The Story of an American Family,* and her book *Dark Testament and Other Poems* came out in 1970.

After deciding to enter the ministry, Murray earned a divinity degree and in 1977 became the first African American woman to be ordained a priest in the Episcopal Church. Murray died in 1985. Her autobiography, *Song in a Weary Throat,* was published two years later.

◆

WHO WAS THE FIRST AFRICAN AMERICAN WOMAN BISHOP OF A MAJOR RELIGIOUS ORGANIZATION?

Leontine Kelly was born in 1920 in Washington, D.C., where her father was a Methodist minister. Before she was ten years old, the family moved to Cincinnati, and her mother cofounded the local Urban League. Kelly graduated from Virginia Union University and later earned a divinity degree from Union Theological Seminary in Richmond, Virginia. A schoolteacher at first, Kelly entered the ministry after the 1969 death of her husband, who had been minister of a Methodist church in Virginia.

In 1984 she was elected a bishop of the United Methodist Church, the first African American woman to hold this position in a major denomination. She was consecrated in a multicultural ceremony in Boise, Idaho, attended by one thousand African Americans, Latinos, Native Americans, and whites. She served as resident bishop of the United Methodist Church for the San Francisco Bay area until her retirement in 1988, when she became a visiting professor at the Pacific School of Religion in Berkeley.

In November 2000, responding to the election of three more African American bishops in her church, the eighty-year-old Kelly said: "I will always be the first African American woman bishop of the United Methodist Church, but praise God I am no longer the only."

After Kelly died in June 2012 at the age of ninety-two, M. Garlinda Burton, an African American woman who was an executive at the United Methodist General Commission on the Status and Role of Women, said, "Bishop Kelly is one of the reasons I'm in leadership in the church right now. She has been a standard-bearer for women of color in leadership, and there will be no one like her, ever."

◆

WHEN DID THE EPISCOPAL CHURCH ORDAIN ITS FIRST WOMAN BISHOP?

In February 1989, the Reverend Barbara Clementine Harris was consecrated a suffragan bishop of the Episcopal Diocese of Massachusetts, making her the first woman bishop in the Anglican Communion—a worldwide organization of churches derived from the Church of England.

Harris, who grew up in Philadelphia, was an early participant in the activities of her local church, starting a youth group there when she was still a teenager. After high school she attended a school of advertising and journalism and went on to hold jobs in public relations. Eventually, Harris made a decision to enter the ministry. She studied at Villanova University and in England and was ordained an Episcopal priest in 1980.

A member of the Union of Black Episcopalians, Harris became

BISHOP BARBARA CLEMENTINE HARRIS

active in many organizations, including the Prisoner Visitation and Support Committee and the National Episcopal AIDS Coalition. As a priest, Harris was an eloquent spokesperson for the rights of women, poor people, and African Americans and other minorities. But because she was a woman, she had to overcome strong opposition from some conservative church members when she was named an Episcopal bishop. Harris retired from the Episcopal Diocese of Massachusetts in November 2002, and the next summer she began serving as an assisting bishop in the diocese of Washington, D.C., a position she filled until 2007.

◆

WHEN DID THE CONFERENCE OF CATHOLIC BISHOPS ELECT ITS FIRST AFRICAN AMERICAN PRESIDENT?

Just after he was elected president of the United States Conference of Catholic Bishops in November 2001, Bishop Wilton D. Gregory said that he regarded his election as "an expression of love of the Catholic Church for people of color."

Bishop Gregory, born in 1947 on Chicago's South Side, said he decided to become a priest when he was about eleven years old,

BISHOP WILTON D. GREGORY

after enrolling in parochial school. He studied at the seminary of Loyola University and Saint Mary of the Lake Seminary, and was ordained a priest for the Archdiocese of Chicago in 1973, later earning a doctorate in sacred liturgy at the Pontifical Liturgical Institute in Rome. He was ordained a bishop in 1983, serving for ten years in Chicago under Cardinal Joseph Bernardin, whom he considered a mentor.

In February 1994 Gregory was installed as the Seventh Bishop of Belleville, a diocese of about 105,000 Catholics that covers a wide area of southern Illinois and includes farming communities as well as the predominantly African American city of East St. Louis. Gregory has spoken out about the need for the church to do more to address racism and has written extensively on the church's opposition to the death penalty and to physician-assisted suicide.

In December 2004, Pope John Paul II appointed him the sixth archbishop of the Archdiocese of Atlanta. At an event in Atlanta in April 2007, Gregory spoke of how his faith was shaped by his parents' spirituality and by attending Catholic school as a boy. "These two personal experiences have made me the man I am," he said, "my African American spiritual heritage, of which I am very proud, and my Roman Catholicism, which has defined my life."

◆

WHO WAS THE FIRST AFRICAN AMERICAN PRESIDENT OF THE SOUTHERN BAPTIST CONVENTION?

In June 2012, the Reverend Fred Luter Jr., pastor of the Franklin Avenue Baptist Church in New Orleans, made history when the Southern Baptist Convention—once a bastion of slavery and segregation—elected him as its first African American president. He was reelected for a second term in June 2013.

Luter was born in 1956 in New Orleans's Lower Ninth Ward. He and his four siblings were raised by their mother, a seamstress. When he was twenty-one he suffered serious injuries in a motorcycle accident. After he recovered, he vowed to dedicate his life to the church. After preaching on the street for sev-

FRED LUTER JR.

eral years and then at two Baptist churches, he was hired in 1986 to lead the small congregation—mostly women and children—of the Franklin Avenue Baptist Church.

Luter set about bringing more people into the church, especially men, whom he'd invite over to watch a sporting event. "When Sugar Ray Leonard and Tommy Hearns fought, I had about twenty-five guys at the house that night," he said. "Many of them are still with us."

His congregation grew rapidly. By 1995, it had reached seven thousand members, and plans were underway to construct a new building. But then Hurricane Katrina destroyed the church and scattered its members. Luter traveled around the country urging them to return, while holding services in a borrowed New Orleans Baptist church. In 2008, his own church had been rebuilt, and his congregation continued to grow.

As president of the Southern Baptist Convention, Luter was leading the largest protestant organization in the country, with more than sixteen million members. Referring to the once all-white organization, Luter said, "Our doors are open to each and everybody, no matter the color, no matter the creed, no matter the background. . . ."

SCIENCE
AND
MEDICINE

WHO MADE THE FIRST CLOCK IN THE AMERICAN COLONIES AND WAS THE FIRST AFRICAN AMERICAN TO PUBLISH AN ALMANAC?

Born on a small tobacco farm near Baltimore, Maryland, in 1731, Benjamin Banneker received an eighth-grade education as the only African American child enrolled in a Quaker school near his home. At the age of twenty-two, using a pocket watch as a guide, he designed and built the first clock in the colonies. Completed in 1753, the clock was entirely hand-carved from wood and struck the hours. It is said to have run for more than forty years.

When he was in his late fifties, Banneker, who had been engaged in farming, began to pursue the study of astronomy, which he learned from books loaned to him by his Quaker friend George Ellicott. He spent many nights outside, wrapped in blankets, observing the stars. Scientists took notice of him when he accurately predicted the solar eclipse of 1789. Three years later he published the first in a series of almanacs that included such valuable information as tide tables, phases of the moon, and times of sunrise and sunset. He sent a copy to Thomas Jefferson, who was secretary of state at the time, along with a letter stating that blacks were intellectually equal to whites and should be given the same rights and opportunities. This began a correspondence between the two men that lasted for several years.

In 1791, George Washington appointed a French engineer, Pierre l'Enfant, to design a plan for the nation's capital, and Banneker was chosen as one of the surveyors. But l'Enfant suddenly returned to France, taking the plans with him. Banneker, working only from memory, quickly reconstructed the entire design.

Banneker died in 1806, but his name lived on. The United States Postal Service issued a commemorative stamp in his honor in 1980, many schools bear his name, and the Benjamin Banneker Historical Park and Museum was dedicated in 1998 in Catonsville, Maryland.

◆

WHO WAS THE FIRST
AFRICAN AMERICAN PHYSICIAN?

Born a slave in 1762 in Philadelphia, James Derham became a prominent doctor, one of the country's leading specialists in throat disorders. Derham learned his medical skills from three doctors, each of whom was his master. Encouraged by his third owner, Dr. Robert Love, Derham saved enough money as a medical assistant and apothecary to buy his freedom in 1783 and open a medical practice in New Orleans.

On a visit to Philadelphia, Derham met Dr. Benjamin Rush, one of the country's most outstanding physicians. Rush took an interest in Derham's career and convinced him to move his practice to Philadelphia, where he gained great respect from his medical colleagues. As his practice expanded, Derham became known throughout the nation as an expert on the relationship between disease and climate.

◆

WHO WAS THE FIRST AFRICAN AMERICAN
INVENTOR TO BE GRANTED A U.S. PATENT?

Thomas L. Jennings became the first African American to patent an invention when, in 1821, he was issued a patent for a dry cleaning process known as "dry scouring." Jennings, who owned a dry cleaning and tailoring business in New York City, was said to have used much of his profits to support the abolitionist cause. An activist for the rights of his people, Jennings served as assistant secretary of the First Annual Convention of the People of Color, in June 1831 in Philadelphia.

◆

WHO WAS THE FIRST AFRICAN AMERICAN
TO EARN A MEDICAL DEGREE?

In 1837, James McCune Smith, born in New York City in 1811, earned a medical degree from the University of Glasgow in Scotland. At a farewell dinner in his honor, he vowed to spend his life fighting slavery. He returned to New York City, opening a medical practice and a pharmacy on West Broadway. An eloquent speaker and writer, Smith played an active role in the abolitionist movement. During the Civil War, he joined a campaign that eventually convinced President Lincoln to allow African Americans to fight in the Union Army. Smith died in 1865.

Another African American doctor, David J. Peck, was the first to earn a medical degree in the United States, graduating from Rush Medical College in Chicago in 1847. Peck practiced medicine in Philadelphia for two years, then became a physician in Nicaragua.

◆

WHO WAS THE FIRST TO PATENT A VACUUM
SYSTEM FOR REFINING SUGAR?

In August 1846, the United States Patent Office issued Norbert Rillieux his first patent for a revolutionary system of refining sugar, an invention that completely changed the sugar industry. Rillieux, born in New Orleans in 1806, was the son of a slave and a French plantation owner. He was sent to Paris to be educated and remained there as a teacher of applied mechanics.

Rillieux eventually returned to New Orleans and became an engineer in the sugar refining business. Before his invention, refining the juice of sugar cane into granular sugar was a laborious and dangerous operation. His vacuum evaporation system was simpler and less expensive, and produced a higher-quality sugar. The system was soon adopted by refineries in Louisiana, Mexico, and the West Indies.

Although Rillieux's invention made him wealthy, his life was severely limited after the passage of the Fugitive Slave Act in 1850. Even though he was free, it was difficult to distinguish between free people of color and those who were slaves or fugitives. In

1854, when he was forced to carry a pass to travel around New Orleans, he left the country and returned to France, taking up archeology and deciphering Egyptian hieroglyphics. When he was seventy-five, he invented a more effective method of processing sugar beets, but when he died in Paris in 1894, the French still had not given him credit for his original sugar refining system, which was later recognized throughout Europe.

◆

WHO INVENTED THE FIRST TOGGLE HARPOON FOR WHALING?

Lewis Temple was born in 1800 in Richmond, Virginia, and eventually settled in New Bedford, Massachusetts, where he worked as a blacksmith. The whaling industry was prominent in New Bedford at the time, and in his blacksmith shop Temple forged many of the harpoons used by whalers.

Told that whales often were able to detach themselves and escape, Temple set to work to solve the problem. In 1848 he invented a toggle harpoon that made it more difficult for the whales to get away. The toggle harpoon was said to be the most important invention in the history of the whaling industry. But Temple neglected to patent his invention and never benefited from its profits.

◆

WHO WAS THE FIRST AFRICAN AMERICAN WOMAN TO EARN A MEDICAL DEGREE?

Rebecca Lee Crumpler was born in Richmond, Virginia, in 1833 and raised in Pennsylvania by an aunt who acted as a doctor to others in her community. Inspired by her aunt, Crumpler became a nurse in Massachusetts in 1852. After her supervisors encouraged her to further her medical education, she entered New England Female Medical College, now Boston College School of Medicine, earning a Doctress of Medicine degree in 1864. She was the first African American woman in the country to earn a medical degree.

Dr. Crumpler practiced medicine in Boston until after the Civil War, when she moved to Richmond, where she provided medical care to newly freed slaves. She eventually returned to Boston, and in 1883 she published a book on the subject to which she had devoted her life—health care for women and children.

◆

WHO DESIGNED THE FIRST AUTOMATIC LUBRICATOR AND INSPIRED THE TERM "THE REAL McCOY"?

The child of escaped slaves, Elijah McCoy was born in 1844 in Canada and attended school in Michigan, where his parents eventually settled. He went to Edinburgh, Scotland, to serve an apprenticeship in mechanical engineering, but back in the United States he was unable to find a job in his field. He finally became a fireman on the railroad, where one of his jobs was to oil the engine, which had to be done by hand while the train was stopped.

McCoy began experimenting with less tedious methods to oil machinery. In 1872 he patented his first invention, an automatic lubricator that supplied oil to moving parts while a machine was operating. He patented improvements over the years, and his lubricating device was soon used by manufacturers everywhere. Eventually customers inspecting pieces of machinery would routinely ask if it was "the real McCoy." The phrase is still used today to indicate authenticity.

McCoy acquired more than fifty patents in his lifetime; along with various lubricating devices, he invented an ironing table and a lawn sprinkler. He founded the Elijah McCoy Manufacturing Company in Detroit, and continued working on inventions until a few years before his death in 1929.

◆

WHO WAS THE FIRST AFRICAN AMERICAN NURSING SCHOOL GRADUATE?

Diminutive and energetic, Mary Elizabeth Mahoney developed an acquaintance with medicine early in life. Born in 1845, she was the eldest daughter in a large family and assisted at the births of several of her younger brothers and sisters. She was in her early thirties when she entered the New England Hospital for Women and Children in Boston, the first nursing school in America.

All student nurses were required to do cleaning and laundry while pursing their studies, and the regimen was so exhausting that only three out of a class of forty graduated in 1879; Mahoney was among them. She was an active suffragist, and after the passage of the Nineteenth Constitutional Amendment giving women the right to vote, she was thought to be the first African American woman in Boston to register. Her nursing career continued for forty years, and in 1936 the National Association of Colored Graduate Nurses, which she helped organize, established the Mary Mahoney Award for African American nurses who made outstanding contributions to their profession.

◆

WHO INVENTED THE FIRST LONG-LASTING CARBON FILAMENT FOR LIGHT BULBS?

The only African American member of the famed "Edison Pioneers," Lewis Latimer was a man of many talents and accomplishments. He was born in 1848 in Chelsea, Massachusetts, to parents who had escaped slavery. His father disappeared when he was ten years old, and when he was about fifteen he joined the Union Army.

After the Civil War, Latimer got a job as an office boy in a firm of patent lawyers, where he learned mechanical drawing. He was promoted to draftsman and prepared drawings for Alexander Graham Bell's application for his telephone patent, which was issued in 1876. Latimer took a job with an electric lighting company in

Connecticut and created improvements in the incandescent light that Thomas Edison had invented one year earlier.

Latimer's most important invention, in 1882, was a long-lasting carbon filament for electric light bulbs. He was asked to install his lighting system in New York City, Philadelphia, and Canada. In 1884, Latimer joined the Edison Electric Light Company in New York, where he served as an expert witness in defending patents in court and wrote a standard textbook, *Incandescent Electric Lighting, A Practical Description of the Edison System*. In 1918 he became one of the twenty-eight charter members of the Edison Pioneers, a group of inventors who worked for Thomas Edison. His interests were broad; he was a talented poet, artist, and musician. He spent his later years immersed in the study of literature, and before his death in 1928 his two daughters published a collection of his poems.

◆

WHO CREATED THE FIRST MACHINE TO MAKE A COMPLETE SHOE?

Jan Matzeliger immigrated to the United States from Dutch Guiana and in 1876, at the age of twenty-four, settled in Lynn, Massachusetts, which was the country's largest shoe manufacturing center. Since he had worked in machine shops in his native country, he was able to find a job in a shoe factory. He soon realized there was no machine that could automatically "last" a shoe, that is, connect the upper part to the sole.

For years Matzeliger experimented with machines that would hold the shoe in place, stretch the leather down, and automatically tack it in place on the sole. Finally, he achieved success, and in 1883 received a patent for the first lasting machine that would turn out a complete shoe. His invention revolutionized the shoe industry; the shoe-lasting machine was in demand throughout the world.

But Matzeliger remained a lonely man. He had devoted all his free time to his invention and the four improvements that followed, and he never married. He developed tuberculosis and died when he was only thirty-seven, before he could benefit from the great profits earned by his invention.

♦

WHAT WAS THE FIRST PATENT AWARDED TO AN AFRICAN AMERICAN WOMAN?

In July 1885 a patent was awarded to Sarah Goode, the owner of a Chicago furniture store, for a "folding cabinet bed," which was similar to today's convertible couch.

♦

WHO INVENTED THE FIRST RAILROAD TELEGRAPH SYSTEM?

Granville T. Woods was born in Columbus, Ohio, in 1856. Forced to leave school when he was just ten years old, he went to work in a machine shop. After moving to Missouri at the age of sixteen, Woods worked on the railroad and in a steel rolling mill. Developing an interest in electricity, he studied the subject in books and college courses. For a time he drove a steam locomotive for the Danville and Southern Railroad, and in the early 1880s he opened his own company in Cincinnati, Ohio, and launched his career as an inventor.

In 1887 Woods patented a railroad telegraph system that was designed to avert accidents by allowing messages to be sent between moving trains and between trains and railroad stations. The same year he invented a system for electric trains that utilized a pole extending to an overhead power line; the system was soon adopted for use with electric trolleys. Woods had secured more than sixty patents by the time he died in 1910. His inventions include the "third rail" that is now used on subways, and a series of devices that led to the automatic air brake.

♦

WHO WAS THE FIRST
AFRICAN AMERICAN WOMAN DENTIST?

Ida Gray was born in Clarksville, Tennessee, in 1867. After attending high school in Cincinnati, where her family then lived, Gray earned a bachelor's degree from Ann Arbor College in Michigan. In 1890, when she graduated from the University of Michigan Dental School, she became the first African American woman in the country to receive a doctor of dental surgery degree. Gray then returned to Cincinnati, where she established a successful dental practice. She married in 1895 and moved to Chicago, becoming active in community health organizations.

◆

WHO PERFORMED THE FIRST
OPEN-HEART SURGERY?

Back in 1893, an African American doctor named Daniel Hale Williams made history when he opened the chest of a young black man who had been stabbed in a fight, repaired the hole in the membrane surrounding his heart, and saved the man's life.

Williams was born in Pennsylvania in 1856. When he was nine years old his father died and his mother moved the family to Baltimore. There he was an apprentice to a shoemaker and learned the barbering trade. He then joined his sister in Wisconsin, where he worked as a barber and attended high school. He was hired as an assistant to a local doctor who, impressed by his competence, sponsored his admission to Chicago Medical School. Williams graduated in 1883 and opened an office in Chicago, where his practice quickly grew.

Williams gained a reputation as a skilled surgeon, and he had both black and white patients. But he was keenly aware that opportunities were limited for African American physicians and that black patients often received inferior treatment. He became determined to open a hospital where African American doctors and nurses could be trained and black patients would receive the best of care. In 1891 Williams founded Provident Hospital in Chicago, the first in the country with an interracial staff.

DR. DANIEL HALE WILLIAMS

When James Cornish was stabbed in a bar brawl in 1893 and sent to Provident Hospital, Williams used an innovative technique to save his life. Without X-rays, antibiotics, or blood transfusions, the gifted surgeon made an incision in Cornish's chest and stitched up the wound. The patient recovered completely and the amazing operation made Williams famous throughout the country.

♦

WHAT IS THE FIRST NATIONAL MONUMENT DEDICATED TO AN AFRICAN AMERICAN?

In July 1943, President Franklin Delano Roosevelt called for the establishment of the George Washington Carver National Monument in Diamond, Missouri, the birthplace of this eminent scientist, who had died six months earlier. Dedicated in 1953, it became the first federal monument honoring an African American.

Carver, born in 1860 to enslaved parents on a plantation owned by Moses Carver, became the first African American graduate of Iowa State College (now Iowa State University), where he earned a bachelor's degree in 1894 and a master's two years later. Carver had many interests, but he concentrated on botany. He went on to teach at Tuskegee Institute, where he headed the agriculture department, a position he held until his death.

A pioneer in agricultural research and plant chemistry, he discovered a new method of organic fertilization, originated crop rotation as a means of restoring soil, and developed the peanut and the sweet potato as staples of farming in the South. He created many new uses for agricultural products, including more than three hundred for peanuts and more than a hundred for sweet potatoes and soybeans. Among these were soap, shampoo, vinegar, and wood stains.

Carver died in 1943 on the campus of Tuskegee Institute. His national monument, a 210-acre park on the land where he was born, includes the Moses Carver home, the Carver family cemetery, and a museum tracing his life.

◆

WHO WAS THE FIRST RECIPIENT OF THE NAACP'S SPINGARN MEDAL?

The Spingarn Medal was instituted in 1914 by J. E. Spingarn, who was then chairman of the board of the NAACP. It was designed to be presented annually for the highest achievement by an African American in any field of endeavor. The first recipient of the Spingarn Medal, in 1915, was Ernest E. Just, then head of the department of zoology at Howard Medical School, for his biological research.

Ernest Just was born in 1883 in Charleston, South Carolina, where he attended an elementary school for African American children. When he was seventeen, his mother decided he should go north to further his education. He made his way to New York

City, where he worked for a summer, earning enough money to enter Kimball Academy in Meriden, New Hampshire. His academic accomplishments there were outstanding and he graduated with honors in only three years.

In 1903 Just entered Dartmouth College, where he became intrigued by the study of biology, especially the development of the egg cell. After graduating magna cum laude, he joined the teaching staff of Howard University and spent his summers conducting research on marine eggs at the Marine Biological Laboratories in Woods Hole, Massachusetts.

In 1912 he was named head of the zoology department at Howard, and earned a Ph.D. from the University of Chicago in 1916, a year after being awarded the Spingarn Medal. Becoming discouraged by his future prospects in his own country, Just went to Europe in 1929 to study and teach, eventually settling in France. He returned to the United States in 1940 and died a year later. During his career, Just published more than sixty papers and a 1939 book, *Biology of the Cell Surface*. His findings gave scientists new insights into the development of the cell.

◆

WHO INVENTED THE FIRST TRAFFIC LIGHT AND FIRST GAS MASK?

In the early days of the automobile, traffic was controlled by a person sitting in a little tower at intersections, manually operating stop-and-go signals. This all changed when Garrett A. Morgan, after seeing an accident between an automobile and a horse-drawn carriage on a busy street, invented and patented the first automatic three-position traffic light in November 1923.

Born in Paris, Kentucky, in 1877, Morgan received an elementary school education before leaving home as a teenager and going north to Cincinnati, where he worked and studied. He moved on to Cleveland, repairing sewing machines and opening his own repair and tailoring shop. While trying to make a lubricant for sewing machine needles, he accidentally discovered a hair straightening solution, which he sold as the G. A. Morgan Hair Refining Cream.

In 1916 Morgan came to public attention in a big way when, using a breathing device he had invented two years earlier, he took part in a dramatic rescue. A disastrous explosion had occurred in a tunnel below Lake Erie, trapping a number of workers. Morgan and his brother, wearing his newly invented device, which he called a "Safety Hood," went into the smoke-filled shaft and pulled the workers to safety.

When they heard about the rescue, fire officials around the country placed orders for the Safety Hood, but many cancelled them when they learned that Morgan was an African American. At this point the army saw the value of Morgan's invention, made some improvements on it, and the Safety Hood became the gas mask that saved thousands of lives in World War I.

◆

WHO SET UP THE COUNTRY'S FIRST BLOOD PLASMA BANK?

Dr. Charles R. Drew, famous for his work in the preservation of blood, was a native of Washington, D.C., who first gained recognition as an outstanding athlete. At Amherst College, where he was a star in track and football, Drew won the Mossman Trophy as the athlete who had contributed the most to the school. Drew dreamed of becoming a doctor but could not afford medical school, so he took a job teaching biology and directing athletics at Morgan State College. Two years later he entered McGill University School of Medicine in Montreal, concentrating on research in blood transfusions.

After graduating from McGill, Drew joined the faculty of Howard University Medical School, where he set up a program of residency training in surgery. A turning point in Drew's life came in 1938, when he won a research fellowship and went to New York City to do postgraduate work at Columbia University. While there, he developed techniques for separating and preserving blood, and determined that plasma could be stored much longer than whole blood. In 1939, Drew was instrumental in setting up a blood plasma bank at New York's Presbyterian Hospital, the first of its kind in the country.

When he finished his studies at Columbia University in 1940, Drew returned to Howard Medical School to teach but was soon asked to head a program to collect and process blood plasma for Britain, where German bombings were creating a critical need for blood. A year later, in 1941, Drew was named head of an American Red Cross effort to collect blood for use by the American armed forces. But the military, in a shocking response, announced that blood from African Americans would not be acceptable. After protests from around the country, the policy was revised: African American blood would be accepted but kept separate!

Drew returned to Howard Medical School as a professor of surgery and chief surgeon of its teaching hospital. He received many honors and awards before his life came to an untimely end in 1950 when, on his way to a medical clinic in Alabama, his car went off the road and he was killed. He was only forty-six years old. But Drew's accomplishments lived on. Schools all over the country have been named after him, and a university of medicine and science in California bears his name.

♦

WHO WAS THE FIRST AFRICAN AMERICAN AERONAUTICAL ENGINEER?

Douglas C. Watson fell in love with aircraft when he was still in grammar school. He set up a workshop in his basement to build model planes, and read every issue of *Model Airplane News*. By the time he was in high school his models were winning competitions among New York City boys' clubs.

When Watson entered New York University in 1937, he chose the engineering school, where he earned bachelor's and master's degrees. Watson graduated third in his class and was awarded the Chance-Vought Memorial Prize for his airplane design. But despite his outstanding record and the enthusiastic praise of his professors, Watson was the only member of his class not hired by an aeronautical company. Finally, with the help of his teachers, he was offered a job by an aircraft company in Pennsylvania, where he helped design a plane that won the firm a large army contract.

Watson spent most of his career with the Fairchild Republic

Aviation Corporation in Farmingdale, New York. During his years there he helped to develop the F-105 and F-84 jet fighters and played a major role in the design of the long-range P-47N, a bomber escort. After his retirement from Fairchild in 1978, he served as president of the Sabre Research Corporation, consulting engineers. He died in June 1993 at the age of seventy-three.

Watson was one of a family of achievers. His father, James S. Watson, was the first African American judge in New York State; his sister, Barbara Watson, was the first African American assistant secretary of state; and his younger brother, James L., was the second African American state senator in New York.

◆

WHO WAS THE FIRST AFRICAN AMERICAN SCIENTIST EMPLOYED BY AT&T'S BELL LABS?

W. Lincoln Hawkins's life was notable for hard work, solid achievement, and the deserved recognition of his peers and country. Born in Washington, D.C., in 1911, he earned a bachelor's degree in chemistry from Rensselaer Polytechnic Institute, a master's from Howard, and a doctorate from McGill University in Montreal.

Hired by Bell Laboratories, the prestigious research arm of AT&T, in 1942, Hawkins's most important inventions were additives that prolonged the life of plastic. He and a colleague invented a chemical additive that prevented the deterioration of the plastic coating on telephone cables. This discovery made universal telephone service possible, thus revolutionizing the telecommunications industry. Hawkins remained with Bell Labs for thirty-four years. In all, he was granted 147 patents related to the development of environmentally advanced materials for communications equipment. He was a leader in efforts to promote scientific careers for other African Americans, and helped expand the science programs of predominantly black colleges.

In 1992, two months before he died, Hawkins was awarded the National Medal of Technology by President George Bush for his efforts on behalf of minority group students.

◆

WHO WAS THE FIRST AFRICAN AMERICAN PROFESSOR AT HARVARD MEDICAL SCHOOL?

D r. William Augustus Hinton, born in Chicago in 1883, earned a medical degree with honors in 1912 from Harvard Medical School. After graduation he worked for the Wasserman Laboratory, which at the time was part of Harvard. In 1918 he became an instructor of preventive medicine and hygiene at the medical school, and in 1949 was promoted to clinical professor. He was the first African American professor at Harvard Medical School, where he taught for thirty-six years.

Hinton became famous throughout the world for his work in developing the Hinton test for the detection of syphilis, and the Davies-Hinton tests of blood and spinal fluid. Although the NAACP wanted to present Hinton with its coveted Spingarn Medal in 1938, the doctor refused to take it, fearing that allowing the world to know he was an African American would be detrimental to the acceptance of his work.

◆

WHO WAS THE FIRST AFRICAN AMERICAN WOMAN SURGEON IN THE SOUTH?

D orothy Brown's life did not have a promising start. Five months after her birth in 1919, her mother left her in an orphanage in Troy, New York, where she remained for thirteen years. The future appeared more hopeful by the time she became a student at Troy High School; she had been taken in by loving, supportive foster parents.

Winning a four-year scholarship, Brown studied at Bennett College in Greensboro, North Carolina, graduating second in her class, and in 1948 she earned an M.D. from Meharry Medical College in Nashville, Tennessee. She completed her internship at Harlem Hospital in New York City, but was rejected for a surgical residency there. She returned to Meharry, serving her residency at the hospital connected with the medical school, and then joined the staff as a surgeon.

This was not her only first. She was the first single woman to adopt a child in the state of Tennessee, and in 1966 she became the first African American woman to serve in the Tennessee State Legislature. On January 31, 2000, on the occasion of her retirement from the practice of medicine, the members of the legislature commended her "for her remarkable career as the Southeast's first African American woman surgeon, but also for the difficult duties she so graciously performed during her term as legislator." Brown died in Nashville in 2004.

◆

WHO WAS THE FIRST AFRICAN AMERICAN MEMBER OF THE NATIONAL ACADEMY OF SCIENCES?

Called the greatest African American mathematician of his time, David Blackwell was in his last year of high school when he discovered that he loved mathematics. Although his parents were

DAVID BLACKWELL

not mathematically inclined, Blackwell said he might have inherited his talent from his grandfather, a schoolteacher and storekeeper. Born in the small town of Centralia, Illinois, in 1919, Blackwell was only sixteen when he enrolled in the University of Illinois, where he remained until he earned a Ph.D. in mathematics and won a fellowship to the Institute for Advanced Study in Princeton, New Jersey.

Blackwell became an assistant professor at Howard University in 1944, and by the time he left ten years later, he had been promoted to head of the math department. He headed west to join the faculty of the University of California at Berkeley, teaching mathematics and statistics, where he remained for the rest of his career. At Berkeley, he did fundamental work in game theory, Bayesian inference, and information theory, and cowrote the classic book *Theory of Games and Statistical Decisions*. He was elected to the National Academy of Sciences in 1965. Blackwell retired from U.C. Berkeley in 1988 and died in 2010.

◆

WHAT AFRICAN AMERICAN WAS THE FIRST TO EARN A PH.D. IN COMPUTER SCIENCE?

When he was a teenager, Clarence "Skip" Ellis, born in Chicago in 1943, took a security job at a local company. One of his responsibilities was to protect the company's new computer, which was large and expensive, and he spent some of his free time reading the manuals that came with the machine. During his last two years of high school, his teachers recommended him for summer programs at a local university, but his family couldn't afford to send him to college after he graduated. With the help of the pastor of his church, he won a scholarship to Beloit College in Wisconsin, where he developed a fascination with computer science.

Ellis graduated from Beloit with a major in mathematics and physics and enrolled in graduate school at the University of Illinois, where he worked on hardware, software, and applications of the Illiac 4 Supercomputer. In 1969 he was awarded a Ph.D. in computer science, the first African American to earn this degree. After graduation he continued his work on supercomputers at Bell Telephone Laboratories, IBM, Xerox, Microelectronics and Computer Technology Corporation, Los Alamos Scientific Labs, and Argonne National Lab. He taught at several institutions before he joined the faculty of the University of Colorado at Boulder in 1992 as a professor of computer science and director of the Collaboration Technology Research Group. One of his projects was working with the African Virtual University to bring Afrocentric computer science to selected sub-Saharan African countries. During the spring semesters of 2006 and 2007, he taught and did curriculum development in Ghana and Cameroon.

◆

WHO WAS THE FIRST AFRICAN AMERICAN WOMAN TO HEAD A MAJOR TEACHING HOSPITAL?

From the time she graduated from high school at the age of fifteen, Florence Small Gaynor had to fight against racial obstacles to become a nurse. She first applied to Jersey City Medical Center, in the city of her birth, but was turned down because it did not admit African Americans. To help support her family, she worked for a time at an electric plant and a doll factory. She was finally admitted to the nursing school at Lincoln Hospital in the Bronx, graduating as a registered nurse in 1946.

Gaynor held several nursing jobs while earning a bachelor's degree in nursing and a master's in public health: she was a public health nurse in New York City's East Harlem, a head nurse at a hospital in Manhattan, and a school nurse in Newark, New Jersey. She spent a summer at the University of Oslo in Norway studying the Scandinavian health system, and when she returned she pursued a career in hospital administration.

Rising through the ranks of hospital administration at a time when there were few women or African Americans in such positions, Gaynor was chosen over nineteen male candidates in 1971 to be executive director of Sydenham Hospital in Harlem. Eighteen months later she was named executive director of Martland Hospital in Newark, a 600-bed teaching hospital—the first African American woman in the country to head a major teaching hospital.

From 1976 to 1980, Gaynor directed hospital and health services at Meharry Medical College in Nashville, and for four years after that she was director of a community mental health group in Philadelphia. She died of a brain hemorrhage in 1993 at the age of seventy-two.

◆

WHO WAS THE FIRST WOMAN TO HEAD PLANNED PARENTHOOD?

Faye Wattleton was the first woman and the first African American to become president of the Planned Parenthood Federation of America, the largest family planning organization in the country. Wattleton was born in 1943 in St. Louis and graduated from Ohio State University Nursing School when she was twenty-one, the first in her family to earn a college degree. She went on to earn a master's from New York's Columbia University in maternal and infant health care.

Affected by her experience with a young woman who died after an illegal abortion, and by her work with teenage mothers and neglected children, Wattleton became a volunteer with Planned Parenthood in Dayton, Ohio, where she worked as a public health nurse. She eventually became executive director of that agency and in 1978 was named president of the Planned Parenthood Federation of America. The youngest person to hold that position, she worked diligently and effectively for the reproductive rights of women until her resignation in 1992. Three years later, Wattleton founded and became president of the Center for Gender Equality, a research, policy development, and educational institution created to promote strategies for dismantling the obstacles that impede full equality for women. In 2010, she joined the global professional services firm Alvarez & Marsal as a managing director.

◆

WHO WAS THE COUNTRY'S FIRST
AFRICAN AMERICAN WOMAN NEUROSURGEON?

Not only was Alexa Canady the first African American woman neurosurgeon in the nation, but she was only thirty-six years old when she was named chief of neurosurgery at the Children's Hospital of Michigan, in Detroit. Canady was born in 1950 in Lansing, Michigan; her father was a dentist, and her mother was the first African American elected to the Lansing school board.

A couple of years after she entered the University of Michigan with a major in theoretical mathematics, Canady lost interest in the subject and couldn't decide on her next move. But a summer job for a minority health care program sparked her interest in medicine, and by 1975 she had earned a medical degree from the University of Michigan College of Medicine, with a specialty in pediatric neurosurgery.

During her years at the Detroit Children's Hospital, she turned the neurosurgery program into one of the top in the nation, and she also developed innovative treatments. Her research led to the invention of a shunt to treat hydrocephalus, an abnormal accumulation of fluid in the brain, for which she shared a patent with two fellow neurosurgeons.

After retiring as chief of neurosurgery at Children's Hospital, Canady joined Sacred Heart Medical Center in Pensacola, Florida, as a pediatric neurosurgeon.

◆

WHO WAS THE FIRST NEUROSURGEON TO
SUCCESSFULLY SEPARATE CONJOINED TWINS
JOINED AT THE HEAD?

Appointed director of pediatric neurosurgery at Johns Hopkins Hospital in Baltimore in 1984, when he was only thirty-three years old, Dr. Benjamin S. Carson soon made medical history. In 1985 he performed a medical procedure known as a hemispherectomy, removing half the brain of a four-year-old girl who was suffering 150 seizures a day. The other half of her brain took over all functions, and the girl went on to grow and develop normally.

DR. BENJAMIN S. CARSON

Carson made news again in 1987 when he led the medical team in a twenty-two hour procedure that for the first time in history successfully separated conjoined twins joined at the head. Ten years later he was the primary surgeon on the team of South African and Zambian surgeons that separated twins joined at the top of the head. It was the first time that such complexly joined twins were separated and remained neurologically normal.

Dr. Carson had to overcome almost overwhelming obstacles to reach his prestigious position. When he was eight years old, living in a poor Detroit neighborhood, his father abandoned the family, and his mother took domestic jobs to support her two sons while struggling to instill in them the importance of education.

In elementary school, Carson was a poor student with a violent temper and little confidence, but by high school he managed to change his outlook and graduated third in his class, winning a scholarship to Yale University and later enrolling in the University of Michigan School of Medicine. As director of pediatric neurosurgery at Johns Hopkins, Carson focuses on such conditions as traumatic brain injury, brain and spinal cord tumors, epilepsy, and neurological and congenital disorders. He was awarded the Presidential Medal of Freedom in 2008.

Carson's autobiography, *Gifted Hands*, chronicled his road from poverty and a broken home to his distinguished position in the field of medicine. His motivational books, *Think Big* and *The Big Picture*, outline his philosophy for a successful life.

A television movie, *Gifted Hands: The Ben Carson Story*, starring Cuba Gooding Jr., aired in 2009. The book *America the Beautiful: Rediscovering What Made This Nation Great*, by Carson and his wife, Cindy Carson, was published in January 2013.

◆

WHO WAS THE FIRST AFRICAN AMERICAN WOMAN DOCTOR TO RECEIVE A PATENT?

Dr. Patricia E. Bath accomplished many firsts. She was the first African American resident in ophthalmology at New York University, the first woman to chair an ophthalmology residency program in the United States, and the first woman doctor to patent a medical invention—a method for removing cataracts.

Bath was born in Harlem in 1942. An excellent student, her aptitude in science was recognized in high school, where she edited the school's science paper and won awards for scientific research. She earned a bachelor's degree from New York's Hunter College, received a medical degree from Howard University College of Medicine, interned at Harlem Hospital, completed a fellowship in ophthalmology at Columbia University, and completed her training at New York University, where she was the first African American resident in that specialty.

Bath began to notice differences between the patients at Harlem Hospital, where almost half were blind or visually impaired, and

DR. PATRICIA E. BATH

Columbia, where there were few incidences of blindness. She determined that blindness among African Americans was double that among whites due to the lack of access to ophthalmic care among African Americans. This conclusion led her to propose a new discipline, community ophthalmology, which is now practiced worldwide.

In 1974, Bath moved to Los Angeles, where she joined the faculties of UCLA and Charles R. Drew University. The next year she became the first woman faculty member in the Department of Ophthalmology at UCLA's Jules Stein Eye Institute. In 1976, she and three colleagues founded the American Institute for the Prevention of Blindness. And in 1988, she received a patent for her invention, the Laserphaco Probe, which uses a laser to remove cataracts. She retired from the UCLA Medical Center in 1993 and was appointed to the honorary medical staff.

In a National Institute of Medicine interview, asked about her biggest obstacles to success, Bath said, "Sexism, racism, and relative poverty were the obstacles which I faced as a young girl growing up in Harlem. There were no women physicians I knew of . . . [and] blacks were excluded from numerous medical schools and medical societies." She was inspired to persevere, she said, by the work of Dr. Albert Schweitzer and the encouragement of her family physician.

◆

WHO WAS THE FIRST AFRICAN AMERICAN TO BE ELECTED PRESIDENT OF THE AMERICAN METEOROLOGICAL SOCIETY?

Dr. Warren M. Washington, an internationally recognized expert on atmospheric science and climate research, added another title to his list of notable positions in May 1995 when President Clinton appointed him to a six-year term on the National Science Board, which helps oversee the National Science Foundation and advises the executive branch and Congress on science-related matters. He was later appointed to a second six-year term that began in 2001. In 1993 Washington became the first African American president of the 11,000-member American Meteorological Society.

Crediting his Portland, Oregon, high school teacher with sparking his interest in science and research, Washington earned degrees in physics and meteorology at Oregon State University, and a doctorate in meteorology at Pennsylvania State University. As a senior scientist at the National Center for Atmospheric Research (NCAR) in Boulder, Colorado, which he joined in 1963, Washington was given the responsibility of overseeing programs to study changes in global climate, and of developing computer models to monitor and analyze these changes. These climate models help scientists to understand such phenomena as the greenhouse effect, the ozone hole, and deforestation. A book that is considered to be the standard reference on the subject, *An Introduction to Three-Dimensional Climate Modeling*, was cowritten by Washington.

DR. WARREN M. WASHINGTON

In 1989 Washington founded the Black Environmental Science Trust to focus attention on the special environmental problems experienced by minority communities, such as exposure to lead, exhaust fumes, and contaminated drinking water, and to increase the number of African American scientists in environmental fields. "There is a history of environmental problems being dumped on the poor and disadvantaged people, not only in this country but worldwide," Washington said in a newspaper interview.

In August 2007, Washington received a lifetime achievement award from the U.S. Department of Energy, which was given to him "in recognition of a lifetime of extraordinary contributions to national and international science," and noted that he had "advised five presidents, given wise and insightful counsel to colleagues, advice to the Department of Energy and other federal agencies, and mentored directly and as a role model to enumerable young people."

Washington, as a member of the Intergovernmental Panel on Climate Change, shared the 2007 Nobel Peace Prize with other members of the panel and former vice president Al Gore. In November 2010, President Obama awarded him the National Medal of Science.

◆

WHO WAS THE FIRST AFRICAN AMERICAN SURGEON GENERAL?

Dr. Joycelyn Elders was born in 1933 in the tiny rural town of Schaal, Arkansas, where a visit to a doctor was a rare occurrence. But Elders grew up to be a pediatrician, the director of the Arkansas Health Department, and, in 1993, the first African American Surgeon General of the United States.

The eldest of eight children whose parents were sharecroppers, Elders graduated from college at the age of eighteen and joined the United States Army, where she was trained as a physical therapist. She attended the University of Arkansas Medical School on the GI Bill, and after graduating in 1960 completed an internship at the University of Minnesota Hospital, and a residency in pediatrics at the University of Arkansas Medical Center. She earned a master's degree in biochemistry, became a pediatrics professor at the University of Arkansas Medical Center, and in 1978 was certified as a pediatric endocrinologist.

In 1987 Bill Clinton, then governor of Arkansas, appointed Elders as the first woman and the first African American to head the Arkansas Department of Health. And in December 1992, President Bill Clinton nominated Elders to be the United States surgeon general. But because of some who opposed her progressive and outspoken views on family planning, sex education, and abortion rights, the Senate did not confirm her until September 1993.

As surgeon general, Elders supported universal health coverage and comprehensive health education in the schools. When a remark she made about sex education led to controversy, she was forced to resign after only fifteen months on the job. She returned to the University of Arkansas Medical Center as a professor of pediatrics. She continued to advocate for public health care, openness in sex education, and drug treatment instead of incarceration. She was quoted as saying that violence, sexually transmitted diseases, poverty, and substance abuse were the biggest threats to the health of American children.

After retiring from medicine in 1999, Elders continued to speak on such issues as AIDS, adolescent sexuality, and national health care.

♦

WHO WAS THE FIRST AFRICAN AMERICAN WOMAN TO HEAD A NATIONAL RESEARCH INSTITUTION?

Dr. Shirley Ann Jackson has said that her career path, which led her to the presidency of Rensselaer Polytechnic Institute, was greatly influenced by two historic events: the 1954 Supreme Court decision that desegregated public schools; and the beginning of the space race three years later when the Soviet Union launched Sputnik, the first earth-orbiting satellite. Because of the 1954 decision, she was able to attend the integrated Roosevelt High School in Washington, D.C., and as a result of the country's new interest in science and technology, she could take advantage of enriched science classes.

After graduating at the head of her class, Jackson earned degrees in physics from MIT, worked as a theoretical physicist at the AT&T Bell Laboratories, and was a professor of theoretical physics at Rutgers University. In 1995 President Clinton appointed her to serve as chairman of the United States Nuclear Regulatory Commission, a post she held until 1999, when she became the eighteenth president of Rensselaer Polytechnic Institute in Troy, New York, and Hartford, Connecticut, the oldest technological university in the United States. In 2005, *Time* magazine referred to Jackson as "perhaps the ultimate role model for women in science." The National

DR. SHIRLEY ANN JACKSON

Science Board selected her as its 2007 recipient of the prestigious Vannevar Bush Award for "a lifetime of achievements in scientific research, education, and senior statesman–like contributions to public policy."

In February 2012, Jackson was honored by the AAAS, an international scientific society, for her "extraordinary leadership of and contributions to the scientific community." And later that year, a top RPI administrator, William N. Walker, told Albany's *Times-Union,* "Under her leadership, the institute has become a top-tier, world-class teaching and research institution with global reach and global impact."

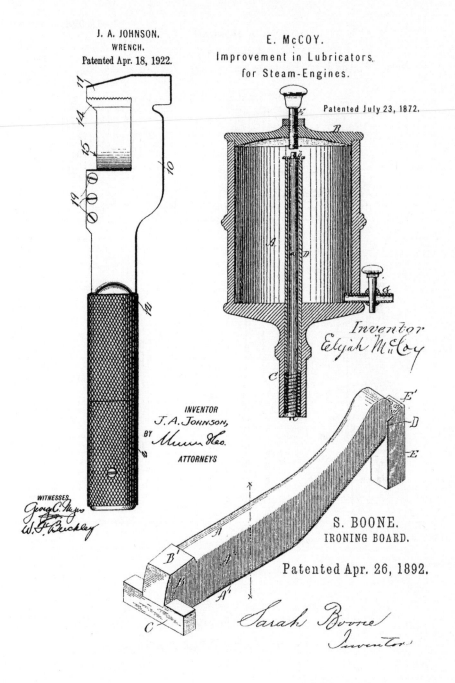

J. A. JOHNSON.
WRENCH.
Patented Apr. 18, 1922.

11
14
15
19
10
12

INVENTOR
J. A. JOHNSON,
BY Munn &co.
ATTORNEYS

WITNESSES
George C. Myers
W. F. Buckley

E. McCOY.
Improvement in Lubricators
for Steam-Engines.

Patented July 23, 1872.

B
A
D
C

Inventor
Elijah McCoy

S. BOONE.
IRONING BOARD.

Patented Apr. 26, 1892.

E'
D
E
A
B'
B
A'
C

Sarah Boone
Inventor

1,475,024

G. A. MORGAN

TRAFFIC SIGNAL

Nov. 20, 1923. Filed Feb. 27. 1922 2 Sheets-Sheet 1

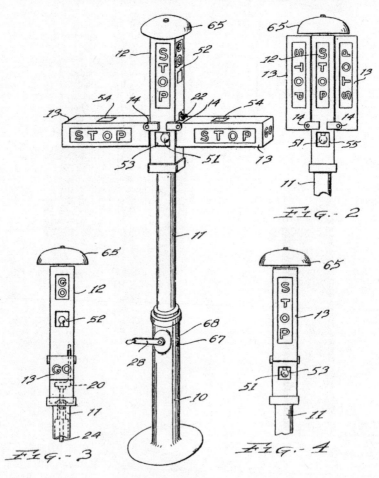

STOP
GO
FIG.-1
FIG.-2
FIG.-3
FIG.-4
INVENTOR
Garrett A. Morgan,
By Baker & Macklin,
ATTORNEYS

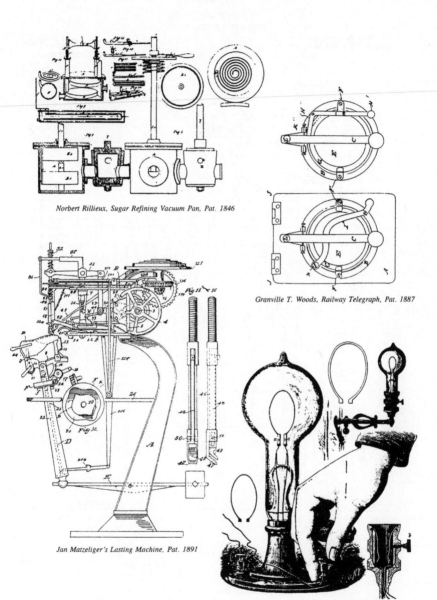

Norbert Rillieux, Sugar Refining Vacuum Pan, Pat. 1846

Granville T. Woods, Railway Telegraph, Pat. 1887

Jan Matzeliger's Lasting Machine, Pat. 1891

Lewis H. Latimer's Electric Lamp, Pat. 1881

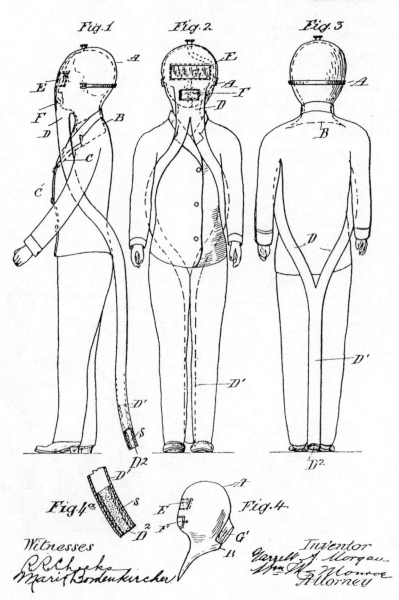

G. A. MORGAN.
BREATHING DEVICE.
APPLICATION FILED AUG. 19, 1912.

1,113,675.

Patented Oct. 13, 1914.
2 SHEETS—SHEET 1.

SPORTS

WHO WAS THE FIRST AFRICAN AMERICAN PLAYER
IN ORGANIZED BASEBALL?

John W. "Bud" Fowler was born John W. Jackson in 1858 in up-state New York and spent his childhood in Cooperstown. He began his career as the first African American player in organized baseball in 1878, playing with teams in Massachusetts. It was then that he changed his name to Bud Fowler. He could play any position in baseball, but was especially talented as a second baseman. He played for many white teams throughout the country, including Keokuk in the Western League in 1885, and Santa Fe in the New Mexico League. Fowler also founded and played for a number of all-black teams, such as the Page Fence Giants, the Smoky City Giants, and the All-American Black Tourists, who played in top hats and tails.

◆

WHO RODE THE WINNING HORSE IN
THE FIRST KENTUCKY DERBY?

From the early days of horse racing until about 1900, most of the handlers, trainers, grooms, and jockeys were African Americans. In the first Kentucky Derby, run in 1875, thirteen of the fifteen jockeys were black. In that race, an African American jockey, Oliver Lewis, rode the winning horse, Aristides, and established an American record for the race. Later that year, Lewis led Aristides to a second place at Belmont. It was reported that after Lewis left racing he worked for a bookmaker, which was legal at the time, and provided detailed information on the characteristics of various racehorses.

◆

WHO WAS THE FIRST JOCKEY TO WIN THE
KENTUCKY DERBY THREE TIMES?

Considered one of the greatest jockeys in racing history, Isaac Murphy was born in 1860 in Fayette County, Kentucky. When his father, who fought in the Union Army, died as a prisoner of war, his mother moved the family to Lexington to live with Isaac's grandfather. The youngster exercised horses for stables in the area, and ran his first professional race when he was only fourteen. Since most of the jockeys of the time were African American, it wasn't difficult for him to enter the profession. When his career began, he changed his last name from Burns to Murphy, in honor of his grandfather, Green Murphy.

ISAAC MURPHY

During his twenty-year career, Murphy raced 1,412 times and won 628 victories. In Saratoga, New York, in 1882, he won forty-nine of his fifty-one races. He won his first Kentucky Derby in 1884, and won it again in 1890 and 1891. Murphy retired from racing in 1895, and died of pneumonia a year later when he was only thirty-five. He was entered in the Halls of Fame of two racetracks: Pimlico and Saratoga.

◆

WHO WAS THE FIRST AFRICAN AMERICAN TO PLAY MAJOR LEAGUE BASEBALL?

Moses Fleetwood Walker was born in 1857 in Mt. Pleasant, Ohio, one of the stops for runaway slaves along the Underground Railroad. His family moved to nearby Steubenville, where his father, one of the first African American doctors in the state, opened a practice. Fleetwood and his younger brother Weldy both entered

MOSES FLEETWOOD WALKER WITH THE TOLEDO BLUE STOCKINGS

Oberlin College, and in 1881 they were the only African Americans on the school's baseball team.

In 1882 Walker enrolled in the University of Michigan Law School, where he played ball for two seasons before leaving to enter professional baseball as a catcher for the Toledo Blue Stockings. When Toledo entered the American Association, a major league, in 1884, Walker became the first African American ballplayer in the majors. During his season with Toledo, he often had to contend with racial insults, especially when traveling in the South. After Toledo let him go, he played for five more years in the minor leagues.

When he was thirty-seven, Walker left baseball and worked for a time as a mail clerk in Syracuse, New York, before returning to Steubenville, where he operated a hotel and he and his brother Weldy published a newspaper. Walker and his wife then moved to Cadiz, Ohio, to manage an opera house. In 1908 he published a book entitled *Our Home Colony: A Treatise on the Past, Present and Future of the Negro Race in America.* After Walker died in 1924, Oberlin alumni put a headstone on his grave that read: "First Black Major League Baseball Player in U.S.A."

◆

WHAT WAS THE FIRST SALARIED AFRICAN AMERICAN BASEBALL TEAM?

During the summer of 1885, the headwaiter at the Argyle Hotel in Babylon, New York, whose name was Frank Thompson, formed a baseball team composed of his fellow African American waiters. They called themselves the Athletics of Babylon. When the hotel closed for the season on October 1, they added more players and hit the road as a professional team.

Impressed by their talents, a wealthy man from New Jersey bought the team, hired an African American manager, and renamed them the Cuban Giants. So they wouldn't be discriminated against as African Americans, the players spoke a kind of doubletalk on the field that they hoped would sound like Spanish.

The first team known to receive weekly paychecks, the Cuban Giants, who were called "marvels of the baseball world," played semipro teams, college teams, and minor league clubs, and almost always won.

◆

WHO WAS THE FIRST AFRICAN AMERICAN JOCKEY TO WIN INTERNATIONAL FAME?

William Simms, known as Willie, was born in Augusta, Georgia, in 1870. He gained fame when he raced in the Kentucky Derby twice—in 1896 and 1898—and finished first both times. He was also the first African American to win each of the Triple Crown races.

Hired to ride in England, Simms became the first American jockey to win on an English racetrack with an American horse, and is credited with introducing the "short stirrup" riding style in England. After retiring from racing, Simms trained horses for a living until he died at the age of forty-seven.

◆

WHO WAS THE FIRST AFRICAN AMERICAN WORLD CHAMPION CYCLIST?

Marshall W. Taylor, born in Indianapolis in 1878, got a job with a local bicycle shop when he was fourteen. He did odd jobs and performed stunts while wearing a military uniform, which earned him the nickname "Major." Around this time he started winning bicycle races, encouraged by his new boss, Lewis Munger, who owned a bike factory. When Munger moved his business to Worcester, Massachusetts, in 1895, Taylor went with him.

Taylor started breaking records, and in 1899 he became a world champion when he won a one-mile race in Montreal. He began competing abroad, racing in Europe, Australia, and New Zealand. At the peak of his success, he had become the most successful and wealthiest athlete of his time.

Taylor retired from racing at the age of thirty-two and began investing his fortune in various business ventures, all of which were unsuccessful. In an effort to save himself from poverty, he moved to a YMCA in Chicago and tried to sell copies of his autobiography, *The Fastest Bicycle Rider in the World*. But he died at the age of fifty-three in the charity ward of Cook County Hospital and was buried in an unmarked grave. There he lay until 1948, when a group of bike racers, including Frank Schwinn, owner of the Schwinn Bicycle Company, moved his remains to a better spot in the cemetery and installed a bronze plaque with an inscription that began: "World's champion bicycle racer who came up the hard way . . ."

In 2000, the Major Taylor Association of Worcester, Massachusetts, chose the Maryland sculptor Antonio Tobias Mendez to create a Major Taylor statue at the Worcester Public Library.

◆

WHEN WAS THE FIRST GOLF TEE CREATED?

In December 1899, Dr. George F. Grant, an African American dentist and an amateur golfer, received a patent for a wooden golf tee. Before his invention, golfers had to balance their balls on mounds of damp sand.

◆

WHO WAS THE FIRST AFRICAN AMERICAN PROFESSIONAL BASKETBALL PLAYER?

When Harry "Bucky" Lew signed up with the Lowell, Massachusetts, Pawtucket Athletic Club in the New England Basketball League in 1902, he became the first African American to sign a professional basketball contract. Lew was born in Lowell in 1884 into a family with a lengthy history in Massachusetts. His great-great grandfather served in the Revolutionary War, and his grandparents' home was a stop on the Underground Railroad.

As a student at Lowell High School, Lew was an excellent student, an outstanding basketball player, and a talented musician, playing a violin solo at his graduation. But on the basketball court, he faced taunts, racial slurs, and rough treatment from white players on opposing teams. In a 1958 interview with the *Springfield Union*, Lew said, "I took the bumps . . . but I gave it right back. It was rough but worth it. Once they knew I could take it, I had it made."

In 1898, Lew joined the local YMCA team, leading it to championships. His expertise on the court led the Pawtucket Athletic Club of the New England Basketball League to recruit him. After the league folded in 1905, Lew stayed in basketball for the next twenty years, managing and playing with teams he'd organized. At the age of forty-two he played his final game, and two years later he moved to Springfield, Massachusetts, where he died in 1963.

◆

WHO WAS THE FIRST AFRICAN AMERICAN BOXER TO WIN A WORLD TITLE?

Joe Gans, born Joseph Gaines in 1874, was still a youngster when he began working as an oyster shucker on the docks of his native Baltimore, Maryland. He started fighting in the back rooms of saloons in what were called battles royal, in which a group of men fought until only one was left standing. Small but tough, Gans was often the winner. He caught the attention of a local restaurant owner and boxing fan, who sponsored his professional debut. Gans became a pro fighter in 1901; a year later he won the lightweight title in a fight in Ontario, Canada, knocking out Frank Erne in the first round.

Gans, who was known as the "Old Master," won a savage fight in 1906 against a Danish boxer called Battling Nelson. Two years later they fought again. Gans, weakened by tuberculosis, lost by a knockout. He died in August 1910 at the age of thirty-six.

◆

WHO WAS THE FIRST AFRICAN AMERICAN PROFESSIONAL FOOTBALL PLAYER?

When Charles Follis signed with the Shelby Blues in Shelby, Ohio, in September 1904, he became the first African American professional football player. Born in Cloverdale, Virginia, in 1879, Follis moved with his family to Wooster, Ohio, when he was a youngster. At Wooster High School, Follis organized the first football team and was elected captain.

He continued to play football after entering the College of Wooster, first for a local amateur team and then for the Shelby Blues, with whom he signed a contract after he graduated in 1904. Follis was severely injured in a Thanksgiving Day game in 1906 and retired from football. He joined the Cuban Giants baseball team, playing with them until 1910, when he died of pneumonia at the age of thirty-one.

◆

WHO WAS THE FIRST AFRICAN AMERICAN ATHLETE TO WIN AN OLYMPIC MEDAL?

In the 1904 Olympics in St. Louis, Missouri, George Poage, a hurdler and quarter-miler, finished third in the 200-meter and 400-meter hurdles, becoming the first African American to win a medal in the Olympic Games. Poage, who represented the Milwaukee Athletic Club, had set a college record for the 440-yard dash and the low hurdles while a student at the University of Wisconsin.

◆

WHO WAS THE FIRST AFRICAN AMERICAN INDUCTED INTO THE RODEO HALL OF FAME?

Bill Pickett, a native Texan born in 1870, learned to ride horses and rope cattle while working as a ranch hand when he was a teenager. While watching herd dogs control cattle by biting their lips, Pickett invented a method of subduing steers that he called bulldogging. While chasing a steer on horseback, he would leap from his horse, grab the steer by its horns, twist its head back, sink his teeth into its upper lip, and wrestle it to the ground. After giving bulldogging exhibitions around Texas, Pickett got to know the Miller brothers, who owned the 101 Ranch near Ponca City, Oklahoma, and signed up with the 101 Ranch Wild West Show. The hair-raising feats of Pickett and his horse, Spradley, attracted crowds throughout the world.

BILL PICKETT

After years of traveling with the show and also appearing in movies, Pickett settled on the 101 Ranch. In 1932, while roping a bronco, he was kicked in the head, suffered a fractured skull, and died two weeks later. In 1971 he became the first African American to be inducted into the National Rodeo Hall of Fame in Oklahoma City, and in 1994 the United States Postal Service issued a stamp in his honor.

◆

WHO WAS THE FIRST AFRICAN AMERICAN WORLD HEAVYWEIGHT CHAMPION?

Born in Galveston, Texas, in 1878, John Arthur Johnson left school after fifth grade and began working as a stevedore on the docks.

Jack, as he was now called, started boxing as a sparring partner and in private clubs, turned professional in 1897, and eventually became a heavyweight champion among African American fighters. But Jim Jeffries, the white champion at the time, refused to fight him because of his race. In 1908, Johnson convinced the then heavyweight champion, Tommy Burns, to agree to a fight. The match took place on Christmas Day in Sydney, Australia, and ended in a victory for Johnson, making him the first African American heavyweight champ.

The boxing establishment, upset with Johnson's win, began to search for a white boxer who could dethrone him. The promoters succeeded in getting former champion Jim Jeffries to agree to a match and billed him as the "Great White Hope." The fight took place in Reno, Nevada, on July 4, 1910. Called the "battle of the century," the brutal match ended in the fifteenth round and Johnson was declared winner by a knockout. Johnson successfully defended his crown until 1915 when, at age thirty-seven, he fought Jess Willard in Havana, Cuba, and was knocked out in the twenty-sixth round.

In 1922 Johnson served a one-year sentence at Leavenworth Federal Prison on an old charge having to do with transporting a white woman over a state line. Few people know that while he was doing his time, Johnson received patents for two inventions, an improved wrench and a theft-prevention device for vehicles.

Johnson, who had held the heavyweight title longer than anyone up to that time, crashed into a light pole in his new Lincoln Zephyr car while traveling to New York and died in a North Carolina hospital on June 10, 1946. He was buried in Graceland Cemetery in Chicago.

◆

WHO WAS THE FIRST AFRICAN AMERICAN TO WIN AN OLYMPIC GOLD MEDAL?

Although his name might be unfamiliar today, back in 1907 the runner John Baxter Taylor was considered the most outstanding quarter-miler in the college world. One year later, Taylor competed in the Olympic Games in London, England, and became the first African American to bring home the gold. Born in 1882 in Washington, D.C., Taylor moved with his family to Philadelphia, where he attended Central High School. He was captain of the track team there, and later, at Brown Preparatory School, he was a member of a team that never lost a race.

In 1903 Taylor entered the University of Pennsylvania's Wharton School, later switching to the School of Veterinary Medicine. His outstanding performance on the university's track teams led the school to championships and enhanced its reputation in the collegiate world of track and field. Taylor's stride measured eight feet, six inches, the longest of any runner at the time. In the summer of 1904, he won races in England and France, and in 1908, at the Olympic Games in London, he was awarded a gold medal as a member of America's one-mile relay team.

Only four months later, at the age of twenty-six, Taylor died of typhoid pneumonia. A *New York Times* article reporting on his funeral began: "Some of the mightiest and speediest athletes of the country stood beside the bier of John B. Taylor . . . and paid their last respects to the former intercollegiate quarter-mile champion and the world's greatest negro runner . . ."

◆

WHO WAS THE FIRST AFRICAN AMERICAN FOOTBALL PLAYER TO PLAY IN THE ROSE BOWL?

Although he wasn't very big—only five feet seven and 160 pounds—Frederick Douglas "Fritz" Pollard was chosen to play football for Brown University after he entered in 1915. He was the first African American player in the school's history and became known as the team's most elusive running back.

In Chicago, where Pollard was born in 1894, he was an outstanding player on the high school football team. A member of the wealthy Rockefeller family who saw him play took an interest in him and paid his tuition to Brown. On New Year's Day 1916, Pollard became the first African American to play in a Rose Bowl game when Brown played Washington State. It was said that when some officials objected to his presence, his Brown University teammates refused to play if he were barred from the game.

FREDERICK DOUGLAS "FRITZ" POLLARD

Pollard left Brown to serve in the army, and in 1919 he signed up with the Akron Pros as one of the first black professional football players. Later, when he was named coach of the Pros, he became the first African American head coach in the National Football League. He continued to coach a number of teams, including an all-black semiprofessional team in New York City called the Brown Bombers. Pollard's accomplishments extended to the business world; he founded the first African American investment banking firm in New York and published the *Independent News,* the first tabloid newspaper in Harlem owned and operated by African Americans. Pollard died in 1986.

♦

WHO FOUNDED THE FIRST AFRICAN AMERICAN
PROFESSIONAL BASEBALL LEAGUE?

A ndrew "Rube" Foster, born in Calvert, Texas, in 1879, organized his first baseball team in elementary school, and before finishing high school he left to become a professional player. At seventeen he joined a traveling Texas team called the Waco Yellow Jackets and went on to pitch for the Chicago Union Giants, the Cuban X Giants, and the Philadelphia Giants. Some considered the six-foot-four, 200-pound ballplayer one of the greatest pitchers of all time. In 1907 Foster joined the Leland Giants of Chicago,

ANDREW "RUBE" FOSTER

later becoming manager, and four years later became part owner of a team called the Chicago American Giants.

In 1920 "the father of black baseball," as Foster has been called, formed the National Association of Professional Baseball Clubs, which became known as the Negro National League. His aim was to provide stability and financial equity for African American ballplayers. With Foster as president, the league's first teams included the Kansas City Monarchs, the Indianapolis ABCs, the Chicago American Giants, the St. Louis Stars, the Dayton Marcos, and the Cuban Giants.

Foster worked night and day running both the league and his own team. The strain took its toll; he suffered a breakdown in 1926 and was committed to a mental hospital. Never recovering completely, he died in 1930. Among the tributes at his funeral was a giant baseball made of white chrysanthemums and roses sent by the directors of the Negro National League.

♦

WHAT WAS THE FIRST AFRICAN AMERICAN OWNED ALL-BLACK PROFESSIONAL BASKETBALL TEAM?

In 1923, a man named Robert Douglas, who owned and managed an all-African American basketball team called the Spartan Braves, approached the owner of the new Renaissance Ballroom and Casino located in the center of Harlem. Douglas asked if the Spartans could play their home games there in exchange for changing the team's name to the New York Renaissance. The owner agreed, and the casino's ballroom became a venue both for basketball games and dancing to big bands. Douglas's team, known as the Rens, was the first African American owned all-black professional basketball team in the country.

The Rens attracted leading basketball stars and played steadily both in New York and around the country. In one season, they won eighty-eight straight games. But victorious games sometimes ended in fights with white players and fans, and the team had to contend with discrimination while on the road. John Isaacs, who died in 2009, was a leading player with the Rens. In 1997,

Isaacs told the *New York Times:* "We would walk into a white-owned restaurant, and the best they could ever do for us was let us eat, standing, in the kitchen, where no one else could see us."

The Rens played teams across the board—professional, semi-pro, and college. But their toughest competitor was the Original Celtics, a leading all-white team from New York. Their games attracted many hundreds of fans. In 1925, when the American Basketball League refused to admit the Rens, the Celtics declined to join in solidarity. Six years later, the Rens defeated the Celtics for the world basketball championship.

After a groundbreaking twenty-six-year career, the Rens disbanded in 1949. John Isaacs once said that when he heard anyone mention that it was the Knicks who brought a championship to New York, he'd say, "Pardon me, but it was the Rens, not the Knicks, who brought home New York City's first official pro basketball title."

WHO WAS THE FIRST AFRICAN AMERICAN BOXER TO WIN THE MIDDLEWEIGHT CROWN?

In February 1926, Theodore Flowers became the first African American middleweight boxing champion when he won the title over Harry Greb in Madison Square Garden. Flowers, a native of Camille, Georgia, who read the Bible before and after every fight, was known as the "Georgia Deacon." A year after winning the championship, he died at the age of thirty-two while undergoing surgery.

◆

WHO WAS THE FIRST AFRICAN AMERICAN GOLFER TO BELONG TO THE PGA?

Dewey Brown learned the game of golf as a caddy in New Jersey, and by the time he was sixteen he had begun his apprenticeship as a professional golfer. At the Shawnee Country Club in Pennsylvania, where Brown started working at the age of twenty,

DEWEY BROWN

he became known as an excellent teacher and a skilled club maker—
President Harding was one of his customers.

In 1928, the Professional Golfers Association, which had no African
American members, accepted Brown's application for membership. Because of Brown's fair skin, he was apparently mistaken for
white. Six years later, his membership was withdrawn with no
explanation.

Brown was a pioneer in a sport dominated by white men, and
he was held in high esteem by all the leading golf pros. In 1947
he moved to the tiny town of Indian Lake in New York's Adiron-
dack Mountains, where he bought the Cedar River House, a resort
hotel with its own nine-hole golf course. He owned and operated
the resort for twenty-five years, leaving it to his son when he retired in 1972.

♦

WHO WAS THE FIRST ATHLETE TO WIN FOUR
GOLD MEDALS IN A SINGLE OLYMPICS?

James Cleveland Owens was born in 1913 in a small Alabama town, the seventh child of poor cotton farmers. His family called him J. C. He was about eight years old when his parents moved to Cleveland, Ohio, in search of better employment. When he started school there, his teacher heard his name as Jesse, and that was how he became known.

In his Cleveland high school, young Jesse Owens was encouraged by the track coach to start training for the team. He became a record-breaking high school track star and went on to make history at Ohio State University when, at a Big Ten track and field meet in May 1935, in less than an hour he set a world record in the broad jump, tied his own world record in the 100-yard dash, and broke two more world records in the 200-yard dash and 220-yard low hurdles.

Owens will always be remembered for winning four gold medals at the 1936 Olympic Games in Berlin, where Hitler had hoped to prove that the Germans were the master race. Owens tied the world record in the 100-meter dash, set Olympic records in the broad jump and the 200-meter dash, and he and his team won gold medals in the 440-meter relay, setting a world record.

When Owens returned to the United States, he was honored by a ticker tape parade in New York City and a reception at the Waldorf-Astoria Hotel. He took a number of jobs in an effort to support his family, eventually working for the Illinois Athletic Commission. Owens died in March 1980, but his glorious victory in Germany will never be forgotten. At the opening ceremony of the 1984 Olympics in Los Angeles, his granddaughter, Gina Hemphill, carried the Olympic torch into the coliseum as a tribute to his memory.

◆

WHO WAS THE FIRST BOXER TO HOLD THE HEAVYWEIGHT CHAMPIONSHIP FOR LONGER THAN A DECADE?

In what some consider the often corrupt world of boxing, Joe Louis was a shining star. Always honorable and dignified, he was idolized by African Americans. He was born Joseph Louis Barrow in 1914 to a poor sharecropper family in Alabama. When his father died and his mother remarried, the family moved to Detroit, where Louis became enthralled by boxing. After winning a string of amateur bouts, he was taken on by a wealthy African American businessman named John Roxborough, who moved him to Chicago in 1934.

By 1935 his reputation as a knockout fighter had earned him the nickname "Brown Bomber." That year Louis fought the former heavyweight champion Primo Carnera in New York's Madison Square Garden and another ex-champ, Max Baer, in Yankee Stadium. He knocked out both. But Louis didn't train hard enough for his next fight, with the German ex-champion Max Schmeling, and lost. His fans were distraught. Then, in 1937, Louis came back; he defeated James Braddock and was crowned heavyweight champion of the world.

In June 1938, with both black and white fans cheering for him, he faced Max Schmeling again. Two minutes and four seconds into the first round, Louis knocked out the German fighter. After going on to beat Billy Conn and Buddy Baer, he joined the army in January 1942 and played a major role in desegregating sports teams in army camps. He returned to the ring in 1946 and defended his title four times over the next three years.

On March 1, 1949, Louis announced his retirement. He had been undefeated world champion for twelve years. But he was overwhelmed with financial problems and owed the government a million dollars in back taxes. He was forced to fight the younger boxers Ezzard Charles and Rocky Marciano, losing badly both times.

Louis wrestled professionally for a time, worked in public relations, and became a bouncer at a Las Vegas club. He suffered a massive heart attack in October 1977. Never fully recovering, he died on April 12, 1981.

◆

WHO WAS THE FIRST AFRICAN AMERICAN IN MAJOR LEAGUE BASEBALL IN MODERN TIMES?

On April 11, 1947, Jackie Robinson played his first game with the National League's Brooklyn Dodgers, becoming the first African American ballplayer in the major leagues since the early days of baseball. (In 1884, Moses Fleetwood Walker was playing with the Toledo Blue Stockings when the team joined the American Association, then a major baseball league.) Robinson was born in Georgia in 1919 and moved with his family to Pasadena, California. An outstanding athlete at the University of California at Los Angeles, he was forced to leave college in 1941 because he could no longer afford the expense. He played professional football before going into the army to serve in World War II.

After his discharge, Robinson signed with a Negro League baseball team, the Kansas City Monarchs. He was noticed by Branch Rickey, owner of the Brooklyn Dodgers, who signed him up in 1945. After a year with the Dodgers farm team in Montreal, Robinson was brought up to the majors in April 1947—the first African American in modern times to play major league baseball. That year he was named Rookie of the Year. He was chosen the National League's Most Valuable Player in 1949, and in 1962 was inducted into the Baseball Hall of Fame.

Robinson played with the Brooklyn Dodgers for his entire career. After his retirement in 1956 he was active in business and social programs. He died in 1972.

◆

WHO WAS THE FIRST AFRICAN AMERICAN BASEBALL PLAYER IN THE AMERICAN LEAGUE?

In July 1947, three months after Jackie Robinson's first game for the Brooklyn Dodgers, Larry Doby signed a contract with the Cleveland Indians, becoming the first African American baseball player in the American League. A World War II veteran and a former second baseman and infielder for the Newark Eagles of the Negro Leagues, Doby became the first African American to score a home run in the World Series, when in 1948 he hit a 425-foot drive into right field.

Doby played in the majors for thirteen years and was named to the American League All-Star team six times. In 1978 he was appointed manager of the Chicago White Sox, becoming the second African American manager in baseball. Twenty years later he was elected to the Baseball Hall of Fame in Cooperstown, New York. Doby died in 2003.

♦

LEROY "SATCHEL" PAIGE

WHO WAS THE FIRST AFRICAN AMERICAN
TO PITCH IN A MAJOR LEAGUE GAME?

Dan Bankhead, one of five brothers who played professional baseball in the Negro Leagues, was born in Empire, Alabama, in 1920. Bankhead signed his first contract with the Birmingham Black Barons in 1940. He left baseball for three years to serve in the Marine Corps, and by 1947 he had become a leading pitcher for the Memphis Red Socks of the Negro American League. It was then that he was scouted by Branch Rickey, the general manager of the National League's Brooklyn Dodgers, who had signed up Jackie Robinson two years earlier. Rickey bought Bankhead's contract from Memphis, and on August 26, 1947, he became the first African American to pitch in a major league game when he took the mound for the Dodgers against the Pittsburgh Pirates at Ebbets Field.

Bankhead pitched in only four games for the Dodgers before returning to the minor leagues. He rejoined the Dodgers for the 1950 season, winning nine games and losing four. He again returned to the minors to stay, and spent most of the rest of his career as a hitter. He died of cancer in Houston in 1956, one day before his fifty-fifth birthday.

◆

WHO WAS THE FIRST AFRICAN AMERICAN PITCHER
IN THE AMERICAN LEAGUE?

Although Dan Bankhead was the first African American pitcher in major league baseball, he was never as celebrated as another pitcher, Leroy "Satchel" Paige. Not only was Paige the first African American baseball player to pitch in the American League, he also was considered by many to be the greatest pitcher in the history of the sport. In the 1930s, while he was still playing for all-black baseball teams, white major leaguers such as Dizzy Dean and Joe DiMaggio who faced Paige in exhibition games called him the best they had ever seen.

Paige was born in Mobile, Alabama. He said the year was 1906, but some have claimed it was earlier. In any case, when he was about seven years old he earned money carrying bags and satchels at the local railroad station. It is said that he dangled several satchels at a time from a long pole, causing the other kids to call him "satchel tree." Eventually shortened to Satchel, the name stayed with him.

Paige also had a job cleaning up at a local ballpark, and it was there that he became interested in baseball. Not able to afford a ball, he practiced by pitching rocks. At age twelve he was caught stealing some cheap rings and was sent to a reform school, where the baseball coach helped him refine his pitching style and learn the game. In 1924 Paige signed on as a pitcher for the Mobile Tigers, and two years later joined the Chattanooga Black Lookouts. He continued to play for various teams in the Negro Leagues, culminating in a string of victories.

Finally, in 1948, a year after Jackie Robinson integrated major league baseball, Paige was signed by the Cleveland Indians. At age forty-two, the tall, lanky player, famous for his fast "bee" ball, became the first African American to pitch in the American League. In 1952, while pitching for the St. Louis Browns, he was chosen for the American League All-Stars. His last job in baseball came in 1968, when he was hired as a coach by the Atlanta Braves. When Paige was elected to the Baseball Hall of Fame in 1971, his inclusion was based on his record in the Negro Leagues. He died eleven years later, leaving a list of rules for a good life, including this one: "Don't look back. Someone may be gaining on you."

♦

WHEN DID THE FIRST AFRICAN AMERICAN WOMAN WIN AN OLYMPIC GOLD MEDAL?

In 1948, at the Olympic Summer Games in London, Alice Coachman became the first African American woman to win the gold, taking first place in the high jump. Her leap of five feet, six and one-quarter inches set a new Olympic record.

This native of Albany, Georgia, where she was born in 1923, became interested in the high jump after watching a track meet for boys. Using ropes and sticks, she and her friends created setups to jump over. Since she wasn't allowed to practice in public facilities, Coachman trained by running barefoot on dirt roads around her town. She excelled in a string of track and field events in high school and as a student at Tuskegee Institute and Albany State College. She had to wait until 1948 to enter the Olympics, since the 1940 and 1944 games had been cancelled because of World War II.

After retiring from competition, Coachman became a physical education teacher and a coach. In 1996, at the Centennial Olympic Games in Atlanta, she was honored as one of the one hundred greatest Olympic athletes.

In a 2010 interview with the National Visionary Leadership Project, Coachman recalled her return to Albany, Georgia, after winning the gold at the 1948 summer Olympics. A welcome-home celebration was held in her honor, but the audience was segregated, she said, and the mayor of Albany congratulated her but wouldn't shake her hand. "I had done this for America, the state of Georgia, and my hometown," Coachman said. "To come back home to your own state and your own city and you can't get a handshake from the mayor, it wasn't a good feeling, but that's the way it was."

◆

WHEN DID THE U.S. LAWN TENNIS ASSOCIATION ALLOW AN AFRICAN AMERICAN TO PLAY IN A TOURNAMENT?

Reginald Weir, an outstanding young tennis player, was captain of his team at City College of New York for three years in a row. Yet in 1929, despite protests by the NAACP, Weir was barred from the National Junior Indoor Tennis Tournament of the U.S. Lawn Tennis Association, the predecessor of today's U.S. Tennis Association. It was 1948 before the Association permitted Weir to participate in a tournament. He won his first match in the Association's National Men's Indoor Championships. By that time, he was thirty-seven years old and a practicing New York City physician and surgeon.

In September 1986, on his seventy-fifth birthday—a little less than a year before he died—a reception was held for him at the Upper Ridgewood Tennis Club in New Jersey. The United States Tennis Association president presented him with a plaque that read: "In appreciation to Dr. Reginald Weir for outstanding and inspirational contributions to the sport of tennis as a player, sportsman, and national champion."

◆

WHO WAS THE FIRST AFRICAN AMERICAN MEMBER OF A U.S. OLYMPIC BASKETBALL TEAM?

When Don Barksdale was growing up in Oakland, California, where he was born in 1923, his high school basketball coach kept him off the team for three years because he didn't want more than one African American player. So Barksdale practiced the game in his neighborhood park, where his skills were noticed by a coach at Marin Junior College, who offered him a slot on his team. Two years later he won a scholarship to UCLA, graduating in December 1947 after taking two years off to serve in the army.

Although Barksdale was chosen to play on the United States basketball team in the 1948 Olympics, he was not allowed to join a professional team because the NBA did not allow African American players. Instead, he signed up with the Oakland Bittners, an Amateur Athletic Union team, and was named AAU All-American three years in a row. In 1951, after the NBA ended its ban, he signed a contract with the Baltimore Bullets, and two years later was traded to the Boston Celtics. In 1953 he was the first African American to play in an NBA All-Star game.

After retiring from basketball, Barksdale hosted a television show, worked as a disc jockey, and opened two nightclubs. He died of cancer in his Oakland home at the age of sixty-nine.

◆

WHO WAS THE FIRST AFRICAN AMERICAN TENNIS PLAYER TO COMPETE AT WIMBLEDON?

Althea Gibson, born in South Carolina in 1927, fought years of racial discrimination to win the most prestigious titles in tennis. Growing up in New York City's Harlem, Gibson started winning tournaments as a paddle tennis player. She was encouraged to learn tennis and soon became a member of the Harlem Cosmopolitan Tennis Club. In 1942 she won the first of numerous events sponsored by the American Tennis Association, an all-black organization, but tennis tournaments outside this association remained closed to her.

Finally, Gibson was allowed to enter the U.S. Championships of 1950 at Forest Hills. A year later she was invited to play at Wimbledon, England—the first African American to compete in that renowned tournament. In 1957 and '58 she returned to Wimbledon, winning women's singles and doubles, and also earned United States championships for women's singles at Forest Hills. After her first victory at Wimbledon, Gibson was greeted with a ticker tape parade in New York City, finally gaining the recognition she deserved. In 1968 she became the first African American inducted into the International Tennis Hall of Fame.

Gibson stopped competing in her forties and became a tennis instructor. She was inducted into the International Tennis Hall of Fame in 1971, and in 1975, she was named New Jersey Commissioner of Athletics, a post she held for ten years. She died in 2003 at the age of seventy-six.

◆

WHO WERE THE FIRST AFRICAN AMERICANS TO PLAY IN THE NATIONAL BASKETBALL ASSOCIATION?

Three African American basketball players were signed by National Basketball Association teams for the 1950–51 season. They were Charles "Chuck" Cooper, who signed with the Boston Celtics; Earl Lloyd, with the Washington Capitols; and Nathaniel "Sweetwater" Clifton, with the New York Knickerbockers. Cooper, a six-feet, six-inch forward from Duquesne University, was the first to be drafted. Lloyd was chosen later in the same draft and became the first African American to play in an NBA game, making his debut on October 31, 1950. Cooper played his first game a day later. Clifton, who was the first to actually sign a contract, debuted with the Knicks on November 4.

◆

WHO WAS THE FIRST AFRICAN AMERICAN TO WIN THE DECATHLON GOLD MEDAL IN THE OLYMPICS?

As a student in his Plainfield, New Jersey, high school, Milt Campbell was known as one of the finest athletes in the country, noted for his skill in track, swimming, wrestling, and football. Campbell's track and field talents were so outstanding that his coach decided to train him for the decathlon in the 1952 Olympics in Helsinki, Finland. The decathlon competition included ten track and field events over two days: the 100-meter sprint, long jump, shot put, high jump, 400-meter race, 110-meter hurdles, discus throw, pole vault, javelin throw, and 1500-meter race.

Campbell's hometown residents raised $1,500 to send him to the West Coast for the Olympic tryouts. At the Games in Helsinki, the eighteen-year-old finished second in the decathlon competition. Four years later, while a student at Indiana University, he won a decathlon gold medal at the Olympics in Melbourne, Australia. After college, where he also played football, Campbell joined two professional teams for a time. He went on to start a school for inner-city youths, run a community center, and establish a personal development company. Campbell died in November 2012 at his home in Gainesville, Georgia.

◆

WHO WAS THE FIRST WOMAN TO PLAY IN THE NEGRO LEAGUES?

When Toni Stone was a teenager in St. Paul, Minnesota, where she was born in 1921, she played softball with a boys' team, switching to baseball after graduating from high school. She moved to California in the early 1940s and played with an African American team called the San Francisco Sea Lions, then traveled to New Orleans, where she joined the Black Pelicans and then the New Orleans Creoles. Although a women's baseball league existed at the time, it was "whites only," so Stone always played on all-male African American teams.

In 1953, Stone was signed to play second base with the Indianapolis Clowns, making her the first woman to play in the Negro Leagues. Stone's image both as a woman and a skilled player attracted new fans to the Negro Leagues, which had been declining since Jackie Robinson ended segregation in the majors. Stone once said that most of her fellow players gave her a hard time, saying things like, "Go home and fix your husband some biscuits."

But she persevered, playing with the Clowns until 1954, when she was sold to the Kansas City Monarchs. She retired at the end of that season and was later honored by the Women's Sports Hall of Fame and the Baseball Hall of Fame in Cooperstown. Stone, who died in 1996, had said that her favorite baseball memory was playing against the famed pitcher Satchel Paige and getting a hit.

◆

WHO WAS THE FIRST AFRICAN AMERICAN MAN TO WIN A MAJOR TENNIS TITLE?

Arthur Ashe began playing tennis as a ten-year-old in a segregated playground in his hometown of Richmond, Virginia. In 1960, at age seventeen, Ashe won his first United States Lawn Tennis Association national title, the Junior Indoors. A year later he became the first African American member of the U.S. Junior Davis Cup Team.

Overcoming the experiences of his early years, when he was sometimes denied entry in tournaments because of his race, Ashe went on to achieve other firsts: he was the first African American to be named to a United States Davis Cup team, in 1963; the first to win the U.S. Open, in 1968; the first to win men's singles at Wimbledon, in 1975; and, ten years later, the first African American man inducted into the International Tennis Hall of Fame. Not

ARTHUR ASHE

political at first, Ashe grew to be a quiet but firm fighter for civil rights, speaking out against injustice in the United States and apartheid in South Africa.

After piling up a multitude of victories, Ashe suffered a heart attack in 1979 and underwent quadruple bypass surgery. In April 1980 he announced his retirement from competitive tennis, and five months later he was named captain of the U.S. Davis Cup team, leading the United States to victory in 1981 and 1982. Ashe published a three-volume history of African American athletes, *A Hard Road to Glory,* in 1988. Just four years later, in an emotional news conference, a gaunt, grim-faced Ashe announced that, apparently as a result of blood transfusions after a second open-heart surgery in 1983, he had contracted the virus that causes AIDS.

Ashe became a leading spokesman in the fight to combat the

disease, creating the Arthur Ashe Foundation for the Defeat of AIDS and speaking before the United Nations on World AIDS Day, December 1, 1992. On February 6, 1993, at the age of forty-nine, Ashe died of pneumonia, a complication of AIDS.

On July 10, 1996, on what would have been his fifty-third birthday, a statue of Ashe was dedicated on Monument Avenue in Richmond. He is depicted carrying books in one hand and a tennis racket in the other. And a year later, the Arthur Ashe Stadium in Flushing, New York, hosted its first U.S. Open. Earlier that year, the president of the U.S. Tennis Association said the stadium was being named in Ashe's honor because he was "the finest human being the sport of tennis has ever known."

◆

WHO WAS THE FIRST WOMAN TO WIN THREE OLYMPIC GOLD MEDALS IN TRACK?

When Wilma Rudolph was a child, no one could have imagined that someday she would be a record-breaking athlete. Born in 1940 in Clarksville, Tennessee, one of nineteen children, she was a sickly child. She came down with scarlet fever and double pneumonia, and when she was four, she was left partially paralyzed by polio and forced to wear leg braces and special shoes. Her family learned to massage and exercise her legs, and by the time she was twelve she could walk on her own.

In high school Rudolph was a star basketball player and top runner. She joined the track team at Tennessee State University, which she entered in 1958, and soon made history. At the 1960 Olympic Games in Rome, she became the first woman to win three gold medals in track, and the Associated Press named her Female Athlete of the Year. At her insistence, a parade and banquet in her honor were the first integrated events ever held in her hometown of Clarksville. After her Olympic victory, Rudolph coached track, was a television sportscaster, and started a foundation to support amateur sports. She died of cancer at her Tennessee home at the age of fifty-four.

◆

WHO WAS THE FIRST HEAVYWEIGHT CHAMPION TO REGAIN THE TITLE?

Floyd Patterson, born in 1935 in Waco, North Carolina, learned to box in a New York State reform school. He won the New York Golden Gloves title in 1951 and '52 and captured a gold medal in the middleweight competition at the 1952 Olympic Games in Helsinki, Finland. The next year he switched to professional boxing, and in 1956 knocked out Archie Moore to become, at twenty-one, the youngest world heavyweight champion in history.

He successfully defended his title four times, but in 1959 he was knocked out by Ingemar Johansson. A year later he KO'd Johansson and regained the title. After losing to Sonny Liston and Muhammad Ali, Patterson retired from boxing at the age of thirty-seven. He later served for a time as New York State Athletic Commissioner. He died in May 2006 at the age of seventy-one at his home in New Paltz, New York.

♦

WHO WAS THE FIRST AFRICAN AMERICAN GOLFER TO PLAY FULL-TIME WITH THE PGA TOUR?

In 1932, when he was ten years old, Charles Sifford got a job as a caddy at the Carolina Country Club near his house in Charlotte, North Carolina. It was then that he discovered the game of golf. When he was seventeen he dropped out of ninth grade and took a bus to Philadelphia, where he got a job as a shipping clerk. He began to play at a public golf course, the first integrated course he had ever seen.

In 1946 Sifford was hired as a private golf instructor by the popular singer Billy Eckstine. For ten years he toured with Eckstine in the winter and in the summer played with the United Golf Association, which sponsored tours for African American golfers. In April 1961 Sifford played in his first Professional Golfers Association (PGA) tournament in Greensboro, North Carolina, the first African American to play in a PGA tour event in the South. Seven months later the PGA dropped its whites-only membership requirement, and Sifford became the first full-time PGA tour member.

Even though Sifford won the Greater Hartford Open in 1967 and the Los Angeles Open in 1969, the Masters Tournament committee chose not to invite him to participate. He played on the PGA circuit for fifteen years and became a regular player on the Senior PGA tour after it was instituted in 1980. In 1992 he published his autobiography, *Just Let Me Play.*

Sifford continued to play in the Super Seniors Tour into his seventies. In 2004, he became the first African American golfer to be inducted into the World Golf Hall of Fame. In an interview on AfroGolf.com, when asked if he was bitter about the racism he'd encountered in his career, he said, "No, I'm not bitter . . . I've put all that negative stuff behind me . . . When I was going through what I did, I focused on proving that a black man can play the game of golf as good as a white man."

◆

WHO WAS THE FIRST AFRICAN AMERICAN FOOTBALL PLAYER TO WIN THE HEISMAN TROPHY?

Ernie Davis was an athlete with great potential. Born in 1939 in New Salem, Pennsylvania, he was raised by his grandparents until the age of twelve, when he went to live with his mother and stepfather in Elmira, New York. An All-American in football and basketball at Elmira Free Academy, he won eleven varsity letters.

After he entered Syracuse University, his skills on the football field led some observers to call him the finest running back in the country. In 1961, his senior year, Davis became the first African American to win the Heisman Memorial Trophy, awarded annually to the country's best college football player.

After college, Davis was signed by the Cleveland Browns, and just before the 1962 season began, he traveled to Chicago to play with a college all-star team against the Green Bay Packers. But a few days before the game, doctors sent him to the hospital for medical tests. He was diagnosed with leukemia. Davis never got to play football with the Cleveland Browns; he died at the age of twenty-three.

◆

WHO WAS THE FIRST BASKETBALL PLAYER TO SCORE ONE HUNDRED POINTS IN A SINGLE GAME?

Although he was physically huge—seven feet, two inches tall and 265 pounds—basketball star Wilt Chamberlain was admired for his speed, grace, and coordination. Chamberlain, born in Philadelphia in 1936, was an outstanding overall athlete in high school. He entered the University of Kansas but left in his third year to join the Harlem Globetrotters. In 1959 he signed with the Phila-

WILT CHAMBERLAIN

delphia Warriors, and in the 1961–62 season he became the first player to score one hundred points in a single game as the Warriors beat the New York Knicks 169-147.

Chamberlain was eventually traded to the Philadelphia 76ers, and got to play with his first NBA championship team in the 1966–67 season, leading the 76ers to victory over the Boston Celtics. He was traded to the Los Angeles Lakers in 1968, and in February 1972 he became the first player in the NBA to score 30,000 points, when he reached that total in a game with the Phoenix Suns. After that season he retired from the NBA and coached for the San Diego Conquistadors for a year. He made a movie and pursued interests in volleyball, tennis, and polo, and in 1978 this legend of the courts was elected to the Basketball Hall of Fame. Chamberlain died in October 1999 of a heart attack in his Bel Air, California, home.

◆

WHO WAS THE FIRST AFRICAN AMERICAN COACH OF A MAJOR LEAGUE BASEBALL TEAM?

Born in 1911 in Carabelle, Florida, John "Buck" O'Neil worked in the celery fields of Sarasota with his father, who encouraged him to follow his dream of becoming a baseball player. He enrolled in Edward Waters College in Jacksonville, playing baseball for the college team, and began his professional career with the Miami Giants in 1934. He served as a first baseman and manager in the Negro Leagues until 1955. As manager of the Kansas City Monarchs, he helped more than three dozen players enter major league baseball.

O'Neil was named coach of the Chicago Cubs in 1962, making him the first African American coach in big league baseball. He never lost his love for the game. In 1991, at the age of seventy-nine, he became chairman of the board of the Negro Leagues Baseball Museum in Kansas City, located near the spot where the Negro National League was started in 1920 by Andrew "Rube" Foster.

In May 2006, O'Neil received an honorary doctorate in education from Missouri Western State University, where he also gave the commencement address. He died five months later in Kansas

JOHN "BUCK" O'NEIL

City. President Bush posthumously awarded him the Presidential Medal of Freedom for his "excellence and determination both on and off the baseball field." O'Neil's autobiography, *I Was Right on Time*, was published in 1996.

◆

WHO WAS THE FIRST AFRICAN AMERICAN TO BE SELECTED AS MVP OF THE AMERICAN LEAGUE?

After graduating from high school in St. Louis, Missouri, where he was born in 1929, Elston Howard joined the Kansas City Monarchs, a Negro Leagues team. In 1955 he became the first African American to play for the New York Yankees, and in 1963 was named the American League's Most Valuable Player.

The catcher was honored with "Elston Howard Day" on August

29, 1964, at Yankee Stadium, and was a Yankee coach until he died in 1980.

◆

WHO WAS THE FIRST AFRICAN AMERICAN TO ACHIEVE THE TITLE OF CHESS MASTER?

Although the involvement of African Americans in chess dates back to at least the nineteenth century, and some players have gained legendary status, their achievements have not received much attention outside of the world of chess. In 1859, James McCune Smith, an African American doctor, wrote an essay promoting chess as a healthy form of entertainment. And later in the nineteenth century, Theophilus Thompson, a domestic servant who was an especially talented chess player, wrote a book, *Chess Problems*.

In 1963, the first African American to achieve the title of national chess master, based on points accrued in tournament play, was Walter Harris, then a scientist at the U.S. Naval Observatory in Washington, D.C. In a December 2005 interview for the Chess Drum website, Harris expressed surprise that he was part of historic chess lore. He said that when he was playing chess, he was not trying to make history, but that the game was an outgrowth of his passion. He was often lonely, he said, as the only notable African American chess player of the time.

◆

WHO WAS THE FIRST AFRICAN AMERICAN DRIVER TO WIN A MAJOR NASCAR RACE?

Before he became a NASCAR racer, Wendell Oliver Scott led a colorful life. Born in 1921 in Danville, Virginia, Scott became known for his speedy motoring as a taxicab driver and a bootlegger in his hometown. It was said that when a promoter of stock car racing asked the Danville police to recommend a driver, they named Scott. He began his career in 1949 at the Danville Fairgrounds Speedway and went on to win 128 races at various tracks. It wasn't easy; some tracks wouldn't let him compete, and at others he was taunted or his tires were slashed.

In 1961 he moved up to NASCAR's top Grand National Circuit, later renamed the Winston Cup Series. On December 1, 1963, he won a hundred-mile event on a half-mile track in Jacksonville, Florida. But before he was declared a winner, officials gave the trophy to another driver, blaming a scoring error. "Everybody in the place knew I had won the race," he later recalled, "but the promoters and NASCAR officials didn't want me out there kissing any beauty queens or accepting any awards."

In a 1973 race in Alabama, Scott was severely injured in a wreck and soon retired from racing. He ran a garage for many years until he died of cancer in 1990. The 1997 Richard Pryor movie, *Greased Lightning,* was loosely based on his life. Scott died in 1990, and in August 2000, he was inducted into the National Motorsports Press Association Hall of Fame.

◆

WHO WAS THE FIRST AFRICAN AMERICAN GOLFER TO WIN A PGA EVENT?

Although he wasn't the first African American to play full time with the PGA tour—that honor belongs to Charles Sifford—Pete Brown was the first to win a PGA event. Born in 1935, Brown grew up in Jackson, Mississippi, where he got his first taste of golf as a teenager when he worked as a caddy at the municipal golf course. Most golf courses of the time were restricted to whites, but Brown discovered a course in New Orleans where African Americans could play on Mondays and Fridays. Other golfers there told him about the United Golf Association tour—the only organization that gave black golfers a chance to compete—and he starting playing in UGA tournaments.

The PGA dropped its whites-only policy in 1961, and Brown got his membership card two years later. In 1964 he became the first African American to win a PGA event, the Waco Turner Open. He won a second tour victory at the Andy Williams Open in 1970. While on tour, he told the writer of a 2006 article in the *Fort Worth Star-Telegram*, "I went to a lot of places that no black person would normally ever go. I didn't lose my temper too much. I could handle things even when I really felt hated."

After playing on the PGA tour for seventeen years, Brown became the head golf pro at Madden Golf Course in Dayton, Ohio.

◆

WHEN DID MAJOR LEAGUE BASEBALL APPOINT ITS FIRST AFRICAN AMERICAN UMPIRE?

"I waited fifteen years for this, and now I'm finally here," said Emmett Ashford before officiating at the opening game of the 1966 baseball season, at which President Lyndon Johnson threw out the first ball. Ashford, a native of Los Angeles, started umpiring baseball games at local schools in about 1947, moving up to officiate at football and basketball games for UCLA and USC. After spending fifteen years as an umpire for the minor leagues on the West Coast, Ashford became the major league's first African American umpire when he joined the American League in the spring of 1966, at the age of forty-eight.

Ashford remained an umpire until 1970, when he worked the World Series game between Baltimore and Cincinnati; he retired at the end of the season. The then-baseball commissioner Bowie Kuhn later hired him as his West Coast representative. Ashford died of a heart attack at the age of sixty-five in Venice, California.

◆

WHO WAS THE FIRST AFRICAN AMERICAN HEAD COACH IN MAJOR LEAGUE SPORTS?

An all-state basketball player in his Oakland, California, high school, Bill Russell won a basketball scholarship in 1952 to the University of San Francisco. There he was his team's captain in his junior and senior years and led the players to two national championships. In 1956 he played on the U.S. team that won an Olympic Gold Medal. He then signed on with the Boston Celtics, leading them in a string of NBA championships.

In 1966 Russell was named player-coach for the Celtics, making him the first African American head coach in major league sports.

After retiring in 1969, he worked as a television sportscaster and coached the Seattle SuperSonics and the Sacramento Kings.

◆

WHO WAS THE COUNTRY'S FIRST AFRICAN AMERICAN OLYMPIC FENCER?

When Uriah Jones was a child in New Rochelle, New York, where his family moved soon after his birth in Harlem in 1924, he imitated swashbuckling Errol Flynn movies by using sticks to fence with his friends. But years went by before he returned to the sport. After attending Hampton Institute, Cooper Union, and Columbia University, he started a career as a civil engineer in New Haven, Connecticut. When he was in his thirties he signed up for fencing lessons at his local YMCA, and then studied with a fencing master in New York City.

In 1968 Jones became the first African American to make a U.S. Olympic fencing team, and in 1971 was the first black fencer to win a United States fencing championship, also winning medals in the Pan American Games.

Jones died in June 2000 in a sauna in a YMCA in Hamden, Connecticut, apparently of a heart attack. He died three weeks before his induction into the United States Fencing Hall of Fame. Commenting on Jones's death, Peter Westbrook, who in 1984 became the first African American fencer to win an Olympic medal, told the *New York Times,* "The first opens doors, like Jackie Robinson. Uriah Jones made it easy for other African Americans. If fencing was a big sport like baseball, he'd be a national hero."

◆

WHO WAS MAJOR LEAGUE BASEBALL'S FIRST AFRICAN AMERICAN MANAGER?

In October 1974 Frank Robinson was named manager of the Cleveland Indians, making him the first African American manager in major league baseball history. He went on to manage the San Francisco Giants, the Baltimore Orioles, and the Montreal Expos.

He managed his final game, for the Washington Nationals, in October 2006.

Born in Texas in 1935, Robinson played baseball while growing up in Oakland, California, and in 1952 was signed by the Cincinnati Reds.

Robinson was the first major leaguer to be voted Most Valuable Player in both leagues—the National League in 1961 as a Cincinnati Red and the American League in 1966 as a Baltimore Oriole. He was elected to baseball's Hall of Fame in 1982.

In April 2012, a bronze statue of Robinson was unveiled in Baltimore's Camden Yards. "Since this is going to be a lifetime thing as far as the statue is concerned," Robinson told the *Baltimore Sun,* "it ranks right up there with the Hall of Fame." Two months later, he was named Major League Baseball's executive vice president of player development.

◆

WHO WAS THE FIRST AFRICAN AMERICAN GOLFER TO COMPETE IN THE MASTERS TOURNAMENT?

Like many other African American golfers, Lee Elder began playing while working as a caddie. Elder was born in Dallas, Texas, in 1935. After moving to Los Angeles with his family, he took lessons from the African American golfer Ted Rhodes. In 1968 he joined the PGA Tour, which had dropped its whites-only clause seven years before, and came in second to Jack Nicklaus at the American Golf Classic in Akron, Ohio.

In 1975 Elder became the first African American golfer to play in the Masters Tournament, held yearly in Augusta, Georgia, which earlier had turned down Charles Sifford. During the months leading up to the Masters, hate mail arrived in Elder's mailbox, but during the week of the tournament he was treated well both by spectators and tournament employees. He played at the Masters five more times and became the first African American golfer to earn more than $100,000 in a season. When Tiger Woods won the Masters in 1997, he gave credit to Lee Elder, Charles Sifford, and other African American golfers who came before him.

◆

WHO WAS THE FIRST FIGHTER TO HOLD THE
WORLD HEAVYWEIGHT TITLE THREE TIMES?

Muhammad Ali, born Cassius Clay Jr. in 1942 in Louisville, Kentucky, began boxing when he was only twelve. At the age of eighteen, after winning an Olympic gold medal, he became a professional fighter. In 1964 he captured the professional heavyweight championship from Charles "Sonny" Liston, knocking him out in seven rounds. That same year, having earlier joined the Nation of Islam, he adopted his new name.

Refusing in 1967 to go into the army because he was opposed to the Vietnam War on religious grounds, Ali was stripped of his title and barred from boxing for four years. In 1970 a court overturned his suspension from boxing and he began a comeback, reclaiming the championship four years later at the age of thirty-two by knocking out George Foreman in the eighth round in Kinshasa, Zaire.

Ali lost the title to Leon Spinks in 1978 but regained it before he retired in 1979. Thus, Ali was World Heavyweight Boxing Champion during 1964–67, 1974–78, and 1978–79. For most of his career he could, as he claimed, "float like a butterfly, sting like a bee."

His autobiography, *The Greatest: My Own Story,* was published in 1975, and many books have been written about him. In 1982 Ali began treatment for Parkinson's disease, which might have been caused by blows to his head. Although he gradually became weaker, he did not give up his involvement in numerous causes. In 1996, with a trembling hand, he lit the flame that opened the Olympic Games in Atlanta. And on December 4, 2001, Ali was back in Atlanta to light the torch that started the Olympic flame on a journey to the 2002 Winter Games in Salt Lake City, Utah. *Ali,* a movie about his life, starring Will Smith, opened on Christmas Day 2001.

Ali was awarded the Presidential Medal of Freedom at a White House ceremony in 2005, and on January 20, 2009, he was back in Washington, sitting with other special guests, as Barack Obama was sworn in as President of the United States.

In September 2013, Ali was awarded the Liberty Medal in a ceremony at the National Constitution Center in Philadelphia.

He was recognized for his efforts in humanitarian causes, civil rights, and religious freedom. According to the *New York Times,* "A frail Ali did not speak, but stood with assistance to receive the medal from his daughter, Laila."

◆

WHO WAS THE FIRST AFRICAN AMERICAN BOWLER TO WIN A PROFESSIONAL BOWLING TITLE?

Born in Detroit in 1963, George Branham III grew up in a bowling family. When the Branhams moved to California, he joined a junior amateur bowling team, winning two tournaments. For this and other victories, he was named Southern California Junior Bowler of the Year in 1983. He thought about going professional but first tested his skill by entering regional tournaments.

After making his mark in the tournaments, Branham decided to join the Professional Bowlers Association, and in 1986, during his second year on tour, he won the Brunswick Memorial World Open, becoming the first African American to win a national tour

GEORGE BRANHAM III

title in the history of the PBA. Seven years later he made history again by winning the Firestone Tournament of Champions, becoming the first African American to capture pro bowling's most prestigious title. In seventeen years as a professional bowler, Branham won five major titles. When he retired in 2004, he was still the only African American bowler to become a PBA champion.

◆

WHEN DID THE NATIONAL FOOTBALL LEAGUE HIRE ITS FIRST AFRICAN AMERICAN REFEREE?

Johnny Grier started officiating at games when he was in eighth grade as part of the physical education program in the Washington, D.C., public schools. He moved to the college level in 1972 at the University of the District of Columbia. In 1981 Grier joined the NFL as a field judge, and at the beginning of the 1988 season, he became the first African American referee in the NFL's history. After he was forced to retire in 2004 because of a leg injury, Grier became an officiating supervisor for the NFL.

◆

WHO WAS THE FIRST AFRICAN AMERICAN ATHLETE TO WIN A MEDAL IN THE WINTER OLYMPICS?

A world-class figure skater and a winner of national and international titles while a freshman at Stanford University in California, Debi Thomas became the first African American to win a medal in the Winter Olympics when she was awarded a bronze medal in the 1988 games in Calgary, Canada. Born in 1967 in Poughkeepsie, New York, Thomas graduated from Stanford in 1991 with a degree in engineering. She studied at Northwestern University Medical School, graduating in 1997 with a specialty in orthopedic surgery. In 2005 she graduated from the orthopedic residency program at Charles R. Drew University in Los Angeles. After completing a one-year training the following year in adult reconstructive surgery, she joined the orthopedic staff at Carle Clinic Association in Urbana, Illinois. By 2012, Thomas had her own medical practice in Richlands, Virginia, specializing in hip and knee surgery.

◆

WHO WAS THE FIRST AFRICAN AMERICAN MANAGER TO LEAD A BASEBALL TEAM TO A WORLD SERIES CHAMPIONSHIP?

In October 1992 the Toronto Blue Jays baseball team defeated the Atlanta Braves and became the first Canadian team to win a World Series. The victory marked another first for baseball: the Blue Jays' manager, Cito Gaston, was the first African American manager to lead a team to a World Series championship. One year later, Gaston once again led his team to victory when Toronto triumphed over Philadelphia to win the 1993 World Series.

Born Clarence Edwin Gaston in 1944 in San Antonio, Texas, the victorious manager had been leading the Blue Jays since 1989, when he was promoted from batting coach. An all-star outfielder who played for eleven seasons with Atlanta and San Diego, Gaston ended his playing career with the Pittsburgh Pirates in 1979.

He began his career with the Blue Jays in 1982 as a batting instructor, becoming manager in 1989. He was the fourth African American manager in major league history. Gaston left the Blue Jays in September 1997 and returned as the team's hitting coach two years later. In October 2001 the Blue Jays announced that Gaston would not return as hitting coach in 2002. But in June 2008, he was rehired as manager of the Blue Jays, and signed a contract that would keep him with the club until 2010. Gaston retired after the 2010 season.

◆

WHO WAS THE FIRST AFRICAN AMERICAN WORLD SUMO CHAMPION?

At six feet, eight inches tall and weighing 740 pounds, Emanuel "Manny" Yarbrough was an impressive figure. But when he hit the headlines in 1995 it wasn't only because of his size.

Yarbrough, then thirty-three years old, had made history by becoming the first African American to win a world championship
in sumo. A Japanese form of wrestling, sumo requires contestants
to perform a number of traditional rituals and then attempt to force
each other out of the ring.

Yarbrough was a football lineman and a wrestler in his Rahway,
New Jersey, high school and later at Morgan State University in
Baltimore. After college he took a number of jobs, including one
as a nightclub bouncer. He was attending a local judo center when
his coach, impressed by his size and talent, encouraged him to
travel to Japan to study sumo. He began competing in 1992, plac-
ing second or third until 1995, when he knocked his opponent out
of the ring in under six seconds, making him world champion.
A celebrity in Japan and the rest of the world, Yarbrough appeared
on talk shows, in commercials, in several movies, and in the HBO
series *Oz*.

In June 2012, Yarbrough, now weighing seven hundred pounds
and included in *Guinness World Records* as the world's heaviest man,
was in the news when Delta Airlines refused to let him fly from
Newark to Italy because of his size, even though he had paid for
three adjoining seats.

◆

WHEN DID THE FIRST AFRICAN AMERICAN
WIN THE TITLE OF INTERNATIONAL
GRANDMASTER OF CHESS?

Growing up in Brooklyn, New York, where his family moved
from St. Andrews, Jamaica, when he was twelve, Maurice Ashley started playing chess with other dedicated young people in
nearby Prospect Park. He began entering local tournaments and
made rapid progress in the game, rising to the rank of national
master in 1986.

After graduating from City College, where he earned a bachelor's degree in English in 1993, Ashley started coaching the Dark
Knights, a prize-winning Harlem middle school chess team. In November of that year, Ashley earned the rank of international master,

the first African American chess player to reach that level. Then, in 1999, at the age of thirty-three, he reached the pinnacle of chess, achieving the title of international grandmaster.

Following through on his desire to make chess available to young people who seldom have access to the game, Ashley opened the Harlem Chess Center, offering free classes to youngsters from the neighborhood. He also designed an award-winning chess tutorial on CD-ROM and initiated an online chess class. His involvement with chess, he said in a 2001 television interview, was "my life's dream come true . . . It's my destiny."

Ashley was named 2003 Grandmaster of the Year by the U.S. Chess Federation, and his book, *Chess for Success*, which crystallizes his vision of using chess to help at-risk youth, was published in 2005.

In the fall of 2011, Ashley set off on a tour of six Caribbean countries, introducing the game of chess to youngsters. In 2012,

MAURICE ASHLEY

he became a joint fellow at Harvard and MIT where, as he wrote on his website, mauriceashley.com, he "worked on bringing the benefits of chess and other classic games to a wider, educational audience through the innovative use of technology." He was also introducing chess to young people involved with the Red Hook, Brooklyn, Juvenile Justice Center.

◆

WHO WAS THE FIRST WOMAN COACH IN MEN'S PROFESSIONAL SPORTS?

In August 2001, Stephanie Ready was named assistant coach of the Greenville Groove, one of eight teams in the NBA's new development organization, known as the National Basketball Development League. Ready, then twenty-five, came to the league after two years as an assistant coach for men's basketball at Coppin State College, in Baltimore.

STEPHANIE READY

After graduating with honors in 1998 from Coppin State, where she was captain of both the women's basketball and volleyball teams during her senior year, Ready was hired as the school's head volleyball coach and, a year later, as assistant men's basketball coach. When she was chosen assistant coach of South Carolina's Greenville Groove, Ready became the first woman in the United States to coach a men's professional team. Commenting on her selection, Greenville Groove coach Milton Barnes said, "Coach Ready knows the game of basketball, has a proven track record at the collegiate level of helping players develop their skills, and comes highly recommended."

Ready coached the Greenville Groove until the team folded in 2003. She served as assistant coach of the Washington Mystics in 2004, and then joined the Charlotte Bobcats as a sideline reporter. She was responsible for in-depth courtside coverage, hosting pre-game shows, and providing features and human-interest stories on the players, coaches, and front-office personnel.

◆

WHO WAS THE FIRST AFRICAN AMERICAN ATHLETE TO WIN A GOLD MEDAL AT THE WINTER OLYMPICS?

Fans of the 2002 Olympic Games in Utah were astonished when the bright-red bobsled partnered by Vonetta Flowers and Jill Bakken zoomed down the track at eighty miles an hour to finish first in the event. The unexpected victory made Flowers, the team's brakewoman, the first African American to win a gold medal at a Winter Olympics. Speaking through tears after receiving her medal, Flowers said, "I hope this won't be the end of it. I hope you'll see other African American girls and boys who want to give winter sports a try, because there are not a lot out there."

Flowers, born in 1973 in Helena, Alabama, was a seven-time all-American track and field star at the University of Alabama at Birmingham, where she later became a track coach. After she tried out for the 2000 United States Olympic track team but failed to qualify, her husband, Johnny Flowers, also a college track star, noticed a flyer near their hotel's entrance that was advertising for a bob-

VONETTA FLOWERS

sled athlete. He urged Vonetta to give it a try. The flyer had been posted by a longtime bobsledder, Bonny Warner, who recruited Flowers to push and brake her sled but later dropped her for someone else. In December 2001, another bobsledder, Jill Bakken, chose Flowers as her brakewoman.

Although ignored as likely winners by Olympic watchers, the duo, after a speedy pushoff by Flowers, raced ahead of two favored German teams and another American team to cross the finish line as number one. It was the first time in fifty-four years that an American bobsled team had won an Olympic gold medal.

"I think there was a lot of focus on the fact that she is the first African American woman to win a gold at the Winter Games," Johnny Flowers said later. "That's great, but at the same time I think her success should not be limited to that label. . . . If Vonetta's success can be a springboard for African American, Asians, Hispanics, and all minorities to try something else, then that's good."

Her book, *Running on Ice: The Overcoming Faith of Vonetta Flowers*, was published in 2005. Flowers was inducted into the Alabama Sports Hall of Fame in May 2011.

◆

WHICH AFRICAN AMERICAN WOMAN SWIMMER WAS THE FIRST TO MAKE A U.S. OLYMPIC TEAM?

Born in 1981 to Guyanese parents in Puerto Rico, Maritza Correia started swimming at the age of seven when doctors recommended the sport as therapy for her scoliosis—curvature of the spine. "My mom took me to the beach and taught me how to float and be safe in the water, and I took to it," Correia told *Wag* magazine in July 2012. "I wouldn't say I was the best athlete. It kind of took a lot, but it taught me to work hard."

When she was nine her family moved to Florida, where she joined the Brandon Blue Wave Swim Club; her older brother, Justin, was already a member. She said that as an African American, "I was kind of an oddball out, along with my brother. It kind of drove me to be successful."

She entered swimming competitions in high school and later at the University of Georgia, winning numerous events. But she almost gave up the sport after a discouraging performance at the 2000 Olympic trials. Realizing she needed more experience, she trained hard and continued to compete, setting records and winning medals. In 2004, she made history as the first African American woman to win a spot on a U.S. Olympic swimming team. She helped her team win a silver medal in the 400-meter freestyle relay at the summer games in Athens.

Correia continued to compete for three more years until arthritis and rotator cuff problems in her shoulders convinced her to retire. She became a spokesperson for Nike and USA Swimming, and she has devoted herself, she said, "to get more minorities into swimming."

◆

WHAT AFRICAN AMERICAN SKATER WAS
THE FIRST TO WIN AN INDIVIDUAL
GOLD MEDAL IN THE WINTER OLYMPICS?

Although Shani Davis was the first African American speed skater to win a spot on the U.S. Olympic team and the first to win a gold medal in the winter Olympics, he said he did not concentrate on making black history. Yet he was clearly making history in the world of speed skating. In January 2009 he was ranked number one in the world in the thousand-meter race.

Born in 1982 in Chicago, and raised by his mother in their South Side neighborhood, Davis started roller-skating when he was two. He became so fast on the roller rink that guards had to chase him to get him to slow down. When he was six, Davis switched to ice. He joined a speed skating club, started competing locally, and was soon winning regional competitions. Since there were no clubs in inner-city Chicago, Davis and his mother moved to the far north side of the city to be closer to a rink. "My mom never thought of herself first," Davis said on his website, "and I credit most of my success to her."

Davis won a spot on the U.S. Olympic team in 2002, and in the 2004–2005 season he became the first United States skater to make all three world teams in the same season (world sprint, world all-round, and world short track), earning medals in each, and ultimately won the world all-round title in Moscow in 2005. He brought home both gold and silver medals from the 2006 Olympics in Turin, Italy, and in January 2009, he returned to Russia to win the world sprint championships, making him the second man to win world championships in both sprint and all-around. After winning the sprint championships, Davis said, "I'm the happiest man in Moscow."

At the 2010 Winter Olympics, Davis once again won the 1,000-meter gold medal and also brought home the 1,500-meter silver. In January 2013, he won the 1,000-meter World Cup speed skating race in Calgary, Alberta. By then, he had set eight world records.

♦

WHICH AFRICAN AMERICAN COACH WAS
THE FIRST TO WIN A SUPER BOWL GAME?

When Tony Dungy retired in January 2009 as head coach of the Indianapolis Colts, he could claim many accomplishments. Not only was he the first African American football coach to lead a team to victory in a Super Bowl game, but he was the author of three books, the founder of a mentoring program for young people, a supporter of several other charities, and a man known for his love of his family and his deep religious faith.

Anthony Kevin "Tony" Dungy was born in 1955 in Jackson, Michigan, where both of his parents were educators. He played

TONY DUNGY

football and basketball in high school, and was on the football team at the University of Minnesota. After graduation he held various coaching positions, and in 1996, was hired as head coach of the Tampa Bay Buccaneers. In 2002 he was named head coach of the Indianapolis Colts, and in 2007, his team became Super Bowl victors when they defeated the Chicago Bears.

Dungy's third book, *Uncommon: Finding Your Path to Significance*, was released two weeks after he announced his retirement. His 2007 book, *Quiet Strength*, reached number one on the *New York Times* best seller list, and a year later he published a children's book, *You Can Do It!*

"Don't shed any tears for me," Dungy said when he announced that he would retire at the end of the 2008–2009 season. "I've gotten to live a dream that most people don't get to live." He said his goals were "to be home a little bit more, be available to my family a little bit more, and do some things to help make our country better."

Soon after he retired, Dungy embarked on a crusade to encourage colleges to hire African American head football coaches. But he didn't stay retired for long. In 2009, he was hired by NBC as an analyst on *Football Night in America*. A prolific writer, Dungy coauthored three books in 2011, and 2012 saw the publication of his book *Uncommon Manhood: Secrets to What It Means to Be a Man.*

◆

WHO WAS THE FIRST AFRICAN AMERICAN SUPER BOWL REFEREE?

In his eighteenth year as a football official, Mike Carey was assigned by the NFL to referee the 2008 Super Bowl game between the New York Giants and the New England Patriots, making him the first African American referee in Super Bowl history. Michael "Mike" Carey, a 1971 graduate of California's Santa Clara University with a degree in biology, suffered an ankle injury as running back after four years on the school's football team, ending his playing career. After graduation he officiated for Pop Warner football games in the San Diego area, and in 1990 was hired by the NFL as a side judge. He was promoted to referee at the start of the 1995 season.

Carey and his wife, Wendy, cofounded Seirus Innovation, a company that manufactures and sells cold weather accessories for skiing and snowboarding. He has invented numerous items of ski apparel, including Cat Tracks, a protective device that slips over the sole of a ski boot.

◆

WHO WAS THE FIRST AFRICAN AMERICAN WOMAN TO WIN OLYMPIC GOLD IN ALL-AROUND WOMEN'S GYMNASTICS?

In August 2012, when she was only sixteen years old, Gabrielle Douglas—often called Gabby—won gold medals in individual and team gymnastics, becoming the first African American cham-

GABRIELLE DOUGLAS

pion in the all-around and the first U.S. gymnast to take home two gold medals in the same game.

Douglas was born in 1995 in Virginia Beach, Virginia. Her mother enrolled her in gymnastics class when she was six, and by the age of eight, she had won a state championship. When she was around thirteen, a renowned coach, Liang Chow, visited her gymnastics clinic and helped Douglas learn a difficult move. Impressed by his coaching style, Douglas became determined to train with him, but that meant leaving her mother, two sisters, and brother and moving to West Des Moines, Iowa, where Chow was located. In 2010, she made the move, accepting an offer to live with a white family with four daughters.

Two years later, still living with her host family and having learned new skills from Chow, Douglas won the Olympic trials in June, guaranteeing her a spot on the 2012 Olympic team. After winning the gold, her grace, charm, and bubbly personality attracted fans from all over the world. Her autobiography, *Grace, Gold, and Glory: My Leap of Faith,* was published that fall.

In February 2013, Douglas received a standing ovation from the Virginia State Senate, which presented her with a framed copy of a resolution honoring her for her accomplishments. The resolution said that Douglas "captured the hearts of millions worldwide with her radiant smile." It added that she brought honor to Virginia and continued to inspire other young women to work hard to achieve their goals.

THEATER
AND
DANCE

WHO WAS THE FIRST AFRICAN AMERICAN ACTOR TO PERFORM BEFORE THE RULERS OF PRUSSIA, SWEDEN, AUSTRIA, AND RUSSIA?

Ira Aldridge was born in 1807 and attended the African Free School in New York City. He later joined a black theater troupe there, the African Company. When the troupe disbanded, Aldridge

IRA ALDRIDGE AS OTHELLO

migrated to England, where he continued his career on the stage. In London, he appeared in the melodrama *The Revolt of Surinam, or A Slave's Revenge,* and in 1833 he received wide acclaim for his performance in Shakespeare's *Othello* at Covent Garden. Although known for his interpretation of the role of Othello, he also gave memorable performances as Macbeth, Lear, Shylock, and Hamlet.

For the rest of his life Aldridge toured England and many other countries, performing Shakespearean roles before royalty and becoming one of the most celebrated actors of his day. Accounts of the time report that students in Moscow, thrilled by his performance, unhitched the horses from his carriage and pulled him from the theater to his hotel. But Aldridge was never able to enact his most famous role, Othello, in his native land; he died in Poland in 1867 while making arrangements for a tour of the United States.

◆

WHAT WAS THE FIRST NEW YORK CITY THEATER TO STAGE AFRICAN AMERICAN PRODUCTIONS?

The African Grove, housed in a modest structure at the corner of Bleecker and Mercer Streets in lower Manhattan, presented all-black versions of Shakespearean plays and other dramas performed by a troupe of actors called the African Company. The famous tragedian James Hewlett, who was the first African American actor to play Othello, appeared at the African Grove in 1821. Ira Aldridge, another great African American tragic actor, also starred in the company's productions.

The actors, who performed for mixed audiences, were sometimes heckled by rowdy white customers and their productions were disparaged by a biased press. The theater was finally forced to close in 1823. Before disbanding, the African Company presented *The Drama of King Shotaway,* about the uprising of Carib Indians on St. Vincent Island against the British navy. Some believe it was the first African American drama to reach the stage.

◆

WHO WAS THE FIRST ACTOR TO
PLAY THE EMPEROR JONES?

Charles Gilpin was the first actor to play the lead in the Eugene O'Neill play, *The Emperor Jones*. Produced in 1920 at the Provincetown Playhouse in New York City, the play starred Gilpin in the role of Brutus Jones, a Pullman porter who becomes the emperor of an island. The NAACP awarded Gilpin its Spingarn Medal for his achievement, the Drama League voted him one of the ten people who had done the most for the theater that season, and he was invited to appear at the White House.

Gilpin was born in Virginia in 1878. He performed in county fairs and vaudeville shows trying to make a career in the theater. When he was in his twenties he helped organize the Pekin Stock

CHARLES GILPIN IN *THE EMPEROR JONES*

Company, a theater group in Chicago, and in 1914 he played the lead in *The Girl at the Fort* with the Anita Bush Company in New York City.

When Gilpin won the role of Brutus Jones, he was supporting himself as an elevator operator in Macy's department store. *The Emperor Jones* gave him the opportunity to become the first African American actor to win fame in a dramatic role. Gilpin later appeared in several other plays, and died at the age of fifty-two.

◆

WHAT WAS THE FIRST DRAMA BY AN AFRICAN AMERICAN PLAYWRIGHT PRODUCED ON BROADWAY?

In May 1923 the one-act play *The Chip Woman's Fortune*, by Willis Richardson, was presented as part of a triple bill by the Ethiopian Art Players, a theater company from Chicago, at the Frazee Theatre on Broadway. Set in the home of an African American family, the play focused on the character of the "chip woman," an old woman who wandered the streets collecting chips of wood and lumps of coal. As the first work by an African American playwright to appear on Broadway, it was well received by the critics.

◆

WHO WROTE THE FIRST FULL-LENGTH PLAY BY AN AFRICAN AMERICAN TO APPEAR ON BROADWAY?

Garland Anderson was working as a bellhop in a busy San Francisco hotel when he wrote his play *Appearances*. A self-educated man who read the Bible and studied psychology, Anderson had never taken a playwriting lesson. Determined to have *Appearances* produced in New York City, Anderson traveled across the country by automobile. When he finally pulled up in front of New York's City Hall, his car was draped with a banner that read: "San Francisco to New York for New York production, 'Appearances' by Garland Anderson, The Black San Francisco Bellhop Playwright."

GARLAND ANDERSON ARRIVING IN NEW YORK

Once in the East, Anderson carried his play from producer to producer, invited New York's governor to attend a reading, and even went to Washington, D.C., in an attempt to get the support of President Coolidge. Anderson's efforts paid off at last; on October 13, 1925, *Appearances* opened at the Frolic Theatre on Broadway. The autobiographical story of a bellhop who believes he can accomplish anything if only he has faith, *Appearances* received little attention from critics. It lasted only twenty-three performances, but was revived in New York in 1929 and was later produced in London.

Having seen his dream come true, Anderson returned to the West Coast and in 1935 became a minister in the Seattle Center of Constructive Thinking.

◆

WHO WAS THE FIRST AFRICAN AMERICAN
DANCER TO GAIN STARDOM?

When Bill "Bojangles" Robinson made his Broadway debut in *Blackbirds of 1928*, he was already fifty years old. As an orphaned youngster in Richmond, Virginia, Robinson sold newspapers and shined shoes for pennies until he learned a few dance styles and began to earn money performing on street corners and in saloons. Around 1890 he joined a touring theater group and ended up in New York City, where critics praised his tap dancing skills in a string of Broadway shows. He was famous for his dance on a staircase and for his ability to run backward.

Although he was middle-aged when his career started to take off, Robinson remained in top physical condition. When he reached

BILL "BOJANGLES" ROBINSON

his sixty-first birthday he was starring in the show *Hot Mikado*. To celebrate, he danced down Broadway from above Columbus Circle to his theater on 44th Street.

It was in Hollywood that Robinson found his greatest fame. He is especially known for the four films he made with Shirley Temple, beginning with *The Little Colonel* in 1935. When he died of a heart condition in 1949, sixty thousand people filed past his coffin as it lay in state in a Harlem armory. After his funeral in the Abyssinian Baptist Church, thousands of people lined the streets as the procession wound down Broadway. It stopped on 47th Street while a band played "Give My Regards to Broadway."

◆

WHO WAS THE FIRST AFRICAN AMERICAN ACTRESS TO STAR IN A BROADWAY PLAY?

Ethel Waters, who had gained fame as a singer, made her dramatic debut in 1939 in the role of Hagar in the Broadway play *Mamba's Daughters*. Raised by various relatives in Pennsylvania, where she was born in 1896, Waters sang in public for the first time in a church program when she was five. Her singing and dancing talents were discovered twelve years later when two vaudeville producers saw her in a talent contest and signed her up for a traveling show.

Billed as "Sweet Mama Stringbean," the slender teenager treated audiences throughout the South to her blues singing and famous shimmy. She moved to New York in 1919 and two years later began a highly successful recording career with the Black Swan label's first blues record, "Down Home Blues" and "Oh, Daddy."

Waters turned to acting in the 1930s, and said that the opening night of *Mamba's Daughters* was the most important event of her life, except when she found religion. She appeared in the 1943 film *Cabin in the Sky*, and portrayed a strong grandmother in *Pinky*, winning a 1949 Academy Award nomination for best supporting actress. Waters returned to Broadway in 1950 in *The Member of the Wedding*, receiving rave reviews and the New York Drama Critics award for best actress; she starred in the film version of the play two years later. After one season in the television series *Beulah*, she published her autobiography, *His Eye Is on the Sparrow.* In 1957 she began many years of touring with the evangelist Billy Graham, and died penniless in 1977.

◆

WHO WAS THE FIRST AFRICAN AMERICAN TO WIN A TONY AWARD?

Twenty-two years after she first appeared on the stage, singer Juanita Hall was honored with a Tony award for her performance as Bloody Mary in the 1949 Broadway production of *South Pacific.* Her renditions of "Happy Talk" and "Bali H'ai" became hits throughout the country.

Hall, born in 1901, studied at the Juilliard School of Music and made her stage debut in 1928 in the chorus of *Show Boat.* For the next several years she was a soloist and an assistant director with the Hall Johnson Choir, and in 1935 formed her own singing group, the Juanita Hall Choir. She gained increasing renown as a choral conductor, and at the 1939 World's Fair in New York City she led a church choir of 300 voices.

In the 1940s Hall played a number of musical and dramatic roles on stage. After her success in *South Pacific,* she appeared in the 1954 production of *House of Flowers* and in *The Flower Drum Song* in 1959, and also performed in nightclubs and concerts and on television. She died in 1968.

◆

WHEN DID THE FIRST AFRICAN AMERICAN DANCER PERFORM ON THE STAGE OF THE MET?

When Janet Collins danced in a 1951 performance of *Aida* at the Metropolitan Opera House in New York City, she became the first African American artist to appear on that stage. Collins, born in 1923 and educated in Los Angeles, moved to New York City to pursue a career in dance. She studied and performed in California before making her New York City debut in 1949. A year later she appeared in the Cole Porter musical *Out of This*

World, dancing the role of Night. After seeing her performance, one critic called Collins a "golden dancing girl."

The country's first African American prima ballerina, Collins danced with the Metropolitan Opera Ballet for four years, appearing in *Carmen, La Gioconda,* and *Samson and Delilah.* During her career she taught at the School of American Ballet, performed in concerts, choreographed, and appeared on television. Collins died in 2003 at the age of eighty-six.

◆

WHO WAS THE FIRST AFRICAN AMERICAN WOMAN PLAYWRIGHT TO WIN AN OBIE?

Alice Childress, born in 1920 in Charleston, South Carolina, came to live with her grandmother in New York City's Harlem when she was nine years old. She attended city schools but had to drop out after her third year in high school, when her grandmother died.

Continuing her education by reading books from the public library, Childress worked at a number of jobs while establishing herself as an actress and writer. She made her acting debut in 1940 in the play *On Striver's Row.* In the early 1940s, she helped found the American Negro Theater and participated in the organization as an actress and a director.

Two plays written by Childress, *Just a Little Simple,* in 1950, and *Gold Through the Trees,* in 1952, were the first by an African American woman to be professionally produced on the American stage. A production of her play *Trouble in Mind* won Childress an Obie in 1955, making her the first African American woman to receive this award for the best off-Broadway play. Throughout her career she wrote four novels and more than a dozen plays. Her novel about teenage drug addiction, *A Hero Ain't Nothin' But a Sandwich,* was made into a 1977 movie starring Cicely Tyson. Childress died in New York in 1994.

◆

WHO WAS THE FIRST AFRICAN AMERICAN MAN TO BECOME A PERMANENT MEMBER OF A MAJOR BALLET COMPANY?

When Arthur Mitchell graduated from the High School of Performing Arts in New York City in the early 1950s, he won a dance award and a scholarship to study at the School of American Ballet. In 1955 Mitchell made his debut with the New York City Ballet, performing in *Western Symphony*. Rising to the position of principal dancer with the company, he performed in all the major ballets in its repertoire, including *A Midsummer Night's Dream, The Nutcracker, Bugaku, Agon,* and *Arcade,* but he remained the only African American dancer with the City Ballet until 1970.

The famous choreographer George Balanchine created the pas de deux from *Agon* especially for Mitchell and the white ballerina Diana Adams. Although Mitchell danced this role with white partners throughout the world, he could not perform it on commercial television in the United States before 1965, because states in the South refused to carry it.

Mitchell left the New York City Ballet in 1966 to appear in several Broadway shows and to direct a dance company. After the assassination of Dr. Martin Luther King Jr. in 1968, Mitchell returned to Harlem, determined to provide opportunities in dance for the children in that community. A year later, he and his teacher, Karel Shook, formed a ballet school and company, the Dance Theatre of Harlem.

◆

WHEN WAS THE FIRST PLAY BY AN AFRICAN AMERICAN WOMAN PRODUCED ON BROADWAY?

Lorraine Hansberry, born in Chicago in 1930, was attracted to the theater while a student at the University of Wisconsin. After moving to New York City in 1950, she took a job as a reporter for Paul Robeson's newspaper, *Freedom*. She left the position to devote herself to playwriting, and in March 1959 her drama *A Raisin in the Sun* opened at New York's Ethel Barrymore Theater. Starring Sidney Poitier, Ruby Dee, and Claudia McNeil, it was directed by Lloyd Richards, who later became dean of the Yale University School of Drama. The play, about an African American family trying to solve its conflicts while seeking to leave a poor Chicago neighborhood, had a highly successful run of nineteen months and was later made into a movie.

A Raisin in the Sun received the New York Drama Critics Circle Award as best play of the 1958–59 season, making Hansberry the first African American playwright to win this award. In 1964 she had another play, *The Sign in Sidney Brustein's Window,* on Broadway and was at work on her autobiography, *To Be Young, Gifted, and Black.* Hansberry died of cancer a year later, but her husband, Robert Nemiroff, completed and published her book.

◆

WHO WAS THE FIRST AFRICAN AMERICAN TO CHOREOGRAPH FOR THE MET?

Katherine Dunham, a choreographer and dancer whose company had performed throughout the world, was asked by the Metropolitan Opera to choreograph its new production of *Aida* for the 1963–64 season. It was the first time the Met had commissioned an African American to choreograph dances for one of its operas.

Dunham's interest in dance began when she was a high school student in her hometown of Joliet, Illinois, where she was born in 1909. As an anthropology major at the University of Chicago, she won a scholarship that allowed her to study dance rituals, rhythms, and movements in Martinique, Trinidad, Jamaica, and particularly in Haiti. Returning home with a collection of authentic West Indian dance forms, Dunham began performing and directing dance companies in Chicago and New York.

In 1940 she and her troupe of dancers performed in *Cabin in the Sky,* a Broadway musical with an African American cast that she helped choreograph. She also choreographed and appeared in several films. Her school of dance in New York City influenced generations of dancers. In 1964 she became an artist-in-residence at Southern Illinois University and was later the director of the school's performing arts center. She then created the Katherine Dunham Centers for Arts and Humanities in East St. Louis, Illinois, which operate a museum and training programs in the arts for young people from the community. A strong advocate of social justice, Dunham, at the age of eighty-two, carried out a forty-seven-day hunger strike in support of improved relations with Haiti. She died in New York City four years later.

♦

WHO WAS THE FIRST AFRICAN AMERICAN PRESIDENT OF ACTORS' EQUITY?

Frederick Douglass O'Neal was born in 1905 in a small Mississippi town and named for the great nineteenth century statesman, Frederick Douglass. After his father, who was a teacher and a merchant, died in 1919, the O'Neal family moved to St. Louis, Missouri. It was there that the twenty-two-year-old aspiring actor made his professional stage debut. He and his friends organized an African American theater group called the Aldridge Players, after the black Shakespearean actor Ira Aldridge.

O'Neal went to New York City in 1936 to study acting. Four years later he helped found the American Negro Theater, an organization of African American actors, playwrights, and producers, and starred in several of its productions. A tall, soft-spoken man, O'Neal made his Broadway debut in 1944 in *Anna Lucasta*; his striking performance earned him several awards. His other stage appearances included *House of Flowers* and *Lost in the Stars,* and he was featured in such films as *Pinky, No Way Out,* and *Something of Value.*

From 1964 to 1973, O'Neal was president of the Actors' Equity Association, an actors' union. A recipient of several honorary degrees and numerous awards, he died in 1992 at the age of eighty-six.

♦

WHO WAS THE FIRST AFRICAN AMERICAN ACTRESS TO PLAY MAJOR ROLES AT THE AMERICAN SHAKESPEARE FESTIVAL?

R uby Dee, born Ruby Ann Wallace in 1923 in Cleveland, Ohio, and raised in Harlem, graduated from New York City's Hunter College and studied acting at the American Negro Theater. She appeared in several plays in the 1940s, including *Anna Lucasta,* in which she played the lead. Her first movie roles were in the 1950 films *No Way Out* and *The Jackie Robinson Story,* playing Robinson's

RUBY DEE

wife. In 1959 she was acclaimed for her performance in Lorraine Hansberry's play *A Raisin in the Sun,* and she later repeated the role in the film.

In 1965, at the American Shakespeare Festival in Stratford, Connecticut, Dee became the first African American actress to play major classical roles, portraying Kate in *The Taming of the Shrew* and Cordelia in *King Lear.* She appeared in the stage and film versions of *Purlie Victorious,* written by her husband, Ossie Davis, and played Lena in the 1971 production of Athol Fugard's *Boesman and Lena,* winning an Obie award for her performance.

This talented actress worked on many stage, film, and television projects with Ossie Davis. Her numerous films include *Do the Right Thing, Jungle Fever,* and *Having Our Say.* She appeared onstage in 1998 in *My One Good Nerve,* and in 2001 in *Saint Lucy's Eyes.* That same year she and Ossie Davis, both active in many social causes, were honored with the Screen Actors Guild Lifetime Achievement Award. A book they wrote together, *With Ossie and Ruby: In This Life Together,* was published in 1998. Davis died in 2005. Two years later, Dee was nominated for an Academy Award for best supporting actress for her portrayal of Mama Lucas in *American Gangster.* In 2013, at the age of ninety, she was still making movies.

◆

WHAT WAS THE FIRST AFRICAN AMERICAN BALLET COMPANY TO BE PERMANENTLY ESTABLISHED?

When Dr. Martin Luther King Jr. was assassinated in 1968, Arthur Mitchell felt he had to do something positive in response. He made a decision to open a school in New York City's Harlem where he could introduce young people to the beauty and discipline of dance. Thirteen years earlier, Mitchell had made his debut with the New York City Ballet; he was the first African American to become a member of a major ballet company.

Mitchell started his new organization, the Dance Theatre of Harlem, with his teacher and mentor, Karel Shook. Beginning as a small ballet school in the basement of a Harlem church, it quickly grew to accommodate more than 400 students. The professional dance company made its debut in 1971 and continued to be enthusiastically received by audiences and critics alike. After its first major New York City season in 1974, the company danced all over the world, giving command performances for royalty and heads of state. It appeared at the White House and at the Kennedy Center for the Performing Arts in Washington, D.C.

In September 1992, the Dance Theatre of Harlem became the first multiracial performing arts group to visit South Africa. In 1997, the company performed Billy Wilson's Concerto in F for the Kennedy Center's twenty-fifth anniversary celebration. The Dance Theatre celebrated its thirty-fifth anniversary in February 2004 with an extensive tour throughout the United States followed by a seven-week tour of the United Kingdom.

Later that year, facing a huge debt, the company went on hiatus. A smaller company returned eight years later, started touring in early 2013, and opened its New York season that April.

◆

WHO WAS THE FIRST AFRICAN AMERICAN PLAYWRIGHT TO WIN A PULITZER PRIZE FOR DRAMA?

An actor, director, playwright, and teacher, Charles Gordone was born in Cleveland in 1925 and educated in California and New York City, where he settled in 1952. He supported himself as a waiter in a Greenwich Village bar and became involved in the theater community, winning an Obie award in 1953 for his performance in *Of Mice and Men*. He spent most of the next ten years directing and then turned to playwriting; his first work was produced in 1964. At about the same time, he led efforts to involve more African Americans in the performing arts.

In 1970 Gordone became the first African American playwright to win the Pulitzer Prize, when he was given the award for his play *No Place to Be Somebody*. The play, set in a bar much like the one in which he had worked, dealt with the problems of an African American bar owner and his customers. Gordone later taught in New Jersey prisons and at the New School for Social Research.

In 1986 he joined the faculty of Texas A&M University, where he taught until his death in 1995.

♦

WHO LED THE FIRST AMERICAN MODERN DANCE COMPANY TO PERFORM IN RUSSIA?

In 1970 the Alvin Ailey American Dance Theater performed in Russia to enraptured audiences, receiving a twenty-three-minute ovation in Leningrad. This illustrious dance company had been formed twelve years earlier by dancer Alvin Ailey, who had always encouraged the work of African American choreographers and composers, used the tunes and rhythms of spirituals and work songs, and provided a showcase for many talented black dancers. Under the auspices of the U.S. State Department, the company began its international travels in 1962, with a thirteen-week tour of Australia and the Far East, and later toured widely in Europe, Africa, and Asia.

Alvin Ailey was born in the tiny farming town of Rogers, Texas, in 1931 and moved with his mother to Los Angeles, where he attended high school. There he followed his interest in music and dance. Inspired by the performances of the African American dancers Katherine Dunham and Janet Collins, he began taking classes with Lester Horton. When Horton died in 1953, Ailey became artistic director of his dance company.

The next year he won a role in the Broadway show *House of Flowers,* and soon settled in New York, where he studied with the top choreographers. He continued to perform on Broadway as well as in movies and on television, and in 1958 made his debut as a choreographer with his own dance company. His 1960 dance *Revelations* became one of his most celebrated creations.

By the time Ailey died in 1989 of an AIDs-related illness, he and his company had won many honors. After his death, more than 4,000 devoted admirers attended his memorial service at the Cathedral of St. John the Divine.

♦

WHO WAS THE FIRST AFRICAN AMERICAN WOMAN TO DIRECT A BROADWAY MUSICAL?

Vinnette Carroll began her professional life as a psychologist, but soon was lured by the theater. Born in New York City in 1922, Carroll moved with her family to Jamaica when she was three. She returned to the United States, earned degrees from Long Island and New York Universities, and worked as a clinical psychologist until 1948, when she entered drama school. For many years she taught theater arts and directed plays as a faculty member of the High School of Performing Arts, and she made her acting debut on Broadway in a 1956 revival of *A Streetcar Named Desire*. In 1967 she founded the Urban Arts Corps, formed to assist minority performers in the theater.

In 1972, collaborating with songwriter Micki Grant, she directed their production of *Don't Bother Me, I Can't Cope*, for which she received a Tony nomination as best director of a musical. The two joined forces again in 1977 with *Your Arm's Too Short to Box With God*, winning another Tony nomination for Carroll. When she relocated to Fort Lauderdale, Florida, she started her own repertory company, the Vinnette Carroll Theater. Carroll died in 2002.

◆

WHO WAS THE FIRST AFRICAN AMERICAN TO WIN A TONY AWARD FOR CHOREOGRAPHY?

George Faison was born in 1945 in Washington, D.C., where he grew up in a comfortable home with a nurturing family. He studied dentistry at Howard University but soon was drawn to the theater, and received his first training and performing experience with the American Light Opera Company. He later toured for three years with the Alvin Ailey American Dance Theater, returning to New York to form his own group, the George Faison Universal Dance Experience.

Faison made his Broadway debut in 1972 as choreographer of the long-running musical *Don't Bother Me I Can't Cope*. Three years later he won a Tony award for his choreography of the all-African American musical *The Wiz*, starring Stephanie Mills.

GEORGE FAISON

He went on to choreograph and direct dozens of musicals, concerts, and television shows. In 2000, he directed and choreographed a revival of the Ntozake Shange play *for colored girls who have considered suicide/when the rainbow is enuf*, presented at New York's American Place Theater.

In 2000, Faison and a partner bought a former firehouse in Harlem and transformed it into a performing arts center, the Faison Firehouse Theater.

◆

WHO WAS THE FIRST AFRICAN AMERICAN WOMAN TO WIN THE PULITZER PRIZE FOR DRAMA?

The Pulitzer Prize for drama was awarded to Suzan-Lori Parks on April 8, 2002, for her play *Topdog/Underdog,* which had opened on Broadway the night before. The play, about two African American brothers with a complicated relationship, was first produced eight months earlier at New York's Public Theater, where it starred Jeffrey Wright and Don Cheadle. In the Broadway production, the rapper Mos Def took over the Cheadle role.

Suzan-Lori Parks, born in Kentucky in 1964, the daughter of an army officer, had lived in six states and Germany before entering Mount Holyoke College in Massachusetts. There, her creative writing teacher, James Baldwin, after hearing her read her short stories aloud, suggested she try writing plays. She took his advice and completed her first drama, *The Sinner's Place,* in her senior year. After college, her original and provocative works soon won the attention of the theater community. In 1989, a *New York Times* drama critic named her the year's most promising playwright. She won Obie awards in 1989 and 1996 for her plays *Imperceptible Mutabilities in the Third Kingdom* and *Venus,* and in 2001 she was awarded a MacArthur Foundation "genius grant."

Remarking on becoming the first African American woman to win a Pulitzer for drama, Parks said, "I wish I were the one hundred and first. You open the door but it's everybody's responsibility to walk through."

Starting in November 2002, Parks wrote a short play every day for a year. The result was *365 Days/365 Plays,* portions of which were performed at theaters throughout the country. Her novel, *Getting Mother's Body,* was published in 2003. In 2008, Parks was awarded the first master writer chair at New York City's Public Theater. And in 2012, Parks wrote an adaptation of the Gershwin opera *Porgy and Bess,* which won a Tony award for the best musical revival.

◆

WHO WAS THE FIRST AFRICAN AMERICAN WOMAN TO WIN A TONY FOR BEST LEADING ACTRESS?

In June 2004, Phylicia Rashad was awarded a Tony as best leading actress for her portrayal of Lena Younger, the matriarch of a struggling African American family, in a revival of Lorraine Hansberry's prize-winning play, *A Raisin in the Sun*. The 2004 Tony awards ceremony was a gratifying evening for African American actresses. Audra McDonald also won a Tony as best featured actress for her role in *A Raisin in the Sun*, and Anika Noni Rose won for best featured actress in a musical for her part in Tony Kushner's *Caroline, or Change*.

Rashad was born Phylicia Ayers-Allen in 1948 in Houston, Texas. Her father was a dentist and her mother was a poet. She graduated from Howard University in 1970 and moved to New York City, where she worked with the Negro Ensemble Company. She made her Broadway debut as a munchkin in the 1975 production of *The Wiz*, followed by a small part in *Dreamgirls*. In 1983 she joined the cast of the daytime soap opera *One Life to Live*, and later gained fame on television in her role as Clair Huxtable in *The Cosby Show*, which ran from 1984 to 1992. She repeated her role in *A Raisin in the Sun* in a 2008 television adaptation of the play, and returned to Broadway that same year in the all-African American production of Tennessee Williams's *Cat on a Hot Tin Roof*, directed by her sister, Debbie Allen. Rashad once again joined a television series in 2012 when she was cast as Dr. Vanessa Young in *Do No Harm*.

VISUAL
ARTS

WHO WAS THE FIRST KNOWN AFRICAN AMERICAN PAINTER?

Although he was a slave, Scipio Moorhead, who was owned by the Reverend John Moorhead of Boston, was allowed to study painting. He learned this craft from Reverend Moorhead's wife, Sarah, an artist. When the poet Phillis Wheatley, herself a slave, was given the opportunity to have her book *Poems on Various Subjects, Religious and Moral* published in England, she asked that Scipio Moorhead draw her portrait for the frontispiece. The drawing depicts the young poet at her desk, in Colonial dress, with her hand holding a quill pen poised over a sheet of paper. Wheatley's book contains a poem inspired by Moorhead, "To S. M., a Young African Painter, on Seeing His Works."

◆

WHO WAS THE FIRST AFRICAN AMERICAN ARTIST TO BE RECOGNIZED AS A PORTRAIT PAINTER?

Although born a slave, Joshua Johnston was eventually able to gain his freedom, develop his artistic talent, and pursue a career as a portrait painter. In 1796, he even advertised his services in a Baltimore newspaper. He claimed in his ad to be "a self-taught genius," but some art experts believe that Johnston studied with another portrait painter of the time, Charles Peale Polk, since their styles are similar.

Most of Johnston's subjects are white aristocrats, although one painting, *Portrait of a Cleric,* shows an African American minister. His subjects, who include many children, are typically shown gazing forward, and certain objects reappear in the paintings, such as baskets of strawberries or cherries, a fuzzy white dog, and chairs studded with brass tacks. More than eighty paintings have been signed by or attributed to this early painter.

◆

WHO WAS THE FIRST AFRICAN AMERICAN PAINTER OF MURALS?

The first African American artist to be recognized abroad, Robert Scott Duncanson was born in upstate New York in 1821 and educated in Canada. Duncanson moved with his mother to a town outside Cincinnati, Ohio, in 1841, and a year later he exhibited his first paintings.

In 1848 he was hired by a wealthy Cincinnati political leader, Nicholas Longworth, to paint a series of murals for his new mansion. Completed over a two-year period, the murals consisted of eight landscape paintings of the American West. This accomplishment made Duncanson the first African American muralist.

Duncanson began traveling abroad, exhibiting in England, Scotland, and Italy and receiving international recognition. In the 1860s a London journal wrote that he was one of the best landscape painters in the world. But in 1872, at the top of his power and fame, he experienced a mental breakdown, and died in a Detroit insane asylum.

◆

WHO WAS THE FIRST PROFESSIONAL AFRICAN AMERICAN ARTIST IN CALIFORNIA?

Grafton Tyler Brown was born in Harrisburg, Pennsylvania, in 1841. Around 1860 he moved to San Francisco, where he lived in a boardinghouse called the What Cheer House and worked as a draftsman and a lithographer. In 1866 he founded his own business and became widely known for his lithographs of California towns and cities, which included a number of scenes of San Francisco. Brown is thought to have been the first African American to work as a professional artist in California.

In 1882 Brown journeyed to Victoria, British Columbia, and joined a group that was conducting a geological survey of sections of Canada. He later produced many detailed watercolors of places he had visited. He became a popular realistic painter in Victoria as well as in Portland, Oregon, producing works that evinced strong feelings for natural settings. His 1891 painting *Grand Canyon of the Yellowstone from Hayden Point* may have been one of his last.

Later in the 1890s he traveled eastward, settling in St. Paul, Minnesota, and working for part of that time as a draftsman for the city's civil engineering department and the U.S. Army Engineers. His career as a painter apparently ended years earlier, since there is no evidence of his work in the 1900s. Brown died in a state hospital in St. Paul in 1918.

◆

WHO WAS THE FIRST PROFESSIONAL AFRICAN AMERICAN SCULPTOR?

The daughter of a Chippewa Indian woman and an African American man, Edmonia Lewis was born about 1845 near Albany, New York. Her parents died when she was young, and she went to live with her mother's sisters in Niagara Falls. The Chippewa people named her Wildfire and taught her to make baskets and embroidered moccasins.

Her brother, a California gold miner, arranged for her to enter Oberlin College in Ohio, where she stayed for two years. Moving to Boston, Lewis studied with a local sculptor and began selling her work. She opened her own studio, where she created a number of pieces, including a bust of Colonel Robert Gould Shaw, the commander of an African American Civil War regiment from Massachusetts, as well as medallion portraits of the abolitionists John Brown and William Lloyd Garrison.

In 1865 Lewis sailed for Europe, settling in Rome to continue her studies. Influenced by the Greco-Roman sculpture she saw there, she began creating works in a neoclassical style. By the time she returned to the United States in 1874, her patrons included distinguished families in this country and abroad. She was given receptions in Philadelphia and Boston and was praised by prominent

EDMONIA LEWIS

art critics. But her popularity dwindled and she eventually vanished from the art world. Lewis's surviving works include *Forever Free,* which was acquired by the Howard University Gallery of Art, and *Death of Cleopatra,* in Washington's National Museum of Art.

◆

WHO WAS THE FIRST AFRICAN AMERICAN TO WIN A NATIONAL ART AWARD?

Edward Mitchell Bannister was born about 1826 in St. Andrews, a small seaport in New Brunswick, Canada, his mother's home. Bannister's father, a native of Barbados, died when the boy was two years old. His mother, who lived only twelve years longer, encouraged her son's interest in art. When he was in his twenties, Bannister settled in Boston, where he studied painting and supported himself as a photographer's assistant and a barber.

In 1855 Bannister painted his first commissioned work, *The Ship Outward Bound,* and his talents were increasingly recognized in artistic circles. In 1869 Bannister and his wife, a successful hairdresser and wigmaker, moved to Providence, Rhode Island, where he achieved a wide reputation as a painter of pastoral landscapes. He became increasingly involved in the cultural life of the city and was one of the founders of the Providence Art Club, which evolved into the renowned Rhode Island School of Design.

The high point of Bannister's career came in 1876 when his landscape *Under the Oaks* was awarded a first place medal at the Centennial Exhibition in Philadelphia, making him the first African American to win a national art award. When he heard that he had won the prize, he rushed to the committee room, where he was treated rudely by the officials and art patrons. They were astonished and apologetic when they learned that he was the winning painter. After Bannister's death in 1901, the Providence Art Club honored him with a memorial exhibit of more than one hundred of his paintings.

◆

WHO WAS THE FIRST AFRICAN AMERICAN PAINTER TO GAIN INTERNATIONAL FAME?

Henry Ossawa Tanner was born in Pittsburgh, Pennsylvania, in 1859, the son of a bishop of the African Methodist Episcopal Church. When he was thirteen, walking in the park with his father, he became fascinated by the sight of a painter at work and soon made up his mind to become an artist. He painted throughout his teens, and at the age of twenty-one he enrolled in the Pennsylvania Academy of Fine Arts, where he studied with the leading American portrait painter, Thomas Eakins.

Tanner moved to Atlanta in 1888, ran a small photo gallery for a time, and taught at Clark College. He held his first solo exhibition in Cincinnati in 1890, and the next year, financed by a bishop and his wife, sailed for Europe. Settling in Paris, he enrolled in a distinguished art school, and decided to stay in France for the rest of his life.

Tanner's early paintings, *Banjo Lesson* and *The Thankful Poor,* portrayed African Americans in everyday life, but he later concentrated on religious themes. His first major religious painting was *Daniel in the Lion's Den* in 1895, followed by *The Resurrection of Lazarus* a year later. He received many honors, including membership in the National Academy of Design and the French Legion of Honor, and in 1900 he won a medal of honor at the Paris Exposition. He died at his home in Paris in 1937.

◆

WHO WAS THE FIRST AFRICAN AMERICAN MEMBER OF THE AMERICAN INSTITUTE OF ARCHITECTS?

A native of Los Angeles, Paul Revere Williams was born in 1894 on downtown Olvera Street, where his parents owned a grocery store. After finishing high school, Williams attended the Los Angeles workshop of New York's Beaux Arts Institute of Design, and later studied architecture at the University of Southern California. He worked for two architecture companies, earned his license in 1921, and a year later, at the age of twenty-eight, started his own firm. In 1928 he joined the southern California chapter of the American Institute of Architects, becoming that organization's first African American member.

Known as the "architect to the stars," Williams designed hundreds of graceful, comfortable houses in such areas as Beverly Hills and Bel Air, including homes for such entertainers as Frank Sinatra, Lucille Ball, and Anthony Quinn. He designed the Los Angeles County Courthouse, was an associate architect of the Los Angeles International Airport, and also designed a number of landmark buildings in the African American communities of Los Angeles, including the First African Methodist Episcopal Church, the Second Baptist Church, and the Golden State Mutual Life Building.

When he retired in 1973, he could look back with pride on the thousands of projects he completed during his fifty-year career. He died in 1980 at the age of eighty-five.

◆

WHO WAS THE FIRST AFRICAN AMERICAN TO
HAVE A ONE-MAN SHOW AT THE MUSEUM
OF MODERN ART?

Born around 1870 in Nashville, Tennessee, William Edmondson never received any artistic training. He worked as a railroad laborer and for many years was an orderly at a Baptist hospital. After the Depression began, he lost his hospital job, but was soon inspired to begin a new career.

Edmondson said that God had appeared at the head of his bed and commanded him to find a mallet and chisel and create tomb-stones. He said that God appeared again, holding models of tomb-stones for Edmondson to copy. Following his vision, he made his first works using pieces of limestone from old curbing and de-molished buildings. Putting up a sign that read "Tomb-Stones for Sale," he progressed to creating limestone figures: birds, rabbits, squirrels, owls, preachers, angels, and brides.

His carvings were discovered by a magazine photographer, who took pictures of Edmondson and his work and showed them to the director of the Museum of Modern Art in New York City. In 1937 he was given a solo exhibition, the first at that museum for an African American artist. Edmondson continued his carving, but in 1947 he was stricken with cancer and gradually grew too ill to work. Over the years between his New York show and his death in 1951, he received little recognition, but in the spring of 2000, a curator at Nashville's Cheekwood Museum of Art put together an exhibition of Edmondson's work, which traveled to Atlanta, Orlando, and the Museum of Folk Art in New York City.

◆

WHO WAS THE FIRST AFRICAN AMERICAN TO
INVENT A FINE ARTS PRINTING PROCESS?

Born in the rural town of Griffin, Georgia, in 1893, Dox Thrash left school after fourth grade but learned to draw through cor-respondence courses. At fifteen he began traveling around the coun-try, working in circuses and vaudeville shows. Arriving in Chicago in 1911, he took a job as an elevator operator and enrolled in evening

DOX THRASH'S *CABIN DAYS*

classes at the Art Institute of Chicago. He enlisted in the army in 1917, served for fourteen months, and eventually returned to Chicago to continue his studies at the Art Institute.

After living for a time in Boston and New York, Thrash finally settled in Philadelphia, where he began the study of printmaking. In the early 1930s he started exhibiting prints, as well as oils and watercolors. In 1937 he joined Philadelphia's Fine Print Workshop, a division of the government-sponsored Federal Arts Project. It was there that he invented the carborgraph printing process, using carborundum crystals to create an image from a copper plate. This new method produced a range of rich tones, from pale gray to deep black.

Thrash used the new process to produce luminous images of war workers, nudes, and scenes of the rural South and the urban North. During the 1940s and '50s, his prints and drawings were shown in cities throughout the country. The Philadelphia Museum of Art began collecting his prints in 1941, and by 1999 had acquired fifty of his approximately 150 works. A major exhibition of his work, entitled "Dox Thrash: An African American Master Printmaker Rediscovered," opened at the museum in October 2001.

◆

WHO WAS THE FIRST AFRICAN AMERICAN WOMAN CARTOONIST TO CREATE NATIONALLY SYNDICATED COMIC STRIPS?

Zelda "Jackie" Ormes began her newspaper career in the 1930s as a sportswriter for her hometown newspaper, the *Pittsburgh Courier*. She started contributing occasional drawings, and in 1937 developed a comic strip called "Torchy Brown in Dixie to Harlem," about the experiences of an intelligent, attractive young African American woman who leaves the South to settle in New York City's Harlem.

In 1946 Ormes introduced another strip, "Patty-Jo 'n' Ginger," about a smart, socially aware young girl who lives with her older sister. The strip first appeared in the *Pittsburgh Courier* and was later syndicated, running in fourteen African American newspapers. Ormes revived Torchy Brown in 1950 in a strip called "Torchy Brown and the Heartbeats," which ran for five years. In all of her comics, Ormes addressed segregation, sexism, and other forms of injustice. As she grew older, arthritis limited her art, and she began a hobby of doll collecting. She died in 1985.

◆

WHO WAS THE FIRST AFRICAN AMERICAN
ART HISTORIAN?

When James A. Porter's book *Modern Negro Art* appeared in 1943, it was the first comprehensive history of African American art to be published. Porter, born in Baltimore in 1905, graduated from Howard University and went to New York to study at Columbia and the Art Students League. He was awarded a grant to travel to several countries, where he studied collections of African arts and crafts, and he later earned a master's degree in art history from New York University.

Porter returned to Howard as an art instructor and eventually was named chairman of the school's art department, a position he held until his death in 1971. During his tenure at Howard, Porter took several trips abroad to study art and to create his own paintings, including many that reflected his impressions of West Africa, Haiti, and Cuba. In 1966 Porter was honored by President Lyndon Johnson as "one of America's most outstanding men of the arts."

◆

WHO WAS THE FIRST AFRICAN AMERICAN
SCULPTOR IN A MAJOR MUSEUM COLLECTION?

Born in 1901 in Bay St. Louis, Mississippi, Richmond Barthé studied at the Art Institute of Chicago, where he concentrated on painting until he was persuaded by a teacher to try modeling in clay. His teacher's enthusiastic response encouraged him to switch to sculpture. In 1919 he went to New York City, where his work attracted the attention of Gertrude Vanderbilt Whitney, an art collector. The Whitney Museum of American Art exhibited his work throughout the 1930s and bought three of his pieces for its permanent collection.

Barthé's work was shown at the 1939 World's Fair, and in 1946 he was commissioned to create a bust of Booker T. Washington for the New York University Hall of Fame. Throughout his long career, his work was popular with museums and private collectors. His sculptures ranged from a graceful African dancer to busts of the actors Paul Robeson and Sir Laurence Olivier. Barthé died at his home in Pasadena, California, at the age of eighty-eight.

◆

WHO WAS THE FIRST AFRICAN AMERICAN PHOTOGRAPHER TO WIN A GUGGENHEIM?

Roy DeCarava was born in New York City in 1919 and lived there all his life. He studied painting and lithography for two years at Cooper Union and then took classes at the Harlem Community Art Center and the George Washington Carver Art School. In the mid-1940s he began taking photographs to document his ideas for paintings, and he gradually gave up painting altogether to concentrate on photography.

In 1950, Edward Steichen, then the curator of photography at the Museum of Modern Art, saw a show of DeCarava's work at a gallery, bought three prints for the museum, and encouraged him to apply for a Guggenheim Fellowship. In 1952 he became the first African American photographer to win the fellowship, and the grant allowed him to pursue his project of photographing everyday life in Harlem. One hundred and forty of these images, accompanied by a Langston Hughes text, were published in the 1955 book *The Sweet Flypaper of Life.*

DeCarava began a series of photographs of jazz musicians in 1956, which were later shown at the Studio Museum of Harlem and, in 2001, published in the book *The Sound I Saw: Improvisations on a Jazz Theme.* DeCarava joined the faculty of Hunter College in 1975 and was later named Distinguished Professor of Art. In 2006, he was awarded the National Medal of Arts. DeCarava died in October 2009, six weeks before his ninetieth birthday.

◆

WHO WAS THE FIRST FULL-TIME PHOTOGRAPHER OF AFRICAN AMERICAN THEATER?

Bert Andrews, who was born in 1929 in Chicago and grew up in New York City's Harlem, started out as a songwriter, singer, and dancer. But his career path changed after he studied photography while in the army in the early 1950s, and he later served as an apprentice to Chuck Stewart, a well-known photographer of jazz musicians. Andrews soon began chronicling African American theater, photographing such productions as *A Soldier's Play*, *Ma Rainey's Black Bottom*, and *The Blood Knot*. He photographed almost every leading black actor of his generation, and documented more than 1,000 productions.

In 1985 Andrews saw thirty years of his work go up in smoke when a devastating fire struck his studio, destroying more than 40,000 prints and 100,000 negatives. With the help of the theater community, Andrews was able to reassemble much of his collection, and about 3,000 of his photographs were housed in Manhattan at the Schomburg Center for Research in Black Culture. Some of the images were reproduced in his book, *In the Shadow of the Great White Way*, which was published in 1989, four years before Andrews's death at the age of sixty-three.

◆

WHO WAS THE FIRST AFRICAN AMERICAN WOMAN TO BECOME A LICENSED ARCHITECT?

Norma Sklarek was born in New York City in 1928 and raised in the Crown Heights section of Brooklyn. Her parents encouraged their only child to enter a profession, and she decided to attend the School of Architecture at Columbia University. She graduated in 1950, a time when few women were entering the field. She became a licensed architect in New York in 1954, and a year later was hired by Skidmore, Owings & Merrill, one of the largest architectural firms in the United States.

Relocating to Los Angeles, Sklarek joined the firm of Gruen Associates, where she was the company's first woman director of architecture. Her projects included the American Embassy in Tokyo, Fox Hills Mall in Culver City, and the San Bernardino City Hall. In 1980 she went to Welton Becket Associates, where she was the firm's first woman vice president and served as project director of Terminal One at Los Angeles International Airport. That same year she became the first African American woman to be made a fellow of the American Institute of Architects.

NORMA SKLAREK

In 2008, when she was semi-retired, Sklarek was honored by the American Institute of Architects as the recipient of the Whitney M. Young Jr. Award, which is given to an architect who exemplifies the profession's responsibility toward current social issues.

Sklarek died of heart failure in February 2012. Roberta Washington, a fellow architect, wrote that she had attended a memorial service for Sklarek because "for me and dozens of black women I knew, Norma was mentor par excellence and inspiration on cloudy days. She was confirmation that neither sexual nor racial classifications were reasons not to embrace a life in architecture."

◆

WHO WAS THE FIRST AFRICAN AMERICAN MAN TO WIN A PULITZER PRIZE?

Moneta Sleet Jr., then a staff photographer for *Ebony* magazine, was awarded a Pulitzer Prize in 1969 for his moving photograph of Coretta Scott King consoling her daughter at the funeral of Dr. Martin Luther King Jr. Born in Kentucky in 1926, Sleet took his first pictures with a camera his parents gave him when he was ten. He enrolled in Kentucky State College, where he assisted the dean, an accomplished photographer, in his photo studio. After serving in the army and then earning a business de-

MONETA SLEET JR.

gree, he took a six-month course in photography in New York City and taught photography at Maryland State College for a year before returning to New York to earn a master's in journalism from New York University.

Sleet reported on sports for a short time for the *Amsterdam News* and in 1950 began his career as a professional photographer for *Our World* magazine. His first assignment was in the emergency room of Harlem Hospital. Five years later he became a staff photographer for *Ebony.* Throughout his career he photographed the most important events of African American life, including the civil rights march from Selma to Montgomery, Alabama, and the 1963 March on Washington. He accompanied Dr. King when he went to Norway in 1964 to accept the Nobel Peace Prize, and traveled to Africa many times to photograph important leaders. He died in September 1996, not long after covering the Olympic Games in Atlanta.

◆

WHO WAS THE FIRST ARTIST TO WIN THE NAACP'S SPINGARN MEDAL?

Jacob Lawrence was honored as an artist, teacher, and humanitarian when the NAACP awarded him the Spingarn Medal in 1970 for his outstanding achievements. Throughout his lengthy artistic career, Lawrence concentrated on depicting the history and struggles of African Americans.

Born in 1917 in Atlantic City, New Jersey, Lawrence was thirteen when he moved with his mother to New York City, where she enrolled him in classes at an arts and crafts settlement house in Harlem. After dropping out of high school at sixteen, Lawrence worked in a laundry and a printing plant and attended classes at the Harlem Art Workshop, taught by his mentor, the African American artist Charles Alston.

Lawrence was not quite twenty-one years old when his series of paintings of the Haitian general Toussaint L'Ouverture was shown in an exhibit of African American artists at the Baltimore Museum of Art. This impressive work was followed by a series of paintings of the lives of Frederick Douglass and Harriet Tubman.

Lawrence was only twenty-three when he completed the sixty-panel set of narrative paintings entitled *Migration of the Negro.* The series, a moving portrayal of the migration of hundreds of thousands of African Americans from the rural South to the North after World War I, was shown in New York and brought him national recognition.

In the 1940s Lawrence was given his first major solo exhibition at the Museum of Modern Art in New York City and became the most celebrated African American painter in the country. In 1974 the Whitney Museum of American Art in New York held a major retrospective of his work, and in 1983 he was elected to the American Academy of Arts and Letters. He taught at several schools, and his work was collected by numerous museums, including the Metropolitan Museum of Art, the Museum of Modern Art, the Whitney Museum, and the Brooklyn Museum.

Lawrence continued to paint until a few weeks before his death in June 2000 at the age of eighty-two. His last public work, the mosaic mural *New York in Transit,* was installed in October 2001 in the Times Square subway station in New York City.

◆

WHO WAS THE FIRST AFRICAN AMERICAN WOMAN TO HAVE A SOLO SHOW AT THE WHITNEY MUSEUM?

When Alma Thomas was given a solo exhibition of her paintings at the Whitney Museum of American Art in New York City in 1972, she had been a professional artist for only twelve years. Born in Columbus, Georgia, in 1891, Thomas graduated from the fine arts department of Howard University and earned a master's in art education from Columbia University. In 1925 she became an art teacher at Shaw Junior High School in Washington, D.C., where she stayed until she retired thirty-five years later. During her years at Shaw, she was deeply involved in the arts, organizing an art project for Washington's African American children and establishing an art gallery in a public school.

In 1950 Thomas began taking classes at American University, where she evolved into an abstract painter, concentrating on color and composition. By the 1960s she was creating images, many inspired by her flower garden, with small dabs of paint laid across the surface of the painting. After seeing Thomas's show at the Whitney Museum, an art critic said her colorful works brought "joy to the painting of the '70s." Thomas died in 1978.

♦

WHO WAS THE FIRST AFRICAN AMERICAN ARTIST TO HAVE A SOLO EXHIBITION AT THE BOSTON MUSEUM OF FINE ARTS?

Lois Mailou Jones, known for her brilliant, decorative paintings of Haitian and African subjects, was a 1927 graduate of the Boston Museum School of Fine Arts, a prestigious art school in

LOIS MAILOU JONES

the city where she was born in 1905. At first she pursued a career as a textile designer, but soon turned to painting. She joined the art department of Palmer Memorial Institute in North Carolina, one of the country's first prep schools for African American students, and two years later, in 1930, became a teacher of watercolor and design at Howard University. She was to remain a member of the Howard faculty for forty-seven years.

Jones's early work was influenced by African themes. After studies in France, she concentrated more on French landscapes, cityscapes, and figures. In 1953 Jones married a Haitian artist, and her travels in Haiti led to a gradual transformation of her paintings; she developed a bright, decorative, two-dimensional style. A visit in 1969 to eleven African countries made a further impression on her work, inspiring her once again to explore African motifs.

In 1973 the Boston Museum of Fine Arts mounted a solo exhibition of Jones's paintings. She was the first African American artist to be so honored by the museum—a notable achievement for the time. After retiring from Howard in 1977, Jones continued to paint and lecture. She died in 1998 at her home in Washington.

◆

WHO WAS THE FIRST AFRICAN AMERICAN WOMAN CARTOONIST SYNDICATED IN MAINSTREAM NEWSPAPERS?

Barbara Brandon, born in Brooklyn in 1958, was exposed to cartoon art early in her childhood; her father, Brumsic Brandon Jr., was the creator of "Luther," a comic strip about an inner-city child that was syndicated nationally from 1968 to the mid-'80s. As a youngster, Brandon assisted her father by filling in colors and drawing borders on his strips.

After graduating from Syracuse University in 1981, she took a job with the magazine *Elan,* for which she created her comic strip "Where I'm Coming From." But the magazine folded before the strip appeared, and she went on to write for *Essence* magazine. "Where I'm Coming From" was reborn in 1989 when it began appearing in the *Detroit Free Press.* Featuring the lives and thoughts of a

BARBARA BRANDON

group of African American women, the weekly strip was picked up by Universal Press Syndicate in 1991. Brandon's illustrations have appeared in a number of publications, including several editions of *Best Editorial Cartoons of the Year,* and her comics were published in two collections in the 1990s: *Where I'm Coming From* and *Where I'm Still Coming From.*

◆

WHICH SCULPTOR CREATED THE FIRST MONUMENT COMMEMORATING THE BUFFALO SOLDIERS?

Twenty thousand people, including General Colin Powell and more than one hundred Buffalo Soldier veterans, attended the dedication of the National Buffalo Soldier Monument at Fort Leavenworth, Kansas, on July 25, 1992. Eddie Dixon, an African American sculptor from Lubbock, Texas, had spent two and a half years creating the work, a twelve-foot bronze statue of a Buffalo Soldier reining in his horse.

EDDIE DIXON'S BUFFALO SOLDIER MONUMENT

"This monument is magnificent and we have waited many, many years for the recognition it bestows," said General Powell, whose idea it was to create a monument honoring the African American men who served in the Ninth and Tenth Cavalry units. Powell officially dedicated the monument on that July day.

The statue's creator, Eddie Dixon, spent his childhood in California and, after high school, served in Vietnam for two years. When he left the service, he and several friends went to Lubbock to study at Texas Tech University, where Dixon earned an undergraduate degree in chemistry and zoology and a master's in entomology. He started sculpting in graduate school, carving the face of an Iberian warrior that was cast in bronze.

Dixon spent the next seven years as a commodities broker in Chicago, where he began delving into African American history, learning all he could about black heroes. One that he discovered was Eugene Jacques Bullard, the first African American fighter pilot; Dixon's sculpture of Bullard was acquired by the Smithsonian Air and Space Museum in 1993. As he continued his career as a sculptor, his work was displayed at the Smithsonian's National History Museum, the Department of the Interior, the Pentagon, and numerous museums.

In September 2000, Dixon was inducted into the West Texas Walk of Fame in Lubbock. That same day he was honored at the dedication of his fourteen-foot bronze sculpture, *Knight of the Llano Estacado,* which was placed on permanent display at the Lubbock Civic Center. The giant sculpture depicts Dixon's vision of a Spanish conquistador who rode across the high plains of West Texas in the mid-1500s.

Dixon's statue of Willie McCool, an astronaut commander and Lubbock native who was killed in the 2003 explosion of the space shuttle *Columbia,* was dedicated in May 2005. The large bronze statue of McCool stands on a marble base with a young boy by his side, holding a toy airplane. In August 2008, Dixon's statue of Dr. James Henry Wayland, the founder of Wayland Baptist University, was unveiled on the school's main campus in Plainview, Texas.

In May 2012, the National Endowment for the Arts awarded $15,000 to Cultural Arts of Waco for a statue, to be created by Dixon, honoring Doris Miller, the first hero of World War II and a native of Waco. In October, Dixon announced that he had been commissioned by the Kansas Historical Commission to sculpt a bust of Colin Powell.

Select Bibliography

PUBLICATIONS

Abdul, Raoul. *Blacks in Classical Music*. New York: Dodd, Mead & Company, 1977.

Abramson, Doris E. *Negro Playwrights in the American Theatre 1925–1959*. New York: Columbia University Press, 1969.

Alexander, James I. *Blue Coats: Black Skin: The Black Experience in the New York City Police Department Since 1891*. Hicksville, New York: Exposition Press, 1978.

Appiah, Kwame Anthony, and Henry Louis Gates, Jr., eds. *Africana, The Encyclopedia of the African and African American Experience*. New York: Basic Civitas Books, 1999.

Asante, Molefi K., and Mark T. Mattson. *The Historical and Cultural Atlas of African Americans*. New York: MacMillan Publishing Company, 1991.

Ashe, Arthur. *A Hard Road to Glory, History of the African American Athlete*. New York: Warner Books, 1988.

Balliett, Whitney. *American Musicians, 56 Portraits in Jazz*. New York: Oxford University Press, 1986.

Bogle, Donald. *Blacks in American Films and Television*. New York: Garland Publishing, 1988.

Bontemps, Arna, ed. *Negro American Heritage*. San Francisco: Century Communications, Inc., 1965.

Brown-Guillery, Elizabeth. *Their Place on the Stage: Black Women Playwrights in America*. New York: Greenwood Press, 1988.

Buckley, Gail. *American Patriots: The Story of Blacks in the Military from the Revolution to Desert Storm*. New York: Random House, 2001.

Cantor, George. *Historic Black Landmarks, A Traveler's Guide*. Detroit: Visible Ink Press, 1991.

Conyers, Charline Howard. *A Living Legend: The History of Cheyney University, 1837–1951*. Cheyney, Pennsylvania: Cheyney University Press, 1990.

Cripps, Thomas. *Slow Fade to Black: The Negro in American Film, 1900–1942*. New York: Oxford University Press, 1977.

DeCarava, Roy, and Langston Hughes. *The Sweet Flypaper of Life*. Washington, D.C.: Howard University Press, 1984.

Dodson, Howard, Christopher Moore, and Roberta Yancey. *The Black New Yorkers: The Schomburg Illustrated Chronology*. New York: John Wiley & Sons, Inc., 2000.

Emory, Lynne Fauley. *Black Dance from 1619 to Today*. Princeton, New Jersey: Princeton Book Company, 1988.

Fletcher, Tom. *100 Years of the Negro in Show Business*. New York: Da Capo Press, 1984.

Franklin, John Hope. *An Illustrated Study of Black Americans*. New York: Time-Life Books, 1970.

Franklin, John Hope, and August Meier, eds. *Black Leaders of the Twentieth Century*. Urbana: University of Illinois Press, 1982.

Gates, Henry Louis, Jr., and Nellie Y. McKay, eds. *The Norton Anthology of African American Literature*. New York: W. W. Norton & Company, Inc., 1997.

Giddins, Gary. *Visions of Jazz*. New York: Oxford University Press, 1998.

Green, Mildred Denby. *Black Women Composers: A Genesis*. Boston: Twayne Publishers, 1983.

Greene, Robert Ewell. *Black Defenders of America, 1775–1973*. Chicago: Johnson Publishing Company, Inc., 1974.

Haber, Louis. *Black Pioneers of Science & Invention*. New York: Harcourt, Brace & World, 1970.

Handy, D. Antoinette. *Black Women in American Bands & Orchestras*. Metuchen, New Jersey: The Scarecrow Press, 1981.

Harrison, Daphne Duval. *Black Pearls: Blues Queens of the 1920's*. New Brunswick, New Jersey: Rutgers University Press, 1988.

Haskins, James. *Black Music in America*. New York: HarperCollins, 1987.

———. *Outward Dreams, Black Inventors and Their Inventions*. New York: Walker Publishing Company, 1991.

Hedgepeth, Chester M., Jr. *Twentieth Century African American Writers and Artists*. Chicago: American Library Association, 1991.

Hine, Darlene Clark, ed. *Black Women in America, An Historical Encyclopedia*. Brooklyn, New York: Carlson Publishing Co., 1993.

Homan, Lynn M., and Thomas Reilly. *Black Knights: The Story of the Tuskegee Airmen*. Gretna, Louisiana: Pelican Publishing Company, 2001.

Hughes, Langston, and Milton Meltzer. *Black Magic: A Pictorial History of the Negro in American Entertainment*. Englewood Cliffs, New Jersey: Prentice-Hall, Inc. 1967.

Hughes, Langston, Milton Meltzer, and C. Eric Lincoln. *A Pictorial History of Black Americans*. New York: Crown Publishers, 1983.

Ittman, John W. *Dox Thrash: An African American Master Printmaker Rediscovered*. Philadelphia: Philadelphia Museum of Art, 2001.

Ives, Patrician Carter. *Creativity and Inventions, The Genius of Afro-Americans and Women in the United States and Their Patents*. Arlington, Virginia: Research Unlimited, 1987.

Kasher, Steven. *The Civil Rights Movement, A Photographic History, 1954–68*. New York: Abbeville Press, 1996.

Katz, William Loren. *The Black West*. New York: Doubleday & Company, Inc., 1971.

Kranz, Rachel C. *The Biographical Dictionary of Black Americans*. New York: Facts on File, 1992.

Lanker, Brian. *I Dream A World: Portraits of Black Women Who Changed America*. New York: Stewart, Tabori & Chang, 1989.

Lewis, Samella. *Art: African American*. Los Angeles: Hancraft Studios, 1990.

Lincoln, C. Eric. *The Negro Pilgrimage in America*. New York: Bantam Books, 1967.

Litwack, Leon, and August Meier, eds. *Black Leaders of the Nineteenth Century*. Urbana: University of Illinois Press, 1988.

Long, Richard A. *Black Americana*. Secaucus, New Jersey: Chartwell Books, Inc., 1985.

Low, W. Augustus, and Virgil A. Clift. *Encyclopedia of Black America*. New York: Da Capo Press, 1981.

Ogg, Alex, with David Upshal. *The Hip Hop Years: A History of Rap*. New York: Fromm International, 2001.

Parks, Gordon. *Half Past Autumn*. Boston: Little, Brown and Company, 1997.

Pastra, Phil. *Dead Man Blues: Jelly Roll Morton Way Out West*. Los Angeles: University of California Press, 2001.

Patton, Sharon F. *African American Art, Oxford History of Art*. New York: Oxford University Press, 1998.

Peterson, Robert W. *Only the Ball Was White*. Englewood Cliffs, New Jersey: Prentice-Hall, Inc., 1970.

Quarles, Benjamin. *The Negro in the Making of America*. New York: MacMillan Publishing Company, 1964.

Riley, James A. *The Biographical Encyclopedia of the Negro Baseball Leagues*. New York: Carroll & Graf Publishers, Inc., 1994.

Sammons, Vivian Ovelton. *Blacks in Science and Medicine*. New York: Hemisphere Publishing Corp., 1990.

Saunders, Doris E., ed. *Special Moments in African American History, 1955–1966, The Photographs of Moneta Sleet, Jr.* Chicago: Johnson Publishing Company, Inc., 1998.

Schuller, Gunther. *Early Jazz, Its Roots and Musical Development*. New York, Oxford University Press, 1968.

Shaw, Arnold. *Black Popular Music in America*. New York: Schirmer Books, 1986.

Sinnette, Calvin H. *Forbidden Fairways, African Americans and the Game of Golf*. Chelsea, Michigan: Sleeping Bear Press, 1998.

Smith, Jessie Carney, ed. *Notable Black American Women*. Detroit: Gale Research, Inc., 1992.

Tirro, Frank. *Jazz: A History*. New York: W. W. Norton & Company, 1977.

Toppin, Edgar A. *A Biographical History of Blacks in America Since 1528*. New York: David McKay Company, Inc., 1971.

Williams, Bert, and Paul Carter Harrison. *In the Shadow of the Great White Way: Images from the Black Theatre*. New York: Thunder's Mouth Press, 1989.

Williams, Juan. *Eyes on the Prize, America's Civil Rights Years*. New York: Viking Penguin, Inc., 1987.

Woll, Allen. *Black Musical Theatre, from Coontown to Dreamgirls*. Baton Rouge: Louisiana State University Press, 1989.

Woods, Paula L., and Felix H. Liddell. *I, Too, Sing America*. New York: Workman Publishing, 1992.

Woodson, Carter G. *The History of the Negro Church*. Washington, D.C.: The Associated Publishers, 1921.

WEBSITES

Aaregistry.com
Allmusic.com
Blackpast.org
Nlbpa.com
Swingmusic.net
Thechessdrum.net

Photo Credits

BUSINESS

Captain Dave Harris, courtesy American Airlines; Louis L. Freeman, courtesy Louis L. Freeman; Delano E. Lewis, courtesy Delano E. Lewis; Ursula Burns, Courtesy of Xerox Corporation.

EDUCATION

Alexander Twilight, courtesy Orleans County Historical Society; George Washington Henderson, Special Collections, Bailey/Howe Library, University of Vermont; Alain Lock, State Historical Society of Wisconsin; Ernest Green, courtesy Ernest Green; Charlayne Hunter-Gault, courtesy the *McNeil/Lehrer Newshour*; Mary Frances Berry, courtesy Mary Frances Berry; Ruth J. Simmons, Brown University/Clark Quin; Sadie Tanner Mossell, University of Pennsylvania; Ruby Bridges, Ruby Bridges Foundation.

ENTERTAINMENT

Josephine Baker, Nat King Cole, State Historical Society of Wisconsin; Harry Belafonte with Dorothy Dandridge in *Carmen Jones*, Museum of Modern Art film stills archive; Adam Wade, CBS photo by Emil Romano; Johnathan Lee Iverson, copyright Feld Entertainment; Ava DuVernay, Brigitte Lacombe.

FILM

Hearts in Dixie, Hallelujah!, Bright Road with Dorothy Dandridge, Museum of Modern Art film stills archive; Stepin Fetchit, State Historical Society of Wisconsin; Etta Moten, Billy Rose Theatre Collection, the New York Public Library for the Performing Arts, Astor, Lenox and Tilden Foundations.

HISTORY

Harriet Tubman, Moorland-Spingarn Research Center, Howard University; Franklin Thomas, courtesy Franklin Thomas; Bessie Coleman, The Miriam

Matthews Collection; Guion Bluford, Mae Jemison, courtesy NASA; Captain William Pinkney, by Chad Lyons, courtesy Amistad America Inc.; Bernard A. Harris, Jr., courtesy Bernard Harris; Sophia Danenberg, courtesy Sophia Danenberg; Barrington Irving, courtesy Barrington Irving.

JOURNALISM

Carl T. Rowan, by Scott McLay, courtesy Carl T. Rowan Jr.; Pearl Stewart, by Gordon Clark; Mark Whitaker, courtesy *Newsweek*; Sherman L. Maxwell, *The Star-Ledger*.

LAW AND GOVERNMENT

Lawrence Douglas Wilder, courtesy Lawrence Douglas Wilder; Jacquelyn Barrett, courtesy Jacquelyn Barrett; Carol Moseley-Braun, courtesy Carol Moseley-Braun; Pamela Fanning Carter, by Sid Rust; Ronald V. Dellums, courtesy Ronald V. Dellums; Elaine R. Jones, by Asman Photo; Beverly J. Harvard, courtesy Beverly J. Harvard; Karen Bass, courtesy Office of Speaker Karen Bass; Barack Obama, Michelle Obama, AP Images/Charles Dharapak; Eric Holder, AP Images/Evan Vucci; Susan Rice, AP Images/ Bebeto Matthews; Charles L. Gittens, courtesy Sharon Quick.

LITERATURE

Richard Wright, courtesy Harper & Row; Audre Lorde, by Dagmar Schullz; Rita Dove, by Fred Viebahn; Virginia Hamilton, courtesy Scholastic, Inc.; Annette Gordon-Reed, by Jerry Bauer.

MILITARY

Robert Smalls, State Historical Society of Wisconsin; Martin Delany, Moorland-Spingarn Research Center, Howard University; Wesley Brown, Samuel Graveley, United States Naval Institute; Benjamin O. Davis Jr., Photographs and Prints Collection, Schomburg Center for Research in Black Culture, the New York Public Library, Astor, Lenox and Tilden Foundations; Marcelite J. Harris, courtesy Marcelite J. Harris; Stayce Harris, courtesy Stayce Harris; Roscoe Robinson, Jr., United States Military Academy.

MUSIC

Robert Cole and J. Rosamond Johnson, the Billy Rose Collection, the New York Public Library for the Performing Arts, Astor, Lenox and Tilden Foundations; James Reese Europe and his Clef Club Orchestra, Louis Armstrong with King Oliver's Creole Jazz Band, John Birks "Dizzy" Gillespie, Erroll Garner, James P. Johnson, Institute of Jazz Studies, Rutgers the State University of New Jersey; Ella Fitzgerald, Institute of Jazz Studies, Rutgers, the State University of New Jersey; Mamie Smith, State Historical Society of Wisconsin; William Grant Still, William Grant Still Music, Flagstaff, Arizona; Mahalia Jackson, by Carl Van Vechten, Moorland-Spingarn Research Center, Howard University; Marian Anderson, Moorland-Spingarn Research Center, Howard University; Robert McFerrin, Metropolitan Opera Archives; Charley Pride, courtesy Charley Pride; Margaret Rosezarian Harris, courtesy Frances Veri, Pennsylvania

Academy of Music; Awadagin Pratt, by Cynthia Johnson; Camilla Williams, Virginia Historical Society (2005. 340. C).

RELIGION

Bishop Richard Allen, Bishop Henry McNeal Turner, Moorland-Spingarn Research Center, Howard University; Bishop Barbara Harris, copyright Reginald Jackson; Bishop Wilton D. Gregory, courtesy Bishop Wilton T. Gregory; Fred Luter, Jr., courtesy Franklin Avenue Baptist Church.

SCIENCE AND MEDICINE

Dr. Daniel Hale Williams, Moorland-Spingarn Research Center, Howard University, David Blackwell, by George Bergman, courtesy David Blackwell; Dr. Benjamin S. Carson, courtesy Dr. Benjamin S. Carson; Dr. Warren M. Washington, courtesy NCAR; Dr. Shirley Ann Jackson, by Mark McCarty; patent drawings, United States Patent Office; Dr. Patricia E. Bath, Patricia Bath, MD.

SPORTS

Isaac Murphy, Kinetic Corp./Churchill Downs, Inc.; Moses Fleetwood Walker with the Toledo Blue Stockings, Andrew "Rube" Foster, Leroy "Satchel" Paige, John "Buck" O'Neil, Negro Leagues Baseball Museum; Bill Pickett, Black American West Museum and Heritage Center; Frederick Douglas "Fritz" Pollard, courtesy Brown University; Dewey Brown, courtesy J. Peter Martin; Arthur Ashe, copyright Jeanne Moutoussamy-Ashe; Wilt Chamberlain, courtesy Basketball Hall of Fame, Springfield, Mass.; George Branham III, courtesy PBA Tours; Maurice Ashley, by Frank Johnson; Stephanie Ready, by Garrett Ellwood/NBAE/Getty Images; Vonetta Flowers, courtesy University of Alabama at Birmingham; Tony Dungy, by Brian MacDonald; Gabrielle Douglas, Associated Press/Julie Jacobson.

THEATER AND DANCE

Ira Aldridge, Photographs and Prints Collection, Schomburg Center for Research in Black Culture, the New York Public Library, Astor, Lenox and Tilden Foundations; Charles Gilpin, Garland Anderson, Bill "Bojangles" Robinson, Billy Rose Theatre Collection, the New York Public Library for the Performing Arts, Astor, Lenox and Tilden Foundations; Ruby Dee, courtesy Ruby Dee; George Faison, courtesy George Faison.

VISUAL ARTS

Edmonia Lewis, Boston Athenaeum; Dox Thrash's *Cabin Days*, Philadelphia Museum of Art: Thomas Skelton Harrison Fund; Norma Sklarek, by Marc Schurer, courtesy Norma Sklarek; Moneta Sleet Jr., by Vernon Smith, courtesy Moneta Sleet Jr.; Lois Mailou Jones, Lois M. Jones Pierre-Noel Trust; Barbara Brandon, courtesy United Press Syndicate; Buffalo Soldier Monument, by Jay Carey, courtesy Eddie Dixon.

Index